Harmonisation of Regulatory Oversight in Biotechnology

Safety Assessment of Transgenic Organisms in the Environment, Volume 9

OECD CONSENSUS DOCUMENTS ON THE BIOLOGY OF CROPS: APPLE, SAFFLOWER, RICE

OECD

BETTER POLICIES FOR BETTER LIVES

Please cite this publication as:
OECD (2022), *Safety Assessment of Transgenic Organisms in the Environment, Volume 9: OECD Consensus Documents on the Biology of Crops: Apple, Safflower, Rice*, Harmonisation of Regulatory Oversight in Biotechnology, OECD Publishing, Paris, https://doi.org/10.1787/e49bd2e8-en.

ISBN 978-92-64-37575-8 (print)
ISBN 978-92-64-98344-1 (pdf)
ISBN 978-92-64-47038-5 (HTML)
ISBN 978-92-64-93105-3 (epub)

Harmonisation of Regulatory Oversight in Biotechnology
ISSN 2414-6854 (print)
ISSN 2311-4622 (online)

Photo credits: Cover ©John Bill/Shutterstock.com.

Corrigenda to publications may be found on line at: www.oecd.org/about/publishing/corrigenda.htm.

Foreword

From their first commercialisation in the mid-1990s, genetically engineered crops (also known as "transgenic" or "genetically modified" plants) have been approved for commercial release in an increasing number of countries, for planting, entering in the composition of foods and feeds, or use in industrial processing. The majority of these productions are for soybean, maize, cotton and rapeseed (canola) bearing pest resistance and herbicide tolerance traits, aiming to improve yields and reduce the costs of production. Other transgenic crops that are increasingly grown to date comprise lucerne (alfalfa), sugar beet, sugarcane, papaya, safflower, potato, eggplant, as well as pumpkin, apple and pineapple in smaller areas. Other traits are increasingly introduced in engineered plants, adapting them to biotic or abiotic stress, such as resistance to drought or tolerance to salt in the growing environment, or changing a characteristic, e.g. modified oil content, reduced lignin content, non-browning or nutritional quality (biofortification). Thus, transgenic crops, where adopted and available on the market, enlarge possibilities for farmers, industry and consumers. They can play a part in addressing global concerns such as the rising need for food and feed in the growing population context or the necessary adaptation of agriculture for better resilience to climate change.

Modern biotechnologies are applied to plants (crops, flowers and trees) but also animals and micro-organisms. The safety of the resulting genetically engineered organisms, when released in the environment for their use in agriculture, forestry, fishery, the food and feed industry, biofuel production or other applications, represents a challenging issue. A scientifically sound approach to their risk assessment should inform biosafety regulators and support national decisions regarding their possible market release. Genetically engineered products are rigorously assessed by their developers during their elaboration and by governments when ready for commercial use, to ensure high safety standards for the environment, human food and animal feed. Such assessments are considered essential for healthy and sustainable agriculture, industry and trade.

In 2019, according to the annual report of the International Service for the Acquisition of Agri-biotech Applications, the five main producers of genetically engineered crops were the United States, Brazil, Argentina, Canada and India (listed by decreasing area) covering a combined 170 million hectares representing more than 90% of the global transgenic crop area. Among the 29 countries having grown genetically engineered crops in that year, 9 of them were OECD countries, listed by decreasing area as follows: the United States, Canada, Australia, Mexico, Spain, Colombia, Chile, Portugal and Costa Rica, representing 45% of the global transgenic crop acreage. This rate might increase significantly in future, with Argentina and Brazil being candidates to OECD membership and for whom discussions in the accession process started in 2022.

In addition, a higher number of countries do not grow genetically engineered plant varieties but import commodities derived from them, in particular for their feed industry. In 2019, a total of 72 countries dealt with transgenic organisms for production and/or consumption purpose: 29 countries planted them, while 43 additional economies imported their products for use as novel food or feed ingredients.

The OECD offers long-standing recognised expertise in biosafety and contributes to facilitating a harmonised approach. Since 1995, the OECD Working Party on the Harmonisation of Regulatory Oversight in Biotechnology (WP-HROB) has brought together national authorities responsible for the environmental risk/safety assessment of products of modern biotechnology in OECD countries and other economies. International organisations and experts involved in biosafety activities are associated with this programme.

The primary goals of the WP-HROB are to promote international regulatory harmonisation and ensure that methods used in the risk/safety assessment of genetically engineered products are as similar as possible. This may open the way to possible recognition and even acceptance of information from the assessments of other countries. The benefits of harmonisation are multiple: it strengthens mutual understanding among countries, prevents duplication of efforts, saves resources and increases the efficiency of the risk assessment process. Overall, it improves safety while reducing unnecessary barriers to trade.

Guidance and tools developed by the WP-HROB to help the environmental risk/safety assessment of transgenic organisms are already being used worldwide. Biosafety consensus documents are major outputs of its work. These publications address the key elements and core set of science-based issues that countries believe are relevant to biosafety assessments. This information is said to be mutually acceptable among OECD members and other economies associated with the work. Because these documents are publicly available, they can also benefit other countries around the world wishing to use these tools following the same principles.

A total of 60 consensus and guidance documents have been published by the WP-HROB. They mainly address the biology of crops, trees, animals and micro-organisms, as well as specific traits introduced in engineered plants. Their scope is growing in line with the new biotechnological developments and wider applications to new fields. The list shown in Annex A of the publication summarises the extent of the species or subjects currently covered and in which volume of the series to find them.

In addition, information on the transgenic crops approved for commercial release in at least one country for use in agriculture and/or foods and feeds processing can be found in the OECD BioTrack Product Database (https://biotrackproductdatabase.oecd.org). Each transgenic product and its unique identifier are described, with information on approvals in different countries. To date, this database covers 387 approved genetically engineered varieties from 24 plant species and will be extended in future years to include additional species and information from a larger group of countries.

The fast development and increasing use of a range of new breeding techniques, including "genome editing", allows for quicker and more efficient development of applications at a lower cost. These techniques are being reviewed by regulators, risk assessors, researchers and developers for their potential impact on risk/safety assessment while favouring a coherent policy approach to facilitate innovation, and the OECD including the WP-HROB offers the relevant platform for it (see for instance the proceedings of the OECD conference "Genome Editing: Applications in Agriculture – Implications for Health, Environment and Regulation" held in 2018).

This Volume 9 contains a compilation of those biosafety consensus documents issued between 2019 and 2021 dealing with the biology of apple, safflower and rice. The chapter on rice revises and replaces the original document issued in 1999 and published in Volume 1. Also included here are the "Revised points to consider on plant biology consensus documents", originally published in 2006 and revised in 2020, updating the related section of Volume 3. The plant species covered by this volume are three major agricultural crops of different nature and uses. All of them are traded internationally as raw commodities and transformed products, and are subject to biotechnology developments with novel varieties proposed on the market. Apple is a well-known fruit cultivated throughout temperate areas, entering in industrial food processing and being consumed worldwide; safflower is an important oilseed plant mostly cultivated for oil production; while rice is an essential staple cereal crop, cultivated mainly in Asia but also in other regions of the world, easy to store and cook, and commercialised everywhere.

Along with the previous volumes, the introduction section explains the purpose of these documents, their relevance to risk/safety assessment, and the process by which the consensus documents are drafted, using a "lead country(ies)" approach. Australia (safflower), Belgium and Germany (apple), Japan (rice) and the United States (points to consider) led or co-led the preparation of the respective chapters.

The set of science-based information and data contained in Volume 9, previously agreed by consensus and published by the OECD, constitute a solid reference recognised internationally, and a tool for use during the biosafety assessment process. As such, this publication should be of value to applicants for commercial and public uses of engineered varieties of safflower, apple or rice, to risk assessors and regulators from national authorities responsible for granting approvals for their release in the environment as well as to the wider scientific community.

This biosafety work is complementary to the activities of the OECD programme on the safety of novel foods and feeds, in particular to the consensus documents developed on the composition of foods and feeds derived from transgenic organisms. These documents describe the key nutrients, anti-nutrients, toxicants and other constituents that can be used in a comparative approach. More information on this programme can be found in the introduction to this volume.

The consensus documents published in Volumes 1 to 9 of the series are also available individually free of charge on the OECD BioTrack website (www.oecd.org/biotrack). Please note, however, that there have been minor updates to some statistical production data and citations in the current edition.

Acknowledgements

This compendium publication results from the common effort of the participants of the OECD Working Party on the Harmonisation of Regulatory Oversight in Biotechnology (WP-HROB). Its chapters include a "guidance document" and three "consensus documents" which were prepared under the leadership of one or several countries, as listed at the end of this volume. During the preparation of their successive drafts, useful input and suggestions were provided by a number of delegates and experts from the WP-HROB, whether from OECD member countries, non-member economies or observer organisations.

Each guidance or consensus document was issued individually, as soon as finalised and agreed on declassification by the OECD Environment, Health and Safety (EHS) Division in the Series on Harmonisation of Regulatory Oversight in Biotechnology. This volume, containing the documents issued from 2019 to 2021, was prepared by Eleonore Morena. It was edited by Akihiro Kagoshima under the supervision of Bertrand Dagallier, at the EHS Division of the OECD Environment Directorate.

The OECD is grateful to the scientists, regulators and authorities who participated in the development of these chapters on the biology of three crop species subject to biotechnology developments, and wishes to thank each of them.

Table of contents

Foreword 3

Acknowledgements 7

Abbreviations and acronyms 13

Executive summary 17

Introduction to the OECD biosafety consensus documents 19
About the OECD's working party for biosafety 20
Regulatory harmonisation 20
The need for harmonisation activities at the OECD 20
Key background concepts and principles 21
A common approach to risk/safety assessment 21
The emergence of the concept of consensus documents 22
The purpose of consensus documents 22
The process through which consensus documents are initiated and brought to publication 23
Current and future trends in the Working Party on Harmonisation of Regulatory Oversight in Biotechnology 24
The OECD Working Party for the Safety of Novel Foods and Feeds 25
Joint projects of the WP-HROB and WP-SNFF 25
Notes 26
Annex A1. OECD biosafety principles and concepts developed prior to the WP-HROB (1986-94) 27
References 29

Part I Facilitating harmonisation 31

1 Revised points to consider on plant biology consensus documents 33
Introduction 34
Section I. General description including taxonomy and morphology 35
Section II. Centres of origin, geographical distribution and agronomic practices 36
Section III. Reproductive biology 38
Section IV. Genetics 40
Section V. Hybridisation and introgression 41
Section VI. General interactions with other organisms (ecology) 42
Section VII. Additional information 43
Section VII. References 43
Appendix 1. Common pests and pathogens 43

Appendix 2. Biotechnological developments 43
Note 44

Part II Biology of crops 45

2 Biology of Apple (*Malus domestica*) 47
Introduction 48
Species or taxonomic group 48
Reproductive biology 54
Genetics 60
Hybridisation and introgression 62
General interactions with other organisms and ecology 64
Annex 2.A. *Malus* species 67
Annex 2.B. Biotechnological developments 69
Annex 2.C. Apple diseases 71
Annex 2.D. Apple pests 75
References 78

3 Biology of Safflower (*Carthamus tinctorius*) 85
Introduction 86
Species and taxonomic groups 86
Reproductive biology 93
Genetics 99
Hybridisation and introgression 107
General interactions with other organisms (ecology) 112
Additional information 116
Annex 3.A. Common pests and pathogens 119
Annex 3.B. Biotechnological developments 121
References 122
Note 129

4 Biology of Rice (*Oryza sativa*) 131
Introduction 132
General description including taxonomy and morphology 132
Centres of origin, geographical distribution and agronomic practices 139
Reproductive biology 144
Genetics 150
Hybridisation and introgression 160
Various interactions with other organisms (ecology) 166
Annex 4.A. Glossary of rice ecological types and their relationships 179
Annex 4.B. Rice diseases 181
Annex 4.C. Rice pests 185
Annex 4.D. Weeds in rice fields 189
Annex 4.E. Transgenic and genome-edited rice (*Oryza sativa*) 191
Transgenic rice 191
Genome-edited rice 192
References 195

Annex A. List of OECD consensus documents on environmental safety assessment, 1996-2021 219

Tables

Table 2.1. Classification and synonyms of *Malus domestica* 48
Table 2.2. Overview of continents, territories and countries where apple is cultivated 53
Table 2.3. Highlights of a typical management schedule for apple production 54
Table 3.1. Taxonomic groups of *Carthamus* sensu 87
Table 3.2. Guide to the positive identification of *Carthamus tinctorius* L. 89
Table 3.3. Nuclear DNA content and other karyological features 100
Table 3.4. Intraspecific crossing rates and gene flow potential in safflower 104
Table 3.5. Geographical distribution of *Carthamus tinctorius* L. (cultivated safflower) and related species 108
Table 3.6. Assessment of self-compatibility, compatibility with *C. tinctorius* L. and genomic formulae for *Carthamus* spp. 109
Table 4.1. Classification and distribution of 23 species in the genus *Oryza* 133
Table 4.2. Comparison of the main characteristics of japonica and indica rice 138
Table 4.3. Production and cultivation of rice in the world, 2020 139
Table 4.4. Classical Mendelian genes and isolated genes for natural variation in heading date in rice 153
Table 4.5. Type and characters of cytoplasmic male sterility (CMS) 156
Table 4.6. Cloned genes affecting hybrid sterility in intraspecific crosses of *O. sativa* L. 158
Table 4.7. Outcrossing rates estimated in wild and cultivated rice species by different methods 160
Table 4.8. Field experiments to detect the frequency of pollen-mediated (trans)gene flow from cultivated rice to weedy rice 162
Table 4.9. Introgression of genes from wild *Oryza* species into cultivated rice 164

Annex Table 2.A.1. Species and hybrid species in the genus *Malus* 67
Annex Table 2.C.1. Bacteria (including phytoplasma) 71
Annex Table 2.C.2. Fungi 71
Annex Table 2.C.3. Protista; Oomycota 72
Annex Table 2.C.4. Viruses and viroids 72
Annex Table 2.D.1. Arthropoda (ranked by order) 75
Annex Table 2.D.2. Nematodes 77
Annex Table 3.A.1. Summary of common insect pests that affect *Carthamus tinctorius* (safflower) 119
Annex Table 3.A.2. Summary of important diseases that affect *Carthamus tinctorius* (safflower) 120
Annex Table 3.B.1. Approvals of genetically engineered safflowers 121
Annex Table 4.A.1. Characteristics of rice ecological types 179
Annex Table 4.B.1. Fungal and oomycete diseases 181
Annex Table 4.B.2. Bacterial diseases 182
Annex Table 4.B.3. Phytoplasmal diseases 183
Annex Table 4.B.4. Viral diseases 183
Annex Table 4.C.1. Arthropoda 185
Annex Table 4.C.2. Nematoda 187
Annex Table 4.C.3. Mollusca 187
Annex Table 4.D.1. Weeds in rice fields (except for weedy rice (*Oryza sativa* L. [f. *spontanea*]) 189
Annex Table 4.E.1. List of gene modifications by genome editing in rice (till 2020) 194

Figures

Figure 2.1. Commercially grown apple cultivars 49
Figure 2.2. Flower and fruit of apple, cut lengthwise, showing the relation of the parts of the flower 50
Figure 2.3. Evolutionary history of the cultivated apple 51
Figure 2.4. Open king flower and closed lateral flowers 56
Figure 3.1. Safflower crop 86
Figure 3.2. Flowers of cultivated safflower 88
Figure 3.3. Recorded global distribution of cultivated safflower (*Carthamus tinctorius* L.) from 1795 until 2019 90
Figure 3.4. Sowing and harvest dates of major global safflower growers 91

Figure 3.5. Development stages and development timeline of a safflower plant 94
Figure 4.1. Panicle, seeds and brown rice of typical cultivated rice 132
Figure 4.2. Habitats of eight species of the *sativa* complex in the genus *Oryza* 134
Figure 4.3. Evolutionary relationships of species in the genus *Oryza* 135
Figure 4.4. Phenotypic characteristics of cultivated rice *O. sativa* 136
Figure 4.5. Establishment of Asian cultivated rice and some key introgression events 140

Annex Figure 4.A.1. Relationships among wild, weedy, volunteer and cultivated rice 179

Abbreviations and acronyms

°C	Degree Celsius
°N	North latitude
°S	South latitude
µm	Micrometre (= 10^{-6} m)
4-HPPD	4-Hydroxyphenylpyruvate dioxygenase
AFLP	Amplified fragment length polymorphism
ALS	Acetolactate synthase
AMF	Arbuscular mycorrhizal fungi
AOA	Ammonia-oxidising archaea
AOB	Ammonia-oxidising bacteria
AOP	Apomictic Offspring Producer
ApMV	Apple mosaic virus
ATP	Adenosine triphosphate
AUDA-NEPAD	African Union Development Agency – New Partnership for Africa's Development
AWC	Australian Wildlife Conservancy
BB	Bacterial blight
BC	Backcross
BCE	Before the Common (or current) Era
BCO	Biological control organism
BPH	Brown planthopper (*Nilaparvata lugens*)
Bt	*Bacillus thuringiensis*
C.	*Carthamus* genus
Cas9	CRISPR associated protein 9
CBC	OECD Chemicals and Biotechnology Committee
cm	Centimetre
cM	Centimorgan (or map unit [m.u.], a unit for measuring genetic linkage)
CMS	Cytoplasmic male sterility
CR	Critically endangered species (IUCN Red List category)
CRISPR	Clustered regularly interspaced short palindromic repeats
CW	Chinese wild rice
DNA	Deoxyribonucleic acid
EGMS	Environment-sensitive genic male sterility
EN	Endangered species (IUCN Red List category)
EPP	Effective pollination period
ETI	Effector-triggered immunity
FAO	Food and Agriculture Organization of the United Nations
FAOSTAT	FAO Statistical Databases

g	Gramme
Gb	Gigabases (= 10^9 base pairs; genome size unit)
GE	Genetically engineered
GMS	Genetic male sterility
GRH	Green rice leafhopper
GRIN	Germplasm Resources Information Network
GRISP	Global Rice Science Partnership
GSI	Gametophytic self-incompatibility
GTP	Guanosine-5'-triphosphate
GUS	Beta-glucuronidase
h	Hour
ha	Hectare
iGLMap	Integrated Genetic Linkage Map
ILSI-CERA	International Life Sciences Institute – Center for Environmental Risk Assessment
IRGSP	International Rice Genome Sequencing Project
IRRI	International Rice Research Institute
IUCN	International Union for Conservation of Nature
kg	Kilogramme
km	Kilometre
L	Honglian (a wild rice CMS type)
LD	Lead rice
LYP9	Liang-You-Pei-Jiu (a hybrid rice strain)
m	Metre
M.	*Malus* genus
m^2	Square metre
MAS	Marker-assisted selection
Mb	Megabases (=10^6 base pairs; genome size unit)
Mbp	Megabases pair
mg	Milligramme
MGMS	Marker-linked GMS
mm	Millimetre
MSU	Michigan State University
Mya	Million years ago
NBS-LRR	Nucleotide-Binding Site Leucine-Rich Repeat
NERICA	New Rice for Africa
NMS	Nuclear male sterility
NT	Near threatened species (IUCN Red List category)
O.	*Oryza* genus
OECD	Organisation for Economic Co-operation and Development
P.	*Pyricularia* genus
PA64S	Peiai 64S (a photo-thermo-sensitive genic male sterile line)
PAM	Protospacer adjacent motif
PAMPs	Pathogen-associated molecular patterns
PCD	Programmed cell death
PEG	Polyethylene glycol (method)
pg	Picogramme (= 10^{-12} g)
PGMS	Photoperiod-sensitive genic male sterility

pH	Potential of hydrogen
PPO	Polyphenol oxidase
PPR	Pentatricopeptide repeat
PR	Pathogenesis-related (protein)
PTI	PAMP-triggered immunity
QTL	Quantitative trait locus (plural form: Q. T. Loci)
RAPD	Random amplified polymorphic DNA
RAP-DB	Rice Annotation Project Database
RBSDV	Rice black-streaked dwarf virus
RDV	Rice dwarf virus
RGSV	Rice grassy stunt virus
RNAi	Ribonucleic acid interference
ROS	Reactive oxygen species
RRSV	Rice ragged stunt virus
RSV	Rice stripe virus
RTBV	Rice tungro bacilliform virus
RTSV	Rice tungro spherical virus
SA	Salicylic acid
SBPH	Small brown planthopper (*Laodelphax striatellus*)
SDN	Site-directed nuclease
SHROB	OECD Series on Harmonisation of Regulatory Oversight in Biotechnology
SNP	Single nucleotide polymorphism
SRAP	Sequence-related amplified polymorphism
SRBSDV	Southern rice black-streaked dwarf virus
S-RNase	Self-incompatibility ribonuclease
SSR	Simple sequence repeat
t	Tonne
TALENs	Transcription activator-like effector nucleases
TGMS	Thermo-sensitive genic male sterility
TILLING	Targeting Induced Local Lesions IN Genomes
TRD	Transmission ratio distortion
UNEP	United Nations Environment Programme
USDA-ARS	United States Department of Agriculture Agricultural Research Service
VU	Vulnerable species (IUCN Red List category)
WA	Wild abortive
WBPH	Whitebacked planthopper (*Sogatella furcifera*)
WP-HROB	OECD Working Party on the Harmonisation of Regulatory Oversight in Biotechnology
WP-SNFF	OECD Working Party for the Safety of Novel Foods and Feeds

Executive summary

This document constitutes the ninth volume of the OECD Series on Harmonisation of Regulatory Oversight in Biotechnology, which relates to the environmental risk/safety assessment of transgenic organisms, also called "biosafety". It is a compendium of individual "consensus documents" published by the Working Party on the Harmonisation of Regulatory Oversight in Biotechnology. The eight previous volumes of the series covered documents issued from 1996 to 2018. The current volume contains the consensus documents published in 2019-21 on the biology of apple, safflower and rice, preceded by the "points to consider" section providing guidance to authors of draft consensus documents.

Modern biotechnologies are applied to crop plants as well as trees, animals and micro-organisms. The safety of the resulting transgenic organisms, when released in the environment for use in agriculture, forestry, fishery, the food and feed industry or other applications, represents a challenging issue. Genetically engineered products are rigorously assessed by their developers during their elaboration and by governments when ready for release, to ensure high safety standards. These risk/safety assessments, conducted through a scientifically sound approach, inform biosafety regulators and support the decision concerning the release of novel organisms in the environment. Such assessments are considered essential for healthy and sustainable agriculture, industry and trade.

The OECD offers long-standing recognised expertise in biosafety and contributes to facilitating a harmonised approach. The environmental risk/safety assessment of transgenic organisms is usually based on the information collected on the characteristics of the host organism, the introduced traits, the environment into which the organism will be released, the interaction between these factors and the intended use of the organism. The OECD consensus documents identify parts of this information that could be commonly used in countries when conducting environmental risk/safety assessment, aiming to encourage information sharing and prevent duplication of effort among countries. They offer practical tools which compile science-based information relevant for this purpose. They are not a substitute for national requirements and locally available data should also be taken into account, but they can contribute to the risk/safety assessment process. These documents are publicly available and considered worldwide as sustainable references for use in biosafety evaluation.

Opening Volume 9, the introduction to the biosafety consensus documents provides additional information on the key background concepts, principles and common approaches prevailing in risk/safety assessment of transgenic organisms. The purpose of the OECD consensus documents is described, as well as the process through which these documents are developed.

Chapter 1 deals with the "Revised points to consider on plant biology consensus documents", originally published in 2006 and revised in 2020. It offers a structured explanatory checklist of relevant points to consider when preparing or evaluating a consensus document on the biology of a cultivated plant species, in relation to biotechnology and environmental risk/safety assessment of novel varieties.

Chapters 2, 3 and 4 deal with the biology of three major agricultural plants whose products are traded internationally, subject to diverse transformations and uses, and consumed worldwide. These cultivated plant species are respectively: a fruit tree, apple (*Malus domestica*); an oilseed crop, safflower (*Carthamus tinctorius*); and a staple cereal, rice (*Oryza sativa*). The final section on rice revises the original publication of 1999 contained in Volume 1. The information contained in the three biology chapters provides, for each of the crops, key insights into the regulatory assessment of the environmental safety of genetically engineered varieties: taxonomy, centres of origin, geographic distribution, reproductive biology, genetics, hybridisation and introgression, as well as ecology. Chapter annexes then present the common diseases and pests for the concerned plant and its current biotechnological developments.

The set of science-based information and data contained in this volume, previously agreed by consensus and published by the OECD, constitute a solid reference recognised internationally and already widely used as part of biosafety assessments. As such, this publication should be of value to applicants for commercial uses of transgenic organisms, to risk assessors and regulators from national authorities responsible for granting approvals for their release in the environment as well as to the wider scientific community.

Introduction to the OECD biosafety consensus documents

This chapter introduces the consensus documents developed by the OECD Working Party on the Harmonisation of Regulatory Oversight in Biotechnology (WP-HROB) which deal with the environmental safety (or biosafety) of products. Information is provided on the Working Party background and its aim towards harmonisation in biotechnology, including key concepts biotechnology, principles and a common approach to risk/safety assessment on which the work is based. The consensus documents published by the WP-HROB are available as tools for helping authorities in their biosafety regulatory assessments. The purpose of these documents and their development process are explained. Then, current and future trends in the WP-HROB and their complementarity with the activities of the Working Party for the Safety of Novel Foods and Feeds are summarised.

About the OECD's working party for biosafety

The OECD Working Party on the Harmonisation of Regulatory Oversight in Biotechnology (WP-HROB) comprises delegates from the 38 member countries of the OECD and the European Commission. Typically, delegates are assigned from those government ministries and agencies responsible for the environmental risk/safety assessment of products of modern biotechnology. The WP-HROB also includes a number of observer delegations and invited experts who participate in its work, from countries such as Argentina and South Africa, the United Nations Environment Programme (UNEP), the Secretariat of the Convention on Biological Diversity (SCBD), the Food and Agriculture Organization of the United Nations (FAO), the African Union Development Agency - New Partnership for Africa's Development (AUDA-NEPAD), and the Business at OECD (BIAC).

In recent years, with the increasing use of biotechnology products in many regions of the world, together with the development of activities relating to tropical and subtropical species, participation was enlarged to invited non-member economies including Bangladesh, Brazil, the People's Republic of China, India, Indonesia, Kenya, Paraguay, the Philippines, Thailand, Uruguay and Viet Nam. Several other countries, which have since become OECD members, participated in the WP-HROB activities as non-members before their accession. From July 2011 to December 2014, a programme was jointly implemented by the World Bank, the ILSI Research Foundation (now the Agriculture & Food Systems Institute AFSI) – Center for Environmental Risk Assessment (ILSI-CERA) and the OECD within the framework of the Partnership for Biosafety Risk Assessment and Regulation, which developed new links, enhanced collaboration and supported the participation of four non-member economies in the activities of the WP-HROB.

Regulatory harmonisation

The Working Party on the Harmonisation of Regulatory Oversight in Biotechnology was established in 1995,[1] at a time when the first commercial transgenic crops were being considered for regulatory approval in a number of OECD countries. From the beginning, one of the group's primary goals was to promote international regulatory harmonisation in biotechnology among members. Regulatory harmonisation is the attempt to ensure that the information used in risk/safety assessments, as well as the methods used to collect such information, is as similar as possible. This should lead to countries recognising or even accepting information from one another's assessments. The benefits of harmonisation are clear. It increases mutual understanding among countries, which avoids duplication, saves on scarce resources and increases the efficiency of the risk/safety assessment process. This, in turn, improves safety while reducing unnecessary barriers to trade (OECD, 2000).

The need for harmonisation activities at the OECD

The establishment of the WP-HROB and its programme of work followed a detailed review by member countries of whether there was a need to continue work on harmonisation in biotechnology at the OECD and, if so, what it should entail. This analysis was undertaken by the Ad Hoc Group for Environmental Aspects of Biotechnology (established by the Joint Meeting)[2] in 1994.

The Ad Hoc Group for Environmental Aspects of Biotechnology took into consideration and built upon earlier work at the OECD which had begun in the mid-1980s. Initially, these OECD activities focused on the environmental and agricultural implications of field trials of transgenic organisms but this was soon followed by a consideration of their large-scale use and commercialisation (a summary of this extensive body of work can be found in the annex to this introductory chapter).

Key background concepts and principles

The Ad Hoc Group for Environmental Aspects of Biotechnology took into account previous work on risk analysis that is summarised in the publication *Safety Considerations for Biotechnology: Scale-up of Crop Plants* (OECD, 1993a). The following quote gives the flavour: "Risk/safety analysis is based on the characteristics of the organism, the introduced trait, the environment into which the organism is introduced, the interaction between these, and the intended application". This body of work has formed the basis for environmental risk/safety assessment that is now globally accepted. In considering the possibilities for harmonisation, the ad hoc group paid attention to these characteristics and the information used by risk/safety assessors to address them.

This was reinforced by the concept of familiarity, also elaborated in the above-mentioned document (OECD, 1993a). This concept "is based on the fact that most genetically engineered organisms are developed from organisms such as crop plants whose biology is well understood. Familiarity allows the risk assessor to draw on previous knowledge and experience with the introduction of plants and micro-organisms into the environment". For plants, familiarity takes account of a wide range of attributes including, for example, knowledge and experience with "the crop plant, including its flowering/reproductive characteristics, ecological requirements, and past breeding experiences" (OECD, 1993a; see also the annex for a more detailed description). This illustrates the role of information related to the biology of the host organism as a part of an environmental risk/safety assessment.

The Ad Hoc Group for Environmental Aspects of Biotechnology also considered document *Traditional Crop Breeding Practices: An Historical Review to Serve as a Baseline for Assessing the Role of Modern Biotechnology* (OECD, 1993b), which focuses on host organisms. It presents information on an initial group of 17 different crop plants, which are used (or are likely to be used) in modern biotechnology. It includes sections on phytosanitary considerations in the movement of germplasm and on the current uses of these crop plants. There is also a detailed section on current breeding practices.

A common approach to risk/safety assessment

An important aspect for the Ad Hoc Group for Environmental Aspects of Biotechnology was to identify the extent to which member countries address the same questions and issues during risk/safety assessment. Big differences would mean difficulties in working towards harmonisation, while a high level of similarity would suggest it is more feasible.

This point was resolved by two studies considered by the ad hoc group: one covered crop plants (OECD, 1995a; 1995b) while the other concerned micro-organisms (OECD, 1995c; 1995d). Both studies involved a survey with national authorities responsible for risk/safety assessment. The aim was to identify the questions they address during the assessment process (as outlined in national laws/regulations/guidance texts) in order to establish the extent of similarity among national authorities. The studies used the information provided in the OECD "Blue Book" on Recombinant DNA Safety Considerations (OECD, 1986) as a reference point, in particular the sections covering: i) general scientific considerations; ii) human health considerations; and iii) environmental and agricultural considerations (Appendices B, C and D). Both studies showed a remarkably high degree of similarity among countries in the questions/issues addressed in risk/safety assessment.

The emergence of the concept of consensus documents

The Working Party on the Harmonisation of Regulatory Oversight in Biotechnology was therefore established with the knowledge that national authorities have much in common in terms of the questions/issues addressed when undertaking risk/safety assessments. It also took into account those characteristics identified as part of the assessment (i.e. the organism, the introduced trait and the environment) around which harmonisation activities could focus.

It was further recognised that much of the information used in risk/safety assessment relating to the biology of host organisms (crop plants, trees, animals or micro-organisms) would be similar or virtually the same in all assessments involving the same organism. In other words, the questions addressed during risk/safety assessment which relate to the biology of the organism, for example the potential for gene transfer within the crop plant species and among related species, as well as the potential for weediness, remain the same for each application involving the same host species. This also applies to some extent to information related to introduced traits.

Consequently, the WP-HROB put forth the idea of compiling information common to the risk/safety assessment of a number of transgenic products and decided to focus on two specific categories: the biology of the host species and traits used in genetic modifications. The aim was to encourage information sharing and prevent duplication of effort among countries by avoiding the need to address the same common issues in applications involving the same organism or trait. It was recognised that biology and trait consensus documents could be agreed upon relatively quickly by member countries (within a few years). This compilation process was formalised in the drafting of consensus documents.

The purpose of consensus documents

The consensus documents are not intended to be a substitute for a risk/safety assessment because they address only a part of the necessary information. Nevertheless, they should make an important contribution to environmental risk/safety assessment.

Consensus documents are intended to be a "snapshot" of current information, for use during the regulatory assessment of products of biotechnology. They are not intended to be a comprehensive source of information covering the full knowledge about a specific host organism or trait; they do, however, address – on a consensus basis – the key or core set of issues that countries believe to be relevant to risk/safety assessment.

The documents aim to share information on these key components of an environmental safety review in order to prevent duplication of effort among countries. The documents are envisaged to be used by: i) applicants as information to be given in applications to regulatory authorities; ii) regulators as a general guide and reference source in their reviews; and 3) governments for information sharing, research reference and public information.

Originally, it was said that the information in the consensus documents is intended to be mutually recognised or mutually acceptable among OECD member countries, though the precise meaning of these terms is still open for discussion. During the period of the Ad Hoc Group for Environmental Aspects of Biotechnology and the early days of the WG-HROB (1993-95), the phrase "mutual acceptance of data" was discussed. This concept, borrowed from the OECD Chemicals Programme, involves OECD Council decisions that have legally binding implications for member countries. In the case of the consensus documents, there has never been a legally binding commitment to use the information they contain, though the WP-HROB is interested in enhancing the commitment of countries to make use of the documents. Participation in the development of documents and the intention by countries to use the information is done in "good faith". It is expected, therefore, that reference will be made to relevant consensus documents during risk/safety assessments. As these documents are publicly available, they can be of interest to any country wishing to use them in national assessments.

The process through which consensus documents are initiated and brought to publication

There are a number of steps in the drafting of a specific consensus document. The first occurs when a delegation, in a formal meeting of the Working Party on the Harmonisation of Regulatory Oversight in Biotechnology, makes a proposal to draft a document on a new topic, typically a crop species or a trait. If the WP-HROB agrees to the proposal, a provisional draft is prepared by either a single country or two or more countries working together ("lead country approach"). Typically, lead countries have had experience with the concerned plant, animal, micro-organism or trait and are able to draw on experts to prepare a provisional draft. Where relevant, an ad hoc group is constituted with experts from several interested countries and observer organisations, bringing the range of current knowledge on the specific topic in order to contribute at best to the drafting exercise.

The provisional draft is first reviewed by the Bureau of the WP-HROB[3] to ensure that it addresses the range of issues normally covered by consensus documents and is of sufficiently high quality to merit consideration by the WP-HROB as a whole.

Based on the comments of the bureau, a first draft is prepared for consideration by the full WP-HROB. This is the opportunity for each delegation to review the text and provide comments based on their national experiences. Input is incorporated in a second draft, which is again circulated to the WP-HROB. At this point, the WP-HROB may decide to recommend that the document should be declassified. Such a recommendation is only forthcoming when all delegations have come to a consensus that the document is complete and ready for publication. Sometimes, however, the text may need a third round or more of discussions within the WP-HROB before declassification can be contemplated.

Once the WP-HROB has agreed for a final document to be ready for publication, it is forwarded to the supervisory committee, the Chemicals and Biotechnology Committee (CBC), recommending declassification. Following the agreement of the CBC, the document is then published.

It is important to note that the review of consensus documents is not limited to formal meetings of the WP-HROB. Ad hoc expert groups might also exchange in meetings or workshops, where feasible. Furthermore, much discussion occurs through electronic means during the whole process, especially via the protected website dedicated to the WP-HROB. This enables a range of experts to have input into drafts.

For a number of documents, it has also been necessary to include information from non-member countries. This wider share of expertise has become increasingly important in recent years with the development of activities relating to tropical and subtropical species. This has been particularly true in the case of crop plants where the centre of origin and diversity occurs in a non-member country(ies). In these cases, UNEP, the FAO, the African Biosafety Network of Expertise of the AUDA-NEPAD and other organisations have assisted in the preparation of documents by identifying experts from relevant countries, including international agricultural research centres as appropriate.

The full series of consensus documents developed by the WP-HROB is also published in compendium documents, as is the case for this volume. Volume 8 was issued in 2018 (covering 2018), Volume 7 in 2017 (covering 2016-17), Volumes 5 and 6 in 2016 (covering 2011-15), Volumes 3 and 4 in 2010 (covering 2007-10), while Volumes 1 and 2 were published in 2006 (covering 1996-2006) (OECD, 2006a, 2006b, 2010a, 2010b, 2016a, 2016b, 2016c, 2017, 2018).

Current and future trends in the Working Party on Harmonisation of Regulatory Oversight in Biotechnology

The WP-HROB continues its work on the preparation of specific consensus documents and on the efficiency of the process by which they are developed. An increasingly large number of crops and other host species (trees, animals, micro-organisms) are being modified, for an increasing number of traits, and the WP-HROB aims to fulfil the current needs whilst preparing for emerging topics.

At the OECD Workshop on Review of Consensus Documents and Future Work in Harmonisation held in Washington, DC in 2003, the WP-HROB considered how to set priorities for drafting future consensus documents among a large number of possibilities. It was also recognised that published consensus documents may be in need of review and updating from time to time, to ensure that they include the most up-to-date information. The WP-HROB considers these aspects on a regular basis when planning future work. For the preparation of future documents, the workshop identified the usefulness of developing a standardised structure of consensus documents. Thus, the working party issued a guidance document on “points to consider” for consensus documents on the biology of cultivated plants that was published in 2006, further revised in 2020 and constituting the first chapter of this Volume 9.

Among the important activities of the WP-HROB, a new document is being developed on the “environmental considerations for the risk/safety assessment for the release of transgenic plants”. Focused on the core of the biosafety work that is applied to crops and trees and taking into account the most recent views from countries of all regions of the world, this document will constitute a key guidance tool for developers, assessors and regulatory authorities. It is expected to be published in 2022.

An important step was taken in 2017 with the publication of the first consensus biology document dedicated to an animal species, the Atlantic salmon (*Salmo salar*). It was followed one year later by the publication on the mosquito *Aedes aegypti*, which represented a key development for the WP-HROB by enlarging further the range of organisms potentially covered and directly contributing to human health issues for the first time. Some genetically engineered strains of *Ae. aegyti* are used to control the virus-vector insect population in the fight against tropical diseases (yellow fever, dengue and others) that have been dramatically extending in many regions of the world over the last decade. A document on the biology of another mosquito, *Anopheles gambiae*, the main vector of malaria disease, is under preparation.

The WP-HROB is also considering projects on micro-organisms, therefore opening up to new areas, for instance bioenergy, with the ongoing preparation of a document on eukaryotic micro-algae. The photosynthetic cyanobacteria are potential providers of renewable energy and are of special interest as they can be cultivated year-round in non-arable areas, alleviating the pressure on farmland and freshwater resources that would be exerted by crops grown for biofuel purposes, as stated in the proceedings of the OECD Conference on Biosafety and the Environmental Uses of Micro-Organisms (OECD, 2015a). Other biotechnology developments applied to micro-organisms might be considered to prepare future documents: an updated review of biofertiliser organisms living in symbiosis in crop roots and optimising the nitrogen fixation, or biocontrol agents acting as plant protection products to control disease and attack by insects and other herbivores. Other exploratory fields may comprise bioremediation by using living organisms for removing contaminants from the environment such as polluted land, or the development of detergents containing micro-organisms.

In recent years, the WP-HROB has initiated the exchange of knowledge and promoted discussion on the new plant breeding techniques and their potential impact on biosafety assessment. An OECD workshop was organised on these matters in 2014; the key message from its report at the time was that “experience to date indicates that current guidance and tools for environmental risk/safety assessment of transgenic plants are applicable to plants developed using [new plant breeding techniques]”, where such assessment may be required (OECD, 2016c). Specific events on new plant breeding techniques are regularly organised at the OECD for increasing awareness and sharing information, including the important Conference on

Genome Editing Applications in Agriculture – Implications for Health, Environment and Regulation held in 2018 (Transgenic Research, 2019). The subject will be kept under review.

The OECD Working Party for the Safety of Novel Foods and Feeds

The OECD Working Party for the Safety of Novel Foods and Feeds (WP-SNFF) addresses aspects of the assessment of human food and animal feed derived from genetically engineered crops. Established in 1999 as a "task force", this body became an OECD working group in 1997 and then a working party in 2021. As with the WP-HROB, the main focus of WP-SNFF work is to ensure that the types of information used in risk/safety assessment, as well as the methods used to collect such information, are as similar as possible amongst countries. The approach is to compare transgenic crops and derived products with similar conventional ones that are already known and considered safe because of their history of safe use. Harmonised methods and the sharing of information are facilitated through the WP-SNFF's activities.

In a similar approach to the biosafety programme, the main outcome of the foods and feeds programme is the set of consensus documents on compositional considerations of new varieties of specific crops. The WP-SNFF documents compile a common base of scientific information on the major components of crop plants, such as key nutrients, anti-nutrients, toxicants, allergens and other constituents. These documents constitute practical tools for regulators and risk/safety assessors dealing with these new varieties, with respect to foods and feeds. To date, 31 consensus documents have been published on major crops and on general considerations for facilitating harmonisation, including regular updates of the oldest issues. They constitute the Series on the Safety of Novel Foods and Feeds which is also available on the OECD's website (www.oecd.org/biotrack). A document on considerations for collaborative work on the safety assessment of foods and feeds derived from rDNA plants is under preparation.

The full series of consensus documents developed by the WP-SNFF is also published in compendium documents. Volume 3 was issued in 2019 (covering 2015-19), Volume 2 and Volume 1 were issued in 2015 (covering 2002-14) (OECD, 2015b, 2015c, 2019).

Joint projects of the WP-HROB and WP-SNFF

The two bodies (WP-HROB and WP-SNFF) are implementing closely related and complementary programmes, focused on environmental aspects for the first and food and feed aspects for the second. Their co-operation on issues of common interest resulted in a document developed jointly by the two bodies, the "Consensus Document on Molecular Characterisation of Plants Derived from Modern Biotechnology", published in 2010 (included in Volume 3 of the current series) (OECD, 2010b). The two bodies also refer to the same "unique identifiers" assigned by developers to transgenic products approved for cultivation and/or for food and feed use; they wish to keep this system defined by the OECD always relevant and adapted to new types of products and new species. The unique identifier system is described in Volume 3 (OECD, 2010b).

Both working parties collaborate on the ongoing update of the OECD legal instrument of interest for risk/safety assessors of genetically engineered organisms, the Recommendation of the Council concerning Safety Considerations for Applications of Recombinant DNA Organisms in Industry, Agriculture and the Environment, for publication expected in 2023. The two bodies are also conducting common events such as workshops and conferences, and other joint activities are being contemplated.

Notes

[1] The original title of the working party was the Expert Group for the Harmonisation of Regulatory Oversight in Biotechnology. It became an OECD working group in 1998 and then working party in 2021.

[2] The Joint Meeting of the Chemicals Committee and the Working Party on Chemicals, Pesticides and Biotechnology (hereafter 'Joint Meeting') was the supervisory body of the Ad Hoc Group for Environmental Aspects of Biotechnology and, as a result of its findings, established the WP-HROB as a subsidiary body. The Joint Meeting became the Chemicals and Biotechnology Committee in 2021.

[3] The bureau comprises the chair and vice-chairs of the working party. The bureau is elected by the working party once a year. At the time of preparing this publication, the chair is from Australia, and vice-chairs from Belgium, Canada, Finland, Japan and the United States.

Annex A1. OECD biosafety principles and concepts developed prior to the WP-HROB (1986-94)

Since the mid-1980s the OECD has been developing harmonised approaches to the risk/safety assessment of products of modern biotechnology. Prior to the establishment of the Working Party on the Harmonisation of Regulatory Oversight in Biotechnology, the OECD published a number of reports on safety considerations, concepts and principles for risk/safety assessment as well as information on field releases of transgenic crops, and a consideration of traditional crop breeding practices. This annex notes some of the highlights of these achievements that were background considerations in the establishment of the working party and its development of consensus documents.

Underlying scientific principles

In 1986, the OECD published its first safety considerations for genetically engineered organisms (OECD, 1986). These included the issues relevant to human health, the environment and agriculture that might be considered in a risk/safety assessment. In its recommendations for agricultural and environmental applications, it suggested that risk/safety assessors:

> *"- Use the considerable data on the environmental and human health effects of living organisms to guide risk assessments.*
>
> *- Ensure that recombinant DNA organisms are evaluated for potential risk, prior to application in agriculture and the environment by means of an independent review of potential risks on a case-by-case basis.*
>
> *- Conduct the development of recombinant DNA organisms for agricultural and environmental applications in a stepwise fashion, moving, where appropriate, from the laboratory to the growth chamber and greenhouse, to limited field testing and finally to large-scale field testing.*
>
> *- Encourage further research to improve the prediction, evaluation, and monitoring of the outcome of applications of recombinant DNA organisms." (OECD, 1986)*

The role of confinement in small-scale testing

In 1992, the OECD published its *Good Developmental Principles* (OECD, 1992) for the design of small-scale field research involving transgenic plants and micro-organisms. It describes the use of confinement in field tests. Confinement includes measures to avoid the dissemination or establishment of organisms from a field trial, for example, the use of physical, temporal or biological isolation (such as the use of sterility).

Scale-up of crop plants – "Risk/safety analysis"

By 1993, the focus of attention had switched to the scale-up of crop plants as plant breeders began to move to larger-scale production and commercialisation of transgenic plants. The OECD published general principles for scale-up, which reaffirmed that:

> *"...safety in biotechnology is achieved by the appropriate application of risk/safety analysis and risk management. Risk/safety analysis comprises hazard identification and, if a hazard has been identified, risk assessment. Risk/safety analysis is based on the characteristics of the organism, the introduced trait, the environment into which the organism is introduced, the interaction between these and the intended application.*

> *Risk/safety analysis is conducted prior to an intended action and is typically a routine component of research, development and testing of new organisms, whether performed in a laboratory or a field setting. Risk/safety analysis is a scientific procedure which does not imply or exclude regulatory oversight or imply that every case will necessarily be reviewed by a national or other authority."* (OECD, 1993a)

The role of familiarity in risk/safety assessment

The issue of scale-up also led to an important concept – familiarity – which is one key approach that has been used subsequently to address the environmental safety of transgenic plants.

The concept of familiarity is based on the fact that most genetically engineered organisms are developed from organisms such as crop plants, whose biology is well understood. It is not a risk/safety assessment in itself (US-NAS, 1989). However, the concept facilitates risk/safety assessments because to be familiar means having enough information to be able to make a judgement on safety or risk (US-NAS, 1989). Familiarity can also be used to indicate appropriate management practices, including whether standard agricultural practices are adequate or whether other management practices are needed to manage the risk (OECD, 1993a). Familiarity allows the risk assessor to draw on previous knowledge and experience with the introduction of plants and micro-organisms into the environment and this indicates appropriate management practices. As familiarity depends also on the knowledge about the environment and its interaction with introduced organisms, the risk/safety assessment in one country may not be applicable in another country. However, as field tests are performed, information will accumulate about the organisms involved and their interactions with a number of environments.

Familiarity comes from the knowledge and experience available for conducting a risk/safety analysis prior to the scale-up of any new plant line or crop cultivar in a particular environment. For plants, for example, familiarity takes account of, but need not be restricted to, knowledge and experience with the following:

> *"- The crop plant, including its flowering/reproductive characteristics, ecological requirements, and past breeding experiences.*
>
> *- The agricultural and surrounding environment of the trial site.*
>
> *- Specific trait(s) transferred to the plant line(s).*
>
> *- Results from previous basic research including greenhouse/glasshouse and small-scale field research with the new plant line or with other plant lines having the same trait.*
>
> *- The scale-up of lines of the plant crop varieties developed by more traditional techniques of plant breeding.*
>
> *- The scale-up of other plant lines developed by the same technique.*
>
> *- The presence of related (and sexually compatible) plants in the surrounding natural environment, and knowledge of the potential for gene transfer between crop plant and the relative.*
>
> *- Interactions between/among the crop plant, environment and trait".* (OECD, 1993a)

Risk/safety assessment and risk management

Risk/safety assessment involves the identification of potential environmental adverse effects or hazards, and when a hazard is identified, determining the probability of it occurring. If a potential hazard or adverse effect is identified, measures may be taken to minimise or mitigate it. This is risk management. Absolute certainty, or "zero risk", in a safety assessment is not achievable, so uncertainty is an inescapable aspect of all risk assessment and risk management (OECD, 1993a). For example, there is uncertainty in extrapolating the results of testing in one species to identify potential effects in another. Risk assessors and risk managers thus spend considerable effort to address uncertainty. Many of the activities in intergovernmental organisations, such as the OECD, address ways to handle uncertainty (OECD, 2000).

References

OECD (2019), *Safety Assessment of Foods and Feeds Derived from Transgenic Crops, Volume 3*, Novel Food and Feed Safety, OECD Publishing, Paris, https://doi.org/10.1787/f04f3c98-en.

OECD (2018), *Safety Assessment of Transgenic Organisms in the Environment, Volume 8: OECD Consensus Document on the Biology of Mosquito Aedes aegypti*, Harmonisation of Regulatory Oversight in Biotechnology, OECD Publishing, Paris, https://doi.org/10.1787/9789264302235-en.

OECD (2017), *Safety Assessment of Transgenic Organisms in the Environment, Volume 7: OECD Consensus Documents*, Harmonisation of Regulatory Oversight in Biotechnology, OECD Publishing, Paris, http://dx.doi.org/10.1787/9789264279728-en.

OECD (2016a), *Safety Assessment of Transgenic Organisms in the Environment, Volume 6: OECD Consensus Documents*, Harmonisation of Regulatory Oversight in Biotechnology, OECD Publishing, Paris, http://dx.doi.org/10.1787/9789264253421-en.

OECD (2016b), *Safety Assessment of Transgenic Organisms in the Environment, Volume 5: OECD Consensus Documents*, Harmonisation of Regulatory Oversight in Biotechnology, OECD Publishing, Paris, http://dx.doi.org/10.1787/9789264253018-en.

OECD (2016c), "Report of the OECD Workshop on Environmental Risk Assessment of Products Derived from New Plant Breeding Techniques (February 2014)", *Series on Harmonisation of Regulatory Oversight in Biotechnology No. 61*, OECD, Paris, www.oecd.org/officialdocuments/publicdisplaydocumentpdf/?cote=env/jm/mono(2016)5&doclanguage=en.

OECD (2015a), *Biosafety and the Environmental Uses of Micro-Organisms: Conference Proceedings*, OECD Publishing, Paris, http://dx.doi.org/10.1787/9789264213562-en.

OECD (2015b), *Safety Assessment of Foods and Feeds Derived from Transgenic Crops, Volume 2*, Novel Food and Feed Safety, OECD Publishing, Paris, http://dx.doi.org/10.1787/9789264180338-en..

OECD (2015c), *Safety Assessment of Foods and Feeds Derived from Transgenic Crops, Volume 1*, Novel Food and Feed Safety, OECD Publishing, Paris, http://dx.doi.org/10.1787/9789264180147-en

OECD (2010a), *Safety Assessment of Transgenic Organisms: OECD Consensus Documents: Volume 4*, Harmonisation of Regulatory Oversight in Biotechnology, OECD Publishing, Paris, http://dx.doi.org/10.1787/9789264096158-en.

OECD (2010b), *Safety Assessment of Transgenic Organisms: OECD Consensus Documents: Volume 3*, Harmonisation of Regulatory Oversight in Biotechnology, OECD Publishing, Paris, http://dx.doi.org/10.1787/9789264095434-en.

OECD (2006a), *Safety Assessment of Transgenic Organisms: OECD Consensus Documents: Volume 2*, Harmonisation of Regulatory Oversight in Biotechnology, OECD Publishing, Paris, http://dx.doi.org/10.1787/9789264095403-en.

OECD (2006b), *Safety Assessment of Transgenic Organisms: OECD Consensus Documents: Volume 1*, Harmonisation of Regulatory Oversight in Biotechnology, OECD Publishing, Paris, http://dx.doi.org/10.1787/9789264095380-en.

OECD (2000), "Report of the Working Group on Harmonisation of Regulatory Oversight in Biotechnology", Prepared for the G8 Summit held in Okinawa, Japan on 21-23 July 2000, C(2000)86/ADD2, OECD, Paris, www.oecd.org/chemicalsafety/biotrack/Report-of-the-Working-Group-on-Harmonisation-of-Regulatory.pdf.

OECD (1995a), "Commercialisation of agricultural products derived through modern biotechnology: Survey results", *OECD Environment Monograph: Series No. 99*, OECD, Paris, www.oecd.org/science/biotrack/1876950.pdf.

OECD (1995b), "Report of the OECD Workshop on the Commercialisation of Agricultural Products Derived through Modern Biotechnology", *OECD Environment Monograph: Series No. 107*, OECD, Paris, www.oecd.org/officialdocuments/publicdisplaydocumentpdf/?cote=OCDE/GD(95)72&docLanguage=En.

OECD (1995c), "Analysis of information elements used in the assessment of certain products of modern biotechnology", *OECD Environment Monograph: Series No. 100*, OECD, Paris, www.oecd.org/officialdocuments/publicdisplaydocumentpdf/?cote=OCDE/GD(95)11&docLanguage=En.

OECD (1995d), *Safety Considerations for Biotechnology: Scale-up of Micro-organisms as Biofertilizers*, OECD, Paris, www.oecd.org/env/ehs/biotrack/Safety-considerations-scale-up-of-micro-organisms-as-biofertilizers.pdf.

OECD (1993a), *Safety Considerations for Biotechnology: Scale-up of Crop Plants*, OECD, Paris, www.oecd.org/env/ehs/biotrack/1958527.pdf.

OECD (1993b), *Traditional Crop Breeding Practices: An Historical Review to Serve as a Baseline for Assessing the Role of Modern Biotechnology*, OECD, Paris, www.oecd.org/env/ehs/biotrack/1946204.pdf.

OECD (1992), *Safety Considerations for Biotechnology – Part Two: Good Developmental Principles (GDP)*, OECD, Paris, www.oecd.org/sti/biotech/2375496.pdf.

OECD (1986), *Recombinant DNA Safety Considerations. Safety Considerations for Industrial, Agricultural and Environmental Applications of Organisms Derived by Recombinant DNA Techniques* ("The Blue Book"), OECD, Paris, www.oecd.org/env/ehs/biotrack/Recombinant-DNA-Safety-Considerations.pdf.

Transgenic Research (2019), "OECD Conference on Genome Editing: Applications in Agriculture – Implications for Health, Environment and Regulation held in June 2018, Proceedings (25 articles)", *Transgenic Research,* Vol. 28/2, https://link.springer.com/journal/11248/volumes-and-issues/28-2/supplement

US-NAS (1989), *Field Testing of Genetically Modified Organisms: Framework for Decisions*, National Research Council, Committee on Scientific Evaluation of the Introduction of Genetically Modified Microorganisms and Plants into the Environment, National Academy Press, Washington, DC, www.nap.edu/catalog/1431/field-testing-genetically-modified-organisms-framework-for-decisions.

Part I Facilitating harmonisation

1 Revised points to consider on plant biology consensus documents

This chapter deals with the revised "points to consider on consensus documents on the biology of cultivated plants", an update of the original 2006 publication. It provides a structured explanatory checklist, regarding both order and contents, of relevant points to consider when preparing or evaluating a consensus document on the biology of a cultivated vascular plant species or other taxonomic groups of interest, in relation to biotechnology and environmental risk/safety assessment. Existing consensus documents are mentioned as illustrative examples for each considered point.

Introduction

This chapter was prepared by the OECD Working Party on the Harmonisation of Regulatory Oversight in Biotechnology, with the **United States** as the lead country. It was initially issued in 2020 as the Revised Points to Consider on Consensus Documents on the Biology of Cultivated Plants, replacing the original document issued in 2006. It was completed in this publication with few examples of references to consensus documents published in 2020 and 2021.

Page numbers quoted in the examples provided throughout the chapter refer to the original consensus documents that can be consulted on the OECD BioTrack website: Consensus Documents for the Work on Harmonisation of Regulatory Oversight in Biotechnology: By number - OECD.

Most environmental risk/safety assessments of transformed (genetically modified or engineered) plants are based upon a broad body of knowledge and experience with the untransformed species (variety, etc.), i.e. familiarity with the crop plant. The biology consensus document intends to describe portions of this body of knowledge directly relevant to risk/safety assessment in a format readily accessible to regulators. The document is not an environmental risk/safety assessment of the species. Rather, the consensus document provides an overview of pertinent biological information on the untransformed species to help define the baseline and scope (the comparator against which transformed organisms will be compared) in the risk/safety assessment of the transformed organism. Consensus documents are not detailed crop handbooks or manuals of agricultural or silvicultural practice or economic botany, but rather focus on the biological information and data that may be clearly relevant to the assessment of newly transformed plants.

This *Points to Consider* chapter is meant as a structured explanatory checklist, regarding both order and contents, of relevant points to consider in preparing or evaluating a consensus document on the biology of a cultivated vascular plant species or other taxonomic groups of interest, in relation to biotechnology and environmental risk/safety assessment. The general approach laid out here may also be pertinent to non-vascular plants (e.g. mosses), fungi, animals and micro-organisms; however, these groups are biologically and ecologically so different that further adaptation and refinement of the general approach will be necessary.

The biology consensus documents that have been published to date as well as most in preparation (excepting those on the oyster mushroom, Atlantic salmon, mosquito species and micro-organisms) are on annual crops, timber trees and fruit trees. The plants of interest that have been the subject of the documents are primarily row crops, or trees managed silviculturally or grown in plantations or orchards. They are vascular plants, either flowering plants (angiosperms) or conifers (gymnosperms).

The points to consider as covered in the present chapter create a basic format and scope to be used for writing or reviewing new consensus documents and updating the earlier documents. While this chapter is meant to provide a basic format and scope, it is not intended to be rigid or inflexible. Of the biology consensus documents to date, some have addressed a particular point in depth, others lightly and some not at all, depending on the relevance of the point to the plant species or other group of interest. Should additional points beyond those covered in this document be needed for a particular plant, the additional information can be included in the body of the consensus document, or in appendices. If a particular point is not covered in a consensus document, the text may briefly explain why the point, in the particular case, is not relevant.

Authors of the draft of a plant biology consensus document should be familiar with this *Points to Consider* chapter as well as existing consensus documents in the OECD Series on Harmonisation of Regulatory Oversight in Biotechnology (SHROB), in order to develop the appropriate scoping and presentation of information and data and for general editorial style. Existing consensus documents,[1] particularly more recent ones, may provide detailed examples (some noted below) that are helpful models or thought-provoking for particular cases. Authors of plant biology consensus documents should also be familiar with any corresponding food/feed composition consensus document developed by the OECD Working Party for the Safety of Novel Foods and Feeds to ensure consistency and avoid any unnecessary duplication (Consensus documents: work on the safety of novel foods and feeds: Plants - OECD).

Those interested in information on the evolution of how pertinent topics are covered in OECD biology consensus documents may specifically consult the "Analysis and Comparison of Consensus Documents" presented as background paper at the OECD Workshop on Review of Consensus Documents and Future Work in Harmonisation, held in Washington, DC, United States in 2003. This chapter on "Points to consider for consensus documents on the biology of cultivated plants" results from a recommendation of that meeting. It was originally declassified in 2006 and subsequently updated in 2020.

An understanding of the biology of the species or other group of interest will aid in determining the kinds of information pertinent to the environmental risk/safety assessment. This *Points to Consider* chapter provides an explanation of why the point (as enumerated below) is important in risk/safety assessment of the transformed plant, and presents a rationale for how the information in the point relates to risk/safety assessment. For a particular environmental risk/safety assessment, biological or ecological information in addition to that presented in the consensus document may be needed to address the regional environments into which the genetically engineered plant is proposed to be released.

Section I. General description including taxonomy and morphology

The focus of each biology consensus document has usually been a species but, in some cases, the focus has been a group of species or a genus, or just a subspecies or a cultivar group (examples are below). The primary focus of this *Points to Consider* chapter is also the species of interest, so appropriate adjustments will be necessary if the focus of the consensus document is broader or narrower.

Classification and nomenclature

Give the scientific name of the cultivated species of interest, with its authors, and pertinent synonyms (i.e. actively used alternative scientific names, if any). If necessary to delimit the plant, also give the horticultural name, e.g. the cultivar group (e.g. *Beta vulgaris* subsp. *vulgaris* Sugar Beet Group). Provide main international common name(s) at least in English for the species of interest. Give the taxonomic context of the species (the family always, perhaps the order and possibly the subfamily, tribe, subgenus or section). If the taxonomy is not settled, be relatively conservative in choosing the taxonomy, and briefly explain the alternative(s). The latest taxonomic or nomenclatural study is not necessarily definitive, and may need time for scientific consensus before it is adopted. A common name for the crop species of interest can be introduced here, to be used in much of the document as a more familiar name (aide-memoire).

Describe the taxonomic relationships of the cultivated species: related species and related genera, particularly if there is a high likelihood for spontaneous hybridisation or the generic limits are unsettled. A list of related species (with brief geographic ranges) should be given and include all relatives with a potential for hybridisation (i.e. cross-compatible relatives). This topic is dealt with in detail in Section V. The listing here may provide brief information on chromosome numbers and ploidy if these data are pertinent to the taxonomic differentiation of the species, whereas a more complete coverage of the relevant details is provided in Sections IV and V.

Rationale: *The scientific name enables an unequivocal understanding (i.e. a circumscription) of the plant of interest, at the appropriate level, such as the species or the subspecies. This addresses what the species (or another group) is and what it is called (i.e. circumscription and name). The list of close relatives could help in subsequent analysis to form an idea of the kinds of pertinent traits such as disease resistance or stress tolerance that may already occur in these direct relatives of the cultivated plant, and may help* *elucidate how genes/traits are shared and move via gene flow amongst related populations. The list of close relatives aids in understanding the range of diversity and variability in the gene pool.*

Examples: OECD Series on Harmonisation of Regulatory Oversight in Biotechnology (SHROB) No. 16 (poplars, Section II, p. 15-18); No. 45 (cotton, Section II, p. 14-15); No. 56 (sugarcane, Section II, p. 17-18); No. 58 (*Eucalyptus*, Section I, pp. 12-14); No. 62 (sorghum, Section I, p. 11-13), and No. 70 (rice, Section I, p. 11-14).

Description

Give a brief non-technical description of the species of interest, understandable to the non-specialist. Provide the habit and general characteristics of the plant, for example, that it is an annual, a long-lived tree or a biennial cultivated as an annual crop and that it is, for instance, grown for fibre, fruit or seeds. Also, provide a concise technical (taxonomic) description sufficient to make a positive identification of the plant (or part). An illustration (line drawing or black-and-white photo) may be useful. To clarify distinctiveness, emphasise the practical diagnostic or distinguishing morphological or other characters. Limit jargon, with precise sentences and familiar words. A table of main differences or taxonomic key may be instructive (e.g. Table 1 in SHROB No. 62 on sorghum). If necessary, when based on recent information or a new approach for example, present or reference the analytical methods by which a differential identification of the similar plants (e.g. species) is now made.

Rationale: *These descriptions provide broad orientation and as well accurate identification. They briefly explain how the species of interest is actually identified in relation to others. Additionally, the description may give particular characteristics of the plant to aid in defining the scope of a risk/safety assessment. Although an exact identification is often based on experience (i.e. recognition) or regional publications, rigorous or subtle analysis using specialist resources is sometimes required.*

Examples: OECD SHROB No. 8 (potato, Section IV, p. 14-15); No. 28 (European white birch, Section I, p. 12-13); No. 45 (cotton, Section I, pp.11-13); No. 54 (*Brassica* crops, Section I, pp.19-31); and No. 62 (sorghum, Section I, pp.13-16).

Section II. Centres of origin, geographical distribution and agronomic practices

This section covers the primary or crop species of interest, including plants that are wild or free-living (whether native or naturalised) or weedy, and as cultivated or managed in the field. Crossable relatives with the relevant information and data on their intraspecific and interspecific crossing are discussed in Sections IV and V.

Centres of origin and diversity

Describe the known or probable primary centre(s) of origin, as well as secondary centres where additional important variability or biodiversity may occur, whether naturally (e.g. *Beta*) or through the process of domestication (e.g. *Zea mays*, *Solanum tuberosum* subsp. *tuberosum*). The evolutionary centres important for natural biodiversity should be mentioned as well as the central areas of domestication and landrace diversity, with an indication of the centres' relative importance. Genetic diversity is covered in Section IV. Provide a brief sketch of the history or extent of domestication including mention of relevant domestication traits (e.g. non-shattering, loss of seed dormancy).

Rationale: *The interaction of the cultivated plant with close relatives, especially in a centre of origin, is an important consideration because gene flow, varietal competition or a change in cultivation practices may alter this especially rich and valuable diversity. If the plant is not expected to be grown near a centre of diversity, the absence of such relatives would also be important. A brief review of domestication may* *provide insight showing the continuity of modification of the species and the degree of the crop plant's adaptation to or dependence on the managed environment.*

Examples: OECD SHROB No. 9 (bread wheat, Section III, p. 13-16); No. 27 (maize, Section IV, p. 18-20); No. 31 (sunflower, Section I, p. 14-15); No. 58 (*Eucalyptus*, Section II, pp.15-16); and No. 63 (tomato, Section I, pp.14).

Geographic distribution

Describe the overall geographic distribution (if helpful including altitudinal range or climatic region), broadly indicating where the species of interest originates (i.e. is indigenous), where it has been naturalised (introduced but free-living) and where it is in cultivation. A general map may be useful.

Rationale: *Knowledge of the geographic distribution sets the context for understanding the potential interaction of the species with its relatives and with the surrounding ecosystems. For example, it is important to make a distinction between the species' native and naturalised occurrence when assessing the potential effects and the importance of gene flow.*

Examples: OECD SHROB No. 13 (white spruce, Section III, p. 15-16); No. 16 (poplars, Section II, p. 15-18); No. 54 (*Brassica* crops, Section I, pp.32-34); No. 57 (cassava, Section II, pp.15); and No. 60 (cowpea, Section I, pp.15-18).

Ecosystems and habitats where the species occurs natively and where it has naturalised

Indicate the natural and non-cultivated or non-managed ecosystems where populations of the species of interest are native (indigenous) and where introduced and now naturalised (free-living) components of the vegetation. Designated natural areas (e.g. protected reserves, parks) where the species may be an invasive problem would be noted here. A weedy species in disturbed waste (e.g. abandoned) areas would be included here, whereas the weedy species in intensively managed areas would be discussed in the following subsection. Those ecosystems and habitats in which the species of interest occurs and its abundance are indicated here, whereas its ecological interactions with biotic components of the ecosystems and habitats are developed in Section VI.

Rationale: *The focus of this subsection is the relatively natural, self-sustaining context, rather than the land areas strongly managed for plant production. Knowledge of where the species occurs indigenously or is free-living provides baseline information for understanding the range of habitats in which the species exists, the range of behaviours exhibited in those habitats and how characteristics of the species determine the range of habitats where it occurs. This information provides an understanding of the species' potential for interaction with its relatives and surrounding habitats.*

Examples: OECD SHROB No. 28 (European white birch, Section III, p. 19-20); No. 49 (black spruce, Section VII, pp.30-31); No. 54 (*Brassica* crops, Section I, pp.34-37); No. 57 (cassava, Section II, pp.16); and No. 60 (cowpea, Section I, pp.18).

Agronomic, silvicultural and other intensively managed ecosystems where the species is grown or occurs on its own, including management practices

Describe where the species is dependent on management for survival or persistence over several years of usual conditions. Areas where the plant may be a weed problem would be discussed here. Areas to be discussed could include habitats such as annual row crops or bordering areas, tree plantations, orchards and vineyards, along regularly managed roadsides, rights-of-way, irrigation ditches, etc. Identify the pertinent general agronomic or other practices, and if relevant, regional differences in practices (including various practices within a region). Information might briefly encompass site preparation after clear-cutting, tillage, sowing or planting, weed control, control of volunteers, harvesting, plant protection practices during crop growth and after harvest, transport practices and the use of harvested materials (e.g. for silage). The relevant ecological interactions of the species with particular organisms in these managed ecosystems are discussed in Section VI.

Rationale: *The focus of this subsection is on the plant's survival in agro-ecological, silvicultural and other such managed areas, to provide the baseline environmental information on how the plant responds to or is managed by accepted agronomic, silvicultural or similar intensive practices. Identification of significant cultivation or management practices provides an understanding of measures available to manage or control the plant.*

Examples: OECD SHROB No. 15 (soybean, Sections II and V, p. 13 and 14); No. 18 (sugar beet, Sections I and II, p. 16-17); No. 49 (black spruce, Section III, p. 34-38); No.59 (common bean, Section I, p. 14-16); and No. 66 (apple, Section I, p. 16-18); and No. 70 (rice, Section II, p. 21-23).

Section III. Reproductive biology

Generation time and duration under natural circumstances and where grown or managed

Important aspects of generation time and duration include the time to first flowering and total life cycle of the plant and time from planting to plow-down. Include the effects of agronomic, silvicultural and similar practices when describing generation time and duration of the cultivated plant. Important differences within both natural and cultivated regions should be noted.

Rationale: *The generation time and duration are indications of the terms in which environmental effects may occur. Precocious generation times and shorter durations in agriculture affect the likelihood of outcrossing with free-living (wild) relatives and give a general indication of when outcrossing may first occur.*

Examples: OECD SHROB No. 18 (sugar beet, Section I, p. 13-14); No. 57 (cassava, Section III, pp.21); No. 60 (cowpea, Section III, p. 21); No. 62 (sorghum, Section II, pp. 21-22); and No. 66 (apple, Section II, p. 19).

Reproduction (production of flowers or cones, fruits, seeds and vegetative propagules)

Include a characterisation of the key stages in the life cycle necessary for the plant to survive, reproduce and disperse. Particular attention is given to any uncommon survival structures or strategies and their importance under natural and cultivation conditions, and the dependence of survival and reproduction on ecological and geographical factors.

Rationale: *The reproductive capabilities of a plant determine the means by which the plant can produce progeny and spread or disperse. Both the plant and its progeny may affect the environment, including other organisms and thus the time frame and geographic area over which effects might occur.*

Reproductive structure

In the case of angiosperms: Describe the general floral dynamics (e.g. flowering season, flowering time, anthesis, selfing and/or outcrossing, diagram and formula floral). Relevant genetic details of the outcrossing and/or selfing are addressed in Section IV.

In the case of gymnosperms: Describe the female (megasporangium) and male (microsporangia) structure.

In both cases (angiosperms and gymnosperms), indicate if the plant is monoecious or dioecious.

Rationale: *This information will assist in understanding some of the factors that affect the potential for gene flow and in assessing particular management strategies for reducing gene flow when outcrossing may occur. Such management strategies may include induced male sterility or asynchronous flowering times.*

Examples: OECD SHROB No. 8 (potato, Section VI, p. 17); No. 21 (Sitka spruce, Section III, p. 15); No. 49 (black spruce, Section III, p. 15); No. 53 (*Cucurbita*, Section V, p. 30-31); and No. 59 (common bean, Section II, p. 18).

Pollination (wind, insects, both, etc.), pollen dispersal, pollen viability

Describe observed modes of pollen dispersal, indicating the most prevalent way. Important insect or other animal pollinators should be indicated. Give data on the range of pollen dispersal through the air and/or by the animal vectors, if known. Note how climatic or regional (e.g. geographic) differences can affect pollination. Provide available information or data on the influence of pollen quantity, movement, viability, load and competition on outcrossing, which is discussed in Sections IV and V. Details on pollination as they pertain to the plant are covered here, whereas details particularly pertinent to the pollinator are covered in Section VI.

Rationale: *Pollen biology is an important component in the assessment of the potential for gene flow and in the evaluation of a need for and the type(s) of pollen confinement strategies such as buffer rows or isolation distances.*

Examples: OECD SHROB No. 8 (potato, Section VI, p. 17); No. 18 (sugar beet, Section IV, p. 22-23); No. 54 (*Brassica* crops, Section II, p. 59-61); No. 62 (sorghum, Section II, p. 22-23); and No. 63 (tomato, Section II, p. 21-22).

Seed production and natural dispersal of fruits, cones and/or seeds

Briefly describe the sexual reproductive structures, including relevant morphological characteristics of fruits (or cones) and seeds, and note any inherent means of dispersal (e.g. shattering, fruit splitting, ballistic). Note the number of seeds produced by a plant (e.g. seeds per fruit and number of fruits). Provide information on the means and range of dispersal (e.g. by gravity, wind, water, on and/or in animals) and, if there are several means, indicate their relative importance. Cover apomixis below, in subsection "Asexual propagation (apomixis, vegetative reproduction)".

Rationale: *The number of seeds and seed/fruit dispersal mechanisms is a factor to consider in understanding the potential for the establishment of free-living plants or populations, and thus the time and geographic area over which environmental effects might occur. The range of variability of these factors is also an important consideration.*

Examples: OECD SHROB No. 15 (soybean, Section IV, p. 14); No. 28 (European white birch, Section IV, p. 23); No. 53 (*Cucurbita*, Section V, p. 31-33); No. 54 (*Brassica* crops, Section II, p. 65-69); and No. 63 (banana, Section V, p. 34).

Seed viability, longevity and dormancy, natural seed bank, germination, and seedling viability and establishment

Discuss factors in the establishment of any seed bank, including its transience or persistence, and the viability, longevity and dormancy of seeds under natural conditions. Note any special conditions that affect dormancy and/or germination (e.g. depth of burial, light and/or temperature, passage through an animal's digestive tract, or need for fire) that might be particularly relevant. Note any special requirements for the establishment and survival of seedlings (e.g. soil qualities or regime), as the organism's fitness may be revealed at this challenging phase in the life cycle.

Rationale: *Seed viability is a key factor to consider in assessing the likelihood of survival of non-cultivated plants. Natural seed banks are often the main source of weeds in cultivated fields, whether they are previous-crop volunteers or non-crop weedy relatives. Whether seedlings can establish is usually a primary limiting factor in continuing the life cycle.*

Examples: OECD SHROB No. 45 (cotton, Section IV, p. 26-27); No. 54 (*Brassica* crops, Section II, p. 70-72); No. 56 (sugarcane, Sections V and IX, p. 39-40 and 57-58); No. 58 (*Eucalyptus*, Sections IV and VII, p. 32-33 and 47-50); and No. 62 (sorghum, Section II, pp. 23-24).

Asexual propagation (apomixis, vegetative reproduction)

Take into account natural vegetative cloning (e.g. in grasses and poplars), the kinds of propagules (special structures and/or fragmented plant pieces), dispersal of the propagules and their viability. Discuss the relative importance of asexual reproduction for the plant, including any differences dependent on habitat or region. For apomixis (non-sexual production of seeds), similarly consider its relative importance and effectiveness.

Rationale: *If a plant has a strategy that includes asexual propagation, this could be a means for considerable or quite different dispersal or spread, and consequently may also affect the time frame and geographic area over which environmental effects might occur.*

Examples: OECD SHROB No. 16 (poplars, Section IV, p. 23); No. 49 (black spruce, Section III, pp.16-17); No. 53 (*Cucurbita*: Section V, p. 35); No. 56 (sugarcane, Section V, pp.37 and 40-41); and No. 57 (cassava, Section III, pp.24).

Section IV. Genetics

Relevant detailed genetic information on the species

Give a basic overview of the relevant genetic constitution and genetic dynamics of the species. If more appropriate in a particular case, some basic genetic information (e.g. ploidy, ancestral/progenitor genomes) may be more fully or otherwise discussed in Section V. In this Section IV (including subsections as needed), cover for example and if appropriate cytogenetics (e.g. karyology, meiotic behaviour), nuclear genome size, possible extent of repetitive or non-coding DNA sequences, main genetic diversity or variability (e.g. among or within populations or varieties, and of alleles at a locus), evidence of heterosis or inbreeding depression, maternal and/or paternal inheritance of organellar genomes, and methods of classical breeding (e.g. utility from employing mutagenesis with the species). The relevance of the information to the species' variability and the potential effects of transformation are paramount in deciding what to include, as the focus is not to provide this genetic characterisation for plant development.

Intraspecific crossing with both non-cultivated strains (e.g. weedy races) and among non-transformed cultivars is appropriately covered here (perhaps with a table or diagram), including any genetic or cytoplasmic constraints or limitations to crossing (e.g. cytoplasmic or nuclear sterility, incompatibility systems). Interspecific crosses are addressed in the following section.

Rationale: *The information in this section includes genetic and breeding data, such as details of genomic or genetic stability (including gene silencing) and intraspecific outcrossing behaviour and potential, only to the extent that such information describes parameters that influence how genetic material (including new material) behaves in particular genetic backgrounds and in outcrossing. Interspecific hybridisation is detailed in a separate section (which follows) as intraspecific crossing is more likely (and familiar) and interspecific hybrids may bring in more extensive concerns.*

Examples: OECD SHROB No. 9 (bread wheat, Sections III and V, p. 13-17 and 2023); No. 12 (Norway spruce, Section VI, p. 21-23); No. 45 (cotton, Section V, p. 28-29); No. 54 (*Brassica* crops, Section III, p. 73-78); No. 66 (apple, Section III, p. 26-28); and No. 68 (safflower, Section III, p. 27-35).

Section V. Hybridisation and introgression

Natural facility of interspecific crossing (extent, sterility/fertility)

Describe interspecific (including intergeneric) crosses observed under natural conditions. Provide a list and perhaps a diagram of the documented hybrids, i.e. the crossings that may occur unaided under usual environmental conditions – if crossable relatives (other species) may be present. The information could include a discussion of ploidy (and ancestral/progenitor genomes). Provide an indication or review of the likelihood of first-generation (F_1) hybrids and later generations of these F_1 hybrids, and as well whether F_1 hybrids are potential bridges for genes to cross into other (non-parental) species. Rare plant species are considered here and in the following subsection. Indicate naturally hybridising species that are weedy (including invasive) in the list of hybridising species (detailed discussion of their weediness in a local environment would be covered in an environmental risk/safety assessment).

Rationale: *The ability of a cultivated species to hybridise with other cultivated or wild species is a significant factor in determining whether genes or traits could be transferred to other species.*

Examples: OECD SHROB No. 9 (bread wheat, Section V, p. 20-23); No. 16 (poplars, Sections III and VI, p. 20 and 28-29); No. 54 (*Brassica* crops, Section II, p. 61-65); No. 56 (sugarcane, Section X, pp. 59-61); and No. 58 (*Eucalyptus*, Section IX and Appendix, pp. 53-55 and 58-61).

Experimental crosses

Discuss the experimental data available on outcrossing under controlled conditions and theoretical possibilities for and barriers to outcrossing. This information is in contrast to that in the previous subsection, which indicates the outcrossing to readily crossable relatives. Experimental data that are the result of forced crosses employing special techniques (e.g. embryo rescue) would be relevant only if such studies help to clarify the degree of relatedness and likelihood of natural crossing. Theoretical considerations or experimental information might be, for example, on cytogenetic data and meiotic behaviour, or sexual incompatibility systems.

Rationale: *Experimental data and theoretical considerations may broaden the understanding of potential (or as yet unknown) unaided (natural) gene transfer. The information and data are only relevant if unaided crossing in the field can occur.*

Examples: OECD SHROB No. 8 (potato, Section VII, p. 19-21); No. 16 (poplars, Section VI, p. 28-29); No. 22 (eastern white pine, Section IV, p. 17); No. 59 (common bean, Section IV, p. 21); and No. 63 (tomato, Section IV, p. 27-29).

Information and data on introgression

Provide an indication or review of the likelihood of F_1 hybrids backcrossing into one or both parents. Provide information on both natural and experimental introgression (extensive backcrossing) and on the (types of) genes or the traits for which introgression has been demonstrated. For example, extensive backcrossing and introgression may be only in one direction, rather than into both parental lines or species' populations. Information should include the extent of likely natural (i.e. unaided) introgression or generations of experimental backcrossing, and the fertility and fecundity of the resultant plants.

Rationale: *Of primary consideration is whether interspecific crossing will lead to the introgression of genes. Interspecific crossing is a necessary but typically not a sufficient step for considerable introgression to occur. Even if introgression occurs, it is not the presence but the expression of the gene or trait that may be of primary importance.*

Examples: OECD SHROB No. 24 (*Prunus* sp. – stone fruits, Section II, p. 30); No. 53 (*Cucurbita*, Section VII, p. 41-43); No. 60 (cowpea, Section IV, p. 26); No. 62 (sorghum, Section III, p. 28-29); and No. 66 (apple, Section IV, p. 30).

Section VI. General interactions with other organisms (ecology)

Interactions in natural ecosystems and in agronomic, silvicultural or other ecosystems where the species is cultivated or managed

Provide a general overview (including subsections as needed) of main functional ecological interactions of the species of interest within these natural and managed ecosystems and habitats (subsections "Ecosystems and habitats where the species occurs natively and where it has naturalised" and "Agronomic, silvicultural and other intensively managed ecosystems where the species is grown or occurs on its own, including management practices" list and briefly characterise the natural (unmanaged) and managed ecosystems and habitats in which the species of interest occurs). Topics addressed in Section VI could include, for example, symbiotic relationships (e.g. rhizobial and mycorrhizal symbioses, plant-pollinator interactions), food webs (e.g. fruit and seed consumers or predators), noxious/toxic or other important interactions, whether direct or incidental, with insects (e.g. chemical defence), other invertebrate and vertebrate animals (e.g. non-domesticated or wild animals), and with plants (e.g. through allelopathy). Tritrophic interactions may also be considered.

Topics related to consumption by humans and/or domesticated animals of plants consumed as food and/or feed are not addressed in consensus documents on the biology of cultivated plants as these topics are outside the scope of the OECD Working Party on Harmonisation of Regulatory Oversight in Biotechnology (WP-HROB). Topics related to consumption by non-domesticated or wild invertebrate and vertebrate animals are however within the scope of the WP-HROB. This section could address, for example, major natural toxicants and common properties of the plant as regards non-domesticated vertebrates (e.g. effects of ingestion of *Cucurbita*) as well as common environmental allergenic (e.g. contact irritants, dermal or aeroallergens) properties regarding humans and domesticated animals in incidental contact with the plant. In some cases, it may be relevant to mention similar information from related species (e.g. toxicants in sexually compatible wild relatives of the plant species).

Animal pollinators (e.g. bees, hummingbirds) and the importance of a pollination system to the animal pollinator is detailed here, whereas the importance of the pollination system to the plant is addressed in subsection "Pollination (wind, insects, both, etc.), pollen dispersal, pollen viability". A listing of pertinent pests and pathogens (and diseases) may be presented as an appendix, with only those that are critically relevant discussed here.

Rationale: *The description of the basic general ecology of the species of interest is useful when determining the scope of interactions that may be used as a baseline for understanding the influences the cultivated plant may have on organisms that are in usual close contact. A general understanding of the interactions of the species with other organisms, including non-domesticated animals if relevant, will aid in determining whether any concerns may arise during cultivation from a change in the genetics of the species. If relevant, a brief description of the effects of cultivation of the plant species on the health of non-domesticated animals (e.g. levels of nitrate) may be included. Effects of incidental contact of humans (e.g. worker safety during cultivation and handling, windborne pollen) and domesticated animals to toxicants and allergens may be relevant. Effects of ingestion on the health of humans and/or domesticated* *animals would be thoroughly treated elsewhere, such as in an OECD consensus document on compositional considerations for food and feed issues. Corresponding OECD compositional documents for the considered plant species, if they exist (see* Consensus documents: work on the safety of novel foods and feeds: Plants - OECD*) should be referenced as appropriate.*

Examples: OECD SHROB No. 13 (white spruce, Section VII, p. 28-31); No. 49 (black spruce, Section VII, pp.31-34); No. 53 (*Cucurbita*, Section IX, pp. 49-51); No. 54 (*Brassica* crops, Section V, pp.89-93); and No. 62 (sorghum, Section IV, p. 34-36).

Section VII. Additional information

The possibility is expressly left open for topics of additional information that is pertinent to environmental risk/safety assessment, as a section in the main text of the document, and/or as appendices.

Examples: OECD SHROB No. 68 (safflower, Section VI, p. 48-49)

Section VII. References

As much as possible, the references should be peer-reviewed literature available internationally and mentioned in full format. After the references directly cited in the text, this section could include a subsection on additional useful references "for further reading".

Example: OECD SHROB No. 66 (apple, p. 42-51).

Appendix 1. Common pests and pathogens

Provide a list of causative organisms for diseases (pathogens) and pests that commonly occur in the crop under agronomic, silvicultural or equivalent conditions.

Rationale: *Provide as considered useful for risk/safety assessment rather than usual production management. Critically important organisms and ecological relationships (e.g. a virus disease that is a principal management issue) are covered in Section VI. The risk/safety assessment would then consider whether the transformation in the crop would be of environmental concern.*

Examples: OECD SHROB No. 18 (sugar beet, Appendix, p. 32-37); No. 31 (sunflower, Section V and Appendices 1 and 2, p. 31 and 37-47); No. 56 (sugarcane, Section VIII and Appendices 1 and 2, p. 46-56 and 65-68); No. 60 (cowpea, Section V and Appendix 1, p. 27 and 30-34); and No. 63 (tomato, Appendices I and II, p. 34-35 and 36-37).

Appendix 2. Biotechnological developments

General information on the kinds of traits being introduced into the species may be included. Provide information directly necessary for defining the scope or detail of biological information that would be useful. For example, transgenes under experimental development for a crop might result in a change in environmental fitness or range and habitats of the plant or its relatives (e.g. disease resistance, and drought, frost or salinity tolerance). Other biotechnological developments (e.g. to assist in marketing) may not be pertinent to address here.

Rationale: *An overview of biotechnological developments may help to assure that the biological information included in a consensus document is pertinent to the environmental risk/safety assessments anticipated. Consensus documents that include the biotechnological developments to bring traits into the crop can be quite useful in explaining the relevance of assessing certain kinds of biosafety information.*

Examples: OECD SHROB No. 27 (maize, Appendix A, p. 39-41); No. 45 (cotton, Section VI, p. 33); No. 58 (*Eucalyptus*, Section II, p. 20-21); No. 63 (tomato, Appendix III, p. 38-40); and No. 66 (apple, Annex B, p. 35-36).

Note

[1] All consensus documents quoted as examples in the text below can be consulted on the OECD BioTrack public website (Consensus documents: work on harmonisation of regulatory oversight in biotechnology - OECD).

Part II Biology of crops

2 Biology of Apple (*Malus domestica*)

This chapter deals with the biology of apple (*Malus domestica*). It contains information for use during the risk/safety regulatory assessment of genetically engineered varieties of apple intended to be grown in the environment (biosafety). It includes elements of taxonomy, centres of origin, cultivation, reproductive biology, genetics, hybridisation and introgression, as well as ecology. Annexes present the *Malus* species, apple's common diseases and pests, and current biotechnology developments.

Introduction

This chapter was prepared by the OECD Working Party on the Harmonisation of Regulatory Oversight in Biotechnology, with **Belgium** and **Germany** as the co-lead countries. It was initially issued in 2019 as the Consensus Document on the Biology of Apple (*Malus Domestica* Borkh.). Production data have been updated in this publication, based on FAOSTAT.

Species or taxonomic group

Classification and nomenclature

The genus *Malus* belongs to the rose family (Rosaceae) which is traditionally divided into four subfamilies on the basis of fruit type. These include: Rosoideae (e.g. *Rosa, Fragaria, Potentilla* and *Rubus*; fruit, achene); Prunoideae (e.g. *Prunus*; fruit, drupe); Spiraeoideae (e.g. *Spirea*; fruit, follicle or capsule), and Maloideae (e.g. *Malus, Pyrus* and *Cotoneaster*, fruit, pome) (Schulze-Menz, 1964). The systematic classification of Rosaceae has changed over the years and molecular analysis has added to the debate on the subfamily groupings (Potter et al., 2007). Using nucleotide sequence data from nuclear and chloroplast regions of 88 genera of Rosaceae, the Rosaceae family was re-classified into three subfamilies: Rosoideae (base chromosome number x = mostly 7), Dryadoideae (e.g. *Cercocarpus*, *Dryas* and *Purshia*; fruit, achene or aggregate of achenes; x = 8 or higher) and Spiraeoideae (mostly x = 8, 9, and rarely x = 15 or 17). All genera previously assigned to Prunoideae (x = 8) and Maloideae (x = 17) were included in the Spiraeoideae (Potter et al., 2007). This subfamily, however, is to be called Amygdaloideae rather than Spiraeoideae under the International Code of Nomenclature (McNeill et al., 2012). The latest classification of the Rosaceae family is thus based on three subfamilies: Rosoideae, Amygdaloideae, including *Malus,* and Dryadoideae. Although the traditional definition of the four major rosaceous subfamilies may be collapsing from a taxonomic view, this grouping still has great utility from an economic and horticultural standpoint and is still commonly used in literature.

The genus *Malus* is currently organised into six taxonomic sections, one being *Malus* to which the species *Malus domestica* belongs (USDA-ARS, 2018; see Table 2.1). Altogether, 59 species of *Malus* (also listed as *M.*) are cited in the taxonomy database of the USDA-ARS Germplasm Resources Information Network (GRIN) and are provided in Annex 2.A. However, the number of species included in the genus is an ongoing subject of debate, revolving around the acceptance of putative hybrids. For example, *M. arnoldiana* (*M. baccata* × *M. floribunda*), which is considered a "secondary species" developed through interspecific hybridisation of "primary species" (Jackson, 2003; Luby, 2003; Rieger, 2006; Hancock et al., 2008).

Table 2.1. Classification and synonyms of *Malus domestica*

Scientific name		*Malus domestica* Borkh.
Pertinent synonym(s)		*Malus Bork* (L.) Britton, nom. inval.; *Malus pumila* auct.; *Malus pumila* var. *domestica* (Borkh.) C. K. Schneider; *Malus sylvestris* auct.; *Malus sylvestris* var. *domestica* (Borkh.) Mansf.; *Pyrus malus* L.
Taxonomic context	Family	Rosaceae Juss.
	Subfamily	Amygdaloideae
	Tribe	Maleae
	Subtribe	Malinae
	Genus	Malus Mill.
	Section	*Malus*
	Species	*Malus domestica* Borkh.

Source: USDA-ARS (2018), *Germplasm Resources Information Network (GRIN)*, https://www.ars-grin.gov (accessed 1 October 2019).

The cultivated apple *M. domestica* is thought to be the result of interspecific hybridisation (see section on centres of origin and diversity). The binomial *M. domestica* Borkh. has been generally accepted as the appropriate scientific name replacing the earlier scientific name *M. pumila* (Korban and Skirvin, 1984; Qian et al., 2010). Throughout its history of cultivation, more than 10 000 cultivars of *M. domestica* have been developed, although many of those are now lost (Way et al., 1990; Janick et al., 1996; Rieger, 2006). Currently, about 100 cultivars are grown commercially, the most popular worldwide including: 'Fuji', 'Delicious', 'Golden Delicious', 'Gala', 'Granny Smith', 'Idared', 'Jonagold', 'Braeburn', 'Cripps Pink', 'Jonathan', 'Elstar' and 'McIntosh' (Jackson, 2003) see Figure 2.1). Most of the cultivars are diploid, while some of them are triploid (e.g. 'Jonagold', 'Mutsu', 'Schöner von Boskoop') and a few are tetraploid (e.g. 'Antonovka Ploskaya', 'Wealthy Tetraploidnyi', 'Papirovka Tetraploidnaya', 'McIntosh Tetraploidnyi').

Figure 2.1. Commercially grown apple cultivars

Note: (a) 'Fuji', (b) 'Delicious', (c) 'Golden Delicious', (d) 'Gala', (e) 'Granny Smith', (f) 'Idared', (g) 'Jonagold', (h) 'Braeburn', (i) 'Cripps Pink', (j) 'Jonathan', (k) 'Elstar' and (l) 'McIntosh'.
Source: Courtesy of Bundessortenamt and Julius Kühn-Institute, Germany.

Description

M. domestica is botanically described as follows:

- **Tree** – a small- to medium-sized, branched, deciduous tree with a single trunk and a broadly spreading canopy. The trees are generally 2-10 m tall (in cultivation, tree size and shape are heavily dependent on rootstock and training [planting] system). Young stems and twigs are somewhat tomentose (hairy), while older branches are glabrous (smooth) (Bailey and Bailey, 1976;

Webster, 2005a). Spurs (very short shoots) grow very slowly and primarily produce flowers and subsequent fruits. They are formed on one-year-old shoots. Root suckers can emerge from the rootstock.

- **Leaves** – are alternately arranged, dark green, simple oval-shaped with a serrated edge, 4-13 cm long x 3-7 cm wide, with irregularly saw-toothed margins, and usually hairy beneath (Webster, 2005a; Rieger, 2006).
- **Buds** – are purplish brown, ovoid and densely hairy. Buds either give rise to shoots/leaves (vegetative buds) or flowers (flower buds). Flower buds are larger and plumper than growth buds and have a downy surface.
- **Flowers** – are 3-4 cm in diameter. Each flower blossom has 5 sepals, 5 petals, varying from white to pink, and about 20 stamens with yellow anthers in three whorls (10+5+5). The pistil comprises of a stigma and five styles united at the base (Jackson, 2003; Hancock et al., 2008). The five styles are slightly longer than the stamen. The ovary is inferior, positioned beneath the sepals, petals and stamen. The peduncle and calyx (all sepals) are usually woolly, and the calyx is persistent in the fruit (Webster, 2005a). Flowers are usually terminal on spurs, although they may grow laterally from one-year-old shoots in some cultivars, borne in groups of 4-6, in inflorescences that have variously been described as corymbs, corymbose racemes, cymes, and false cymes (Jackson, 2003; Rieger, 2006).
- **Fruit** – is an ellipsoid to obovoid, globe-like pome indented at the base and the apex (see Figure 2.2). The fruits are usually greater than 5 cm in diameter weighing 200-350 grammes. Fruits vary in colour and can be uniformly red, green or yellow or bi-coloured. Bi-coloured fruit can be striped or blushed red on a yellow or green background (see Figure 2.1). Each fruit contains a cortex of (edible) flesh between the skin and the core line. The central core has a fleshy pith with a papery capsule of five fused carpels. Each carpel typically contains two seeds. Seeds are smooth, shiny, and chestnut brown (Jackson, 2003; Rieger, 2006).

Figure 2.2. Flower and fruit of apple, cut lengthwise, showing the relation of the parts of the flower

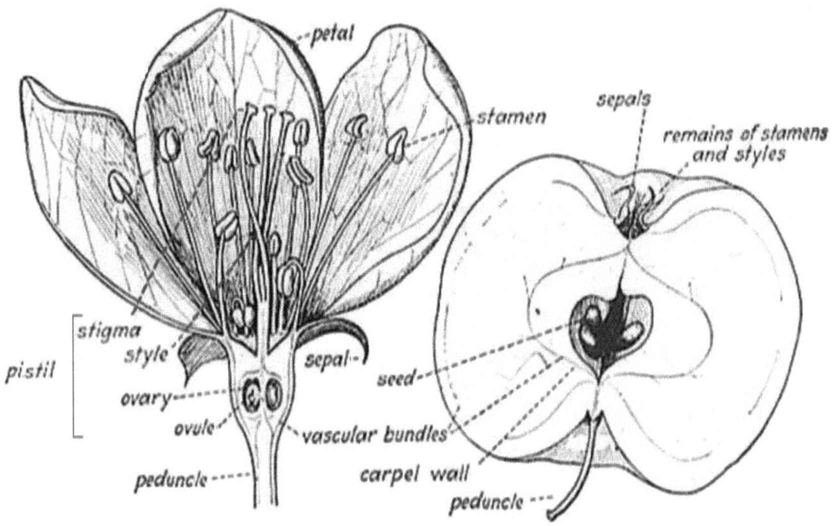

Source: Adapted from Iowa State University (2003), *Reproductive Terms*.

- **Roots** – consist of a horizontal layer of permanent, thickened, spreading scaffold roots less than 50 cm from the surface, and numerous vertical "sinkers" descending to an impermeable layer or water table (Jackson, 2003).

Centres of origin and diversity, geographic distribution, natural and managed ecosystems and habitats, cultivation and management practices

Centres of origin and diversity

The centre of origin for domesticated apple species lies within the Tian Shan Forest regions of Central Asia, including Kazakhstan, Kyrgyzstan and Tajikistan (Vavilov, 1951; Dzhangaliev, 2003). The wild species *Malus sieversii* (Ledeb.) M. Roem. occurring in these forest regions has been identified as the initial progenitor to the genome of the cultivated *M. domestica* on the basis of morphological, historical and molecular evidence (Robinson et al., 2001; Harris, Robinson and Juniper, 2002; Velasco et al., 2010; Duan et al., 2017).

The domestication of *Malus* occurred around 8 000 to 2 000 BCE in Central Asia, possibly near Almaty, Kazakhstan (Vavilov, 1930, as referred to in Robinson et al., 2001; Zohary, Hopf and Weiss, 2012). Apple seeds and trees from selected forms were then dispersed along the trade routes of the Silk Route from Central Asia, east to the People's Republic of China (hereafter 'China') and west to Europe (Harris, Robinson and Juniper, 2002), resulting in the random establishment of apple germplasm along the Silk Route (see Figure 2.3).

Figure 2.3. Evolutionary history of the cultivated apple

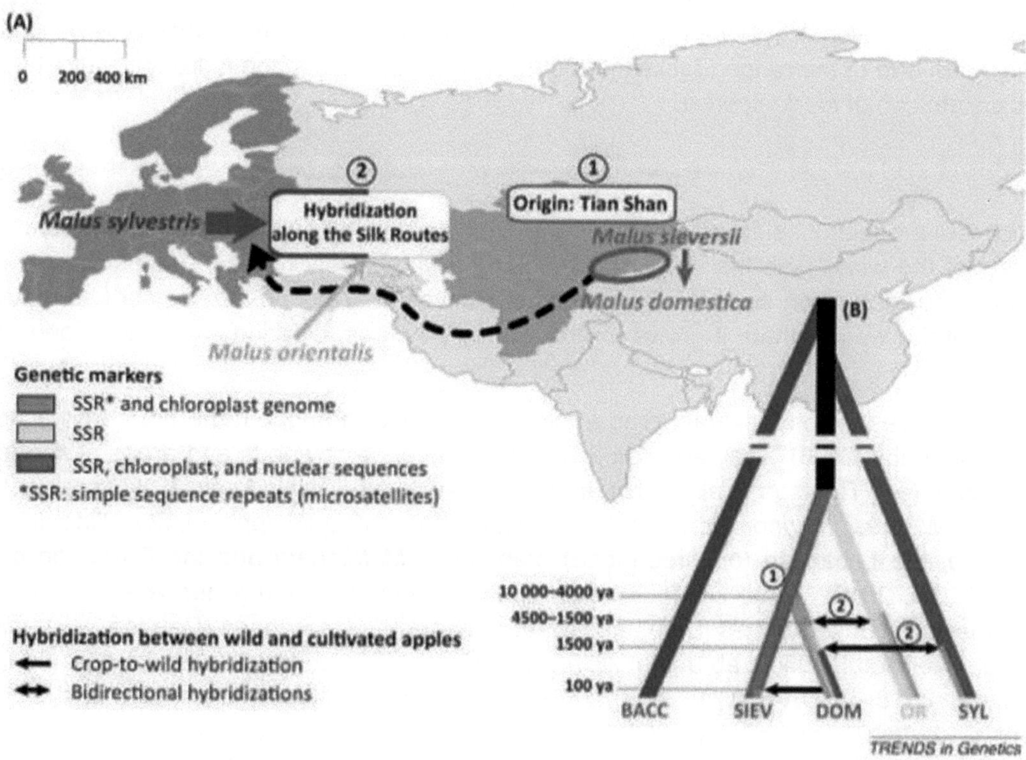

Note:

(A) Origin in the Tian Shan Mountains (1) followed by dispersal (2) from Asia to Europe along the Silk Route. Arrow thickness is proportional to the genetic contribution of various wild species to the genetic makeup of *Malus domestica*.

(B) Genealogical relationships between wild and cultivated apples. Approximate dates of the domestication and hybridisation events between wild and cultivated species are detailed in the legend. Abbreviations: BACC, *M. baccata*; DOM, *M. domestica*; OR, *M. orientalis*; SIEV, *M. sieversii*; SYL, *M. sylvestris*; ya, years ago.

Source: Cornille, A. et al. (2014), "The domestication and evolutionary ecology of apples", *Trends in Genetics*, Vol. 30, p. 57-65.

Hybridisations occurred between the apples coming from Central Asia and closely related species present along the Silk Route. This gave rise to diverse forms of hybrids from which the present-day cultivated apple might have been selected and propagated by vegetative means. Several species contributed to the genetic background of the current apple populations: some of the ones that are considered to have contributed are the Siberian crab apple *M. baccata* L. (Borkh.), the Caucasian crab apple *M. orientalis* Uglitzk. and the European crab apple *M. sylvestris* L. Mill. (Cornille et al., 2012). The wild European crab apple *M. sylvestris*, in particular, is considered to be a major contributor to *M. domestica* in Western Europe, as it is genetically more closely related to this species than to its Central Asian progenitor, *M. sieversii* (Cornille et al., 2012, 2014; Duan et al., 2017).

Geographic distribution

M. domestica is cultivated throughout temperate areas of the world. In general, *M. domestica* is well adapted to a range of climates but its ideal growing conditions are the cool-temperate zone between about 35-50° latitude with high light intensity, warm days and cool nights (Webster, 2005b; Rieger, 2006). Its range is farther north than most other fruit crops due to its relatively late blooming and cold hardiness (Rieger, 2006). It is also cultivated in less suitable climates (i.e. semi-arid, subtropical and tropical) where irrigation, altitude and various farming practices are used to overcome climatic limitations (Westwood, 1993; Hampson and Kemp, 2003). An example of the range of temperatures over which apples are successfully produced is provided by Jackson (2003). At the extreme cold end of the range, Poland, with winter monthly minimum temperatures of -17°C and summer monthly maximum temperatures of 30°C, has successful apple cultivation. Egypt with winter minimums of 1°C and summer maximums of 43°C reflects the extreme warm end of the range (Jackson, 2003). Global climate change is likely to affect the current geographic distribution of *M. domestica*.

Ecosystems and habitats where the species occurs natively and where it has naturalised

M. domestica is a product of selection by human intervention and hybridisations over thousands of years in many parts of the world (see the section describing the intensively managed ecosystems where the species is grown or occurs on its own). Outside of its cultivation areas, *M. domestica* has naturalised in different parts of the world, where it grows in abandoned pastures, clearings, roadsides and borders of woods (Randall, 2017).

Wild apple populations, also known as "crab apples", are native throughout the northern hemisphere in temperate areas (Luby, 2003). They are mainly found on the edge of woods and areas of scrub, in moist or coastal regions (e.g. Routson et al., 2012). In Europe, there are five endemic *Malus* species: the crab apple from Sicily *M. crescimannoi*, the Florentine (or Hawthorn-leaf) crab apple *M. florentina*, the Paradise apple *M. pumila*, the Lebanese (or three-lobed) crab apple *M. trilobata* and the European crab apple *M. sylvestris* (IUCN, 2019). There are four *Malus* species native to North America – the Southern crab apple *M. angustifolia* (United States [US]), the Sweet crab apple *M. coronaria* (Canada, US), the Oregon crab apple (also termed Pacific crab apple) *M. fusca* (Canada, US) and the prairie crab apple *M. ioensis* (US) (VASCAN, 2018; USDA-NRCS, 2018). *M. sieversii* is native to western China and Central Asia (Richards et al., 2008; Gharghani et al., 2009; Gross et al., 2012; Nikiforova et al., 2013; Volk et al., 2013) but has become a rare and threatened plant in China (Yan et al., 2008; IUCN, 2019).

Crab apple accessions of different *Malus* species may be grown as ornamentals in landscaping, parks or gardens (Fiala, 1994). Many of these accessions offer prolific spring bloom and a wide range of decorative fruits differing in size, shape and colour (Fiala, 1994). Further, crab apples may be used as pollinisers in apple orchards.

Intensively managed ecosystems where the species is grown or occurs on its own, including management practices

The apple *M. domestica* is one of the most widely cultivated tree fruits (Table 2.2). Cultivation started as early as 4 000 BCE in the Near East (Figure 2.3) and apples reached the eastern Mediterranean region by 2 000 BCE and Greece and Italy by 900 and 800 BCE.

Table 2.2. Overview of continents, territories and countries where apple is cultivated

Continent	Territories and countries
Africa	Algeria, Egypt, Kenya, Libya, Madagascar, Malawi, Morocco, South Africa, Tunisia, Zimbabwe.
Americas	Argentina, Bolivia, Brazil, Canada, Chile, Colombia, Ecuador, El Salvador, Grenada, Guatemala, Honduras, Mexico, Paraguay, Peru, Saint Vincent and the Grenadines, United States, Uruguay.
Asia	Afghanistan, Armenia, Azerbaijan, Bhutan, People's Republic of China, Cyprus, Democratic People's Republic of Korea, Georgia, India, Iran, Iraq, Israel, Japan, Jordan, Kazakhstan, Korea, Kyrgyzstan, Lebanon, Nepal, Pakistan, Syria, Tajikistan, Turkey, Turkmenistan, Uzbekistan, Yemen.
Europe	Albania, Austria, Belarus, Belgium, Bosnia and Herzegovina, Bulgaria, Croatia, Czech Republic, Denmark, Estonia, Finland, France, Germany, Greece, Hungary, Ireland, Italy, Latvia, Lithuania, Luxembourg, Montenegro, Moldova, Netherlands, North Macedonia, Norway, Poland, Portugal, Romania, Russian Federation, Serbia, Slovak Republic, Slovenia, Spain, Sweden, Switzerland, Ukraine, United Kingdom.
Oceania	Australia, New Zealand.

Source: FAO (2022), *FAOSTAT*, www.fao.org/corp/statistics/en (accessed 16 February 2022).

The Roman armies carried apples across Europe, planting seeds wherever they settled. By the 1200s, cultivated apples were becoming increasingly popular in the Nile Delta and throughout Europe, where they appeared in the gardens of both royalty and commoners. By the 1600s, there were at least 120 cultivars of apple described (Luby, 2003). European colonists introduced *M. domestica* to the Americas (1500-1600s), South Africa (1650s), Australia (1788) and New Zealand (1814). By the late 1800s, *M. domestica* had been introduced into southern and eastern Asia, where it supplanted the Chinese soft apple *M. x asiatica Nakai*, the primary cultivated apple in that region for over 2 000 years (Luby, 2003; Hancock et al., 2008). Today, the global apple market is dominated by European and North American *M. domestica* varieties.

M. domestica is a labour-intensive, highly managed crop, especially by the time an orchard has reached maturity and is ready for commercial production. Although barely any fruit is produced during the first year(s) after plantation, there is still a number of agronomic issues that must be properly managed to ensure good tree growth. These include nutrient amendments (through fertigation or direct soil application), disease and pest control, irrigation, weed control and pruning. Table 2.3 highlights a typical management schedule for apple production. Trees and fruit are prone to a number of fungal, bacterial and pest problems (see section on pests and diseases), which can be controlled by a number of non-organic and organic means. Many commercial orchards pursue a programme of chemical sprays but a trend in orchard management is the use of biological control methods, which include, for instance, the introduction of a natural predator to reduce the population of a particular pest (see section on biological control organisms).

M. domestica is not regarded as a weed of agriculture (Randall, 2017). Volunteer plants originating from seed in apple orchards are rare due to the perennial nature of the crop and orchard management practices that include herbicide treatment of the tree row and mowing of the alley between rows (Stover and Marks, 1998).

Table 2.3. Highlights of a typical management schedule for apple production

Time of year – Phase	Action
Winter – Dormancy	- Prune dormant trees - Remove root suckers - Perform root pruning - Analyse soil composition - Apply soil fertiliser and lime - Apply herbicides
Spring – Fruit set	- Perform pruning (mechanical) - Apply mulching - Perform irrigation - Apply frost protection - Place bees in orchards when blossom begins - Apply chemical and/or mechanical thinning - Monitor and control pests (insects and diseases) - Monitor and control weeds
Summer – Fruit growth	- Perform irrigation - Apply hand thinning - Perform summer pruning - Remove root suckers - Apply mulching - Apply foliar fertiliser (calcium to prevent bitter pit) - Monitor and control pests (insects and diseases) - Monitor and control weeds - Prepare soil for planting
Fall – Harvest period	- Harvest apples - Store apples in cold or controlled atmosphere storage - Apply leaf fall spraying - Build the trellis (support) system for new trees - Perform tree planting

Source: Adapted from AAFC (2013), Crop Profile for Apple in Canada, 2013, Pesticide Risk Reduction Program, Pest Management Centre, Agriculture and Agri-Food Canada, Ottawa.

Reproductive biology

Generation time and duration under natural circumstances, and where grown or managed

The whole sexual reproduction cycle (fertilisation, seed formation and seedling growth) only occurs naturally in the wild (see "Life cycle of apple under natural conditions"), in the production of some rootstocks and in apple breeding programmes (for the latter two, see section on breeding approaches). The life cycle of apple in managed ecosystems starts from the adult phase (see "Life cycle of apple in managed ecosystems").

The life cycle of apple under natural conditions

Under natural circumstances, the life cycle of wild apple starts from a seed, released by frugivorous animals or by the rotting of fruit during winter on the ground. After germination, the juvenile growing period follows. During this period morphological and physiological characteristics of the plant differ relative to the adult stage. The inability to flower and produce fruit and seeds is one of the main characteristics of the juvenile period. The plant enters the adult stage once flower bud differentiation occurs. During the adult stage, the plant is fertile and will flower almost every year. The juvenile period of wild apple plants under natural conditions usually takes between 6-12 years and is influenced by environmental as well as genetic factors. Years with a high crop load can be followed by years with low to no crop load, a phenomenon known as biennial bearing (Tromp, Webster and Wertheim, 2005).

The life cycle of apple in managed ecosystems

In managed commercial orchards, one- or two-year-old trees are planted that were propagated in fruit tree nurseries by budding or grafting on rootstocks. The buds or grafts are collected from mature commercial apple cultivars. This means that the resulting trees are no longer juvenile. Nevertheless, it is unlikely that one-year-old trees will bear fruit. In commercial orchards, the first yield will be obtained from the second year on and will progressively increase until a maximum yield is reached after 5-7 years.

The life span of a commercial high-density apple orchard is about 15 years, although many orchards do maintain a sufficient production beyond this age. A number of factors, including tree health, pests, apple cultivar, soil quality, environmental factors (i.e. heat units, winter injury), market opportunities, etc., play a role in the life span of a commercial orchard.

Generally, apple fruits reach maturity about 120-150 days after flowering but some cultivars mature in as little as 70 days, others in as long as 180 days (Rieger, 2006). Time to maturity varies with temperature (e.g. warmer temperatures reduce time to maturity) and is therefore geographically dependent. However, rankings of "early" or "late" maturing varieties relative to each other are fairly consistent (Jackson, 2003). Short-season cultivars tend to have a wide climatic tolerance; they do well in colder, northerly apple-producing regions such as Canada (e.g. 'McIntosh') and may also be grown as early-season crops in countries like France and New Zealand (e.g. 'Cox') (Jackson, 2003). Long-season cultivars like 'Braeburn', 'Fuji', 'Cripps Pink' and 'Granny Smith' generally cannot be grown successfully in northern areas and do best in the milder climates, mainly in the southern hemisphere (Hampson and Kemp, 2003; Jackson, 2003).

Reproduction (production of flowers, fruits, seeds and root suckers)

Floral biology

Flower development

In apple, flower development lasts between nine and ten months, starting with the formation of floral primordia in the mixed flower buds (i.e. buds producing flowers in addition to leaves and shoots) in summer and early autumn. At leaf fall, flower and leaf primordia are present in a large portion of the flower buds (Kotoda et al., 2000; Dennis, 2003; Jackson, 2003; Koutinas, Pepelyankov and Lichev, 2010). During winter, development slows due to bud inhibition by (endo)dormancy. Bud break follows after winter-chilling and heat-unit requirements are met. The king (apical) flower of the apple inflorescence opens first, followed by the lateral flowers (Jackson, 2003). Flowering occurs in spring when white to deep pink flowers develop in a cyme-like inflorescence of 4-6 flowers (Figure 2.4). Apple flowers can be borne in both terminal and lateral flower buds on both spurs and shoots. Flower clusters on lateral buds open later than do those on terminal buds and generally produce smaller fruit (Jackson, 2003). The flowering period takes 1-4 weeks, depending on the weather conditions, beginning with the (king flower of the) terminal flower buds and ending with the (lateral flowers of the) lateral flower buds.

Flowering is affected by many biotic (endogenous phytohormones, previous year's crop load, pathogens and pests) and abiotic (light, water stress, nutrients, temperature and exogenously applied chemicals) factors. Also, cultivation practices drive flowering and include grafting, pruning, scoring and/or ringing the base of the tree (Jackson, 2003). The flowering period can significantly differ between cultivars. The difference in flowering time between commercial cultivars and local cultivars can be more than one month in colder temperate regions (e.g. Northwestern Europe) and about 2-3 weeks in warmer regions (e.g. Southern Europe).

Figure 2.4. Open king flower and closed lateral flowers

Source: Courtesy of A. De Schrijver.

Effective pollination period

The length of the flowering period during which viable pollen is produced varies depending on weather conditions and generally lasts from 7 to 30 days (Jackson, 2003). During flowering, the stigma produces extracellular secretions which provide a moist environment for pollen deposition and germination (Jackson, 2003). Once the pollen grains have germinated, the pollen tubes grow down the style into an ovule where fertilisation of the egg cell (to form a zygote) and polar nuclei of the egg sac (to form the endosperm) occur (Dennis, 2003). Successful fertilisation depends on the pollen grains reaching the ovule before it degenerates.

The time during which the flower can be fertilised, if pollination is not limited, is assessed by the effective pollination period (EPP) (Williams, 1966). The EPP is defined as the number of days during which pollination is effective in producing fruit and is determined under orchard conditions by recording the initial fruit set (fruit set after pollination) and final (mature) fruit set in hand-pollinated flowers. Variation in EPP values has been claimed to be due both to environmental effects, mainly temperature (Tromp and Borsboom, 1994), and to flower quality (Jackson, 2003). The EPP values are highly variable among cultivars, years and sites. Typically, EPP values vary between 2 and 9 days (Sanzol and Herrero, 2001).

Gametophytic self-incompatibility, cross-incompatibility and semi-incompatibility

Fruit set in most apple cultivars is less than 10% after self-pollination (Komori et al., 1999). Self-fertilisation is inhibited due to the presence of a multi-allelic *S* locus, which contains pistil *S* and pollen *S* genes, that is responsible for S-RNase-mediated gametophytic self-incompatibility (GSI) (see Sassa, 2016 and reference therein). Cultivars with the same *S* alleles cannot fertilise each other. When an *S* haplotype in the haploid pollen matches one of the two *S* haplotypes in the pistil, then the pollen is recognised as "self" and the pollen tube formation is blocked at the upper part of the style, whereas the "non-self" pollen tubes can grow along the style and reach the ovary. Because of this self-incompatibility, outcrossing is promoted, resulting in the majority of cultivars displaying high levels of allelic heterozygosity. However, self-incompatibility in Rosaceae is broken down by polyploidisation and has been demonstrated in tetraploids of apple (Adachi et al., 2009).

Although many species are believed to be strongly self-incompatible, variations between species in self-incompatibility strength have been observed. The increase in self-compatibility in species with a functional self-incompatibility mechanism, like apple, can be caused by a variety of environmental variables such as temperature and flower age (Ferrer et al., 2009). Such species are called partial or pseudo-self-compatible, partially self-compatible or pseudo-self-fertile (Levin, 1996). Self-incompatibility in apple can also vary in strength depending on the apple cultivar. De Witte et al. (1996) found 'Fuji' and 'Golden Delicious' to give only 1% and 1.8% set respectively, following self-pollination under conditions, where pollination of these cultivars with the ornamental apple 'Baskatong' gave 24% and 25% set respectively. Much higher levels of self-fertility were found in 'Idared' (12.3%) and 'Elstar' (7%) although very few of the resulting fruits contained seeds (De Witte et al., 1996).

Instances of cross-incompatibility and semi-compatibility exist (Janick and Moore, 1975; Ramírez and Davenport, 2013). These are also controlled by the *S* locus that plays a role in self-incompatibility. Depending on their *S* loci, pairs of apple cultivars can be incompatible when both loci are identical and semi-compatible when they carry one different and one similar *S* locus. Pairs of apple cultivars are fully compatible when they differ in their *S* loci.

Pollination, pollen dispersal and pollen viability

Pollen dispersal and pollination depend on the pollinator (pollen vector), weather conditions, surrounding habitat and polliniser (pollen donor tree).

Pollinator

Insects, most notably honeybees, but also bumblebees, other wild bees and to a lesser extent some flies, are the primary vectors for pollination in apple. Apple pollen is relatively heavy and not easily carried by the wind (Dennis, 2003; Jackson, 2003).

Apple growers typically rent honeybee hives during the bloom period and it is recommended that they are placed at a density of four or five strong colonies per hectare in a mature orchard (Dennis, 2003). Although honeybees are the insects most used in orchards, they are not as efficient pollinators as some solitary bees and bumble bees. A lot of honeybees take nectar from the flower without even touching the anthers (Delaplane and Mayer, 2000) and do not contribute to pollination. Moreover, Sapir et al. (2017) found that adding bumblebees to honeybees increased cross-pollination. Adding bumblebees had multiple effects on pollination: not only the number of pollinating insects increased but these were now also working in adverse weather conditions and even the foraging behaviour of the honeybees was enhanced.

Weather

Rain during the flowering period may have a negative impact on the pollination of apples, by lowering the foraging activities of pollinators which reduces pollen transfer (Abrol, 2012). Another possibility is that rain inhibits the germination and growth of pollen on the stigma (AHDB, 2017). Similarly, wind can also have negative influences on apple pollination. Strong winds will make it harder for pollinators to transfer pollen from flower to flower (Jackson, 2003). At wind speeds of 15 km/h or more, honeybees do not fly and the limited amount of pollen that would have been transferred will rapidly desiccate (Tromp, Webster and Wertheim, 2005).

During flowering, a minimum temperature of 10°C is needed for effective pollen germination. When the temperature increases to 20°C, pollen germination rate (Yoder et al., 2009; Abrol, 2012) and hence pollen tube growth (Jefferies and Brain, 1984) increases with higher chances of successful fertilisation. Spring frosts can cause severe damage especially for early flowering cultivars and the damage is not always visible immediately after frost (Jackson, 2003; Tromp, Webster and Wertheim, 2005).

Surrounding habitat

Small habitats in the environment support wild pollinators with food and housing and encourage the diversity of wild bees (Sheffield, Ngo and Azzu, 2016). The surrounding habitat needs to be diverse in plant species and provide the bees with adequate nectar and pollen while also offering suitable nesting opportunities (Garibaldi et al., 2013; Sheffield et al., 2013).

Polliniser

The polliniser (i.e. pollen donor tree) used in the orchards is also an important factor for fertilisation. There are two main aspects in choosing the right polliniser: bloom overlap and compatibility with the acceptor tree.

Bloom overlap takes place when two apple cultivars flower synchronously, promoting effective pollen transfer. When pollen is deposited before the receptive period, the pollen should remain viable and fertile for a long enough period to allow successful pollination. Differences in pollen viability have been reported for different cultivars (Petrisor et al., 2012; Moshtagh et al., 2015). Pollen fertility of most apple cultivars is close to 100% but is reduced in some cultivars by unknown factors or triploidy.

The second important aspect is compatibility. In the case of cross-incompatibility, not all cross-pollination will result in fertilisation and seed formation. Semi-compatibility, however, is not a problem if there are enough pollinators, blossom abundance and pollen supply is high and conditions for pollination are good.

Pollen dispersal and dispersal studies

Many apple species are self-incompatible and, hence, fruit production only occurs with pollen transfer between cultivars. Most orchards consist of a limited number of cultivars, which are arranged in monotypic blocks or rows. The economic costs due to fruit yield loss as a result of inadequate pollination highlights the need to more accurately predict patterns of pollen movement in orchards (Kron et al., 2001). Pollen dispersal in apples has received considerable attention. However, most studies are based on apparent rather than realised pollen dispersal (Free and Spencer-Booth, 1964; Wertheim, 1991) and only a few studies have attempted to relate factors other than the distance to pollination success. In apple orchards, the majority of honeybee foraging flights are between flowers on the same tree and secondarily between adjacent trees in the same row and to a lesser extent across rows (Free and Spencer-Booth, 1964; Free, 1966). However, in a study by Kron et al. (2001) in which they examined pollen dispersal by molecular markers, they found the same number of seeds sired by the polliniser along and across the row.

Early research on pollen dispersal was conducted using a pollen donor carrying a dominant gene for red leaf colour, such as 'Baskatong'. Researchers monitored gene flow in apple orchards by observing the percentages of red-leafed seedlings borne from trees at increasing distances from the 'Baskatong' polliniser. A study using this approach found that 69% and 91% of the fertilised seeds occurred within the first 10 m and 60 m of the pollen donor respectively (Reim et al., 2006). Kron et al. (2001) used allozyme markers to determine the parentage of seeds to track pollen flow in orchards where 'Idared' was planted as a polliniser. Pollen dispersal generally declined with increasing distance, as 50% of total seeds sired by 'Idared' occur within the first four rows, or approximately 20 m (Kron et al., 2001). In a survey of a wild population of the crab apple *M. sylvestris*, Larsen and Kjær (2009) used microsatellite loci data in conjunction with spatial distances of the individual trees in the population to monitor pollen movement in a natural environment. These authors found that successful pollination occurred mostly between nearby trees, with a median distance of about 23 m. The data suggest that the majority of cross-pollination occurs between receptive flowers and proximate pollen sources. A significant factor affecting pollination intensity is the distance from the pollen source. Other important factors include weather, pollinator presence, cultivar compatibility and flowering synchrony (Kron et al., 2001). Maximum pollen dispersal distances in orchard settings were reported up to 40 m (Wertheim, 1991), 86 m (Kron et al., 2001), 104 m (Reim et al., 2006), 137 m (Tyson, Wilson and Lane, 2011) and 150 m (Soejima, 2007). In-hive transfer of viable pollen between bees foraging in geographically distant areas may explain long-distance pollen flow (Degrandi-Hoffman, Hoopingarner and Klomparens, 1986).

To predict bee-vectored pollen transfer, Tyson, Wilson and Lane (2011) developed a mechanistic model based on monitoring beta-glucuronidase (GUS) activity in seeds borne from trees located at increasing distances from a row of transgenic GUS-expressing 'Gala' trees. The authors use the model to examine the effect of buffer rows and isolation distances on outcrossing rates. The model demonstrates that the level of outcrossing is affected by the relative sizes of the nearby orchards. As the size of the orchard with conventional trees becomes smaller relative to the orchard with transgenic trees, the isolation distance required to limit the frequency of outcrossing is increased. Furthermore, the incorporation of buffer rows between the two orchard types generally reduces the isolation distance required in order to limit outcrossing frequency (Tyson, Wilson and Lane, 2011).

Seed production and natural dispersal of fruits and seeds

Seed production

Seed production is the result of fertilisation of the egg cell present in the apple flower and the male gamete present in the pollen. Seeds develop and reside in the central core of the fruit, in the carpels. Each carpel has two ovules that develop into seeds following fertilisation. In general, the seed number of fruit varies between two and seven, depending on the fertilisation intensity.

Natural dispersal of fruits and seeds

The primary means of movement and dispersal of apple seeds in natural settings is through frugivorous mammals, such as bears, foxes and deer (Willson, 1993; Myers et al., 2004) as well as birds (Witmer, 1996 and references therein). For example, white-tailed deer travel a range of many hectares on a daily basis and are considered dispersers of low numbers of apple seeds (Myers et al., 2004). Seeds may accidentally be attached to vertebrates or fruits could be ingested and digested, thereby deliberating the seeds (Galetti, 2002; Herrera, 2002; Myers et al., 2004). Seeds pass through the digestive tract of animals and can germinate and generate a new apple tree. It is also possible that apple seeds are dispersed by humans during the transport of fruit or after eating the fruit.

Seed viability, germination, seedling viability and establishment

In apple, it is accepted that there is no seed bank formed in nature, although this has not been studied in detail. During the winter, cold temperatures (< 5°C) and high humidity break the dormancy of mature seed. This process is known as stratification. The stratification time depends on the genotype. Seeds will either germinate during spring or die. Seed germination rate is very high and can reach up to 95% under controlled conditions of stratification and sowing.

The survival of seedlings in nature is rather low but precise data are not available. Seedling growth in the first year is minimal compared to the later years. Seedlings can grow in very different soil and climate conditions of temperate regions with enough precipitation, although they can grow also in semi-arid regions.

Asexual propagation

Apomixis

Apomixis, a form of asexual reproduction in flowering plants, is common in agriculturally important crops, except for apple and citrus fruits. Apomixis *sensu stricto* refers to asexual seeds that are genetically identical to the mother plant. Apples are facultative apomicts which means that they contain both sexually and asexually produced seeds in their fruits. The process of apomixis is very similar to sexual reproduction and also leads to viable seeds. However, in contrast to sexual reproduction, there is no fusion of male and female gametes and embryo sac formation occurs without meiosis. The embryo is thus only derived from maternal somatic tissue and is, therefore, a clone of the mother plant (Koltunow, 1993).

Vegetative reproduction

Another form of asexual reproduction in apple trees is the formation of root suckers. Root suckers are sprouts that arise from the roots. Because commercial apple trees are planted on rootstocks, these root suckers are originating from the rootstock and not from the commercial cultivar itself. Several commercial rootstocks, including M.7, M.9 and G.202, tend to produce a lot of root suckers which need to be removed regularly because they compete for water and nutrients with the commercial tree and because they form a potential entry point for fire blight (Miller and Racsko, 2011). These root suckers will not have the chance to flower in commercial orchards. However, after felling, the apple tree's remaining roots can produce root suckers that flower after several years when the land is not further managed.

Parthenocarpy

Apples can develop fruits without fertilisation, known as parthenocarpic fruits. Parthenocarpic fruits are seedless. There are two distinct types of parthenocarpy: vegetative and stimulative. Vegetative parthenocarpy is spontaneous and arises without pollination or any other externally applied stimulus. Several apple cultivars are intrinsically parthenocarpic, e.g. 'Spencer Seedless', but they are rarely of economic value (Jackson, 2003). Stimulative parthenocarpy can be induced by pollination without fertilisation (e.g. with irradiated pollen) or by plant hormones, primarily gibberellins. Although parthenocarpy can be induced with growth regulators in apple, the response is limited and such treatments are not used commercially (Jackson, 2003).

Genetics

Detailed genetic information

Whereas the haploid (x) chromosome numbers of most species in the family Rosaceae are 7, 8 or 9, the Maleae tribe, including *Malus domestica*, is distinct in having a haploid chromosome number of 17 (x = 17). Two hypotheses are still under investigation to explain the chromosome number of Maleae. The first hypothesis postulates that Maleae originated from ancient hybridisations between species in the Prunoideae (x = 8) and the Spiraeoideae (x = 9), followed by chromosome doubling. The original hybrids would have been sterile and only after chromosome doubling would they have formed fertile allopolyploids (Way et al., 1990; Luby, 2003; Webster, 2005a). The second hypothesis postulates that the genome originated more than 50 million years ago from a genome-wide duplication event of the x = 9 ancestral (most probably) *Gillenia* chromosomes followed by loss of 1 chromosome (Velasco et al., 2010). As a genome-wide duplication pattern was found for all chromosomes (Velasco et al., 2010; Daccord et al., 2017), this hypothesis likely explains the 17 chromosomes in *M. domestica*.

Most *Malus* species, including *M. domestica*, are diploid with 2n = 34 chromosomes; however, different levels of ploidy (tri-, tetra-, penta- and hexaploidy) are also known (Höfer and Meister, 2010). The mean value for the 2C nuclear deoxyribonucleic acid (DNA) content of *M. domestica* is 1.514 picograms (pg) per nucleus (Höfer and Meister, 2010).

The nuclear genome of *M. domestica* cultivar 'Golden Delicious' has been sequenced and represents the apple reference genome (Velasco et al., 2010; Daccord et al., 2017). Using the 'Golden Delicious' reference, nearly 200 apple genotypes have been re-sequenced. In addition to the nuclear DNA, whole organelle genomes (chloroplast and mitochondrial DNA) of apple were also sequenced (Goremykin et al., 2012; Nikiforova et al., 2013; Duan et al., 2017).

Genetic linkage mapping has contributed significantly to our current understanding of the structure of the *Malus* genome. First genetic linkage studies on apple were done in the late 1980s (Chevreau and Laurens, 1987; Manganaris and Alston, 1987; 1988a,b) and were followed by international apple genome mapping projects in Europe (King et al., 1991) and New Zealand (Gardiner et al., 1996). The first linkage map of the apple genome was published by Hemmat et al. (1994). With the establishment of simple sequence repeat (SSR) and single nucleotide polymorphism (SNP) markers, the number of linkage studies increased rapidly. Today, there are more than 60 different apple linkage maps available in the Genome Database for Rosaceae (https://www.rosaceae.org/). These maps were established using different parental genotypes, with different types of DNA markers, and were established for traits ranging from disease resistance to fruit quality, aroma, flower and fruit development, harvesting time and tree growth parameters, etc. The biggest advance in this field of research is the development of a multi-parental, high-density, integrated Genetic Linkage Map (iGLMap) of apple, comprising 15 417 SNP markers (Di Pierro et al., 2016).

The first apple reference transcriptome was published by Velasco et al. (2010) and significant improvements were made by Bai, Dougherty and Xu (2014). The use of high-throughput proteomics and metabolomics approaches in apple research has been increasing exponentially during the last few years (for reviews see Liu et al. (2017)).

Breeding approaches

The commercial apple tree, as in the case of other fruit trees, is a composite of a rootstock and a scion. The rootstock constitutes the root system and a small proportion of the lower trunk whereas the scion grafted or budded onto the rootstock forms the upper fruiting part (Webster and Wertheim, 2003). Rootstocks influence the performance of the grafted scion and can affect traits like drought and disease resistance of the tree, and vigour, precocity and fruiting of the scion (Webster and Wertheim, 2003). Various compounds, such as minerals, proteins, ribonucleoproteins, ribonucleic acid (RNA) and small RNAs are transferred between the rootstock and scion, but the molecular mechanisms of how the rootstock influences scion phenotypes is not yet clarified in detail (Kumari et al., 2015).

The scion is the cultivar or the part of the tree that has name recognition, such as 'Jonagold'. Once a commercial cultivar is obtained, they are always propagated asexually (Webster and Wertheim, 2003). Sexual propagation is not preferred as each seed is genetically unique with considerably different properties of the parental genotypes, which would result in a plant that is not "true-to-type". Additionally, cultivars propagated from seeds generally bear fruits of poor size, appearance and quality. Although rootstocks can be propagated via seeds, the propagation of rootstocks is becoming increasingly asexual (Tromp, Webster and Wertheim, 2005). Rootstocks and scions are generally *Malus* species or interspecific *Malus* hybrids.

Breeding in apple is focused on the development of better rootstock and scion cultivars. The main accomplishment in apple rootstock breeding was the development of dwarfing apple rootstocks, which started in the early 1920s, by the East Malling Research Station in Kent, England (United Kingdom) (Tukey, 1964; Mudge et al., 2009). The M.9 rootstock, released by this research station, and its improved selections belong until now to the most used rootstocks worldwide. Other efforts in rootstock breeding resulted, for example, in the selection of dwarfing rootstocks tolerant to winter cold or in resistance to fire blight, collar rot and other diseases (Cummins and Aldwinckle, 1994). In apple scion breeding, obtaining a combination of high fruit quality (fruit size, inner fruit quality, fruit colour, flavour and aroma) with disease and pest resistance is the main objective. Furthermore, a range of other traits is considered important in the selection of new (scion) cultivars, like high and regular yielding, the percentage of marketable fruits (Peil et al., 2011), adaptation to climatic conditions and storability of fruits. Low allergenic or high flavonoid content, red fruit flesh or low chilling are minor objectives.

There are several characteristics of *M. domestica* that inhibit rapid genetic improvement of cultivars, most notably: a long juvenile period, self-incompatibility, the high level of heterozygosity resulting from the necessary cross-pollination and inbreeding depression (Brown and Maloney, 2003). The breeding programmes follow, in general, a common strategy, which establishes a series of back-crossings between hybrids exhibiting a trait of interest and susceptible commercial cultivars. Usually, the source of resistance genes comes from sexually compatible wild apple relatives. The traditional breeding method that is most commonly used is a modified backcross, where a different recurrent parent is used in each generation of backcrossing to circumvent self-incompatibility. This process is laborious and time-consuming because it demands several generations to recover near-isogenic lines of high commercial value expressing the desired trait. Typically, the process takes more than 20 years. For example, it took several decades to successfully introgress a scab resistance trait from crab apple into a commercial cultivar (Gessler and Pertot, 2012).

Recent advances in genomic technologies allow for the acceleration of the development of cultivars of apple. Modern breeding programmes using molecular tools have been shown to allow for early screening (typically at the seedling stage) for certain inherited traits, like scab resistance (e.g. Bus et al., 2000; Patocchi et al., 2009; Baumgartner et al., 2015) without the need to phenotype the plants themselves. Two important international research programmes, RosBREED (www.rosbreed.org) in the United States and FruitBreedomics (www.fruitbreedomics.com) (Laurens et al., 2012) in Europe, have provided such molecular tools for screening and developed pre-breeding material. Although simple sequence repeats (SSR) are still used for marker-assisted selection of traits, the development of single nucleotide polymorphism (SNP) markers (Jänsch et al., 2015) and the establishment of an apple 480k SNP genotyping array (Bianco et al., 2016) can allow for genomic selection of traits, such as fruit quality traits as demonstrated by Kumar et al. (2012).

Recombinant DNA technology developments can also address some of the breeding bottlenecks in the development of elite cultivars and rootstocks of apple (for more information, see Annex 2.B.). Successful reduction of the juvenile period to one single year was achieved via constitutive expression of the *BpMADS4* gene from silver birch in early flowering apple lines (Flachowsky et al., 2007, 2009, 2011, 2012). Further, it is a promising tool as it can be used for the direct introduction of specific genes (traits) into a particular cultivar while retaining all other desirable qualities. For example, scab-resistant transgenic apple cultivars were obtained via *Agrobacterium*-mediated transfer and further attempts resulted in the first successful report of a cisgenic apple (Vanblaere et al., 2011).

Hybridisation and introgression

The natural facility of interspecific crossing (extent, sterility and fertility)

Most species in the genus *Malus* can be readily hybridised after artificial cross-pollination (Luby, 2003; Hancock et al., 2008) but interspecific crossing can also occur under natural conditions. The latter is the case in forests in Flanders where 7% of the sampled *Malus sylvestris* trees were hybrid forms of *M. sylvestris* and *M. domestica* (Keulemans, Roldan-Ruiz and Lateur, 2007). The capacity for inter-species hybridisation within the genus *Malus* is evident by the numerous hybrids among *Malus* sp. (e.g. Korban, 1986; Schuster and Büttner, 1995; USDA-ARS, 2018). The majority of *Malus* sp. are diploid and inter-fertile, as there are no apparent physiological or genetic barriers (Korban, 1986; Vanwynsberghe, 2006). Triploid and tetraploid commercial apple cultivars exist but introgression of their genes into wild species seems unlikely since triploids are considered sterile and tetraploid introgression in diploid wild species will give sterile triploid progeny.

Outside of the genus *Malus*, the potential for natural hybridisation with other genera appears to be limited. While there has been extensive intergeneric hybridisation reported among closely related taxa (e.g. in the former subfamily Maloideae), a summary presented by Robertson et al. (1991) indicates no intergeneric crosses involving *Malus* sp. outside of breeding programmes. A reported *Malus* × *Chaenomeles* hybrid was subsequently discounted by Rudenko (1976, cited in Robertson et al., 1991) and a proposal that the species *M. florentina* (Zuccagni) C. K. Schneid. was the product of hybridisation between *Malus* and *Sorbus* sect. *Torminaria* (called × *Malosorbus*) was also subsequently challenged by several authors who considered it a relictual species of *Malus* (e.g. Huckins, 1972, cited in Robertson et al., 1991). This has been further supported by more recent taxonomic work (Qian et al., 2008).

Experimental crosses

Artificial interspecific hybrids are easily produced (Luby, 2003). *M. domestica*, which is thought to be of hybrid origin (Korban, 1986), can be readily hybridised with its congeners in the genus *Malus* (Korban, 1986; Vanwynsberghe, 2006; Kron and Husband, 2009). Interest in controlled hybridisation for the improvement of cultivated apples dates back to the 1700s and reports of successful experimental interspecific hybridisations began in the late 1800s (Korban, 1986). Since then, interspecific hybridisation has played a major role in genetic improvement and a large number of crosses have been made among *Malus* sp. in research and breeding programmes throughout the world, primarily to improve the cultivated apple or to develop new hybrid species with distinctive characteristics (Korban, 1986). A list of experimental interspecific hybrids that have been documented in the genus *Malus* is provided by Korban (1986) and includes about 60 different species combinations. Some new interspecific combinations with *M. domestica* have been added to this list (Vanwynsberghe, 2006).

Breeding programmes have produced intergeneric hybrids between apple and pear (*Malus* × *Pyrus*), and apple and hawthorn (*Malus* × *Crataegus*) as reported in Robertson et al. (1991); however, these relied on techniques such as embryo rescue (Banno et al., 2003). Forced intergeneric hybridisation of *Cydonia* (quince) with *Malus* resulted in fertile genotypes which have been identified as an artificial hybrid genus × *Cydomalus*. However, the seedlings produced are generally weak and of low viability and germinability (Bell and Leitão, 2011). F2 progeny from F1 genus × *Cydomalus* hybrids seem to originate from apomictic seeds (Information communicated to the authors by W. Keulemans). Hybridisation barriers between *Malus* and related species are complex and involve several processes: reduced pollen germination, although pollen adhesion on the stigma seems not affected, reduced pollen tube growth in the style and the ovary, and incongruity of pollen and egg cell. Almost no seeds are formed after an intergeneric cross and seeds are in most cases not viable (Vanwynsberghe, 2006).

Information and data on introgression

A number of studies show that there is a potential for gene introgression from *M. domestica* into native *Malus* species. Coart et al. (2003, 2006) evaluated hybridisation between *M. domestica* and the European wild crab apple *M. sylvestris* in Belgium using nuclear microsatellites and found that 11% of the sampled *M. sylvestris* trees were of hybrid origin. Larsen et al. (2006) on the other hand, did not find *M. domestica* x *M. sylvestris* hybrid individuals in natural *M. sylvestris* populations in Denmark despite the overlap in geographical distribution and flowering time of *M. domestica* and *M. sylvestris*. The fact that handmade interspecific crosses between these two species yield viable seeds which exhibited normal growth and development up to young seedlings suggests there is some other, still unknown, reproductive barrier operating to maintain genetically distinct populations (Larsen, Jensen and Kjær, 2008). A study conducted by Kron and Husband (2009) in southern Ontario examined populations of the introduced *M. domestica* and the native tetraploid crab apple *M. coronaria* and found that their geographic ranges and flowering times overlapped sufficiently for cross-pollination to occur. The study found that 27.7% of seeds from open-pollinated fruit was of hybrid origin. However, the ability of the resulting hybrid plants to survive and backcross with *M. coronaria* is unknown at this time, and the adult trees within the populations were all identified to be distinct species (either *M. domestica* or *M. coronaria*). Successful backcrosses seem unlikely since the hybrids are expected to be triploids, which are normally not fertile.

General interactions with other organisms and ecology

Interaction with natural and other ecosystems where the species is cultivated or managed

Interactions between cultivated apple *Malus domestica* and other organisms include those with agricultural diseases and pests, beneficial organisms, soil organisms, as well as with other *Malus* species. For the latter, please refer to the section "Natural facility of interspecific crossing".

Pests and diseases

M. domestica is susceptible to a number of fungal and bacterial plant diseases (see Annex 2.C.). The most economically important disease of apples worldwide is apple scab caused by the fungal pathogen *Venturia inaequalis* (Cooke) Wint. Another significant disease reported in all major apple production regions with a widespread yearly occurrence and high pest pressure is fire blight caused by the bacterium *Erwinia amylovora* (Burrill) Winslow et al. Fire blight can, under the right conditions, wipe out entire orchards within a growing season (AAFC, 2013). Other significant fungal diseases reported as having localised yearly occurrence with high pest pressure or widespread sporadic occurrence with high pest pressure include, respectively, black rot (in Ontario), caused by the *Botryosphaeria obtusa* (Schwein.) Shoemaker and powdery mildew, caused by the *Podosphaera leucotricha* (Ellis & Everh.) E.S. Salmon (AAFC, 2013). Viruses and viroids can occur in apple orchards but many of them are symptomless in most commercial cultivars. The apple mosaic virus (ApMV) is one of the most widespread apple viruses (Reddy, 2010).

A variety of pests can threaten apple trees and fruits (Carlson, 2008; Sherwani, Mukhtar and Wani, 2016). One of the most common pests of apples is the codling moth (*Cydia pomonella*). This insect eats holes and burrows the core of the apple fruit. Different scale insects, including the San Jose scale (*Quadraspidiotus perniciosus*) and many bugs, like the brown marmorated stink bug (*Halyomorpha halys*), living on apple, impact fruit quality. A group of insects that damages fruit trees are mites. The European red mite (*Panonynchus ulmi*), the twospotted spider mite (*Panonynchus urticae*) and the apple rust mite (*Aculus schlechtendali*) are major mite pests in apple orchards. Leaf rollers can damage both fruits and leaves, while the woolly apple aphid (*Eriosoma lanigerum*) affects leaves, bark and rootstocks. An overview of pests is presented in Annex 2.D.

Some vertebrates can also be considered pests to apple growers. Birds, such as pigeons and crows, can peck holes in the fruit or wood (Tromp, Webster and Wertheim, 2005; AAFC, 2013).

Beneficial insects

Pollinators

The interaction between honey bees, bumble bees and apple trees are mutually beneficial: the bees aid in fertilisation (see section on flower development) and receive nectar and pollen in return.

Biological control organisms

In managed systems, one can exploit the mutual interactions between organisms living on apple and the apple host. In some specific cases, it is possible to manage and control pests and diseases with biological control organisms (BCOs). The application of BCOs in cultivated apple has been investigated in several parts of the growth cycle, from flowering (Pusey, Stockwell and Mazzola, 2009) to post-harvest storage (Jamalizadeh et al., 2011). The use of arthropods against pests which damage the leaves and fruits of the apple plants, such as aphids and mites, is common (Asante, 1997; Nicholas, Spooner-Hart and Vickers, 2005; Brown and Mathews, 2007; Zhou et al., 2014; Walker, Suckling and Wearing, 2017). Even birds can be deployed as BCOs for the predation of caterpillars (Mols and Visser, 2002) but this measure is rarely applied in commercial orchards. This is also the case for bacteria that have been used as BCOs to suppress pathogens like blue mould (Etebarian et al., 2005) and grey mould (Jamalizadeh et al., 2008), or for the fungus *Trichoderma* to control *Phytophthora* in apple seedlings (Roiger and Jeffers, 1991).

Alternative strategies are under investigation to use BCOs as antagonists against *E. amylovora*. One approach for instance is the use of bumblebees as a vector to bring the BCOs to the flowers during bloom (entomovectoring) (Remy et al., 2016, 2017).

Animals

Various mammals, including rodents, rabbits, hares and deer feed on tree tissues, including girdling of bark and feeding on roots, young branches, leaves and buds (AAFC, 2013). Various birds, such as crows and woodpeckers, and some mammals, including bears, feed on fruits.

Apple seeds contain small amounts of amygdalin, a cyanogenic glycoside, which is a naturally occurring plant pre-toxin considered to play a role in plant defence against herbivores due to bitter taste and release of toxic hydrogen cyanide upon tissue disruption (Dar et al., 2016). The presence of small amounts of toxicants and other metabolites (organic acids, phenolic compounds) in apple and products derived from apple and the effect this may have on humans are addressed in the OECD Consensus Document on Compositional Considerations for New Cultivars of Apple (OECD, 2019a).

Soil micro-organisms

Soil micro-organisms interacting with apple are poorly studied. In most cases, rhizosphere micro-organisms are studied in relation to replant diseases in commercial apple plantations (e.g. Čatská et al., 1982; Jiang et al., 2017) or specific treatments on the crop like triazole fungicides (Sułowicz and Piotrowska-Seget, 2016). In some cases, rhizosphere micro-organisms can be used for biological control of soil-borne diseases in apple (Sindhu, Rakshiya and Sahu, 2009) or to improve growth and nutrient uptake (Rengel and Marschner, 2005; Rumberger, Merwin and Thies, 2007).

Annex 2.A. *Malus* species

Annex Table 2.A.1. Species and hybrid species in the genus *Malus*

	Scientific name	Common name (English)
1	*M.* × *adstringens* Zabel	
2	*M. angustifolia* (Aiton) Michx	Southern crab apple
3	*M.* × *arnoldiana* (Rehder) Sarg. ex Rehder	
4	*M.* × *asiatica* Nakai	
5	*M.* × *astracanica* (hort. ex Dum) Cours	
6	*M.* × *atrosanguinea* (hort. ex Späth) C. K. Schneid.	
7	*M. baccata* (L.) Borkh.	Siberian crab apple
8	*M. baoshanensis* G. T. Deng	
9	*M. brevipes* (Rehder) Rehder	
10	*M. chitralensis* Vassilcz.	
11	*M. coronaria* (L.) Mill.	Sweet crab apple
12	*M. crescimannoi* Raimondo	
13	*M.* × *dawsoniana* Rehder	
14	*M. domestica* Borkh.	Apple
15	*M. doumeri* (Bois) A. Chev.	
16	*M. florentina* (Zuccagni) C. K. Schneid.	Hawthorn-leaf crab apple
17	*M. floribunda* Sieb. ex Van Houtte	Japanese crab apple
18	*M. fusca* (Raf.) C. K. Schneid.	Oregon crab apple
19	*M.* × *gloriosa* Lemoine	
20	*M. halliana* Koehne	Hall crab apple
21	*M.* × *hartwigii* Koehne	
22	*M. honanensis Rehder*	
23	*M. hupehensis* (Pamp.) *Rehder*	Chinese crab apple, Hupeh crab
24	*M. ioensis* (Alph. Wood) Britton	Iowa crab apple, prairie crab apple
25	*M. kansuensis* (Batalin) C. K. Schneid.	
26	*M. komarovii* (Sarg.) Rehder	
27	*M. leiocalyca* S. Z. Huang	
28	*M.* × *magdeburgensis* Hartwig	
29	*M. mandshurica* (Maxim.) Kom. ex Skvortsov	Manchurian crab apple
30	*M.* × *micromalus* Makino	Kaido crab apple
31	*M.* × *moerlandsii* Door.	
32	*M. muliensis* T. C. Ku	
33	*M. ombrophila* Hand.-Mazz.	
34	*M. orientalis* Uglitzk.	
35	*M. orthocarpa* Lavallee ex anon.	
36	*M.* × *platycarpa* Rehder	
37	*M. prattii* (Hemsl.) C. K. Schneid.	

	Scientific name	Common name (English)
38	*M. prunifolia* (Willd.) Borkh.	Chinese crab apple, plum-leaf crab apple
39	*M. pumila* Mill.	Paradise apple
40	*M.* × *purpurea* (A. Barbier) Rehder	
41	*M.* × *robusta* (Carrière) Rehder	Siberian crab apple
42	*M. sargentii* Rehder	Sargent's crab apple
43	*M. scheiderckeri* (L. H. Bailey) Späth ex Zabel	
44	*M. sieversii* (Ledeb.) M. Roem.	
45	*M. sikkimensis* (Wenz.) Koehne ex C. K. Schneid.	
46	*M.* × *soulardii* (L. H. Bailey) Britton	Soulard crab apple
47	*M. spectabilis* (Aiton) Borkh.	Asiatic apple, Chinese crab apple
48	*M. spontanea* (Makino) Makino	
49	*M.* × *sublobata* (Dippel) Rehder	
50	*M. sylvestris* (L.)Mill.	European crab apple
51	*M. toringo* (Siebold) de Vriese	Toringo crab apple
52	*M. toringoides* (Rehder) Hughes	
53	*M. transitoria* (Batalin) C. K. Schneid.	
54	*M. trilobata* (Poir.) C. K. Schneid	
55	*M. tschonoskii* (Maxim.) C. K. Schneid.	
56	*M.* × *xiaojinensis* M. H. Cheng & N. G. Jiang	
57	*M. yunnanensis* (Franch.) C. K. Schneid.	Yunnan crab apple
58	*M. zhaojiaoensis* N. G. Jiang	
59	*M. zumi* (Matsum.) Rehder	

Source: USDA-ARS (2018), *Germplasm Resources Information Network (GRIN)*, https://www.ars-grin.gov (accessed 1 October 2019).

Annex 2.B. Biotechnological developments

Apple has become a model species for Rosaceae genetic and genomic research. James et al. published in 1989 the first *Agrobacterium tumefaciens*-mediated leaf disc transformation in apple. In the subsequent years, the main objective in several laboratories around the world was to improve the methodology and to create a "clean vector technology" for marker-free transgenic apples. Due to the lack of availability of "apple own" genes giving a commercially interesting advantage (e.g. disease resistance), the first achievements in genetic engineering of apple (from the early 1990s on) mainly relied on genes from other species and have been reviewed by Gessler and Patocchi (2007), Hanke and Flachowsky (2010) and Rai and Shekhawat (2014). The main target traits in apple transformation are disease and pest resistance, in particular fungal resistance to scab and powdery mildew and resistance to the bacterial fire blight disease. Other traits in apple on which research has been conducted include: i) stress tolerance; ii) herbicide resistance; iii) self-incompatibility; iv) fruit ripening and other fruit characteristics; v) allergens; vi) precocity and flower induction; and vii) dwarfing and rooting ability in rootstock genotypes.

To date, only a few apple genes of potential interest have been mapped. Four disease resistance genes of apple have become available for transformation: two genes (*Rvi6*, Belfanti et al., 2004; *Rvi15*, Schouten et al., 2014) providing resistance to apple scab, one gene (*Fb-Mr5*, Broggini et al., 2014) leading to fire blight resistance and one gene (*Pl2*, Rikkerink et al., 2016) mediating resistance to powdery mildew. Other candidate resistance genes have been identified but map-based cloning of these genes is still in progress (Gessler and Pertot, 2012; Broggini et al., 2014; Schouten et al., 2014). Although most efforts have been done on the cloning of *R* genes, a few genes encoding for other traits in apple have also been identified, like the *Ma* genes controlling the content of malic acid in apple fruits and the *Co* gene leading to a columnar like growth habit of the tree (Xu et al., 2012; Okada et al., 2016). New research initiatives, such as TranscrApple, may increase the number of genes that become available for transformation.

Transgenic apples on the market and transgenic apples for which biosafety research is ongoing are summarised below:

- **Disease resistance:** Scab-resistant transgenic apple cultivars were obtained via *Agrobacterium*-mediated transfer of scab resistance genes *Rvi6* from *M. floribunda*, a species of crab apple that shows natural resistance to some strains of the apple scab fungus, to cultivar 'Gala' (Barbieri et al., 2003; Belfanti et al., 2004; Silfverberg-Dilworth et al., 2005; Malnoy et al., 2008). Further research resulted in the first intragenic and cisgenic apple lines of the cultivar 'Gala' with scab resistance (Joshi et al., 2011; Vanblaere et al., 2011, 2014; Krens et al., 2015), containing the *Rvi6* gene from *M. floribunda* under the control of the promoter from the apple Rubisco gene or the native *Rvi6*-promoter respectively. These plants were planted in a field trial to study scab resistance in an orchard situation (Krens et al., 2015). In 2015, the development of the first cisgenic apple with increased resistance to fire blight was reported (Kost et al., 2015). A cisgenic apple line C44.4.146 of the susceptible apple cultivar 'Gala Galaxy' was regenerated using the *FB_MR5* gene from the wild apple *M. robusta*.
- **Breeding cycle acceleration:** Fruit trees typically have long breeding cycles. Successful reduction of the juvenile period of apple to one single year was achieved via constitutive expression of the *MADS4* transcription factor gene from silver birch (*Betula pendula* Roth.) in early flowering apple cultivars 'Pinova' (Flachowsky et al., 2007, 2009, 2011, 2012), 'Gala', 'Mitchgl Gala' and 'Santana' (Weigl et al., 2015). The BpMADS4-based breeding technology allows for more rapid introgression of agronomically relevant traits (e.g. disease resistances) from wild apples into domestic apple cultivars (e.g. Schlathölter et al., 2018).

- **Fruit quality:** Apples have been engineered using a gene-silencing technique called ribonucleic acid interference (RNAi), in order to reduce the production of polyphenol oxidases (PPO), which causes the apple's flesh to brown when sliced or bitten (Xu, 2013). Transgenic versions of the varieties 'Golden Delicious', 'Granny Smith' and 'Fuji' have been approved for marketing (OECD, 2019b).

Annex 2.C. Apple diseases

The following lists include the most relevant diseases in terms of economic losses.

Annex Table 2.C.1. Bacteria (including phytoplasma)

Scientific name	Common name (English)
Agrobacterium rhizogenes	Hairy root
Agrobacterium tumefaciens	Crown gall
Erwinia amylovora	Fire blight
Phytoplasma	Apple chat fruit
Pseudomonas syringae	Blister spot
Apple-proliferation phytoplasma	

Annex Table 2.C.2. Fungi

Scientific name	Common name (English)	Occurrence
Alternaria alternata	Alternaria rot	W
Alternaria mali	Alternaria blotch	A, AF, NA
Armillaria mellea	Root rot	W
Athelia rolfsii	Southern blight	AF, NA, SA
Biscogniauxia marginata	Blister canker	NA
Botryosphaeria berengeriana	Apple ring rot and canker	A
Botryosphaeria dothidea	Apple ring rot	AF, NA, SA, O
Botryosphaeria stevensii	Black rot, frog eye leaf spot, canker	AF, E, NA, SA, O
Botrytis cinerea	Grey mould rot	W
Butlerelfia eustacei	Fish-eye rot	A, E, NA
Cadophora malorum	Side rot	A, NA
Cladosporium spp.	Mouldy core, core rot	W
Colletotrichum spp.	Bitter rot	E
Corticium stevensii	Thread blight	NA
Cytospora ceratosperma		A
Diplocarpon mali	Marssonina blotch	A, E, NA
Epicoccum spp.	Mouldy core, core rot	W
Fusarium spp.		E
Geastrumia polystigmatis	Sooty-blotch complex	W
Gloeopeniophorella sacrata	Peniophora root canker	O
Grovesinia moricola		A
Gymnosporangium clavipes	Quince rust	NA
Gymnosporangium globosum	American hawthorn rust	NA
Gymnosporangium juniperi-virginianae	Cedar apple rust	NA
Gymnosporangium libocedri	Pacific Coast pear rust	NA

Gymnosporangium yamadae	Japanese apple rust	A
Helicobasidium longisporum		O
Helminthosporium papulosum	Black pox	NA
Lepteutypa cupressi	Monochaetia twig canker	NA
Leptodontidium trabinellum	Sooty-blotch complex	
Leucostoma cinctum	Leucostoma canker, dieback	E, NA
Monilinia fructigena	European brown rot	A, AF, E
Monilinia laxa	European brown rot	A, AF, E
Monilinia mali	Monilinia leaf blight	A
Mucor spp.	Mucor rot	
Mycosphaerella pomi	Brooks fruit spot	NA
Nectria cinnabarina	Nectria twig blight	E, NA, O
Nectria ditissima	Nectria canker	A, AF, NA, SA, O
Neofabraea malicorticis	Anthracnose canker, bull's eye rot	E, NA, O
Paraconiothyrium fuckelii	Blossom-end rot, Leptosphaeria canker, fruit rot	W
Peltaster fructicola	Sooty-blotch complex	W
Penicillium spp.	Blue mould	
Peyronellaea obtuse	Black rot, frog eye leaf spot, canker	AF, E, NA, SA, O
Phacidiopycnis malorum		E
Phomopsis prunorum	Phomopsis canker, fruit decay, rough bark	A, E, NA
Phyllosticta solitaria (Blotch)		NA
Podosphaera leucotricha	Powdery mildew	W
Rosellinia necatrix	Rosellinia root rot	W
Schizothyrium pomi	Fly-speck	W
Scytinostroma galactinum	White rot	NA
Sphaeropsis spp.		E
Stemphilium spp.		E
Trichothecium roseum	Pink mould rot	W
Venturia inaequalis	Apple scab	W
Xylaria mali	Black root rot	NA
Xylaria polymorpha	Black root rot	W

Note: A: Asia, AF: Africa, E: Europe, NA: North America, O: Oceania, SA: South America, W: worldwide.

Annex Table 2.C.3. Protista; Oomycota

Scientific name	Common name (English)
Phytophthora cactorum	Phytophthora crown, collar, root and fruit rot
Phytophthora syringae	Phytophthora crown, collar, root and fruit rot

Annex Table 2.C.4. Viruses and viroids

Common name (English)	Acronym
Apple chlorotic leaf-spot virus	ACLSV
Apple stem-grooving virus	ASGV

Common name (English)	Acronym
Apple mosaic virus	APMV
Tulare apple mosaic ilarvirus	TAMV
Apple stem-pitting foveavirus	ASPV
Tomato ringspot nepovirus	TomRSV
Apple fruit-crinkle viroid	AFCVd
Apple dimple-fruit viroid	ADFVd
Apple scar-skin viroid	ASSVd

Source (annex): Ogawa, J.M. and H. English (1991), *Diseases of Temperate Zone Tree Fruit and Nut Crops*, University of California, Division of Agriculture and Natural Resources, Publication 3345; Grove, G. (2003), "Diseases of apple", in D.C. Ferree and I.J. Warrington (eds.), *Apples: Botany, Production and Uses*, CAB International, Wallingford, UK, pp. 459-488; Hadidi, A. et al. (2003), *Viroids*, CSIRO Publishing, Collingwood, Australia; Betere Bomen (2019), *Malus*; VIDE (2018), Virus Identification Database Exchange - *Known susceptibilities of Rosaceae*, Malus.

Annex 2.D. **Apple pests**

Annex Table 2.D.1. Arthropoda (ranked by order)

Scientific name	Common name (English)
Coleoptera (beetles, weevils)	
Anthonomus piri	Apple bud weevil
Anthonomus pomorum	Apple blossom weevil
Curculionidae nenuphar	
Polydrusus	
Sitona lineatus	Pea leaf weevil
Xyleborus dispar	Pear blight beetle
Diptera (flies)	
Anastrepha fraterculus	South American fruit fly
Ceratitis capitata	Mediterranean fruit fly
Dasineura mali	Apple leaf curling midge
Rhagoletis pomonella	Apple maggot
Tephritidae	Tephritid fruit flies
Hemiptera	
Anuraphis farfarae	
Aphis pomi	Apple aphid
Campylomma verbasci	Mullein plant bug
Dysaphis plantaginea	Rosy apple aphid
Eriosoma lanigerum	Woolly apple aphid
Edwardsiana crataegi	
Halyomorpha halys	The brown marmorated stink bug
Lepidosaphes ulmi	Apple mussel scale
Lygocoris pabulinus	Common green capsid
Lygus lineolaris	Tarnished plant bug
Parthenolecanium corni	European fruit lecanium
Psylla mali	Apple sucker
Quadraspidiotus ostreaeformis	European fruit scale
Rhopalosiphum insertum	Apple-grass aphid
Hymenoptera (sawflies, wasps ants, bees)	
Ametastegia glabrata	Dock sawfly
Hoplocampa testudinea	Apple sawfly
Isopoda (woodlouse)	
Oniscidea spp.	

Lepidoptera (moths)	
Adoxophyes orana	Summer fruit tortrix
Adoxophyes reticulana	
Amphipyra pyrimadoides	Humped green fruitworm
Archips rosana	Rose tortrix
Archips podana	Large fruit-tree tortrix
Archips breviplicanus	Asiatic leafroller
Archips argyrospila	Fruittree leafroller
Clepsis spectrana	Cabbage leafroller
Coccus cossus	Goat moth
Coleophora hemerobiella	Fruit tree case moth
Cydia pomonella	Codling moth
Epiphyas postvittana	Light brown apple moth
Grapholita molesta	Oriental fruit moth
Lithophane antennata	Widestriped green fruitworm
Lacanobia subjuncta	Lacanobia fruitworm
Malacosoma Neustria	Lackey moth
Operophtera brumata	Winter moth
Orthosia incerta	
Orthosia spp.	
Phlogophora meticulosa	Angle shades
Phyllonorycter blancardella	Spotted tentiform leafminer
Phyllonorycter crataegella	Apple blotch leafminer
Phyllonorycter elmaella	Western tentiform leafminer
Spilonota ocellana	Bud moth
Stigmella malella	Banded apple pigmy
Stigmella incognitella	Grey apple pigmy
Synanthedon myopaeformis	Red-belted clearwing
Yponomeuta malinellus	Apple ermine
Zeuzera pyrina	Leopard moth
Thysanoptera (thrips)	
Thripidae spp.	Thrips
Trombidiformes (mites)	
Aculus schlechtendali	Apple rust mite
Eriophyes pyri	Pearleaf blister mite
Epitrimerus pyri	Pear rust mite
Panonychus ulmi	European red mite
Phyllocoptes malinus	
Tetranychus mcdanieli	McDaniel spider mite
Tetranychus urticae	Twospotted spider mite
Tetranychus viennensis	Fruit tree spider mite

Annex Table 2.D.2. Nematodes

Scientific name	Common name (English)
Meloidogyne arenaria	
Meloidogyne hapla	
Meloidogyne incognita	
Meloidogyne javanica	
Pratylenchus penetrans	
Pratylenchus vulnus	
Xiphinema americanum	American dagger nematode
Xiphinema rivesi	

Sources (annex): Grove, G. (2003), "Diseases of apple", in D.C. Ferree and I.J. Warrington (eds.), *Apples: Botany, Production and Uses*, CAB International, Wallingford, UK, pp. 459-488; Betere Bomen (2019), *Malus*; UCANR (2018), *How to Manage Pests: Apple*, University of California Agriculture and Natural Resources, http://ipm.ucanr.edu/PMG/selectnewpest.apples.html (accessed 1 October 2019); Fruit pluktuin (2019), *Schadelijke insecten*, http://www.fruitpluktuin.nl/fruit/Insecten/schadelijke-insecten# (accessed 1 October 2019); Groenkennisnet (2019), *Appel*, https://wiki.groenkennisnet.nl/display/BEEL/Appel (accessed 1 October 2019).

References

AAFC (2013), *Crop Profile for Apple in Canada, 2013*, Pesticide Risk Reduction Program, Pest Management Centre, Agriculture and Agri-Food Canada, Ottawa.

Abrol, D.P. (2012), *Pollination Biology–Biodiversity Conservation and Agricultural Production*, Springer, New York, United States.

Adachi, Y. et al. (2009), "Characteristics of fruiting and pollen tube growth of apple autotetraploid cultivars showing self-compatibility", *Journal of the Japanese Society for Horticultural Science*, Vol. 78/4, pp. 402–409.

AHDB (2017), *Apple Best Practice Guide*, Agriculture and Horticulture Development Board, UK, https://apples.ahdb.org.uk/agronomy-pollination-and-fruit-set.asp (accessed 1 October 2019).

Asante, S.K. (1997), "Natural enemies of the woolly apple aphid, *Eriosoma lanigerum* (Hausmann) (Hemiptera: Aphididae): A review of the world literature", *Plant Protection Quarterly*, Vol. 12/4, pp. 166-172.

Bai, Y., L. Dougherty and K. Xu (2014), "Towards an improved apple reference transcriptome using RNA-seq", *Molecular Genetics and Genomics*, Vol. 289, pp. 427-438.

Bailey, L.G. and E.Z. Bailey (1976), *Hortus Third: A Concise Dictionary of Plants Cultivated in the United States and Canada*, McMillan Publishing Co., New York, US.

Banno, K. et al. (2003), "Breeding and characteristics of symmetric intergeneric hybrids between apple and pear", *Acta Horticulturae*, Vol. 622, pp. 265-276.

Barbieri, M. et al. (2003), "Progress of map-based cloning of the *Vf*-resistance gene and functional verification: Preliminary results from expression studies in transformed apple", *Horticultural Science*, Vol. 38, pp. 329–331.

Baumgartner, I.O. et al. (2015), "Breeding elite lines of apple carrying pyramided homozygous resistance genes against apple scab and resistance against powdery mildew and fire blight", *Plant Molecular Biology Reporter*, Vol. 33, pp. 1573-1583.

Belfanti, E. et al. (2004), "The HcrVf2 gene from a wild apple confers scab resistance to a transgenic cultivated variety", Proceedings of the National Academic of Sciences of the USA, Vol. 101, pp. 886-890.

Bell, R.L. and J.M. Leitão (2011), "Cydonia", in C. Kole (ed.), *Wild Crop Relatives: Genomic and Breeding Resources*, Springer-Verlag, Berlin Heidelberg, pp. 1-16.

Betere Bomen (2019), *Malus*.

Bianco, L. et al. (2016), "Development and validation of the Axiom®Apple480K SNP genotyping array", *The Plant Journal*, Vol. 86, pp. 62-74.

Broggini, G.A.L. et al. (2014), "Engineering fire blight resistance into the apple cultivar 'Gala' using the *FB_MR5* CC-NBS-LRR resistance gene of *Malus* x *robusta* 5", *Plant Biotechnology Journal*, Vol. 12/6, p. 728-733.

Brown, M.W. and C.R. Mathews (2007), "Conservation biological control of rosy apple aphid, *Dysaphis plantaginea* (Passerini), in eastern North America", *Environmental entomology*, Vol. 36/5, pp. 1131-1139.

Brown, S.K. and K.E. Maloney (2003), "Genetic improvement of apple: Breeding, markers, mapping and biotechnology", in D.C. Ferree and I.J. Warrington (eds.), *Apples: Botany, Production and Uses*, CAB International, Wallingford, UK, pp. 31-60.

Bus, V.G.M. et al. (2000), "Marker assisted selection for pest and disease resistance in the New Zealand apple breeding programme", *Acta Horticulturae*, Vol. 538, pp. 541-547.

Carlson, E. (2008), *Major Insect Pests of Apple in Georgia*, https://wiki.bugwood.org/Major_insect_pests_of_apple/Georgia (accessed 1 October 2019).

Čatská, V. et al. (1982), "Rhizosphere micro-organisms in relation to the apple replant problem", *Plant and Soil*, Vol. 69, pp. 187-197.

Chevreau, E. and F. Laurens (1987), "The pattern of inheritance in apple: Further results from leaf isozyme analysis", *Theoretical and Applied Genetics*, Vol. 75, pp. 90-95.

Coart, E. et al. (2006), "Chloroplast diversity in the genus *Malus*: New insights into the relationship between the European wild apple (*Malus sylvestris* (L.) Mill.) and the domesticated apple (*Malus domestica* Borkh.)", *Molecular Ecology*, Vol. 15, pp. 2171-2182.

Coart, E. et al. (2003), "Genetic variation in the endangered wild apple (*Malus sylvestris* (L.) Mill.) in Belgium as revealed by amplified fragment length polymorphism and microsatellite markers", *Molecular Ecology*, Vol. 12, pp. 845–857.

Cornille, A. et al. (2014), "The domestication and evolutionary ecology of apples", *Trends in Genetics*, Vol. 30, p. 57-65.

Cornille, A. et al. (2012), "New insight into the history of domesticated apple: Secondary contribution of the European wild apple to the genome of cultivated varieties", *Public Library of Science Genetics*, Vol. 8/.5 e1002703.

Cummins, J. and H. Aldwinckle (1994), "New resistant rootstocks from Geneva", *Fruit Varieties Journal (USA)*, Vol. 48, p. 39.

Daccord, N. et al. (2017), "High-quality *de novo* assembly of the apple genome and methylome dynamics of early fruit development", *Nature Genetics*, Vol. 49/7, pp. 1099-1108.

Dar, S.A. et al. (2016), Plant-Insect Interactions – Cyanogenic Glucosides, *Imperial Journal of Interdisciplinary Research*, Vol. 2, pp. 1107-1118.

De Witte, K. et al. (1996), "Fruit set, seed set and fruit weight in apple as influenced by emasculation and cross-pollination", *Acta Horticulturae*, Vol. 423(December), pp. 177-184.

Degrandi-Hoffman, G., R. Hoopingarner and K. Klomparens (1986), "Influence of honey bee (Hymenoptera: Apidae) in-hive pollen transfer on cross-pollination and fruit set in apple", *Environmental Entomology*, Vol. 15/3, pp. 723-725.

Delaplane, K.S. and D.F. Mayer (2000), "Crop pollination by bees", *Zoosystematics and Evolution*, Vol. 78/1, pp. 192-192.

Dennis, F. (2003), "Flowering, pollination and fruit set, and development", in D.C. Ferree and I.J. Warrington (eds.), *Apples: Botany, Production and Uses*, CAB International, Wallingford, UK, pp. 153-166.

Di Pierro, E.A. et al. (2016), "A high-density, multi-parental SNP genetic map on apple validates a new mapping approach for outcrossing species", *Horticulture Research*, Vol. 3, p. 16057.

Duan, N. et al. (2017), "Genome re-sequencing reveals the history of apple and supports a two-stage model for fruit enlargement", *Nature Communications*, Vol. 8, p. 249.

Dzhangaliev, A.D. (2003), "The wild apple tree of Kazakhstan", *Horticultural Reviews*, Vol. 29, pp. 63-303.

Etebarian, H.R. et al. (2005), "Biological control of apple blue mold with *Pseudomonas fluorescens*", *Canadian Journal of Microbiology*, Vol. 51/7, pp. 591-598.

FAO (2022), *FAOSTAT*, Food and Agriculture Organization of the United Nations Statistics Division, www.fao.org/corp/statistics/en (accessed 16 February 2022).

Ferrer, M.M. et al. (2009), "Effect of variation in self-incompatibility on pollen limitation and inbreeding depression in *Flourensia cernua* (Asteraceae) scrubs of contrasting density", *Annals of Botany*, Vol. 103/7, pp. 1077-1089.

Fiala, L. (1994), *Flowering Crabapples: The Genus* Malus, Timber Press Inc., Portland, US.

Flachowsky, H. et al. (2012), "Genetic control of flower development in apple and the utilisation of transgenic early flowering apple plants in breeding", *Acta Horticulturae*, Vol. 967, pp. 29-34.

Flachowsky, H. et al. (2011), "Application of a high-speed breeding technology to apple (*Malus* x *domestica*) based on transgenic early flowering plants and marker-assisted selection", *New Phytologist*, Vol. 192, pp. 364-377.

Flachowsky, H. et al. (2009), "A review on transgenic approaches to accelerate breeding of woody plants", *Plant Breeding*, Vol. 128, pp. 217-226.

Flachowsky, H. et al. (2007), "Overexpression of the *BpMADS4* gene from silver birch (*Betula pendula* Roth.) induces early-flowering in apple (*Malus* x *domestica* Borkh.)", *Plant Breeding*, Vol. 126, pp. 137-145.

Free, J.B. (1966), "The foraging areas of honeybees in an orchard of standard apple trees", *The Journal of Applied Ecology*, Vol. 3/2, pp. 261.

Free, J.B. and Y. Spencer-Booth (1964), "The foraging behaviour of honey bees in an orchard of dwarf apple trees", *Journal of Horticultural Science*, Vol. 39/2, pp. 78–83.

Fruit pluktuin (2019), *Schadelijke insecten*, http://www.fruitpluktuin.nl/fruit/insecten/schadelijke-insecten# (accessed 1 October 2019).

Galetti, M. (2002), "Seed dispersal of mimetic fruits: Parasitism, mutualism, aposematism or exaptation?", in *Seed Dispersal and Frugivory: Ecology, Evolution and Conservation*, Third International Symposium-Workshop on Frugivores and Seed Dispersal, São Pedro, Brazil, pp. 6-11.

Gardiner, S.E. et al. (1996), "A detailed linkage map around an apple scab resistance gene demonstrates that two disease resistance classes both carry the V_f gene", *Theoretical and Applied Genetics*, Vol. 93, pp. 485-493.

Garibaldi, L.A. et al. (2013), "Wild pollinators enhance fruit set of crops regardless of honey bee abundance", *Science*, Vol. 339/March, pp. 1608-1611.

Gessler, C. and A. Patocchi (2007), "Recombinant DNA technology in apple", *Advances in Biochemical Engineering/Biotechnology*, Vol. 107, pp. 113-132.

Gessler, C. and I. Pertot (2012), "*Vf* scab resistance of *Malus*", *Trees*, Vol. 26, pp. 95-108.

Gharghani, A. et al. (2009), "Genetic identity and relationships of Iranian apple (*Malus × domestica* Borkh.) cultivars and landraces, wild *Malus* species and representative old apple cultivars based on simple sequence repeat (SSR) marker analysis", *Genetic Resources Crop Evolution*, Vol. 56, pp. 829-842.

Goremykin, V.V. et al. (2012), "The mitochondrial genome of *Malus domestica* and the import-driven hypothesis of mitochondrial genome expansion in seed plants", *The Plant Journal*, Vol. 71/4, pp. 615-626.

Groenkennisnet (2019), *Appel*, https://wiki.groenkennisnet.nl/display/BEEL/Appel (accessed 1 October 2019).

Gross, B.L. et al. (2012), "Identification of interspecific hybrids among domesticated apple and its wild relatives", *Tree Genetics and Genomes*, Vol. 8, pp. 1223-1235.

Grove, G. (2003), "Diseases of apple", in D.C. Ferree and I.J. Warrington (eds.), *Apples: Botany, Production and Uses*, CAB International, Wallingford, UK, pp. 459-488.

Hadidi, A. et al. (2003), *Viroids*, CSIRO Publishing, Collingwood, Australia.

Hampson, C.R. and H. Kemp (2003), "Characteristics of important commercial apple cultivars", in D.C. Ferree and I.J. Warrington (eds.), *Apples: Botany, Production and Uses*, CABI International, Wallingford, UK, pp. 61-90.

Hancock, J.F. et al. (2008), "Apples", in J.F. Hancock (ed.), *Temperate Fruit Crop Breeding: Germplasm to Genomics*, Springer Media B.V., New York, US.

Hanke, M.V. and H. Flachowsky (2010), "Fruit Crops", in F. Kempken and C. Jung (eds.), *Genetic Modification of Plants, Biotechnology in Agriculture and Forestry*, Vol. 64, Springer, Berlin Heidelberg, Germany.

Harris, S.A., J.P. Robinson and B.E. Juniper (2002), "Genetic clues to the origin of the apple", *Trends in Genetics*, Vol. 18, pp. 426-430.

Hemmat, M. et al. (1994), "Molecular marker linkage map for apple", *Journal of Heredity*, Vol. 85/1, pp. 4-11.

Herrera, M.C. (2002), "Seed dispersal by vertebrates", in C.M. Herrera and O. Pellmyr (eds.) *Plant-Animal Interactions: An Evolutionary Approach*, Blackwell Science, Oxford, UK, pp. 328.

Höfer, M. and A. Meister (2010), "Genome size variation in *Malus* species", *Journal of Botany*, Vol. 2010, Article ID 480873, http://dx.doi.org/10.1155/2010/480873 (accessed 1 October 2019).

Iowa State University (2003), *Reproductive Terms*,

IUCN (2019), *The IUCN Red List of Threatened Species,* http://www.iucnredlist.org (accessed 1 October 2019).

Jackson, J.E. (2003), *Biology of Apple and Pears*, Cambridge University Press, Cambridge, UK.

Jamalizadeh, M. et al. (2011), "A review of mechanisms of action of biological control organisms against post-harvest fruit spoilage", *EPPO Bulletin*, Vol. 41/1, pp. 65-71.

Jamalizadeh, M. et al. (2008), "Biological control of gray mold on apple fruits by *Bacillus licheniformis* (EN74-1)", *Phytoparasitica*, Vol. 36/1, pp. 23.

James, D.J. et al. (1989), "Genetic transformation of apple (*Malus pumila* Mill.) using a disarmed Ti-binary vector", *Plant Cell Report*, Vol. 7, pp. 658-661.

Janick, J. and J.N. Moore (1975), *Advances in Fruit Breeding*, Purdue University Press, Indiana, US.

Janick, J. et al. (1996), "Apples", in J. Janick and J. Moore (eds.), *Fruit Breeding Vol. II, Tree and Tropical Fruits*, Wiley, New York, US.

Jänsch, M. et al. (2015), "Identification of SNPs linked to eight apple disease resistance loci", *Molecular Breeding*, Vol. 35, pp. 1-21.

Jefferies, C.J. and P. Brain (1984), "A mathematical model of pollen-tube penetration in apple styles", *Planta*, Vol. 160/1, pp. 52-58.

Jiang, J. et al. (2017), "Microbial community analysis of apple rhizosphere around Bohai Gulf", *Nature Scientific Reports*, Vol. 7, e8918.

Joshi, S.G. et al. (2011), " Functional analysis and expression profiling of HcrVf1 and HcrVf2 for development of scab resistant cisgenic and intragenic apples", *Plant Molecular Biology*, Vol. 75, pp 579-591.

Keulemans, W., I. Roldan-Ruiz and M. Lateur (2007), *Studying Apple Biodiversity: Opportunities for Conservation and Sustainable Use of Genetic Resources (apple)*, SPSDII, Belgian Science Policy, Brussels, Belgium.

King, G.J. et al. (1991), "The 'European Apple Genome Project' – Developing a strategy for mapping genes coding for agronomic characters in tree species", *Euphytica*, Vol. 56, pp. 89-94.

Koltunow, A.M. (1993), "Apomixis: Embryo sacs and embryos formed without meiosis or fertilisation in ovules", *The Plant Cell*, Vol. 5/10, pp. 1425-1437.

Komori, S. et al. (1999), "Discrimination of cross incompatibility by number of seeds per fruit and fruit set percentage in apples", *Bulletin of the National Institute of Fruit Tree Science*, Vol. 33, pp. 97-112.

Korban, S.S. (1986), "Interspecific hybridization in *Malus*", *Horticultural Science*, Vol. 21/1, pp. 41-48.

Korban, S.S. and R.M. Skirvin (1984), "Nomenclature of the cultivated apple", *Horticultural Science*, Vol. 19, pp. 177-180.

Kost, T.D. et al. (2015), "Development of first cisgenic apple with increased resistance to fire blight", *Public Library of Science One*, Vol. 10/12: e0143980.

Kotoda, N. et al. (2000), "Expression pattern of homologues of floral meristem identity genes *LFY* and *AP1* during flower development in apple", *Journal of the American Society for Horticultural Science*, Vol. 125/4, pp. 398-403.

Koutinas, N., G. Pepelyankov and V. Lichev (2010), "Flower induction and flower bud development in apple and sweet cherry", *Biotechnology and Biotechnological Equipment*, Vol. 24/1, pp. 1549-1558.

Krens, F.A. et al. (2015), "Cisgenic apple trees; Development, characterisation, and performance", *Frontiers Plant Science*, Vol. 6, p. 286.

Kron, P. and B.C. Husband (2009), "Hybridization and the reproductive pathways mediating gene flow between native *Malus coronaria* and domestic apple, *M. domestica*", *Botany*, Vol. 87/9, pp. 864-874.

Kron, P. et al. (2001), "Across- and along-row pollen dispersal in high-density apple orchards: Insights from allozyme markers", *The Journal of Horticultural Science and Biotechnology*, Vol. 76/3, pp. 286-294.

Kumar, S. et al. (2012), "Genomic selection for fruit quality traits in apple (*Malus* x *domestica* Borkh.)", *Public Library of Science One*, Vol. 7/5: e36674.

Kumari, A. et al. (2015), "Grafting triggers differential responses between scion and rootstock", *Public Library of Science One*, Vol. 10/4: e0124438.

Larsen, A.S. and E.D. Kjær (2009), "Pollen mediated gene flow in a native population of *Malus sylvestris* and its implications for contemporary gene conservation management", *Conservation Genetics*, Vol. 10/6, pp. 1637-1646.

Larsen, A.S., M. Jensen and E.D. Kjær (2008), "Crossability between wild (*Malus sylvestris*) and cultivated (*M.x domestica*) apples–implications for genetic resource management", *Silvae Genetica*, Vol. 57/3, pp. 127-130.

Larsen, A.S. et al. (2006), "Hybridization and genetic variation in Danish populations of European crab apple (*Malus sylvestris*)", *Tree Genetics and Genomes,* Vol. 2/2, pp. 86-97.

Laurens, F. et al. (2012), "Review of fruit genetics and breeding programmes and a new European initiative to increase fruit breeding efficiency", *Acta Horticulturae*, Vol. 929, pp. 95-102.

Levin, D.A. (1996), "The evolutionary significance of pseudo-self-fertility", *The American Naturalist*, Vol. 148/2, pp 321-332.

Liu, L. et al. (2017), "Apple, from omics to systemic function", *Plant Growth Regulation*, Vol. 83/1, pp. 1-11.

Luby, J.J. (2003), "Taxonomic classification and brief history", in D.C. Ferree and I.J. Warrington (eds.), *Apples: Botany, Production and Uses*, CABI International, Cambridge, UK, p. 1-14.

Malnoy, M. et al. (2008), "Two receptor-like genes, *Vfa1* and *Vfa2*, confer resistance to the fungal pathogen *Venturia inaequalis* inciting apple scab disease", *Molecular Plant-Microbe Interactions*, Vol. 21/4, pp. 448-458.

Manganaris, A.G. and F.H. Alston (1988a), "Inheritance and linkage relationships of glutamate oxaloacetate transaminase in apple: 2. The genes *GOT-2* and *GOT-4*", *Theoretical and Applied Genetics*, Vol. 76/3, pp. 449-454.

Manganaris, A.G. and F.H. Alston (1988b), "The acid phosphatase gene *ACP-1* and its linkage with the endopeptidase gene *ENP-1* and the pale green lethal gene *1* in apple", *Acta Horticulturae*, Vol. 224, pp. 177-184.

Manganaris, A.G. and F.H. Alston (1987), "Inheritance and linkage relationships of glutamate oxaloacetate transaminase isoenzymes in apple: 1. The gene *GOT-l*, a marker for the *S* incompatibility locus", *Theoretical and Applied Genetics*, Vol. 74/1, pp. 154-161.

McNeill, J. et al. (2012), *International Code of Nomenclature for Algae, Fungi and Plants (Melbourne Code) Adopted by the Eighteenth International Botanical Congress Melbourne, Australia, July 2011 (Regnum Vegetabile 154),* Koeltz Scientific Books, Germany.

Miller, D.D. and J. Racsko (2011), "Rootstock effects on fruit drop and quality of 'Gala Galaxy' and 'Golden Delicious Reinders' apples", *Acta Horticulturae*, Vol. 903/August, pp. 397-404.

Mols, C.M. and M.E. Visser (2002), "Great tits can reduce caterpillar damage in apple orchards", *Journal of Applied Ecology*, Vol. 39/6, pp. 888-899.

Moshtagh, F. et al. (2015), "Investigation on pollen viability, germination and tube growth in some apple cultivars in climate conditions in Shirvan", *Journal of Applied Environmental and Biological Sciences*, Vol. 4/12, pp. 295-302.

Mudge, K. et al. (2009), "A history of grafting", *Horticultural Reviews*, Vol. 35, pp. 437-493.

Myers, J. et al. (2004), "Seed dispersal by white-tailed deer: Implications for long-distance dispersal, invasion, and migration of plants in eastern North America", *Oecologia*, Vol. 139, pp. 35-44.

Nicholas, A.H., R.N. Spooner-Hart and R.A. Vickers (2005), "Abundance and natural control of the woolly aphid *Eriosoma lanigerum* in an Australian apple orchard IPM program", *BioControl*, Vol. 50/2, pp. 271-291.

Nikiforova, S.V. et al. (2013), "Phylogenetic analysis of 47 chloroplast genomes clarifies the contribution of wild species to the domesticated apple maternal line", *Molecular Biology Evolution*, Vol. 30, pp. 1751-1760.

OECD (2019a), "Consensus document on compositional considerations for new cultivars of apple (*Malus x domestica* Borkh.): Key food and feed nutrients, allergens, toxicants and other metabolites", *Series on the Safety of Novel Foods and Feeds*, No. 31, Organisation for Economic Corporation and Development, Paris, http://www.oecd.org/officialdocuments/publicdisplaydocumentpdf/?cote=ENV-JM-MONO(2019)23%20&doclanguage=en (accessed 1 October 2019).

OECD (2019b), *OECD BioTrack Product Database*, OECD, Paris, https://biotrackproductdatabase.oecd.org/ (accessed 1 October 2019).

Ogawa, J.M. and H. English (1991), *Diseases of Temperate Zone Tree Fruit and Nut Crops*, University of California, Division of Agriculture and Natural Resources, Publication 3345.

Okada, K. et al. (2016), "Expression of a putative dioxygenase gene adjacent to an insertion mutation is involved in the short internodes of columnar apples (*Malus* x *domestica*)", *Journal of Plant Research*, Vol. 129/6, pp. 1109-1126.

Patocchi, A. et al. (2009), "Towards improvement of marker assisted selection of apple scab resistant cultivars: *Venturia inaequalis* virulence surveys and standardisation of molecular marker alleles associated with resistance genes", *Molecular Breeding*, Vol. 24, pp. 337-347.

Peil, A. et al. (2011), "Apple breeding – From the origin to genetic engineering", *Fruit, Vegetable and Cereal Science and Biotechnology*, Vol. 5/1, pp. 118-138.

Petrisor, C. et al. (2012), "The rate of pollen germination and the pollen viability at ten apple cultivars in the climatic conditions of Transylvania", *Bulletin UASVM Horticulture*, Vol. 69/1, pp. 417-418.

Potter, D. et al. (2007), "Phylogeny and classification of Rosaceae", *Plant Systematics and Evolution*, Vol. 266, pp. 5-43.

Pusey, P.L., V.O. Stockwell and M. Mazzola (2009), "Epiphytic bacteria and yeasts on apple blossoms and their potential as antagonists of *Erwinia amylovora*", *Phytopathology*, Vol. 99, pp. 571-581.

Qian, G.Z. et al. (2010), "Proposal to conserve the name *Malus domestica* against *M. pumila*, *M. communis*, *M. frutescens* and *Pyrus dioica* (Rosaceae)", *Taxon*, Vol. 59/2, pp. 650-652.

Qian, G.Z. et al. (2008), "Taxonomic study of Malus section Florentinae (Rosaceae)", *Botanical Journal of the Linnean Society*, Vol. 158, pp. 223-227.

Rai, M.K. and N.S. Shekhawat (2014), "Recent advances in genetic engineering for improvement of fruit crops", *Plant Cell, Tissue and Organ Culture*, Vol. 116, pp. 1-15.

Ramírez, F. and T.L. Davenport (2013), "Apple pollination: A review", *Scientia Horticulturae*, Vol. 162, pp. 188–203.

Randall, R.P. (2017), *A Global Compendium of Weeds, 3rd Edition*, Department of Agriculture and Food, Western Australia, South Perth, Australia.

Reddy, P.P (2010), *Bacterial and Viral Diseases and Their Management in Horticultural Crops*, Scientific Publishers, Jodhpur, India.

Reim, S. et al. (2006), "Assessing gene flow in apple using a descendant of *Malus sieversii* var. *sieversii* F. Niedzwetzkyana as an identifier for pollen dispersal", *Environmental Biosafety Research*, Vol. 5/2, pp. 89-104.

Remy, S. et al. (2017), "Biocontrol to protect apple and pear flowers against fire blight using bumblebees", *Communications in Agricultural and Applied Biological Sciences*, Vol. 82, pp. 311–320.

Remy, S. et al. (2016), "Protection of apple and pear flowers against fire blight infections using biocontrol organisms applied via bumble bees", *IOBC-WPRS Bulletin*, Vol. 117, p. 113.

Rengel, Z. and P. Marschner (2005), "Nutrient availability and management in the rhizosphere: Exploiting genotypic differences", *New Phytologist*, Vol. 168, pp. 305-312.

Richards, C.M. et al. (2008), "Genetic diversity and population structure in *Malus sieversii*, a wild progenitor species of domesticated apple", *Tree Genetics and Genomes*, Vol. 5, pp. 339-347.

Rieger, M. (2006), *Introduction to Fruit Crops*, Food products Press, Binghamton, US.

Rikkerink, H.A. et al. (2016), *Resistance Gene and Uses Thereof*, US9512442B2.

Robertson, K.R. et al. (1991), "A synopsis of genera in Maloideae (Rosaceae)", *Systematic Botany*, Vol. 16/2, pp. 376-394.

Robinson, J.P. et al. (2001), "Taxonomy of the genus *Malus* Mill. (Rosaceae) with emphasis on the cultivated apple, *Malus domestica* Borkh", *Plants Systematics and Evolution*, Vol. 226, pp. 35-58.

Roiger, D.J. and S.N. Jeffers (1991), "Evaluation of *Trichoderma* sp. for biological control of Phytophthora crown and root rot of apple seedlings", *Phytopathology*, Vol. 81/8, pp. 910-917.

Routson, K.J. et al. (2012), "Gene variation and distribution of pacific crabapple", *Journal of the American Society for Horticultural Science*, Vol. 137/5, pp. 325-332.

Rumberger, A., I.A. Merwin and J.E. Thies (2007), "Microbial community development in the rhizosphere of apple trees at a replant disease site", *Soil Biology and Biochemistry*, Vol. 39/9, pp. 1645-1654.

Sanzol, J. and M. Herrero (2001), "The 'effective pollination period' in fruit trees", *Scientia Horticulturae*, Vol. 90/1-2, pp. 1-17.

Sapir, G. et al. (2017), "Synergistic effects between bumblebees and honey bees in apple orchards increase cross-pollination, seed number and fruit size", *Scientia Horticulturae*, Vol. 219, pp. 107-117.

Sassa, H. (2016), "Molecular mechanism of the S-RNase-based gametophytic self-incompatibility in fruit trees of Rosoceae", *Breeding Science*, Vol. 66/1, pp. 116-121.

Schlathölter, I. et al. (2018), "Generation of advanced fire blight-resistant apple (*Malus* x *domestica*) selections of the fifth generation within 7 years of applying the early flowering approach", *Planta*, Vol. 247, pp. 1475-1488.

Schouten, H.J. et al. (2014), "Cloning and functional characterisation of the *Rvi15* (*Vr2*) gene for apple scab resistance", *Tree Genetics and Genomes*, Vol. 10, pp. 251-260.

Schulze-Menz, G.K. (1964), "Rosaceae", in H. Melchior (ed.), *Engler's Syllabus der Pflanzenfamilien II, 12th Edition*, Gebrüder Borntraeger, Berlin.

Schuster, M. and R. Büttner (1995), "Chromosome numbers in the *Malus* wild species collection of the genebank Dresden-Pillnitz", *Genetic Resources and Crop Evolution*, Vol. 42, pp. 353-361.

Sheffield, C.S., H.T. Ngo and N. Azzu (2016), *A Manual on Apple Pollination*, FAO, Rome.

Sheffield, C.S. et al. (2013), "Bee (Hymenoptera: Apoidea) diversity within apple orchards and old fields in the Annapolis Valley, Nova Scotia, Canada", *The Canadian Entomologist*, Vol. 145/1, pp. 94-114.

Sherwani, A., M. Mukhtar and A.A. Wani (2016), "Insect pests of apple and their management", in A.K. Pandey and P. Mall (eds.), *Insect Pest Management of Fruit Crops*, Biotech, New Delhi, India, pp. 295-306.

Silfverberg-Dilworth, E. et al. (2005), "Identification of functional apple scab resistance gene promoters", *Theoretical and Applied Genetics*, Vol. 110, pp. 1119-1126.

Sindhu, S.S., Y.S. Rakshiya and G. Sahu (2009), "Biological control of soilborne plant pathogens with rhizosphere bacteria", *Pest Technology*, Vol. 3/1, pp. 10-21.

Soejima, J. (2007), "Estimation of gene flow via pollen spread for the orchard layout prior to the field release of apple transformants", *Acta Horticulturae*, Vol. 738(March), pp. 341-345.

Stover, M.E. and P.L. Marks (1998), "Successional vegetation in cultivated and pasture land in Tomkins County, New York", *Journal of the Torrey Botanical Society*, Vol. 125, pp. 150-164.

Sułowicz, S. and Z. Piotrowska-Seget (2016), "Response of microbial communities from an apple orchard and grassland soils to the first-time application of the fungicide tetraconazole", *Ecotoxicology and Environmental Safety*, Vol. 124, pp. 193-201.

Tromp, J. and O. Borsboom (1994), "The effect of autumn and spring temperature on fruit set and on the effective pollination period in apple and pear", *Scientia Horticulturae*, Vol. 60/1-2, pp. 23-30.

Tromp, J., A.D. Webster and S.J. Wertheim (2005), "Fundamentals of temperate zone tree fruit production", *Tree Physiology*, Vol. 25/12, pp. 1571-1572.

Tukey, H.B. (1964), *Dwarfed Fruit Trees*, Macmillan Co., New York, and Collier-Macmillan Ltd, London.

Tyson, R.C., J.B. Wilson and W.D. Lane (2011), "A mechanistic model to predict transgenic seed contamination in bee-pollinated crops validated in an apple orchard", *Ecological Modelling*, Vol. 222/13, pp. 2084-2092.

UCANR (2018), *How to Manage Pests: Apple*, University of California Agriculture and Natural Resources, http://ipm.ucanr.edu/PMG/selectnewpest.apples.html (accessed 1 October 2019).

USDA-ARS (2018), *Germplasm Resources Information Network (GRIN)*, National Plant Germplasm System, United States Department of Agriculture, Agricultural Research Service, https://www.ars-grin.gov (accessed 1 October 2019).

USDA-NRCS (2018), *Plants Database*, United States Department of Agriculture, Natural Resources Conservation Service, https://plants.usda.gov/java (accessed 1 October 2019).

Vanblaere, T. et al. (2014), "Molecular characterisation of cisgenic lines of apple 'Gala' carrying the *Rvi6* scab resistance gene", *Plant Biotechnology Journal*, Vol. 12, pp. 2-9.

Vanblaere, T. et al. (2011), "The development of a cisgenic apple plant", *Journal Biotechnology*, Vol. 154, pp. 304-311.

Vanwynsberghe, L. (2006), "Description of, and possibilities to increase genetic diversity in modern apple", Dissertationes de Agricultura, nr. 714, Faculteit Bio-ingenieurswetenschappen KU Leuven, Belgium.

VASCAN (2018), *The Database of Vascular Plants of Canada*, http://data.canadensys.net/vascan/search (accessed 1 October 2019).

Vavilov, N.I. (1951), *The Origin, Variation, Immunity and Breeding of Cultivated Plants,* The Chronica Botanica Co., Waltham, Massachusetts, US.

Velasco, R. et al. (2010), "The genome of the domesticated apple (*Malus* x d*omestica* Borkh.)", *Nature Genetics*, Vol. 42, pp. 833 -839.

VIDE (2018), Virus Identification Database Exchange - *Known susceptibilities of Rosaceae,* Malus.

Volk, G.M. et al. (2013), "*Malus sieversii*: A diverse central Asian apple species in the USDA-ARS National Plant Germplasm System", *Horticultural Science*, Vol. 48, pp. 1440-1444.

Walker, J.T.S, D.M. Suckling and C.H. Wearing (2017), "Past, present, and future of integrated control of apple pests: The New Zealand experience", *Annual Review of Entomology*, Vol. 62, pp. 231-248.

Way, R.D. et al. (1990), "Apples (*Malus*)", *Acta Horticulturae*, Vol. 290, pp. 3-62.

Webster, A.D. (2005a), "The origin, distribution and genetic diversity of temperate tree fruits", in J. Tromp et al. (eds.), *Fundamentals of Temperate Zone Tree Fruit Production*, Backhuys Publishers, Leiden, The Netherlands.

Webster, A.D. (2005b), "Sites and soils for temperate tree-fruit production: Their selection and amelioration", in J. Tromp, A.D. Webster and S.J. Wertheim (eds.), *Fundamentals of Temperate Zone Tree Fruit Production*, Backhuys Publishers, Leiden, The Netherlands.

Webster, A.D. and S. Wertheim (2003), "Apple rootstocks", in D.C. Ferree and I.J. Warrington (eds.), *Apples: Botany, Production and Uses*, CAB International, Wallingford, UK, pp. 91-124.

Weigl, K. et al. (2015), "BpMADS4 on various linkage groups improves the utilization of the rapid cycle breeding system in apple", *Plant Biotechnology Journal*, Vol. 13, pp. 246-258.

Wertheim, S.J. (1991), "*Malus* cv. Baskatong as an indicator of pollen spread in intensive apple orchards", *Journal of Horticultural Science*, Vol. 66/5, pp. 635-642.

Westwood, M.N. (1993), *Temperate-zone Pomology: Physiology and Culture*, Timber Press, Portland, US.

Williams, R.R. (1966), *Pollination Studies in Fruit Trees. III. The Effective Pollination Period for Some Apple and Pear Varieties*, Report of the Agricultural and Horticultural Research Station, University of Bristol, UK.

Willson, M.F. (1993), "Mammals as seed-dispersal mutualists in North America", *OIKOS*, Vol. 67/1, pp. 159-176.

Witmer, M.C. (1996), "Do some bird-dispersed fruits contain natural laxatives? A comment", *Ecology,* Vol. 77, pp. 1947-1948.

Xu, K. (2013), "An overview of Artic apples: Basic facts and characteristics", *New York State Horticultural Society,* Vol. 21/3, pp. 8-10.

Xu, K. et al. (2012), "Genetic characterisation of the *Ma* locus with pH and titratable acidity in apple", *Molecular Breeding*, Vol. 30, pp. 899-912.

Yan, G. et al. (2008), "Genetic polymorphism of *Malus sieversii* populations in Xinjiang, China", *Genetic Resources and Crop Evolution*, Vol. 55, pp. 171-181.

Yoder, K. et al. (2009), "Effects of temperature and the combination of liquid lime sulfur and fish oil on pollen germination, pollen tube growth and fruit set in apples", *Horticultural Science*, Vol. 44/5, pp. 1277-1283.

Zhou, H. et al. (2014), "Biological control of insects pests in apple orchards in China", *Biological Control*, Vol. 68/1, pp. 47-56.

Zohary, D., M. Hopf and E. Weiss (2012), *Domestication of Plants in the Old World*, Oxford University Press, New York.

3 Biology of Safflower (*Carthamus tinctorius*)

This chapter deals with the biology of safflower (*Carthamus tinctorius*). It contains information for use during the risk/safety regulatory assessment of genetically engineered varieties of safflower intended to be grown in the environment (biosafety). It includes elements of taxonomy, centres of origin, cultivation, reproductive biology, genetics, hybridisation and introgression, as well as ecology. Annexes present safflower's common pests and pathogens, and current biotechnology developments.

Introduction

This chapter was prepared by the OECD Working Party on the Harmonisation of Regulatory Oversight in Biotechnology, with **Australia** as the lead country. It was initially issued in 2020 as the Consensus Document on the Biology of Safflower (*Carthamus tinctorius* L.). Production data have been updated in this publication, based on FAOSTAT.

Species and taxonomic groups

Classification and nomenclature

Cultivated safflower (*Carthamus tinctorius* L.) is an annual oilseed crop (Figure 3.1) that is a member of the family Asteraceae (Compositae), tribe Cardueae (thistles) and subtribe Centaureinae (Bérvillé et al., 2005). Asteraceae is recognised as the largest family of flowering plants and contains more than 1 500 genera and 22 000 species ranging from annual herbs to woody shrubs. Safflower is known by many other names, such as kusum, kasunmba, kusumbo, kusubi, kabri, ma, sufir, kar/karar, sendurgam, agnisikha, hebu, su, suban and others. The Arabic usfur is thought to have been the root for the English name via a number of other terms – affore, asfiore, asfrole, astifore, asfiori, zaffrole or zaffrone, saffiore to, finally, safflower – while in the People's Republic of China (hereafter 'China') it is known as *hung-hua* or "red flower" (Chavan, 1961, and sources cited therein) and under many other names around the world as summarised by Smith (1996).

Figure 3.1. Safflower crop

Source: muratart/Shutterstock.com.

The taxonomy of *Carthamus* has changed substantially as data for this group has been obtained and interpreted (McPherson et al., 2004; Sehgal and Raina, 2011). There have been as few as four species in the genus (with related species in a separate genus) to as many as 25 species and subspecies divided into up to five sections. The sections were based on five chromosome groups identified by Ashri and

Knowles (1960), being n = 10, 11, 12, 22 and 32. Safflower belongs to the *Carduncellus-Carthamus* complex. Morphological and cytological characteristics have not been sufficient to delimit the species into discrete sections and genera. Depending on the taxonomist and the emphasis on particular morphological characteristics, species have been moved between the genera *Carthamus* and *Carduncellus* (McPherson et al., 2004). Determining species relationships is made more difficult by the low levels of genetic variation that occur when clear morphological differences are present (Mayerhofer et al., 2011).

The classification scheme followed in this document is that of López-González (1990), as shown in Table 3.1, which recognises 16 species within *Carthamus* and another closely related species, *Femeniasia balearica*. The species have been further divided into three sections based on chromosome numbers, the section *Carthamus* (n = 12), section *Odonthagnathis* (n = 10 or 11), section *Atractylis* (n = 22 or 32) and two species of uncertain placement.

Carthamus oxyacanthus and *Carthamus persicus* were thought to be the parent species of *C. tinctorius* (Ashri and Knowles, 1960). More recent genetic analysis and geographic evidence indicate that *Carthamus palaestinus* is the wild progenitor of safflower and originated in the Middle East, and is fully cross-compatible with safflower (Pearl et al., 2014).

Table 3.1. Taxonomic groups of *Carthamus* sensu

Section	Species	Number of chromosomes
Carthamus L.	*C. tinctorius* L.	2n = 2x = '24,' n = 12
	C. oxyacanthus Bieb.	2n = 2x = '24,' n = 12
	C. palaestinus Eig	2n = 2x = '24,' n = 12
	C. persicus Willd. (basionym *C. flavescens* auct.)	2n = 2x = '24,' n = 12
	C. curdicus Hanelt.	2n = 2x = '24,' n = 12
	C. gypsicolus Ilj.	2n = 2x = '24,' n = 12
Odonthagnathis (DC.) Henelt	*C. divaricatus* Beguinot & Vacc.	2n = 2x = '22,' n = 11
	C. leucocaulos Sm.	2n = 2x = '20,' n = 10
	C. glaucus Bieb.	2n = 2x = '20,' n = 10
	C. tenuis (Boiww. & Bl.) Bornm.	2n = 2x = '20,' n = 10
	C. dentatus (Forssk.) Vahl	2n = 2x = '20,' n = 10
	C. boissieri Halácsy	2n = 2x = '20,' n = 10
Atractylis Reichemb.	*C. lanatus* L.	2n = 4x = '44,' n = 22
	C. creticus L. (syn *C. baeticus* (Boiss & Reuter) Nyman)	2n = 6x = '64,' n = 32
	C. turkestanicus Popov	2n = 6x = '64,' n = 32
Uncertain placement	*C. nitidus* Boiss.	2n = 2x = '24,' n = 12
	Femeniasia balearica Susanna	2n = 2x = '24,' n = 12

Source: Based on the classification proposed by López-González, G. (1990), "Acerca de la clasificación natural del género" Carthamus" L., s. l.", *Anales del Jardín Botánico de Madrid*, Vol. 47, pp. 11-34.

Description

Safflower is one of humanity's oldest crops yet it remains a minor crop compared to other oilseeds (FAOSTAT, 2022). Safflower is now mostly cultivated for the production of vegetable oil (Kumar et al., 2015).

Safflower is an erect, herbaceous, highly branched, spiny, thistle-like annual plant that grows from 30 to 150 cm in height (Singh and Nimbkar, 2006; Kumar and Kumari, 2011). Young safflower plants form a rosette and remain in this vegetative state for many weeks, during which leaves and a deep taproot system develop. This deep taproot system, with abundant thin horizontal roots, allows the plant to extract water and nutrients from deeper layers of soil than many other crop plants (Li and Mündel, 1996; GRDC, 2010). The rosette stage is followed by rapid stem elongation, extensive branching then flowering, with leaves being arranged on both sides of the stem (Li and Mündel, 1996; Singh and Nimbkar, 2006). The flower colour of cultivated safflower is typically brilliant orange (Figure 3.2). Leaf size varies with variety and position on the plant, although typical leaves are 2.5-5 cm wide and 10--15 cm long. The leaf morphology is described as alternate, sessile and ovate-lanceolate (Teotia et al., 2017). Upper leaves often develop hard spines, while those lower on the stem are usually spineless. These spines make the crop difficult to walk through but act as a deterrent to larger animals such as pigs and kangaroos (GRDC, 2010). As plants mature, they become stiff, woody and resistant to some environmental stressors such as hail and wind. Safflower growth cycle, floral biology and pollination are considered in greater detail in the reproductive biology section below.

Figure 3.2. Flowers of cultivated safflower

Source: High Montain/Shutterstock.com.

Positive identification of safflower plants is important to ensure not only the purity of seed at harvest but also to prevent outcrossing with wild relatives. Safflower has a similar morphological appearance to some close relatives and also to other thistle species. An identification guide and their respective global distribution are shown in Table 3.2. Unfortunately, many of the distinctions can only be made once the plants have reached flowering.

Table 3.2. Guide to the positive identification of *Carthamus tinctorius* L.

Species (common name)	Identification by morphology	Global distribution
Carthamus tinctorius (cultivated safflower)	Brilliant orange flowers, with traces of red and yellow (Figure 3.2)	Cultivated globally (Figure 3.3)
Cirsium vulgare (spear thistle)	Pink or purple flowers	Germany, France, Spain, Japan
***Carduus* sp.** (sheep, slender and plumeless thistles)	Pink or purple flowers	France, Germany, Spain, Netherlands, Sweden, United Kingdom, Japan
Carthamus lanatus (saffron/distaff thistle)	Divided leaves and lighter yellow flowers	Spain, France, Italy, Portugal, United States, Japan
Centaurea solstitialis (Barnaby star thistle)	Yellow flowers; small, round and spiny capitula	France, Germany, United States, Spain, Australia, Greece, Netherlands, Italy, Japan
Centaurea melitensis (Maltese cockspur or Malta star thistle)	Narrow and non-spiny leaves; yellow flowers; small and round capitula	Spain, Australia, United States, France, Portugal, Argentina, Mexico, South Africa, Japan
Scolymus hispanicus (golden thistle)	Denticulate leaves; yellow flowers; flat seeds	Spain, France, Portugal, Australia, Greece, Italy, Israel
Scolymus maculatus (spotted golden thistle)	Obovate leaves; yellow flowers	Spain, Israel, France, Portugal, West Bank and Gaza Strip, Australia
Carthamus dentatus (toothed thistle)	Pink or purple flowers	Australia, Greece, Turkey
Carthamus leucocaulos (Whitestem distaff thistle)	Purple flowers	Greece, Australia, United States
Carthamus glaucus (glaucous star thistle or Mediterranean thistle)	Purple flowers	Israel, West Bank and Gaza Strip, Turkey, Syrian Arab Republic, Lebanon, Greece, Australia

Sources: HerbiGuide (2014a), *Safflower*, (accessed 13 May 2020); HerbiGuide (2014b), *Weeds*, (accessed 13 May 2020); GBIF (2020), *Global Biodiversity Information Facility*, https://www.gbif.org/ (accessed 13 May 2020).

Geographic distribution, natural and managed ecosystems and habitats, cultivation and management practices, and centres of origin and diversity

Geographic distribution

Safflower is a dryland oilseed crop but was traditionally grown for the extraction of dyes for textiles and food (Weiss, 1971; Zohary, Hopf and Weiss, 2012) throughout South and Central Asia and the Mediterranean (Weiss, 1971; Li and Mündel, 1996; Zohary, Hopf and Weiss, 2012). Today, the cultivation of safflower occurs in arid and semi-arid conditions wherever the crops have established a tolerance to hot and dry conditions. The geographical distribution of safflower cultivation is depicted in Figure 3.3.

Figure 3.3. Recorded global distribution of cultivated safflower (*Carthamus tinctorius* L.) from 1795 until 2019

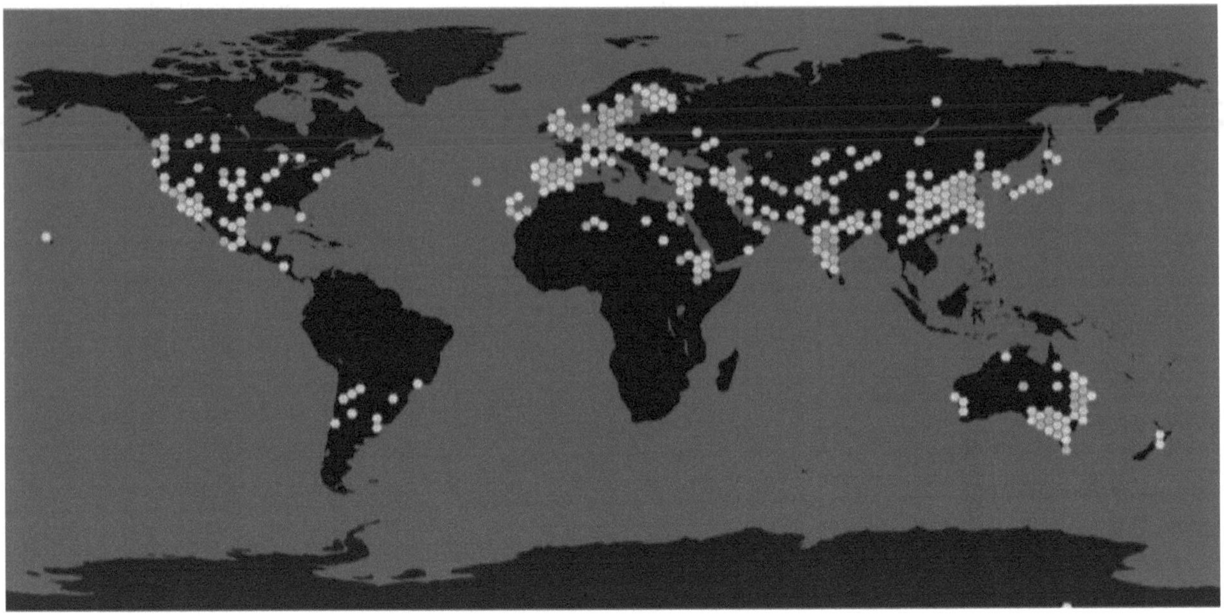

Note: Yellow (or light grey) dots indicate georeferenced occurrences.
Source: GBIF Backbone Taxonomy (2017), "*Carthamus* L.", in *GBIF Secretariat, licensed under CC BY 4.0* https://creativecommons.org/licenses/by/4.0/legalcode.

Ecosystems and habitats where the species occurs natively and where it has naturalised

A naturalised species is one that has the potential to be self-sustaining and exhibits population spreading without human assistance but does not necessarily impact the environment. The capacity for a species to naturalise in foreign environments is a good indicator of its weed potential (Randall, 2017). Safflower has been found to naturalise in many of the countries where it is commonly cultivated including Australia, Chile, China, Croatia, Estonia, Italy, Japan, the Democratic People's Republic of Korea, the Lao People's Democratic Republic, Mexico, Norway, Portugal, Romania, the Russian Federation (hereafter 'Russia'), Ukraine, the United Kingdom and the United States (Randall, 2017).

Agronomic ecosystems where the species is grown, including management practices

Production regions

Traditionally, safflower was grown in hot arid dry regions but it is a highly adaptable plant. In the Americas, commercial production extends from southern Canada, south into Argentina (Li and Mündel, 1996). Although safflower is considered a minor crop compared to other oilseed crops, it is grown in over 20 countries, occupying over 700 000 hectares of agricultural land and producing around 650 000 tonnes of seed in 2020 (FAOSTAT, 2022). The top four producers of safflower from 2018 to 2020 consistently included, in decreasing order, Russia, Kazakhstan, Mexico and the United States. Other significant producers of safflower include Turkey, India, Argentina and China. Worldwide, yields generally range from approximately 0.5 to 1.7 tonnes per hectare (t/ha) (FAOSTAT, 2022). Trial data has shown that safflower yields are variable, dependent on many factors such as planting date (winter vs. spring), sowing rates, temperature, cultivars and water availability (Wachsmann et al., 2008).

Agronomic practices

Safflower is an annual plant with a long growing season. The sowing dates vary among different countries, summarised in Figure 3.4. Similar to other oilseed crops, the sowing date has been shown to affect seed oil content (Mirshekari et al., 2013). Safflower may be sown later than other winter crops, which allows it to be used for weed management or as an option when earlier planted winter crops have failed to establish (GRDC, 2010).

Figure 3.4. Sowing and harvest dates of major global safflower growers

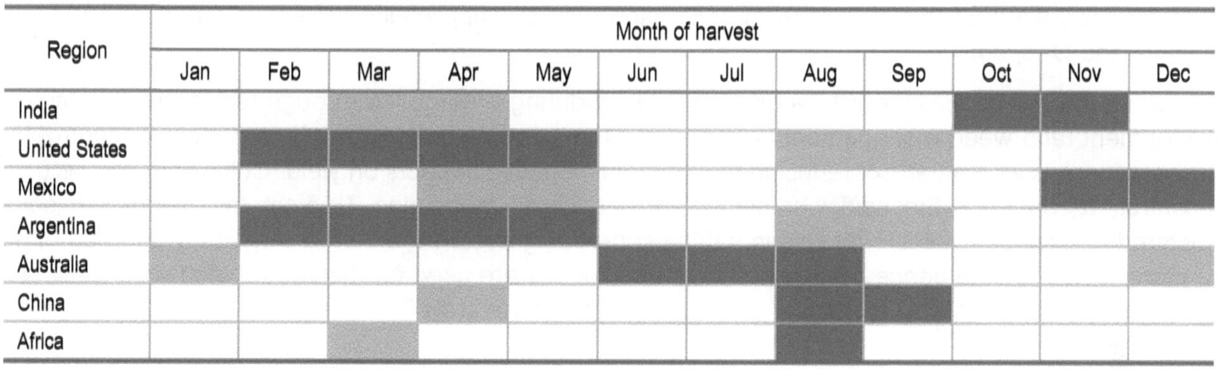

Note:
Sowing period.
Harvest period.
Source: Adapted from Gilbert, J. (2008), "International safflower production - An overview", Paper presented at "Safflower: Unexploited Potential and World Adaptability, 7th International Safflower Conference", Wagga Wagga, NSW, Australia.

Sowing rates of safflower depend on the region and moisture availability. The sowing rates have a broad range from 12-15 kg/ha in northern Australia (drier conditions) and 18-24 kg/ha in southern Australia (irrigated conditions), with plant densities being 20-25 plants/m^2 and 30-40 plants/m^2 respectively (GRDC, 2010). Safflower in the United States is sown at a high seeding rate of 28-39 kg/ha, although the crop develops at a significantly higher density of approximately 65 plants/m^2, promoting better weed competition (Oelke et al., 1992).

Ideally, sowing should be into moist soil, typically between 2 and 5 cm deep but this will vary with soil type and conditions. Delayed emergence and reduced early vigour can occur due to deeper sowing, leaving plants susceptible to pests, diseases and competition from weeds (Mikkelsen et al., 2008). Safflower is normally planted with standard cereal sowing equipment in rows 18-36 cm apart. Narrower rows help suppress weeds, whilst wider spacing allows for better airflow for disease control (GRDC, 2010).

Safflower has a deep root system, which makes it ideal for rainfed cropping systems (Singh and Nimbkar, 2006). Tap roots from safflower may extend 2-3 m into the soil (Oyen and Umali, 2007; Heuzé et al., 2015). Well-drained, deep, fertile, sandy loam soils provide maximum safflower yields (GRDC, 2010). In Australia, due to its deep tap root system, safflower is often used on problem soils to break up hard pans and to improve both water and air infiltration in the subsoil (GRDC, 2010).

Although safflower has high water requirements, it does not tolerate waterlogging well. Safflower has the ability to extract water from deeper layers of soil compared to many other crop plants due to its taproot and thus is considered quite drought tolerant (Li and Mündel, 1996; GRDC, 2010). Irrigation can extend the growing season by two weeks, whereas drought, salinity, increased temperatures or day length will hasten maturity. Safflower is considered to have moderate to high salinity tolerance, being similar to barley or cotton (GRDC, 2010). Safflower is also moderately frost tolerant during the rosette stage but is susceptible to frost damage from the stem elongation stage to maturity. It is also relatively resistant to hail or wind damage (Mündel et al., 2004).

One tonne of safflower seed removes 25 kg of nitrogen, 4.3 kg of phosphorous and 4 kg of sulphur from the soil. Most soils (with the possible exception of sandy soils) contain adequate levels of potassium and sulphur (GRDC, 2010). Although safflower can access nutrients from deeper in the soil profile than cereal crops, fertilisers tend to increase yields and oil levels, especially in irrigated or higher rainfall areas. Fertiliser application rates are dependent on expected yields based on available soil moisture (or irrigation), which also varies significantly between different cultivars. For safflower grown in Pakistan, a study of different nitrogen application rates determined that plant height, number of branches, number of capitula and total seed yield were all significantly increased with the application rate of nitrogen at 120 kg/ha (Siddiqui and Oad, 2006).

Safflower is a poor competitor with weeds, particularly during emergence through to the rosette stage of development, and weed management is essential when growing this crop. It is important to control the number of weeds as a means of reducing the potential negative impacts on yield. Cultivation can be used to control weeds when the safflower plants are seedlings, measuring 7-15 cm tall. There are some registered herbicides available for use in safflower cropping systems, which are typically used as either pre-planting or pre-emergence herbicides. These herbicides are used for the control of in-crop grass and broadleaf type weeds (see sub-section "Weediness of safflower crops").

Harvest

Safflower sown in winter is usually ready for harvest four to six weeks later than wheat sown at a similar time. Safflower is ready for harvest once all the leaves have turned brown and the latest flowering heads are no longer green. At maturity, the seeds should be white and easily threshed by hand (Oelke et al., 1992). For the major global safflower growers, the harvest dates are variable, summarised in Figure 3.4, which helps to ensure the supply of safflower seed throughout the year. In Australia, the recommended seed moisture at the time of harvest should be less than 8% to avoid overheating and mould formation during processing and storage. It is also recommended that harvest occurs as soon as possible as rain can cause staining or early sprouting of the seed, both of which reduce the value of the seed (Oelke et al., 1992; Bockisch, 1998; GRDC, 2010). In parts of Canada, the seed is harvested at a moisture content of 12-15% and then dried by aeration (Mündel et al., 2004).

Safflower is generally harvested without swathing. Safflower is suitable for harvest by direct heading since the capitula do not shatter easily. The same machinery used for cereals can be used for safflower but ground speeds are slower to reduce seed loss (Oelke et al., 1992; Thalji and Alqarallah, 2015). Periodic cleaning of equipment to remove bristles from radiators and hot engine components may be necessary to minimise the risk of fire (GRDC, 2010). In addition, harvesting in cooler or more humid parts of the day is recommended both to reduce the risk of fire and to increase seed cleanliness (Jochinke et al., 2008). In Australia, seed loss during harvest (direct heading) is about 3-4% (GRDC, 2010).

Centres of origin and diversity

Safflower is an ancient crop that is believed to have a single origin of domestication from approximately 4 000 years ago in the Fertile Crescent (Pearl et al., 2014). This region ranges from southern Israel to western Iraq (Chapman et al., 2010). Safflower has been grown for centuries in India, China and northern Africa.

Seven "centres of similarity", or "centres of culture", were identified by Knowles (1969a), namely the Far-East, India-Pakistan, the Middle-East, Egypt, Sudan, Ethiopia and Europe. Ashri (1971) added more centres, however, these were not centres of diversity or origin but of very similar safflower types. Considerable genetic diversity exists across different genotypes. When 60 representative genotypes from

India and other countries were examined it was observed that plant height, seed yield, branching height and seed weight accounted for 80% of the diversity (Patel et al., 1989). Patel et al. (1989) identified 14 clusters of genetic diversity but distribution into clusters was random showing that geographic isolation is not the only factor causing genetic diversity. Up to ten centres of similarity throughout the world were identified based on morphology. Nuclear microsatellite analysis of accessions suggests the presence of five genetic clusters, one in each of the following regions: Europe; Turkey-Islamic Republic of Iran (hereafter 'Iran')-Iraq-Afghanistan; Israel-Jordan-Syrian Arab Republic (hereafter 'Syria'); Egypt-Ethiopia; and Far East-India-Pakistan (Chapman et al., 2010).

The different species of *Carthamus* are all believed to have one common ancestor, probably from Iraq and north-western Iran. With the exception of cultivated safflower, the species are all spiny weeds that grow in the wild. There appear to be three wild species that are closely related. *Carthamus flavescens* (= *C. persicus*) is usually found in wheat fields in Lebanon, Syria and Turkey. *C. oxyacanthus* is a serious weed in the area from western Iraq to north-western India and northward into the southern parts of some former republics of the Union of Soviet Socialist Republics (USSR). *C. palaestinus* is found in the desert regions of Iraq, Israel and Jordan. These species readily cross with *C. tinctorius* to produce fertile progeny. It is thought that early in its evolution, safflower spread to Egypt, Ethiopia, South Asia and the Far East, where distinct types have evolved (as reviewed by Smith, 1996).

Domestication of safflower has resulted in traits such as reduced shattering, smooth seeds, reduced duration of the early vegetative growth stage, restriction of branching to the upper part of the stem and reduced seed dormancy (Bérvillé et al., 2005, and references cited therein). Breeding programmes have resulted in the release of cultivars with higher oil content and/or increased disease resistance (GRDC, 2010).

Reproductive biology

Generation time and duration under natural circumstances and where grown or managed

Traditionally safflower was grown in the Mediterranean regions but today cultivation of safflower occurs in arid and semi-arid conditions, wherever the crops have established a tolerance to the hot and dry conditions (Weiss, 1971; Li and Mündel, 1996; Kumar et al., 2015). Typically, the generation time of safflower is within the range of 182-217 days (Figure 3.5), although there have been reports of growing seasons being as short or long as 81 days and 239 days respectively (Cerioni et al., 1999, as cited in Bellé et al., 2012). Generation time is influenced by variety, management practices and environmental conditions. Safflower cultivation during the fall/winter or the spring/summer season has a significant effect on the generation time (Bellé et al., 2012).

Figure 3.5. Development stages and development timeline of a safflower plant

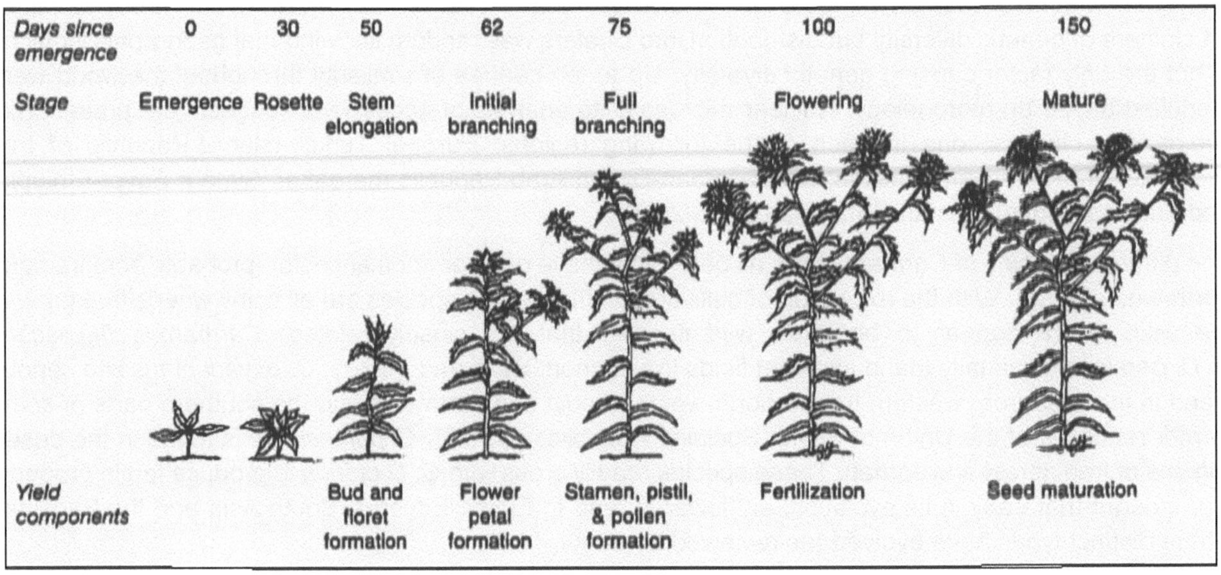

Source: Kaffka, S.R. and T.E. Kearney (1998), "Safflower production in California", *University of California Agriculture and Natural Resources*, Vol. 21565, as adapted from GRDC (2010), *Raising the Bar with Better Safflower Agronomy*, ACT, Australia, Grains Research and Development Corporation.

Safflower emerges 1-3 weeks after sowing. Emergence takes longer under cooler temperatures, increasing the risk of damage by insects and disease. The first emerging leaves form a rosette. The duration of this vegetative rosette stage determines the generation time of safflower. This stage generally lasts between 20 and 39 days post-emergence but the duration varies with variety and growing conditions (temperature and photoperiod for example) and can be as long as several months (Anderson, 1987; Corleto, 2008; Emongor, 2010). During the rosette stage, the deep tap roots begin to develop but no stem is formed. The large tap root system can elongate up to three metres (Li and Mündel, 1996; Bockisch, 1998).

The rosette stage is followed by rapid stem elongation and extensive branching (Li and Mündel, 1996; Singh and Nimbkar, 2006). As temperature and day length increase the stem begins to elongate and branch. Lateral branches develop on stems that are about 20-40 cm high and these lateral branches may branch further to produce secondary and tertiary branches. The branching habit is classified as narrow, with branching angles (branch to stem) ranging from 30 to 75° in respect to the primary stem (Singh and Nimbkar, 2006). The level of branching is greatly influenced by the variety, environment and also plant density (Bockisch, 1998; Bellé et al., 2012). Significantly more branching occurs when plants are sown at lower densities than when sown at higher plant densities (Weiss, 1971; Kaffka and Kearney, 1998).

Higher seed yields can be achieved with a greater number of branches per plant since each branch ends in a flower head. The timing of flowering is mainly influenced by day length, requiring long days to initiate flowering (Gilbert, 2008). After flowering, the time to maturity is around four weeks.

Reproduction (production of flowers and seeds)

Floral biology

Safflower reproduction occurs through the development of seed (USDA-APHIS, 2008). Safflower flowers are typically brilliant orange (Figure 3.2), yellow or red, or more rarely white. The inflorescence is of the composite type characteristic of the family Asteraceae, with each plant producing 3-50 or more flowering heads, called capitula, on the ends of the branches. Capitula on the primary branches flower first, followed by those on secondary and tertiary branches. The flowering of the individual florets in each capitulum starts at the margin of the head and proceeds inward over 3-5 days. Each head normally contains between 20 and 180 individual florets (GRDC, 2010), although there can be as many as 250 florets, with bristles being interspersed between the flowers (Singh and Nimbkar, 2006).

Each flower is composed of five petals which are all attached to a corolla tube. There are also five fused anthers attached to the corolla tube, which surrounds both the style and stigma. It may take between 10 and 45 days for all flowers on a plant to reach anthesis, during which pollen can be shed (Li and Mündel, 1996). Safflower anthers contain 150-300 pollen grains (Pandey and Kumari, 2008). The stigma is receptive for approximately 32-56 hours post-anthesis, after its exertion from the corolla tube (Knowles, 1980). At the base of the corolla tube, it is attached to an inferior ovary, which develops into a single-seeded fruit called an achene (seed) following pollination.

Pollination, pollen dispersal, pollen viability

Pollination

Safflower is primarily self-pollinating and cross-pollination rates vary between lines (Knowles, 1969a). Australian commercial varieties are largely self-pollinating with cross-pollination rates of less than 10% (GRDC, 2017). Self-pollination is predominant because the style and stigma grow through the surrounding anther column; after elongation, the stigma is usually covered with pollen from the same floret (Claassen, 1950). Individual safflower florets are largely self-pollinating, as safflower florets produce pollen that will outcompete with adjacent florets. However, an un-pollinated elongated stigma can remain receptive for several days, and outcrossing rates and seed set can be increased by insect pollinators (Claassen, 1950; Li and Mündel, 1996; GRDC, 2010). Outcrossing rates vary depending mainly on insect pollinators but also on variety, pollen source size and environment. Intra- and interspecific cross-pollination are considered in greater detail in sub-sections on intraspecific crossing and natural facility of interspecific crossing respectively.

Pollen dispersal

Wind

Safflower pollen is yellow and relatively large with a mean diameter of 53-56 µm (USDA-APHIS, 2008). It is not transferred significantly by wind (Claassen, 1950; Li and Mündel, 1996). Claassen (1950) examined outcrossing rates for safflower plants grown either with or without insect exclusion cages. Depending on the cultivar, uncaged plants had outcrossing rates averaging 8.2-35% (range 6.3-58%), whereas the caged plants averaged 0.4-1.2% outcrossing (range 0-3.2%). The author acknowledged that the outcrossing observed in the caged plants could have been due to wind or to insect pollination of a few stigmas that had grown through the cage. In a glasshouse study, which excluded insects, no outcrossing was detected among the safflower plants (Claassen, 1950).

In the same study, pollen traps were placed at heights of 46, 76 and 122 cm above ground level while the safflower plants were in full flower. Safflower pollen was only detected at 46 cm, which was below the level of some of the flowers (Claassen, 1950). The height of the safflower plants was not given. Based on the assumption that some flowers were at or near the 46 cm height, there was no wind-dispersed pollen detected at distances of about 30-76 cm from the flowers. The results of these studies suggest that wind does not facilitate significant outcrossing or transport of safflower pollen and outcrossing is primarily due to insect-mediated pollen movement.

Insect pollinators

Safflower florets are largely self-pollinating but outcrossing rates and seed set can be increased by insect pollinators (Claassen, 1950; Li and Mündel, 1996; GRDC, 2010). Cross-pollination is thought to occur in safflower at approximately 10% but this is highly variable and honey bees, bumblebees, beetles and other insects can increase the level of cross-pollination (Emongor, 2010).

Pollination studies showed that honey bees (*Apis mellifera* and *Apis* spp.) are the major pollinators of safflower crops (Kumari and Pandey, 2005; Pandey and Kumari, 2008) but other insects such as other species of bees and non-hymenopterous insects do forage in safflower (AOSCA, 2012). In studies in the United States, 80-90% of insects observed visiting safflower plants were honey bees and over 80% of these observations occurred between 8 am and noon (Boch, 1961; Levin and Butler, 1966; Bukero et al., 2015). Greatly depleted pollen loads of safflower stigmas were observed in the late mornings, explaining the timeframe of honey bee foraging activity (Langridge and Goodman, 1980).

Bumblebees (*Bombus* spp.) play a role in the transfer of pollen in the northern hemisphere where they represent less than 10% of insect pollinators in safflower (Cresswell, 1999, 2000). Other insects which have been observed to be involved in the pollination of safflower include species from the families of Halictidae (Apoidea bees) and Syrphidae (flies, particularly hoverflies) (Langridge and Goodman, 1980).

Pollinator behaviour

Safflower ranks highly among the commercial crops which are preferred by honey bees. Chaney (1985, as cited in Van Deynze, Sundstrom and Bradford, 2005) found that honey bee pollen collectors bypass cotton and fly 8 km to safflower while nectar collectors forage in nearby cotton. Conclusions from a Californian trial were that the population density of bees in trial crops (onion, carrot and safflower) was primarily a function of the quality and quantity of foraging resources and secondarily a function of competition from nearby colonies (Gary et al., 1977). Nectar gatherers were observed to be the predominant visitors in Australia on "Gila" safflower fields but many were well dusted with pollen (Langridge and Goodman, 1980). The distance of pollen dispersal or movement is dependent on pollinator behaviour and also on plant density, for example sparse areas of plants receive fewer pollinator visits (Kunin, 1997). Long-distance bee foraging has been documented with 1 bee (of 2 000 marked) collected in a safflower field 7.1 km from the hive (Gary et al., 1977). Foraging distances of pollen-collecting honey bees is longer in simple sparse landscapes than complex landscapes with ample vegetation (AOSCA, 2012).

Studies of the foraging habits of honey bees on safflower fields in India observed honey bees making foraging trips that lasted 15 minutes, visiting 5 to 8 flowers per trip, with 15 seconds to 2 minutes spent per flower (Kumari and Pandey, 2005; Pandey and Kumari, 2008). In a study of safflower fields (variety Gila) in Australia, honey bees were observed to visit on average 9 flowers per head, usually visiting 1 head per plant and spending 12.2 seconds per plant. One bee visited 54 plants in 15 minutes while another visited 48 plants in under 8 minutes (Langridge and Goodman, 1980).

Pollen viability

The likelihood of successful pollination or cross-pollination is both dependent on pollen dispersal and on how long the pollen grain remains viable. In general, pollen viability is dependent on a number of factors including temperature and humidity. Safflower is usually grown in dry conditions, where pollen is expected to desiccate rapidly (USDA-APHIS, 2006). There is limited information on safflower pollen viability. However, one study indicated that safflower pollen has a short life, showing a reduction in viability to 73.6% only 24 hours after anthesis (Pandey and Kumari, 2008).

Seed production and natural dispersal of seeds

Seed production

Each safflower head or capitulum usually produces 15-60 seeds. Safflower seeds are contained within a thick hull, this type of fruit is known as an achene, which matures 4-5 weeks after flowering (Li and Mündel, 1996; Singh and Nimbkar, 2006). The composition of mature safflower seed is described as 27-32% oil, 5-8% moisture, 14-15% protein, 2-7% ash and 32-40% crude fibre (Weiss, 2000). The seeds are usually white but can also be striped. Safflower seeds are relatively large measuring 6-10 mm long, tetragonal in shape, with an average weight of 30-40 mg (25 000 seeds/kg) (Bockisch, 1998; GRDC, 2010; Bellé et al., 2012).

The white hulled varieties are used for the birdseed and pet food markets. Seed with brown stripes or with mould or staining is not acceptable (Mündel et al., 2004). Seeds are typically smooth but some varieties have tufts of hairs (pappus) on the ends, which is not desirable in commercial cultivars (Li and Mündel, 1996). Therefore, most seeds of cultivated safflower lack a pappus or, if present, it is reduced (Bérvillé et al., 2005). Since safflower seeds are typically smooth, due to the absence of or reduced pappus, the likelihood of dispersal through wind or adherence (to human clothes or animal fur) is significantly minimised (Vander Wall, Kuhn and Beck, 2005; Wichmann et al., 2008; Mayerhofer et al., 2011).

Natural dispersal of seeds

Wind

Safflower seed is not appreciably dispersed by wind. During domestication of safflower, traits that increased seed recovery at harvest were selected and as a result, cultivated safflower is highly shatter-resistant compared to its wild relatives (Bérvillé et al., 2005; McPherson et al., 2009b). Safflower does not lodge readily but branches/flower heads could be dispersed by strong winds, particularly if the plants or stems were weakened due to pathogen infections or damaged through the activity of birds or other animals (McPherson et al., 2009b; GRDC, 2010). The distance of safflower seed dispersal by wind has not been investigated, although studies with *Brassica* sp. seed can provide indicative information. The wind dispersal of *Brassica* sp. seed was low, dispersing seed less than 250 m due to their spherical shape and high terminal velocities (Bullock and Clarke, 2000; Wichmann et al., 2008). It would be expected that this distance would be significantly less for safflower seeds due to their tetragonal shape and increased seed weight (Bockisch, 1998; Bellé et al., 2012).

Water

No data has been found on the seed transport rates by water of safflower seed. Overall, the dispersal of seed by water has not been widely studied (Wichmann et al., 2008). It is likely that seed could be carried by heavy rains and flooding either shortly after planting or at harvest. If there were heavy rainfalls, the transported seed is likely to germinate because safflower seed has little or no dormancy. Safflower is sensitive to excess moisture/water either as heavy rainfalls, standing water (waterlogging) or humidity. This is due to the increased chance of disease (e.g. *Phytophthora cryptogea*) under these conditions and can lead to substantial yield losses (Nimbkar, 2008; GRDC, 2010), hence it would be expected that dispersal by water has minimal contribution in the dispersal of safflower.

Humans

Human-mediated dispersal can take many forms. Spillage during movement of seed on equipment for planting, harvest or post-harvest storage and/or shipping provides the greatest potential for dispersal of safflower seed. Seed could be spilled during transport and may also be dispersed if inadvertently transported on the machinery (e.g. on muddy wheels). It is also possible for small amounts of seed to be transported on or in clothing (e.g. pockets and cuffs) or boots (especially muddy boots) of workers. Detailed information in regards to the frequencies and distances of human-mediated seed dispersal is still unknown, although some research has focused on the dispersal distances associated with walking (Bullock and Primack, 1977; Mack and Lonsdale, 2001; Wichmann et al., 2008). It has been reported that seed retention and dispersal via clothing (e.g. shirts and trousers) can occur up to 250 m (Bullock and Primack, 1977). Small seeds of some plant species may persist on shoes for more than 5 km, with the predicted potential to be over 10 km (Wichmann et al., 2008). However, for germination and establishment to occur, the seeds must be located in a suitable environment.

Animals

Safflower seeds are a food source for a range of species including mammals, birds and invertebrates. Secondary seed dispersal may also occur and some seeds may be transported intact by ants, dung beetles or scatter-hoarding rodents (Vander Wall, Kuhn and Beck, 2005). Safflower seeds are firmly held within the seed heads and are highly shatter-resistant, therefore limiting access by rodents. Post-harvest dispersal of seeds by small mammals, i.e. rodents, is most likely with predation of seeds present on the soil surface. Safflower seeds may be either dispersed or hoarded by rodents.

For some larger animals such as cattle, foraging or grazing is minimal due to the spiny nature of mature safflower plants (Cummings et al., 2008) but sheep and goats are not irritated by the spines. Feral pigs or boars are destructive and difficult to exclude from fields (Rao et al., 2015). Native animals may also feed on safflower. The viability of safflower seed after passing through the digestive gut of grazing animals is poorly understood.

Safflower dispersal by birds is most likely as some safflower seed varieties are sold as birdseed. Small birds, such as sparrows, can feed on maturing safflower seeds and larger birds, such as cockatoos, can chew safflower plants at the base in order to access seeds (GRDC, 2010). Safflower seed dispersal by several bird species (blackbirds, mallard ducks, pigeons and pheasants) was examined and it was observed that seed did not pass through the digestive tract but did remain viable in the oesophagus and gizzard regions for several hours. The safflower seed viability was measured as a percentage of germination, where the germination rate was in the range of 16-30% and 4-29% for seed collected from the oesophagus and gizzards of birds respectively (Cummings et al., 2008). A few seeds were also transported externally on soil attached to feet or legs of pheasants and pigeons (Cummings et al., 2008; Vazačová and Münzbergová, 2013). Seeds did not attach to plumage possibly due to the fact that safflower seeds are smooth. The researchers also mentioned other bird species that hoard or cache seeds such as ravens, jays and crows as potential transport vectors of safflower seeds.

Seed viability, longevity and dormancy, natural seed bank, germination and seedling viability

Seed longevity, dormancy and germination

Safflower seed has been selected for reduced dormancy during domestication (Bervillé et al., 2005; McPherson et al., 2009b). Seeds of modern cultivars generally lack dormancy and can germinate in the head if rainfall occurs at harvest time (Zimmerman, 1972; Li and Mündel, 1996). A study was conducted to examine the germination of freshly harvested seed from 1973 accessions from over 50 countries, with seed germinated at 20°C. The average time to achieve at least 60% germination was 60 hours for approximately 99% of the accessions. The remaining 1% required more than 120 hours to reach at least 60% germination (Li et al., 1993, as cited by Li and Mündel, 1996). Low levels of dormancy have been observed in safflower, with some variation between cultivars; however, this low level of dormancy was lost during storage. For example, dormancy was lost after 24 weeks of storage at room temperature (Kotecha and Zimmerman, 1978).

Safflower is ideally sown into moist soil at a depth of 2.5-4 cm. Shallow sowing promotes uniform emergence, while deeper sowing increases the susceptibility of the seed to *Pythium* (Oelke et al., 1992; GRDC, 2010). Germination can occur at temperatures as low as 2-5°C and takes between 3 and 8 days, depending on the temperature (Li and Mündel, 1996; Emongor, 2010). However, germination is poor when soil temperatures are below 5°C. Safflower seedlings are frost resistant to about -7°C. Sowing depth, light, temperature and moisture all have an influence on germination (McPherson et al., 2009b). The timing of emergence also depends on temperature but, generally, plants emerge 1-3 weeks after sowing (GRDC, 2010; Bellé et al., 2012).

Seed banks/persistence

Dormancy can affect the persistence of seeds in the soil but, as discussed above, safflower generally has no or little long-term seed dormancy which limits its persistence in seed banks (Bérvillé et al., 2005).

In Australia, safflower seed loss during harvest is about 3-4% (GRDC, 2010). Similarly, harvest losses in California (United States), were estimated at 3-4%, or 192-384 seeds/m^2 on yields of 2 200 to 3 400 kg/ha (Knowles et al., 1965). In one study conducted over 6 sites in Alberta (Canada), seed losses ranged from 230 to 1 070 seeds/m^2 with 80-520 viable seeds/m^2, representing a range of 26% to 84% viable seed depending on the site (McPherson et al., 2009b). It is not rare that a large portion of seed lost during harvest is non-viable. Combine harvester settings (e.g. sieve size, wind speed) are normally such that low weight and small-sized seed are dispersed during harvest. Such seed is usually immature and is unlikely to be viable. However, these levels are relatively high and represent up to five times the recommended seeding rate for that region. The researchers did state that similar pre-harvest and harvest losses are found in wheat fields. Despite these large losses, densities of safflower volunteers emerging in spring ranged from 3 to 11 seedlings/m^2. Volunteers did not survive in fields under chemical fallow. In only 3 of 10 cereal fields surveyed, a few volunteers (0.05-0.33 plants/m^2) survived the first year and generated viable seeds (1-4 seeds per plant). However, volunteer populations did not persist beyond two years (McPherson et al., 2009b).

Seed viability of safflower on the soil surface and buried at two different depths was also examined (McPherson et al., 2009b). The viability of the seed was evaluated after burial in artificial seed banks or spreading the seed on the surface. Seeds did not persist beyond 2 years at the soil surface and beyond 1 year if buried at 2 cm or 15 cm. Thus, the authors recommended tillage to reduce the persistence of the seed bank because the buried seed lost viability faster than the seed on the soil surface. The authors also demonstrated that chemical fallow is an effective control measure, eliminating the presence of safflower volunteers from the fields (McPherson et al., 2009b).

Asexual propagation (apomixis, vegetative reproduction)

Safflower reproduces by seed and is not known to reproduce asexually (USDA-APHIS, 2008).

Genetics

Relevant detailed genetic information on the species

Genetic composition

Cultivated safflower (*C. tinctorius* L.) is a genetically diverse diploid (2n = 2x = 24) with the genus consisting of 16 species (further discussed in the section "Hybridisation and introgression"). In recent years there has been extensive research concentrating on the genetics and genomics of safflower to develop an understanding of both diversity and trait mapping to enable crop improvement through breeding.

The haploid genome size for safflower is approximately 1.4 gigabases (Gb) (Ali et al., 2019), although the genome size varies among populations from different origins (Garnatje et al., 2006). Analysis of genome sizes for those species within the *Atractylis* section reveals that, through the development of allopolyploids, the nuclear DNA content is either the sum of the parental genomes or non-additive, resulting in a smaller hybrid genome size than predicted (Table 3.3). These non-additive changes in genome size function to stabilise polyploidy genomes, which is an adaptive pre-programmed response to genomic stress induced by hybridisation and allopolyploidy (Ozkan, Tuna and Arumuganathan 2003). It was demonstrated that the monoploid genome size (1Cx) decreases with increasing ploidy levels (Garnatje et al., 2006). The sum of the nuclear DNA contents can be used to evaluate the origins and the evolution of hybrid species. For example, the 2C value for *Carthamus creticus* is lower than the sum of the hypothesised parents being *Carthamus lanatus* and *Carthamus leucocaulos*. Similarly, this was also observed for the allopolyploid *Carthamus turkestanicus*, a hybrid of *C. lanatus* and *Carthamus glaucus* (Garnatje et al., 2006).

Table 3.3. Nuclear DNA content and other karyological features

Taxa	2C ± s.d. (pg)	2C (Mbp)	2*n*	Ploidy level	1Cx
		Section *Atractylis*			
C. alexandrines	3.02 ± 0.20	2 953.56	20	2×	1.51
C. anatolicus	2.96 ± 0.03	2 894.22	20	2×	1.48
C. boissieri	2.94 ± 0.01	2 875.32	20	2×	1.47
C. criticus	6.89 ± 0.07	6 738.42	64	6×	1.15
C. dentatus	2.70*	2 640.60	20	2×	1.35
C. glaucus	3.00 ± 0.08	2 934.00	20	2×	1.50
C. lanatus	4.75 ± 0.05	4 645.50	44	4×	1.19
C. leucocaulos	2.26 ± 0.02	2 210.28	20	2×	1.13
C. nitidus	2.44 ± 0.04	2 386.32	24	2×	1.22
C. tenuis	2.74 ± 0.07	2 679.72	20	2×	1.37
C. turkestanicus	7.32 ± 0.11	7 158.96	64	6×	1.22
		Section *Carthamus*			
C. gypsicolus	2.71 ± 0.06	2 650.38	24	2×	1.36
C. oxyacanthus	2.62 ± 0.06	2 562.36	24	2×	1.31
C. palaestinus	2.82 ± 0.06	2 757.96	24	2×	1.41
C. persicus	2.65 ± 0.06	2 591.70	24	2×	1.33
C. tinctorius	2.77 ± 0.04	2 709.06	24	2×	1.39

Source: Garnatje, T. et al. (2006), "Genome size variation in the genus *Carthamus* (Asteraceae, Cardueae): Systematic implications and additive changes during allopolyploidization", *Annals of Botany*, Vol. 97, pp. 461-467.

Repetitive DNA sequences may influence both chromosome structures and recombination events, hence playing an active role in the process of evolution through genome differentiation. Consequently, their abundance, sequence divergence and chromosomal distribution are all important factors in acquiring a complete understanding of genome organisation (Yan et al., 2002). The repetitive elements within the safflower genome have been investigated to better understand their characteristics including size, sequence, location on chromosomes and whether they are unique to safflower (Raina et al., 2005). The location of one element (pCt*Kpn*I-1) in the subtelomeric region of many safflower chromosomes (Raina et al., 2005), a region involved in recombination events during mitosis, suggests a role for this element in the genetic diversity of safflower and its environmental adaptability (Brown et al., 2010). The homology of another element (pCt*Kpn*I-2) with a gene family of *Centaurea stoebe* (Asteraceae) has suggested a role in driving tissue-specific gene expression (Macas, Navrátilová and T. Mészáros et al., 2003; Raina et al., 2005). Further investigations utilising these sequence repeats may help to develop a better understanding of evolution within the Asteraceae family, specifically the *Carthamus* species.

Genetic diversity

The genetic diversity of safflower has been investigated through various molecular techniques including random amplified polymorphic DNA (RAPD), sequence-related amplified polymorphism (SRAP), single nucleotide polymorphisms (SNPs), amplified fragment length polymorphism (AFLP) and simple sequence repeats (SSR), of which the AFLP technique was found to be the most accurate measure (Sehgal et al., 2009). AFLP fingerprinting was further utilised to elucidate associations between genetic differentiation and geographical distribution of globally sourced safflower accessions and cultivars (Kumar et al., 2015).

The Far East region has been described as one of the most conserved centres for safflower, which was confirmed by analysis of genetic diversity, highlighting that most of the accessions analysed formed isolated clusters. Proposed as centres of origin (Knowles, 1969a), the Near East and Iran-Afghanistan regions exhibited high levels of genetic diversity with accessions being distributed across many clusters. It has been suggested that the increased diversity may have been facilitated through genetic exchanges between wild and cultivated germplasm (Ashri, 1971). The accessions from Turkey were fragmented into two clusters that were genetically similar to either accession from the Near East or Iran-Afghanistan regions. A high level of genetic diversity was found within accessions from the Indian subcontinent, with accessions being distributed across multiple clusters. However, the Indian commercial cultivars were found to cluster together, highlighting the untapped potential for the local germplasm to be used for crop improvement by means of introgression. Breeding lines from America also are clustered with the same geographical accessions, indicating low genetic diversity (Kumar et al., 2015). The use of molecular markers, such as AFLP fingerprinting, reflects the diversity of safflower at the DNA level as opposed to morphological markers, thus eliminating the environmental element of observed phenotypes.

Chromosome pairing and cytomixis

During diversification of the safflower cultivars, quantitative genome changes can occur through the exchange of genetic information between chromosome arms, showing variation in DNA content from 2.68 to 2.79 pg (Garnatje et al., 2006; Sheida, Sotoode and Nourmohammadi, 2009). Approximately 75% of this variation can be attributed to mean chromosome length and the lengths of both the short and long arms of chromosomes. The exchange of genetic information occurs during chromosome pairing and the formation of chiasma, where chromosomes crossover, following the chromosomal decondensation phase of meiosis. Genetic linkages are formed during translocation at the point of chiasma, which is mostly associated with chromosome 3 (Pillai, Kumar and Singh 1981). Consequently, increases in chiasma frequencies would enable enhanced genetic diversity. The shedding of elements in the synaptonemal complex,[1] modification of histone proteins and the adaptation to adverse environmental conditions are proposed reasons for genetic diffusion. Simple translocations can also be artificially induced using gamma-irradiation (Singh, Pillai and Kumar 1981).

Methods of breeding

Classical breeding

As with other crops, the ultimate goal of safflower breeding is to accumulate favourable traits into a cultivar. The most commonly utilised breeding method for the development of safflower cultivars is selection for desired traits. This is a multi-step process, which begins with the selection of parents having desirable traits. Examples of desirable traits include seed yields, seed oil content and disease resistance (Singh and

Nimbkar, 2006). Consequently, the selection of parents plays a crucial role in determining the success of any crop improvement breeding programme (Joshi, 1979; Singh and Nimbkar, 2006). The parent plants are then crossed to generate a breeding population. This first hybrid generation (F_1) is allowed to self-pollinate. The traits of interest segregate in the F_2 population. The next step of the breeding process is to select the best performing individuals from within the F_2 and subsequent generations and then to let them self-fertilise in order to generate homogenous lines (homozygous genotypes) exhibiting fixed traits. Homogenous lines are evaluated at multiple geographical locations to identify which ones are best adapted to different environments.

The different safflower varieties and their wild relatives provide the starting material for new crop cultivars. When a new breeding programme is initiated, the selected parental varieties are crossed. Crossing generates genetic variation through genetic recombination at meiosis. Since safflower is mostly self-pollinated, the crossing of the parental lines to generate hybrids would most likely occur in the controlled environment of a glasshouse. Another reason for performing breeding programmes in glasshouses is that it eliminates the likelihood of unknown or unwanted insect-mediated outcrossing that may occur in the field (Li and Mündel, 1996). Another method to ensure that only planned crosses occur is to emasculate the flowers by removing the anther tubes in the late budding stage. Once the styles have elongated, the emasculated florets are then fertilised with pollen from another preselected flower (Knowles, 1980). The F_2 and subsequent generations are processed by a selection process, which is a method of determining the relative worth of individuals in a segregating population. The selective breeding methods are described below (Singh and Nimbkar, 2006).

- **Pedigree selection:** In this method of breeding, individual plants from the F_2 population (5-10% of the population) are further propagated, with the genealogy of each line being recorded. The selected lines are self-fertilised for each generation to ensure the development of homozygous progeny. The pedigree breeding method is the most labour-intensive method but provides the greatest detail of genetic information. It is generally used to create new lines and cultivars that combine the best traits from elite parental lines. This method has been used to breed in desirable traits such as improved seed yields and increased seed oil content (Knowles, 1969b; Ranga Rao, Ramachandram and Arunachalam 1977).
- **Bulk selection:** In this method, plants are chosen which express individual advantages and a sample of the collective seed is propagated in the next inbreeding cycle. The breeder often relies extensively on natural selection or relatively simple selection techniques within the bulk population for removing unwanted types or retaining desirable types, as the population is harvested *en masse* with no individual progeny testing. Consequently, the strong natural selection pressure favours the development of higher-yielding varieties. Another advantage of this method is that breeders are able to handle multiple bulk populations concurrently.
- **Single-seed descent selection:** Involves self-fertilisation of a random sample of F_2-derived plants in each generation and advancing only one seed per plant, with the intent to achieve homozygosity whilst practising minimal selection. When inbred lines have been produced, selection can be based on data from replicated field trials for desirable attributes including agronomic performance, biotic and abiotic stress tolerance, and/or end-use quality testing. This method is usually applied when crossing elite safflower cultivars in which many of the desirable alleles are already fixed.
- **Recurrent selection (backcrossing):** Backcrossing is a method of recurrent selection, used to introduce a desirable trait into a specific genetic background, typically a widely adopted variety (referred to as the recurrent parent). The parental source of the desirable trait is designated the donor parent and the parent in which the trait is introduced is the recurrent parent. After numerous backcrosses, the recurrent parent will have acquired the new desired trait. After the final backcrossing cycle, the selected elite plants are self-fertilised to produce progeny that is both homozygous for the new trait and similar to the recurrent parent. The backcrossing method has been used effectively as a breeding strategy to incorporate dominant genes for the control of

devastating diseases, such as root rot caused by *Phytophthera drechsleri* (Thomas, Rubis and Black 1960; Rubis, 2001) and in the development of high oleic acid safflower (Knowles, 1968; Hamdan et al., 2009).

If a trait of interest does not occur in the existing genetic resources, there are methods to generate genetic variation. Mutagenesis is a technique that induces changes in the genomic DNA sequence, which can be induced by exposing safflower seeds to chemical mutagens or ultraviolet or ionising radiation. TILLING (Targeting Induced Local Lesions IN Genomes) is one example of a mutagenesis technique that uses ethyl methanesulfonate (EMS) to induce short insertion/deletion (INDELS) mutations (Sikora et al., 2011; Kashtwari, Wani and Rather 2019). This mutagenesis is non-targeted, that is genes are mutated at random and this may generate a trait of interest. To date, this technique has not yet been explored for the potential crop improvement of safflower, although it has been used for *Helianthus annus* L. (sunflower), another member of the Asteraceae family (Sabetta et al., 2011).

Hybrid breeding

Hybrid breeding, often referred to as hybridisation, is mainly practised as a method to integrate the desirable traits of two or more varieties into one elite cultivar (Ashri and Knowles, 1960; Baydar, Gökmen and Friedt 2003). Similar to classical breeding methods, parental selection is critical in determining the success of crop improvement breeding programmes involving hybrid breeding (Joshi, 1979; Singh and Nimbkar, 2006). The existence of heterosis for capitula numbers, seed yields and other commercially important traits makes safflower a suitable candidate crop for the exploration and exploitation of hybrid vigour (Urie and Zimmer, 1970).

The very high linoleic acid (*lili*) content in safflower, controlled by recessive alleles at a single locus (*Li*), is a unique trait that is not found in any other commercial oilseed crop (Mattson, Sun and Koo 2004; Hall, 2016). A close genetic repulsion-phase linkage has been demonstrated between traits of nuclear male sterility (NMS; controlled by the gene *Ms*) and very high linoleic acid content (Hamdan et al., 2008). When the safflower parental lines of CL-1 (NMS; linoleic content of 74%) and CR-142 (high linoleic: 88%) were crossed, the recombination frequency of these two genes was evaluated to be 10%, which resulted in most of the progeny being both male-sterile and having an intermediate linoleic acid content. For breeding programmes that involve the very high linoleic acid trait, this genetic linkage enables simple selection of the trait through only progressing fertile progeny (Hamdan et al., 2008).

Development of hybrids

Dominant and recessive genetic male sterility (GMS), cytoplasmic male sterility (CMS) and thermosensitive genetic male sterility (TGMS) systems for producing hybrid safflower plants have been developed (Anjani, 2005; Singh, Ranaware and Nimbkar 2008; Meena et al., 2012; Deshmukh, Wakode and Ratnaparakhi 2014). Identification and development of GMS lines have assisted the release of non-spiny (NARI-NH-1) and spiny (NARI-H-15) safflower hybrids in India (Singh, 1996; Singh, Deshpande and Nimbkar 2003), which exhibit increases in both total seed yield and oil content by 20-25%. Similarly, CMS and TGMS lines are also commercially available in India (Meena et al., 2012). The average yield and oil content of CMS hybrid lines were greater than the open-pollinated lines in field trials run across sites in the United States, Canada, Pakistan, Mexico and Spain (Li and Mündel, 1996). In Australia, the comparison of four US derived CMS lines against open-pollinated lines was inconclusive with regard to yield (Wachsmann et al., 2003).

For hybrid seed production and breeding programmes, GMS lines are used as they reduce the manual labour involved in flower emasculation (Knowles, 1980). In naturally occurring GMS lines, male-sterile and fertile plants can only be distinguished at the time of flowering, with identification typically being dependent on flower morphology and the presence of pollen (Singh, 1996). For the female parent, all fertile plants have to be emasculated before flowering to avoid self-fertilisation, hence eliminating the risk of reductions in both seed yields and seed purity. Genetic linkage has been identified between the recessive alleles of male sterility (*Ms*) and dwarfism (*dw*), which produce dwarf male-sterile (DMS) plants when present in the homozygous state (Singh, 1997). At approximately 30-40 days after sowing, the male-sterile plants are only 5-10 cm tall, whereas the male-fertile plants are significantly taller at 20-25 cm.

Similar to the dwarf trait, a marker-linked GMS (MGMS) line was developed with sterile and fertile plants being distinguishable at the elongation stage, where plants are approximately 40-45 days old (Kammili, 2013), enabling identification approximately 45-50 days prior to the flowering stage. Genetically linked segregation was observed for the male sterility and the non-spiny traits, with sterile plants being identified morphologically by non-spiny leaves, whereas the leaves of fertile plants had spines (Kammili, 2013). The benefits of early identification of male-fertile plants, aided through the traits of either dwarfism or non-spiny leaves, include increased yields, the production of pure hybrid seed and the faster breeding of elite varieties (Singh, 1997; Kammili, 2013).

Intraspecific crossing: Outcrossing and gene flow potential

Vertical gene transfer is the transfer of genetic information from an individual organism to its progeny. In flowering plants, vertical gene transfer mainly occurs via pollen dispersal and cross-pollination between related sexually compatible plants. Intraspecific crossing refers to fertilisation between *C. tinctorius* (safflower) plants (Ashri and Efron, 1964; Imrie and Knowles, 1970). Gene flow captures all of the mechanisms that result in the movement of genes between populations of species that are cross-compatible, whether they are the same or different species or subspecies (Ridley and Alexander, 2016). Outcrossing in safflower is mainly insect-mediated with wind-mediated outcrossing playing a minor role (see sub-section on pollination, pollen dispersal, pollen viability). Honey bees and bumblebees are the main pollinators of safflower. Worldwide, studies show that outcrossing rates appear to be quite variable (Table 3.4) and may depend on a number of factors such as pollen source size and shape, environmental climatic conditions, insect numbers and type and the variety/cultivar.

Table 3.4. Intraspecific crossing rates and gene flow potential in safflower

Study and country	Outcrossing range % (average %)	Distance
Kadam and Patankar (1942): India	1-28 (10)	Close proximity
	0.8-5.9 (1.9)	13.7 m
Claassen (1950): United States	8.3-100 (34.2)	1 m
	0-26 (14.9) low outcrossing lines	1 m
	31.8-93.6 (57.3) high outcrossing lines	1 m
Rudolphi, Becker and von Witzke-Ehbrecht (2008): Germany	6-33 (9.7-18)	Close proximity
	0-11.5 (6.5)	At least 5 m
McPherson et al. (2009a): Canada and Chile	0.48-1.7	0.3-3 m
	0-0.86	≈ 10 m
	0-0.26	≈ 20 m
	0-0.10	≈ 30 m
	0.03-0.16	≈ 40 m
	0.0024-0.04	50 m
	0.01	≈ 100 m
	Nil	≈ 300 m
Cresswell (2010)	0.005-0.05 (mathematical model)	Field to field
Velasco, Fischer and Fernandez-Martinez (2012): Spain	0.5-35.9 (10.3)	1-1.5 m
Nabloussi, Velasco and Fernandez-Martinez (2013): Morocco	8-53 (26.6)	1-1.5 m

Sources: Full reference information listed in the reference section below.

Although safflower is typically considered to be self-pollinating (described in sub-section on pollination, pollen dispersal, pollen viability), if self-pollination- does not occur, pollen may fall from other flowers or pollination may occur through the transfer of pollen from insects such as bees. Due to the limited wind-mediated movement of pollen, less than 1.2 m, cross-pollination of safflower is prominently insect dependent (Claassen, 1950). There are many factors that can influence successful outcrossing including pollinator effects (pollinator species and distance to pollen sources), abiotic factors (distance to compatible plants, wind direction and velocity) and crops characteristics (ploidy level, pollen of donor and receptor plants, pollen longevity, floral synchrony and cross-compatibility) (Kadam and Patankar, 1942; Rudolphi, Becker and von Witzke-Ehbrecht 2008; McPherson et al., 2009a). Although the intraspecific outcrossing potential varies significantly between varieties, consistently it has been demonstrated that the frequency of outcrossing decreases as the distance increases (Kadam and Patankar, 1942; Kumari and Pandey, 2005; Cresswell, 2010). The self-compatibility of different safflower varieties is an important attribute to consider for the evaluation of self-pollination and the potential for intraspecific crossing since self-pollination rates have been shown to range from 9.3% to 81.5% (Claassen, 1950).

One of the earliest studies to examine intraspecific crossing in a number of safflower cultivars, using corolla colour as a morphological marker, was conducted in the United States (Claassen, 1950), with results summarised as follows. Outcrossing levels between rows spaced approximately 1 m apart ranged from 0% to over 50% for some cultivars, although most were less than 10%. Individual plants varied considerably with outcrossing frequencies ranging from 0% to 100%. In inbred varieties selected for high yield and high oil content, the average outcrossing between rows was less than 5%. When outcrossing rates were measured in two different regions within Nebraska, no significant differences were found between the two regions (Claassen, 1950).

In an earlier study conducted in India, also using corolla colour as a marker, cross-pollination rates ranged from 1% to 28%, with an average of 10%, between safflower plants in close proximity (exact distance not given). At a distance of 13.7 m, the average outcrossing rate ranged from 0.8% to 5.9% (average 1.9%) (Kadam and Patankar, 1942).

In 2008, a small study in Germany found the level of outcrossing between plots of safflower ranged from 0% to 33%, with averages of 6.5-18% depending on the location of the sampled plant (Rudolphi, Becker and von Witzke-Ehbrecht 2008). Outcrossing rates were also measured between plants grown together in the same plot and dropped from 63% in 2004 to 30% in 2005. The large variation between the two years of the study may have been due to different environmental conditions (Rudolphi, Becker and von Witzke-Ehbrecht 2008).

A study in Spain, as a model for a typical Mediterranean environment, examined outcrossing from a high oleic content cultivar (CR-6) to a low oleic content cultivar (Rancho) separated by 1-1.5 m. The CR-6 plants were surrounded by Rancho plants and high oleic acid was used as a biochemical marker to estimate outcrossing. The experimental crops were grown at three different times, winter sowing in 2009, winter sowing in 2010 and spring sowing in 2010. Average outcrossing rates of 5.7%, 12.1% and 13.2% were observed respectively. Higher outcrossing frequencies were detected at the single plant level (up to 35.9%) and the single-head level (up to 58.3%) (Velasco, Fischer and Fernandez-Martinez 2012).

Nabloussi, Velasco and Fernandez-Martinez (2013) used the same cultivars and field layout as Velasco, Fischer and Fernandez-Martinez (2012) to determine the outcrossing frequencies under Moroccan conditions. The average outcrossing rate at 1-1.5 m was 26% with a range of 8.3-53% at the plant level. This rate was approximately twice that reported by Velasco, Fischer and Fernandez-Martinez (2012). As this and the Velasco study used the same cultivars and field layout, collectively these studies demonstrate the influence of the environment, and possibly the pollinators, on outcrossing rates.

The frequency of natural intraspecific crossing from genetically engineered (GE) safflower to non-GE safflower was measured under field conditions in three different environments. Outcrossing experiments were conducted in the province of Santiago, Chile (2002) and the Canadian provinces of British Columbia

(2002) and Alberta (2004) (McPherson et al., 2009a). The GE safflower contained the *pat* gene (*phosphinothricin acetyltransferase*), conferring tolerance to the herbicide glufosinate, with this trait used to confirm outcrossing to the non-GE safflower. The three trial sites varied in design layout including the distance from the GE safflower to the first rows of non-GE safflower (0.3-3.0 m), the distance over which outcrossing was measured, and size of the GE pollen source (99-900 m^2) (McPherson et al., 2009a).

The highest rate of outcrossing of 1.67% was detected at the British Columbia site at a distance of 3 m, which was the nearest distance measured. Outcrossing was observed at each distance sampled at this site (from 3 to 101 m), except for a single measurement at 300 m where no outcrossing was detected. At the site in Santiago, outcrossing was observed at nearly every distance (0.7-60.5 m) with the highest outcrossing rate of 0.48% again observed in samples taken at the closest distance of 0.7 m. No outcrossing was detected at most distances measured at the Alberta site (from 0.3 to 49.5 m), the highest outcrossing rate observed was 0.62% at 0.3 m (McPherson et al., 2009a). The highest levels of outcrossing occurred closest to the pollen source and significantly declined over distance for all three sites, with the frequency of outcrossing reduced by 96-100% at 50 m.

Outcrossing frequencies were as heterogeneous between the three sites as they were between blocks (replicates). Researchers indicated this variation may be due to the non-random movement of pollen by insects, as wind is not a significant factor in safflower outcrossing (Claassen, 1950; McPherson et al., 2009a). Additionally, the pollen source size was suggested to be influencing outcrossing. The area of the British Columbia pollen source was about 9 times larger (900 m^2) than either of the other 2 sites (99 and 110 m^2) and outcrossing close to the pollen source at this site was 4 times greater. The larger site also demonstrated a slower decline in outcrossing with distance (McPherson et al., 2009a). Other differences in site design may have affected outcrossing rates. The Alberta site had a barren zone between the GE and non-GE safflower and this may have affected insect-mediated cross-pollination. Differences in insect populations at the sites have been proposed as a possible cause for the lack of outcrossing observed at the Alberta site (McPherson et al., 2009a). Directionality was also considered at the three trial sites and it was noted that there were predominately westerly winds during flowering. However, greater outcrossing was not found on the leeward side of the trial sites, which supports Claassen's (1950) findings that wind-mediated pollination plays a minor role, if any, in outcrossing of safflower.

For the distance range of 0.3-3 m, the intraspecific crossing rates in the study by McPherson et al. (2009a) ranged from 0-1.7%, which is an order of magnitude lower than other studies for distances of 1-1.5 m (see Table 3.3). One reason for this is the environmental differences that can influence outcrossing rates. For example, both Velasco, Fischer and Fernandez-Martinez (2012) and Nabloussi, Velasco and Fernandez-Martinez (2013) used the same cultivars and field designs in different countries (Spain versus Morocco) but had a twofold difference in outcrossing rates. The outcrossing rates could also be influenced by the cultivars included in the study. This was demonstrated through the work by Claassen (1950) where a huge variability in outcrossing was observed (14.9% and 57.3% in low and high outcrossing lines respectively). Additionally, the rate of outcrossing can be influenced by the type and number of pollinators at the trial site.

McPherson et al. (2009a) did point out that this work cannot predict maximum distances of pollen movement by pollinators due to long-distance foraging by bees, as pollen can potentially be dispersed by bees foraging over a range of kilometres. In addition, the researchers found that the outcrossing rate in safflower was spatially heterogeneous as was the case observed by Nabloussi, Velasco and Fernandez-Martinez (2013), indicating that bee and other insect visitations occur in a random and unbalanced way. There is evidence of long-distance insect-mediated pollen transfer in other self-pollinated crops, such as cotton and oilseed rape, due to the long-distance foraging capability of honey bees and bumblebees (AOSCA, 2012).

Bumblebees have been suggested as being more effective at field-to-field pollination of safflower than honey bees. Using a mathematical model of field-to-field gene flow due to insect pollination, the maximum level of bee-mediated gene flow between large fields was estimated at 0.005-0.05% (Cresswell, 2010). The highest value occurred when it was assumed that fields were pollinated exclusively by bumblebees. Values for the model were determined using observations of honey bee and bumblebee behaviour on a 40-ha field of safflower in Canada. Bees made long foraging bouts within the field, making between field pollinations rare. This factor, as well as safflower's high capacity for self-pollination, resulted in the very low estimates of pollinator mediated gene flow between fields (Cresswell, 2010).

Hybridisation and introgression

The natural facility of interspecific crossing (extent, sterility/fertility)

Interspecific crossing refers to the outcrossing of safflower to related species (Ashri and Efron, 1964; Imrie and Knowles, 1970; Garnatje et al., 2006). This hybridisation of different species or subspecies needs to be considered with respect to potential evolutionary and ecological consequences (Ridley and Alexander, 2016).

Studies have revealed that safflower can hybridise with other *Carthamus* species to produce allopolyploid plants (Sheidai, Sotoode and Nourmohammadi 2009), typically associated with differences in the DNA content (Table 3.3; sub-section on genetic composition). During meiosis, chromosome migration can occur within cytomictic channels (inter-meiocyte connections) of the anther, which can lead to aneuploidy of meiocytes. The aneuploidy meiocytes are precursors to the formation of unreduced ($2n$) pollen grains, hence enabling the production of plants with higher levels of ploidy (Sheidai, Sotoode and Nourmohammadi 2009).

Natural interspecific hybridisation between safflower and its wild relatives can only occur if there is synchronous flowering (temporal sympatry) and proximity (spatial sympatry) (Ellstrand, Prentice and Hancock 1999). Hybridisation between safflower and wild *Carthamus* species has probably played a role in the evolution of *C. tinctorius* in the Mediterranean and Asia where they are sympatric (McPherson et al., 2004). Spatial sympatry can be seen in Table 3.5., which summarises the geographical distribution of all *Carthamus* species (McPherson et al., 2004; GBIF Backbone Taxonomy, 2017). Successful experimental (artificial) hybridisation of any two species is not an accurate measure of success in nature, although it does describe the potential for cross-compatibility. The self-compatibility and compatibility with *C. tinctorius* have been summarised in Table 3.6.

Table 3.5. Geographical distribution of *Carthamus tinctorius* L. (cultivated safflower) and related species

Taxon	Geographical distribution
Section *Carthamus* (2n = 24)	
C. curdicus Hanelt	Iran only
C. gypsicolus Iljin	Iran, Iraq, Kazakhstan, Azerbaijan, Armenia, Lebanon, Turkey, Syrian Arab Republic, Uzbekistan
C. oxyacanthus Bieb.	Pakistan, Iran, Afghanistan, Iraq, Turkey, India, Uzbekistan, Azerbaijan, Armenia, Australia
C. palaestinus Eig.	Israel, Iraq
C. persicus Willd. (syn. *C. flavescens* Spreng.)	Israel, Turkey, Iraq, Syrian Arab Republic, Ethiopia, Lebanon, Jordan, Iran
C. tinctorius L.	Widely cultivated (safflower, *refer to Figure 3*)
Section *Odonthagnathis* (DC.) Hanelt (2n = 20, 22)	
C. boissieri Halácsy	Greece, France, Cyprus
C. dentatus Vahl	Australia, Greece, Turkey, Bulgaria, Cyprus, Hungary, Iran, Macedonia
C. divaricatus Beguinot and Vacc.	Libya
C. glaucus Bieb.	Israel, West Bank and Gaza Strip, Turkey, Syrian Arab Republic, Lebanon, Greece, Azerbaijan, Afghanistan, Egypt, Ukraine, Armenia, Jordan, Iraq, Russia, Australia
C. leucocaulos Sm.	Greece, Australia, United States, Germany, Turkey, Argentina
C. tenuis (Boiss. and Bl.) Bornm.	Israel, West Bank and Gaza Strip, Lebanon, Greece, Cyprus[3], Jordan, Egypt, Syrian Arab Republic, Turkey
Section *Atractylis* Reichenb. (2n = 44, 64)	
C. creticus L.	Greece, Spain, United States, Portugal, Denmark, Morocco, New Zealand, Australia, France, Egypt, Iraq, Turkey
C. lanatus L.	Spain, France, Italy, Portugal, United States, Greece, Argentina, Ethiopia, Morocco, Turkey, Germany, Brazil, Netherlands, India, Pakistan, Australia
C. turkestanicus Popov	Afghanistan, Iran, Armenia, Turkey, Uzbekistan, Pakistan
Uncertain placement (2n = 24)	
C. nitidus Boiss	West Bank and Gaza Strip, Israel, Jordan, Syrian Arab Republic, Saudi Arabia, Lebanon, Egypt

Sources: McPherson, M.A. et al. (2004), "Theoretical hybridization potential of transgenic safflower (*Carthamus tinctorius* L.) with weedy relatives in the New World", *Canadian Journal of Plant Science*, Vol. 84, pp. 923-934; GBIF Backbone Taxonomy (2017), "*Carthamus* L.", in *GBIF Secretariat*.

Table 3.6. Assessment of self-compatibility, compatibility with *C. tinctorius* L. and genomic formulae for *Carthamus* spp.

Taxon	Self-compatibility	Compatibility with *C. tinctorius*	Fertility comments	Genomic formula
Section *Carthamus* (2n = 24)				
C. curdicus Hanelt	Compatible	Unknown	–	–
C. gypsicolus Iljin	Compatible	Unknown	–	–
C. oxyacanthus Bieb.	Both known	Yes	Fertile	BB
C. palaestinus Eig.	Compatible	Yes	Fertile	B_1B_1
C. persicus Willd. (syn. *C. flavescens* Spreng.)	Incompatible	Yes	Fertile	B_1B_1
C. tinctorius L.	Compatible	Yes	Fertile	BB
Section *Odonthagnathis* (DC.) Hanelt (2n = 20, 22)				
C. boissieri Halácsy	Unknown	Unknown	–	–
C. dentatus Vahl	Incompatible	No	–	A_1A_1
C. divaricatus Beguinot and Vacc.	Incompatible	Yes	Fertile self-incompatible hybrids	–
C. glaucus Bieb.	Unknown	Yes	Infertile hybrids	AAA_3A_3
C. leucocaulos Sm.	Compatible	Yes	Infertile hybrids	A_2A_2
C. tenuis (Boiss. and Bl.) Bornm.	Unknown	Unknown	–	–
Section *Atractylis* Reichenb. (2n = 44, 64)				
C. creticus L.	Compatible	Yes	Fertile	$A_1A_1B_1B_1A_2A_2$
C. lanatus L.	Compatible	Yes	Infertile hybrids	$A_1A_1B_1B_1$
C. turkestanicus Popov	Compatible	Yes	–	$A_1A_1B_1B_1A_3A_3$
Uncertain placement (2n = 24)				
C. nitidus Boiss	Compatible	Yes	Infertile hybrids	–

Source: McPherson, M.A. et al. (2004), "Theoretical hybridization potential of transgenic safflower (*Carthamus tinctorius* L.) with weedy relatives in the New World", *Canadian Journal of Plant Science*, Vol. 84, pp. 923-934, and references cited therein.

Section *Carthamus* (n = 12)

- Natural hybrids have been identified between *C. tinctorius* and *C. oxyacanthus* and *C. palaestinus*, which are all members of the *Carthamus* section (Table 3.1) (Ashri and Knowles, 1960). *C. oxyacanthus* and *C. tintorius* have a relatively high rate of natural hybridisation when grown side by side and the F_1 plants showed hybrid vigour (Deshpande, 1952). Natural hybrids between these species have been identified in both India and Pakistan where they are sympatric. In contrast, hybrids between *C. tinctorius* and either *C. oxyacanthus* or *C. palaestinus* did not demonstrate any hybrid vigour, increased fitness or weediness (Mayerhofer et al., 2011).
- A review by Knowles and Ashri (1995) indicates that *C. flavescens* (= *C. persicus*), *C. oxyacanthus* and *C. palaestinus* can easily be artificially crossed with *C. tinctorius* and occasionally will form natural hybrids. Hybrids of *C. tinctorius* and *C. oxyacanthus* have been documented in greenhouses and in the field in India and Pakistan where they are sympatric (McPherson et al., 2004, and references cited therein). *C. oxycanthus* is rated as one of the top ten weeds in Pakistan. Hybrids of safflower and *C. palaestinus* have been found in Israel where the two species are sympatric (Knowles and Ashri, 1995). Hybrids of these two species were also found where alternate rows of *C. tinctorius* and *C. palaestinus* were planted in field trials. Seeds from the plants were collected and planted in the field in the following seasons and hybrids with either species

as the female parent were identified morphologically (Ashri and Rudich, 1965). The review also noted that the possibility of natural hybrids occurring between *C. tinctorius* and *C. gypsicolus* or *C. curdicus* had not been determined (Knowles and Ashri, 1995).

Section *Odonthagnathis* (n = 10, 11)

- Naturalised populations of wild safflower species, specifically, *C. leucocaulos, C. dentatus* and *C. glaucus*, have been reported in Australia (Groves et al., 2003; GBIF Backbone Taxonomy, 2017). *C. leucocaulos* is a noxious weed in Australia and California (the United States) (Mayerhofer et al., 2011). There are no reports of species within this section crossing with *C. tinctorius* under natural conditions.
- The potential for natural crossing between *C. tinctorius* and *C. tenuis* or *C. boissieri* (both n = 10) has not been determined.

Section *Atractylis* (n = 22, 32)

- Naturalised populations of *C. lanatus* (n = 22) have been reported in Australia (Groves et al., 2003) and has also been reported as a noxious weed in both Australia and the United States (California) (Mayerhofer et al., 2011). Hybridisation between species with either n = 10 or n = 12 with *C. lanatus* all produce infertile hybrids as a result of the irregular pairing of chromosomes during meiosis (McPherson et al., 2004 and references cited therein), hence the probability of a fertile hybrid occurring naturally is highly unlikely.
- Artificial crosses between *C. tinctorius* and *C. creticus* have resulted in the production of fertile F_1 hybrids, thus it is likely that natural interspecific crossing could occur between these two species if both temporal and spatial sympatry existed (McPherson et al., 2004).

Species of uncertain placement (n = 12)

- Crosses between *C. tinctorius* and *C. nitidus* result in the production of F_1 hybrids which are infertile (Knowles and Schank, 1964).

Experimental crosses

Cross-compatibility has been demonstrated with some of its weedy and wild relatives (McPherson et al., 2004; Garnatje et al., 2006; Mayerhofer et al., 2011; Ali et al., 2019). Both the selfcompatibility and outcrossing potential of safflower with its related species have been investigated, with results summarised in Table 3.6 (Ashri and Efron, 1964; Knowles and Schank, 1964; Imrie and Knowles, 1970; Estilai and Knowles, 1976; Heaton and Klisiewicz, 1981; McPherson et al., 2004; Garnatje et al., 2006; McPherson et al., 2009a; Mayerhofer et al., 2011). Typically experimental crosses are performed by using emasculation and hand-pollination (Mayerhofer et al., 2011). Although hand-pollination is not an appropriate technique for investigating the potential for outcrossing, since the process does not simulate natural pollination and seed production (Ellstrand, Prentice and Hancock, 1999), it does provide information on cross-compatibility.

Section *Carthamus* (n = 12)

- Most *Carthamus* species with n = 12 chromosomes (*C. tinctorius*, *C. oxyacanthus* and *C. palaestinus*) can be crossed successfully to produce fertile progeny (Ashri and Knowles, 1960; Mayerhofer et al., 2011). As discussed in the sub-section on the natural facility of interspecific crossing, natural hybrids of these species have also been identified. The success rate of these interspecific hybridisations occurring under artificial conditions was 30% with *C. palaestinus* and 56% with *C. oxyacanthus*. In comparison, *C. tinctorius x C. tinctorius* control crosses occurred at a rate of 40% (Mayerhofer et al., 2011).

- Crosses between *C. tinctorius* and *C. flavescens* (= *C. persicus*) produced fertile F_1 and F_2 progeny (Imrie and Knowles, 1970), while a review by Knowles and Ashri (1995) indicates that *C. flavescens* (= *C. persicus*), *C. oxyacanthus* and *C. palaestinus* can easily be artificially crossed with *C. tinctorius*. The possibility of artificial hybrids occurring between *C. tinctorius* and *C. gypsicolus* or *C. curdicus* was not determined (Knowles and Ashri, 1995).

Section *Odonthagnathis* (n = 10, 11)

- Safflower has also been crossed with four species outside the section *Carthamus*, to produce viable hybrids. *C. tinctorius* has been artificially crossed with *C. divaricatus* (n = 11) and produced self-sterile F_1 hybrids which show some female fertility in backcrosses with *C. tinctorius*, although at low rates (Knowles and Ashri, 1995). However, backcrossing these hybrids with *C. tinctorius* results in offspring with low fertility (Estilai and Knowles, 1976).
- Artificial crosses between *C. tinctorius* and other members of the species with = 10, are reported to be difficult to achieve and the F_1 hybrids are highly sterile (Knowles and Ashri, 1995; McPherson et al., 2004). Ashri and Knowles (1960) crossed *C. tinctorius* with *C. tenuis* and *C. glaucus*, obtaining sterile hybrids in both cases. Crosses of *C. tinctorius* with *C. leucocaulos* or *C. glaucus* were performed (Mayerhofer et al., 2011). The cross with *C. leucocaulos* resulted in sterile offspring (seed was produced but would not germinate). Although the cross with *C. glaucus* produced fertile F_1 plants, the authors noted that there was some uncertainty about the identity of the *C. glaucus* seeds used. Different regional variants of *C. glaucus* behave differently in interspecific crosses, therefore some subspecies or varieties may produce viable hybrids with *C. tinctorius* (McPherson et al., 2004). Hybrid vigour or increased fitness or weediness was not observed in the F_1 hybrids (Mayerhofer et al., 2011).
- Artificial crosses were performed to investigate the potential for outcrossing between genetically engineered safflower, containing resistance to glyphosate (*pat* gene), and wild relatives. All experimental crosses produced F_1 hybrids that retained the intact transgene, except for one species and demonstrated that hybrid fitness was equal to or greater than the respective parents involved (Ellstrand, Prentice and Hancock, 1999; Mayerhofer et al., 2011). The transgene was completely deleted in approximately 21% of the F_1 progeny resulting from crosses between transgenic *C. tinctorius* and *C. glaucus*, which suggests that some *Cathamus* species possess a negative selection mechanism against foreign DNA (Mayerhofer et al., 2011). The transfer of any gene in nature is typically controlled by selective advantage, a trait that promotes a better chance of both selection and survival (Haygood, Ives and Andow 2003; Chapman and Burke, 2006).
- The potential for artificial or natural crossing between *C. tinctorius* and *C. dentatus* or *C. boissieri* (both n = 10) has not been determined. However, cytogenetic analysis of the interspecific hybrids within this section showed a high frequency of chromosome pairing at meiosis, indicating the close relationship among them (see review by Kumar, 1991). In contrast, analysis of crosses between *C. leucocaulos* or *C. tenuis* (both n = 10) with *C. tinctorius* (n = 12) showed very low chromosome pairing at meiosis, poor pollen stainability and a failure of the hybrids to produce seeds. A review of the potential for safflower to hybridise with other *Carthamus* species indicated that crosses between species with n = 10 and *C. tinctorius* produced sterile hybrids (McPherson et al., 2004). Similarly, Knowles (1980) indicated that most n = 10 species will cross *C. tinctorius* but the hybrids are highly sterile. Thus, it is highly likely that crosses between *C. tinctorius* and *C. dentatus* or *C. boissieri* will also have very low levels of chromosome pairing at meiosis and generate sterile offspring.

Section *Atractylis* (n = 22, 32)

- Successful crosses between *C. tinctorius* and *C. lanatus* (n = 22) have been achieved, especially with *C. tinctorius* as the female parent, but all resulting F_1 plants are sterile (Ashri and Knowles, 1960; Heaton and Klisiewicz, 1981; Mayerhofer et al., 2011). Fertile hybrid plants could only be achieved by treating rescued embryos with colchicine (Heaton and Klisiewicz, 1981). The F_1 hybrids did not exhibit any hybrid vigour or increased fitness or weediness (Mayerhofer et al., 2011).

- Experimental crosses between *C. tinctorius* and the two members of the section *Atractylis*, *C. creticus* and *C. turkestanicus* (both n = 32), produced viable fertile offspring (McPherson et al., 2004; Bérvillé et al., 2005) but with low success rates of < 2% and 0.3% respectively (Mayerhofer et al., 2011).

Species of uncertain placement (n = 12)

- *C. nitidus* (n = 12) has been artificially crossed with *C. tinctorius* with the F_1 hybrid being sterile (Knowles and Ashri, 1995). Attempts to cross *C. nitidus* with other *Carthamus* species produced viable but sterile hybrids (Knowles and Schank, 1964; Knowles, 1989). There is no information on the potential for crossing between *C. tinctorius* and *F. balearica.*

Information and data on introgression

Knowledge, access and exploitation of available genetic diversity in domesticated and wild relatives are essential for expanding the genetic base of safflower cultivars to achieve increases in both crop stability and performance (Sujatha, 2008). Interspecific hybridisation experiments for safflower have typically been targeted towards the assessment of cross-compatibility relationships and the characterisation of F_1 hybrids (see sub-section on experimental crosses). Wild *Carthamus* species potentially possess a wealth of genetic diversity with respect to traits of environmental adaptation, biotic and abiotic stress resistance, and oil content and quality. The largest barrier to the introgression of desirable traits from wild safflowers into cultivated safflower is the difference in basic chromosome number (2*n*; see Table 3.6), hence sexual incompatibility.

The Australian Wildlife Conservancy (AWC) collection was developed through simultaneous open pollination of the thin-hulled safflower line, A4138, with 12 different *Carthamus* species including *C. alexandrines*, *C. arborescens*, *C. creticus*, *C. caeruleus*, *C. dentatus*, *C. flavescens*, *C. glaucus*, *C. oxyacanthus*, *C. syriacus*, *C. palaestinus*, *C. tenuis* and *C. lanatus* (Rubis, 1981). Following flood treatment of the resulting progeny, the thin hull phenotype facilitated the recurrent selection of lines that demonstrated resistance to *P. dreschsleri* root rot. For example, the line PI 537690 exhibited 95% survival, whereas commercial variety checks were 100% killed by disease. The exact pedigree of the surviving plants is unknown, although the plant and seed characteristics indicate that the introgressive germplasm most likely came from either *C. flavescens* or *C. oxyacanthus* (Rubis, 1981).

A disease-resistant allopolyploid was developed from a cross between *C. tinctorius* and *C. lanatus* (Heaton and Klisiewicz, 1981). The resulting allopolyploid contained 34 chromosomes. It is proposed that 22 came from *C. lanatus* and 12 from *C. tinctorius*, with the doubled haploid being 2*n* = 64 chromosomes. The progeny exhibited morphology similar to *C. lanatus*, and demonstrated resistance to a variety of important safflower pathogens, including *Alternaria carthami*, *Fusarium* spp., *Verticillium dahliae*, and bacterial blight. The resulting allopolyploid is self-fertile but is unable to backcross to *C. tinctorius* due to the sterility associated with the majority of chromosomes being non-homologous (Heaton and Klisiewicz, 1981).

General interactions with other organisms (ecology)

Interactions in natural and agronomic ecosystems

Pollination studies showed that honey bees (*Apis mellifera* and *Apis* spp.) are the major pollinators of safflower crops (Kumari and Pandey, 2005; Pandey and Kumari, 2008). Studies in the United States observed that 80-90% of insects visiting safflower plants were honey bees. Safflower ranks highly among the commercial crops which are preferred by honey bees. Honey bees have been found bypassing cotton and corn fields, flying distances more than 8 km, to collect pollen from safflower plants, while nectar collectors remain foraging in nearby cotton (Gary et al., 1977; Van Deynze, Sundstrom and Bradford, 2005). Honey bees that were located in an alfalfa seed field-collected alfalfa pollen until the nearby safflower flowered, after which the honey bees preferentially collected safflower pollen (Torchio, 1966; Wichelns, Weaver and Brooks 1992).

The dense and aggressive root structure of safflower penetrates deeper into the soil than many other crops, having the ability to utilise surplus water from deep in the soil profile. Consequently, safflower can be used to dry saturated soil profiles, for example following irrigated crops such as cotton (GRDC, 2010). Drying the soil profile has additional benefits of disease control in the following crop, for example, root rot caused by *Rhizoctonia solani* (Cook, Schillinger and Christensen 2002; GRDC, 2010). However, safflower does have a high water consumption value, which may result in decreased water availability from the water table for subsequent crops (Pfister et al., 2011). The channels created by safflower roots are able to improve the movement of air and water through the effects of cracking and aeration, which facilitates improved root development of succeeding crops (Gilbert, 2008; GRDC, 2010).

Safflower often requires less pest management than other crops. Growers have found large numbers of beneficial insects such as ladybirds (*Coccinellidae* spp.), spiders and green lacewing (*Chrysoperla carnea*) in safflower fields. These beneficial insects feed on the pest insects (described in sub-section on pests and also listed in Annex Table 3.A.1) and thus reduce the need for spraying insecticides (Hanumantharaya et al., 2008; GRDC, 2010).

Pests and diseases

Safflower is usually grown as a rainfed crop which means the incidence of disease is relatively low. However, safflower has developed from wild species growing in arid desert environments and is particularly susceptible to a large number of insects (especially in regions where it evolved) (Li and Mündel, 1996), to foliar diseases (favoured by moist environments) and root rot organisms (favoured by irrigation), summarised in Annex 3.A. If grown under irrigation, humid conditions and waterlogging favour the development of disease (GRDC, 2010).

Pests

Insects

The most serious crop damage by insects usually occurs as a result of infestations either at the time of germination or flowering, where young seedlings or developing capitula are the targets of attack (Esfahani et al., 2012; Vaani, Udikeri and Karabhantanal, 2016b).

Aphids are a major pest in many countries, having a severe rating of incidence in India, the Middle East, Asia, Russia, Africa, Spain, Australia and the United States (Li and Mündel, 1996; Esfahani et al., 2012) and infestations have caused yield losses of up to 84%, through a combination of affecting both total seed yield and seed oil content (Nimbkar, 2008; Vaani, Udikeri and Karabhantanal, 2016b). In Australia, the main insect pests of safflower are aphids (plum, green peach, leaf curl), cutworms (*Agrotis* spp.), native budworm or heliothis (*Helicoverpa* spp.), Rutherglen bugs (*Nysius vinitor*), red-legged earth mites (*Halotydeaes destructor*) and blue oat mite (*Penthaleus major*), all of which can be readily controlled with insecticides and some with biological control (GRDC, 2010; Vaani, Udikeri and Karabhantanal, 2016a).

In Iran, the serious insect pests that are associated with safflower include the safflower capsule fly (*Acanthiophilus helianthi*), aphids (*Uroleucon carthami*), capsule borer (*Helicoverpa peltigera*), spider mites (*Tetranychus urtica*) and caterpillars (*Perigaea capensis*) (Esfahani et al., 2012). Similarly, the most prevalent pests associated with safflower grown in India include aphids, the capsule borer and caterpillars

(Hanumantharaya et al., 2008). The safflower capsule fly, aphids and capsule borer are the most important pests as they can cause extensive damage to the plants and significant loss of crop yields (Saeidi et al., 2011a). Heavy infestations of the safflower capsule fly is typically associated with the reproductive phase as eggs are laid inside the developing heads, on the inner side of the bracts (Saeidi, Mirfakhraei and Mehrkhou 2012), throughout flowering. The hatched larvae then feed on the capitula bracts or seeds, which has severe impacts on both seed quality and yield, and also seed marketability (Ricci and Ciriciofolo, 1983). The safflower fly is also one of the main limiting factors on production of the crop in several countries, including countries within Africa, Asia and Europe (Saeidi et al., 2011a; Saeidi, Mirfakhraei and Mehrkhou 2012). Resistance to safflower fly has been found in wild accessions of *C. oxyacanthus* and may be used in breeding programmes to develop fly-resistant safflower cultivars (Sabzailian et al., 2010).

Other animals

The majority of crop yield loss occurs as a result of either insects (sub-section on pests) or disease (sub-section on diseases), with damage often being devastating. During a cropping season, safflower seeds can provide a food source for a range of mammals, birds and invertebrates and damage to crops can occur while they are searching for food. For some larger animals such as cattle, grazing is minimal due to the spiny nature of mature safflower plants being a deterrent (Cummings et al., 2008) but sheep and goats are not irritated by the spines. Feral pigs or boars can be destructive and have proven difficult to exclude from fields (Rao et al., 2015).

Damage to safflower crops by animals is most likely to be caused by birds, whether by feeding on the developing capitula or by chewing plants off at the base to access either developing or mature seed (GRDC, 2010; Hall, 2016). Small birds, such as sparrows, can feed on maturing safflower seed, whereas larger birds, such as cockatoos, can chew safflower plants at the base in order to access seeds (GRDC, 2010). Several other bird species have been identified by researchers as potential safflower pests including blackbirds, mallard ducks, pigeons, pheasants, ravens and crows (Cummings et al., 2008; Vazačová and Münzbergová, 2013).

Diseases

When under irrigation, diseases are much more prevalent than if purely rainfed (Nimbkar, 2008; Mirshekari et al., 2013). Safflower is susceptible to many fungal, bacterial and viral diseases and some of these can cause considerable damage (Singh and Nimbkar, 2006), with fungal disease being the most prevalent. Outbreaks of disease can devastate safflower crops.

Leaf blight, caused by the fungus *A. carthami*, is a major disease for safflower grown in India and Australia, having the potential to cause significant seed yield losses in the range of 10-50% (Irwin, 1976; Jackson, Irwin and Berthelsen 1982; Sehgal and Raina, 2011; Taware, Gholve and Dey, 2014). The disease is identifiable from the small brown to dark spots with concentric rings that form on the lower leaves of the safflower plants. These spots can coalesce and form irregular lesions. Seeds can also be infected with this fungus, identified by dark sunken lesions on the testa. If infected seeds germinate, the same spots and concentric rings will become visible on the cotyledons (Taware, Gholve and Dey 2014). The disease is favoured by temperatures in the range of 25-30°C and relative humidity of 80% (Murumkar et al., 2008).

Wilt, a seed-borne disease caused by the fungi *Fusarium proliferatum* and *F. oxysporum*, has been identified as a serious disease for safflower crops grown in India, affecting 40% to 80% of the annual crops (Singh and Kapoor, 2018). This disease has also been documented in Egypt, Australia and the USnited States (Zayed et al., 1980; GRDC, 2010) and more recently in crops grown in Korea (Kim et al., 2016). Safflower crops have been reported as having disease incidence up to 80%, resulting in significant seed yield losses. The severity of the disease significantly affects the extent of seed yield loss, which can vary from 7.2% to 100% (Govindappa, Rai and Lokesh 2011). The disease is visually identified early by the yellowing of leaves and brown discolouration of stems and roots, followed by wilting and dropping of the leaves (Govindappa, Rai and Lokesh 2011). White fungal masses can also be found in the base of the stem. As the disease progresses the infected plants may wither and die. Severe infection is typically associated with delayed flowering and in many cases, the ovaries will fail to develop seeds (Govindappa, Rai and Lokesh 2011; Kim et al., 2016). Disease resistance has been proposed as the most efficient strategy of controlling the disease (Sastry and Chattopadhyay, 2003).

Sclerotinia sclerotiorum causes head rot in safflower, which can lead to significant losses in both total seed yield and oil content (Mündel, Huang and Kozub 1985). Sclerotinia head rot is an important agronomic disease in Canada, India and the United States (Morrall and Dueck, 1982). The disease is typically isolated to the developing capitula, with diseased capitula easily identified by the discolouration of the bracts. Crop rotation is recommended to assist in the control of sclerotinia head rot, although this practice has limited success due to both the persistence in soil and the broad range of hosts including sunflower, rapeseed and soybean (Hoes and Huang, 1976; Huang and Hoes, 1980). The severity of disease was positively correlated with seed yield losses which varied significantly between different cultivars, indicative of potential resistance to sclerotinia head rot. Healthy plants, compared to their diseased controls, also had an average increased seed oil content of 4.4% (Mündel, Huang and Kozub 1985).

Charcoal rot, caused by *Macrophomina phaseolina*, has recently emerged as an important disease affecting safflower (Esfahani, Yazdi and Ostovar 2018), particularly in Iran. This disease has also been identified as a potential problem for safflower crops grown in Australia (GRDC, 2010). This causal fungus is soilborne and has also been attributed to seedling blight and root rot. Symptoms of the disease infection remain latent until the safflower plants approach the stages of flowering or maturity, although the initial infection occurs during the seedling stage (Esfahani, Yazdi and Ostovar 2018). The first symptom is wilting in high temperatures, irrespective of sufficient water. The vascular bundles become covered with fungal microsclerotia, resulting in restrictions of water and nutrient flow to higher parts of the plant. Due to the restricted flow of nutrients, the stress of high temperatures and drought often leads to premature plant death. This fungus can cause the death of approximately 25% of the crop, hence having significant impacts on seed yields (Govindappa, Lokesh and Ravishankar Rai 2005). In the absence of disease-resistant cultivars, the proposed disease management strategies include crop rotation, lowering plant densities and scheduling of both planting and irrigation dates.

Another important disease that affects safflower is root rot, which is caused by a variety of organisms including *Phytophthera cryptogea*, *P. drechsleri*, *Fusarium solani* and *Pythium ultimum* (Nasehi et al., 2013; Esfahani, Yazdi and Ostovar 2018). Although *P. cryptogea* has been reported to be the major cause of root rot (Heritage and Harrigan, 1984), *P. ultimum* has been attributed as the prominent causal agent of seed rot and seedling damping-off (Pahlavani et al., 2009). Reports of the disease have been made in Australia, the United States, Iran, Canada and Argentina (Klisiewicz, 1968; Kochman and Evans, 1969). The yield losses can be high, particularly in conditions where soils with poor drainage coincide with excess water through either irrigation or heavy rainfall. A higher incidence of infections is found when soil temperatures are in the range of 25-30°C (Erwin, 1950; Heritage and Harrigan, 1984; GRDC, 2017). Affected plants are identified by symptoms of vascular wilting, followed by desiccation and collapse of the infected tissues (Thomas, 1970; Esfahani, Yazdi and Ostovar 2018). Early symptoms of stem and root discolouration can appear 4-5 days following rain or irrigation (GRDC, 2017). The best approach to controlling the incidence of root rot and seed rot has been screening for and breeding resistant varieties (Harrigan, 1987; Mailer et al., 2008).

Rust is another fungal disease of safflower caused by *Puccinia carthami*, which has been identified as an important disease in Australia, Italy and Oman (Cappelli and Zazzerini, 1988; Deadman et al., 2005; GRDC, 2017). The disease can lead to significant yield losses, especially when the seeds or soil are contaminated with fungal spores, resulting in the death of seedlings. Significant yield losses can also occur as a result of foliar infections later in the season, leading to the loss of plant biomass (Cappelli and Zazzerini, 1988). Similar to the other fungal diseases affecting safflower, *P. carthami* favours warm and humid conditions (GRDC, 2017). Rust affected plants are identified by the presence of pustules on the leaves, which can be white, yellow or chestnut brown in appearance (Deadman et al., 2005; GRDC, 2017).

Weeds

Weeds that compete with safflower include grass and broadleaf weeds. Later in the season, many weeds can outgrow safflower in height and the resulting shading can reduce crop yields significantly (Li and Mündel, 1996). Control of weeds in safflower is essential for optimum yields.

Safflower can be sown later than other winter crops which gives farmers more time to control weeds prior to sowing. Harrowing when the safflower plants are 7-15 cm tall can give satisfactory control of small, later germinating weeds but damage to the young plants can occur if the soil is ridged or if the plants were sown too deep (Oelke et al., 1992). Safflower is more tolerant of some pre-emergent herbicides than wheat and knock-down herbicides may be used, as well as cultivation which assists in minimising resistance to selective herbicides (GRDC, 2017). Some herbicides can be used before planting the safflower crop to reduce the weed seed bank on the surface of the soil. Several pre-emergent herbicides control broadleaf and grass weeds. Post-emergent herbicides are used for the control of grass weeds, while others are used for the control of broadleaf weeds (Croissant, Johnson and Shanahan 1986; Oelke et al., 1992; GRDC, 2010). However, in Australia, in-crop herbicide options are limited for safflower, especially with respect to controlling broadleaf weeds (GRDC, 2017). Additionally, care must be taken to ensure sufficient time between the use of herbicides and subsequent planting with safflower crops (GRDC, 2017).

Additional information

Weediness of safflower crops

As with all crops cultivated and harvested at the field scale, some seed may be lost during harvest and remain in the soil until the following season when it germinates either before or following seeding of the succeeding crop. In some instances, the volunteers may provide competition to the seeded crop and warrant chemical and/or mechanical control. Volunteers can also be expected away from the planting site, for example, along roadsides and around storage facilities, as a result of spillage during transport.

Safflower lacks characteristics that are common to weeds, such as very high seed output, high seed dispersal, long-distance seed dispersal, seed shattering, persistent seed banks and rapid growth to flowering. During the rosette stage and early stages of growth, safflower is slow-growing and a poor competitor with fast-growing weeds (Li and Mündel, 1996; GRDC, 2010). Safflower is considered a minor weed of agricultural and natural ecosystems; primarily, it is an agricultural or ruderal weed found in disturbed land use areas such as debris, roadside or disused fields (Groves et al., 2003).

Safflower seed may be inadvertently dispersed into neighbouring fields or non-agricultural areas by water, wind and animals (see sub-section on seed production and natural dispersal of seeds). It is also deliberately and inadvertently spread by humans during transport and on farming equipment.

In a Canadian study, safflower volunteers had reduced plant height, seed heads per plant, seeds per head and per plant, viable seeds per plant, as well as lower seed weight, plant biomass and harvest index, in comparison to safflower crop plants. In addition, the volunteer seed viability was 50% compared to 95% for seed from crops (McPherson et al., 2009b). They were poor competitors with subsequent wheat and barley crops. These studies, conducted over several years in Canada (see sub-section on seed viability, longevity and dormancy) suggest that safflower seed and volunteers would not persist beyond two years and that common herbicide and tillage practices would control any volunteer safflower (McPherson et al., 2009b). Moreover, experienced growers in the areas surveyed were not concerned with the control of safflower in volunteers (McPherson et al., 2009b).

Lack of seed dormancy in safflower (see sub-section on seed viability, longevity and dormancy) reduces the weediness potential and volunteers after harvest are uncommon (USDA-APHIS, 2008). However, some feral populations of safflower have become established in agro-ecosystems in several states of the United States, including California, Illinois, Iowa, Kansas, New Mexico, Ohio and Utah (Bérvillé et al., 2005, and references cited therein). There is little information on how long these populations persist but anecdotal reports suggest safflower does not become established outside of agricultural areas (Bérvillé et al., 2005).

Toxicity and allergenicity

Safflower has a long history of cultivation for seed, oil and meal production primarily, although flowers and pollen are also used. Safflower products are used for food and feed, as food additives, dyes and for medicinal and industrial uses. These uses are discussed by a number of authors (see, for example, Oelke et al., 1992; Li and Mündel, 1996; Mündel et al., 2004; AOSCA, 2012). Although safflower components may contain some toxins and allergens, it is generally considered non-toxic to animals and humans.

Safflower oil is non-allergenic and suitable for use in injectable medications and cosmetics (Smith, 1996). To date, only a single case of Immunoglobulin E (IgE)-mediated response to dried safflowers (occupational asthma) has been reported (Compes et al., 2006).

Annex 3.A. Common pests and pathogens

The tables below summarise the common insect pests (Annex Table 3.A.1) and diseases (Annex Table 3.A.2) that have been associated with significant agronomic importance to the cultivation of safflower. For more information, refer to sub-section on pests and diseases.

Annex Table 3.A.1. Summary of common insect pests that affect *Carthamus tinctorius* (safflower)

Common name	Scientific name(s)	Stage affecting crop	Plant part(s) affected
Agronomically important insects			
Aphids (plum, green peach, leaf curl)	*Aphis fafia* *Brachycaudus helichrysi* *Capitophorus eleagni* *Dactynotus carthami* *Dactynotus orientalis* sp. *Dactyonotus jaceae* *Macrosiphum* sp. *Myzus persicae* *Pleotrichophorus glandolosus* *Uroleucon carthami* *Uroleucon compositae*	Nymphs and adults	Whole plant
Safflower capsule fly	*Acanthiophilus helianthi* *Chaetorellia carthami* *Terellia luteola*	Larvae	Capitula
Capsule borer <u>or</u> Silver moth	*Helicoverpa peltigera*	Larvae	Capitula and leaves
Thrips	*Aeolothrips collaris* *Haplothrips* sp. *Thrips tabaci*	Adults	Capitula and leaves
Grasshopper <u>or</u> leafhopper	*Circulifer haematoceps* *Empoasca decipiens* *Euscelis alsius* *Macrosteles laevis* *Neoaliturus fenestratus* *Psammotettix striatus*	Nymphs and adults	Whole plant
Lygus bug <u>or</u> seed bug	*Lygus hesperus* *Lygus* sp. *Oxycarenus hyalipennis* *Oxycarenus pallens*	Adults	Capitula
Other insects			
Mites: - Red-legged earth mites - Blue oat mite - Spider mites	 *Halotydeaes destructor* *Penthaleus major* *Tetranychus urtica*	Adults	Seedlings and leaves
Native budworm <u>or</u> heliothis	*Helicoverpa* spp.	Larvae	Flower buds, capitula and leaves
Cutworms and caterpillars	*Agrotis* spp. *Perigaea capensis*	Larvae	Leaves and stems
Rutherglen bug	*Nysius vinitor*	Adults	Flower buds, upper stems and capitula

Sources: GRDC (2010), *Raising the Bar with Better Safflower Agronomy*, ACT, Australia, Grains Research and Development Corporation; Saeidi, K. et al. (2011b), "Pests of safflower (*Carthamus tinctorious* L.) and their natural enemies in Gachsara, Iran", *South Asian Journal of Experimental Biology*, Vol. 1, pp. 286-291; Esfahani, M.N. et al. (2012), "The main insect pests of safflower on various plant parts in Iran", *Journal of Agricultural Science and Technology*, Vol. A2, pp. 1281-1288.

Annex Table 3.A.2. Summary of important diseases that affect *Carthamus tinctorius* (safflower)

Disease	Causal organism	Plant part(s) affected
Leaf blight	*Alternaria carthami*	Leaves, stems, capitula and seeds
Wilt	*Fusarium oxysporum* *Fusarium proliferatum* *Verticillium dahlia*	Roots, stems and leaves
Charcoal rot	*Macrophomina phaseolina*	Stem
Rust	*Puccinia carthami*	Leaves
Head rot	*Sclerotinia sclerotiorum*	Developing capitula and bracts
Root rot	*Fusarium solani* *Pythium ultimum* *Phytophthera cryptogea* *Phytophthera drechsleri* *Rhizoctonia solani*	Roots and stems

Sources: Irwin, J.A.G. (1976), "*Alternaria carthami*, a seed-borne pathogen of safflower", *Australian Journal of Experimental Agriculture*, Vol. 16, pp. 921-925; Mündel et al. (1985); Sastry, R.K. and C. Chattopadhyay (2003), "Development of Fusarium wilt-resistant genotypes in safflower (*Carthamus tinctorius*)", *European Journal of Plant Pathology*, Vol. 109, pp. 147-151; GRDC (2010), *Raising the Bar with Better Safflower Agronomy*, ACT, Australia, Grains Research and Development Corporation; Esfahani, M.N., J. Yazdi and T. Ostovar (2018), "The major diseases associated with safflower and some of the resistant sources", *Horticulture International Journal*, Vol. 2, pp. 185-192.

Annex 3.B. Biotechnological developments

The table below lists the genetically engineered safflowers which have been approved, including the type of use(s) for which they are approved, the country in which they are approved and the year in which they were approved.

Annex Table 3.B.1. Approvals of genetically engineered safflowers

OECD unique identifier	Trait(s)	Approving country	Type of approval	Date
GOR-73226-6	Increased production of oleic acid	Australia	Cultivation, Food, Feed, Processing[1]	2018, 2019
GOR-7324Ø-2	Increased production of oleic acid	Australia	Cultivation, Food, Feed, Processing[1]	2018, 2019
IND-1ØØØ3-4	Production of bovine pro-chymosin enzyme; glufosinate tolerance	Argentina	Commercial production[2]	2017
IND-1ØØ15-7	Production of bovine pro-chymosin enzyme; glufosinate tolerance	Argentina	Commercial production[2]	2017
IND-1ØØØ3-4 x IND-1ØØ15-7	Production of bovine pro-chymosin enzyme; glufosinate tolerance	Argentina	Commercial production[2]	2017

Sources:

1. OECD, *BioTrack Product Database*, https://biotrackproductdatabase.oecd.org/ (accessed 13 May 2020); CBD (n.d.), *Biosafety Clearing House Central Portal*, http://bch.cbd.int/ (accessed 13 May 2020); ISAAA, *GM Approval Database*, http://www.isaaa.org/gmapprovaldatabase/default.asp (accessed 13 May 2020); FSANZ (n.d.), *Current GM Applications and Approvals*, https://www.foodstandards.gov.au/consumer/gmfood/applications/Pages/default.aspx.
2. MAGyP (n.d.), *Resolution RESOL-2017-103-APN-SECAV#MA Approving GM Safflower Varieties for Commercial Production*, https://www.magyp.gob.ar/sitio/areas/biotecnologia/ogm/_archivos/RS-2017-31775583.pdf.

References

Ali, F. et al. (2019), "Mobile genomic element diversity in world collection of safflower (*Carthamus tinctorius* L.) panel using iPBS-retrotransposon markers", *PLOS ONE*, Vol. 14, e0211985.

Anderson, R.L. (1987), "Broadleaf weed control in safflower (*Carthamus tinctorius*) with sulfonylurea herbicides", *Weed Technology*, Vol. 1, pp. 242-246.

Anjani, K. (2005), "Development of cytoplasmic-genic male sterility in safflower", *Plant Breeding*, Vol. 124, pp. 310-312.

AOSCA (2012), *AOSCA Standards and Procedures for Producing Certified Safflower Seed*, Association of Official Seed Certifying Agencies.

Ashri, A. (1971), "Evaluation of the world collection of safflower, *Carthamus tinctorius* L. II. Resistance to the safflower fly, *Acanthophilus helianthi* R.", *Euphytica*, Vol. 20, pp. 410-415.

Ashri, A. and Y. Efron (1964), "Inheritance studies with fertile interspecific hybrids of three *Carthamus* L. species", *Crop Science*, Vol. 4, pp. 510-514.

Ashri, A. and P.F. Knowles (1960), "Cytogenetics of safflower (*Carthamus* L.) species and their hybrids", *Agronomy Journal*, Vol. 52, pp. 11-17.

Ashri, A. and J. Rudich (1965), "Unequal reciprocal natural hybridization rates between two *Carthamus* L. species", *Crop Science*, Vol. 5, pp. 190-191.

Baydar, H., O.Y. Gökmen and W. Friedt (2003), "Hybrid seed production in safflower (*Carthamus tinctorius*) following the induction of male sterility by gibberellic acid", *Plant Breeding*, Vol. 122, pp. 459-461.

Bellé, R.A. et al. (2012), "Safflower grown in different sowing dates and plant densities", *Ciência Rural*, Vol. 42, pp. 2145-2152.

Bérvillé, A. et al. (2005), "Issues of ferality or potential for ferality in oats, olives, the *Vigna* group, ryegrass species, safflower and sugarcane", in *Crop Ferality and Volunteerism*, CRC Press, pp. 231-255.

Boch, R. (1961), "Honeybee activity on safflower (*Carthamus tinctorius* L.)", *Canadian Journal of Plant Science*, Vol. 41, pp. 559-562.

Bockisch, M. (1998), "Vegetable fats and oils", in M. Bockisch (ed.), *Fats and Oils Handbook*, AOCS Press, pp. 174-344.

Brown, C.A. et al. (2010), "Rapid expansion and functional divergence of subtelomeric gene families in yeasts", *Current Biology*, Vol. 20, pp. 895-903.

Bukero, A. et al. (2015), "Floral activity time period of pollinators on safflower *Carthamus tinctorius* L.", *Science International*, Vol. 27, pp. 347-348.

Bullock, J.M. and R.T. Clarke (2000), "Long distance seed dispersal by wind: Measuring and modelling the tail of the curve", *Oecologia*, Vol. 124, pp. 506-521.

Bullock, S.H. and R.B. Primack (1977), "Comparative experimental study of seed dispersal on animals", *Ecology*, Vol. 58, pp. 681-686.

Cappelli, C. and A. Zazzerini (1988), "Safflower rust (*Puccinia carthami* Cda.) in Italy: seed contamination, seed-plant transmission and seed dressing for disease control", *Phytopathologia Mediterranea*, Vol. 27, pp. 145-147.

CBD (n.d.), *Biosafety Clearing House Central Portal*, Convention on Biological Diversity, UN Environment Programme, http://bch.cbd.int/ (accessed 13 May 2020).

Cerioni, G.A. et al. (1999), "Comportamiento de cultivares de cártamo ("*Carthamus tinctorius*" L.) en la región de Río Cuarto, Córdoba (Argentina)", *Investigación agraria Producción y protección vegetales*, Vol. 14, pp. 203-216.

Chapman, M.A. and J.M. Burke (2006), "Letting the gene out of the bottle: The population genetics of genetically modified crops", *New Phytologist*, Vol. 170, pp. 429-443.

Chapman, M.A. et.al. (2010), "Population genetic analysis of safflower (*Carthamus tinctorius*; Asteraceae) reveals a Near Eastern origin and five centers of diversity", *American Journal of Botany*, Vol. 97, pp. 831-840.

Chavan, V.M. (1961), *Niger and Safflower*, Hyderabad, Indian Central Oilseeds Committee.

Claassen, C.E. (1950), "Natural and controlled crossing in safflower, *Carthamus tinctorius* L.", *Agronomy Journal*, Vol. 42, pp. 381-384.

Compes, E. et al. (2006), "Occupational asthma from dried flowers of *Carthamus tinctorius* (safflower) and *Achillea millefolium* (yarrow)", *Allergy*, Vol. 61, pp. 1239-1240.

Cook, R.J., W.F. Schillinger and N.W. Christensen (2002), "*Rhizoctonia* root rot and take-all of wheat in diverse direct-seed spring cropping systems", *Canadian Journal of Plant Pathology*, Vol. 24, pp. 349-358.

Corleto, A. (2008), "A note on safflower plant ideotype suitable for Mediterranean environments", paper presented at "Safflower: Unexploited Potential and World Adaptability, 7th International Safflower Conference", Wagga Wagga, NSW, Australia.

Cresswell, J.E. (2010), "A mechanistic model of pollinator-mediated gene flow in agricultural safflower", *Basic and Applied Ecology*, Vol. 11, pp. 415-421.

Cresswell, J.E. (2000), "A comparison of bumblebees' movements in uniform and aggregated distributions of their forage plant", *Ecological Entomology*, Vol. 25, pp. 19-25.

Cresswell, J.E. (1999), "The influence of nectar and pollen availability on pollen transfer by individual flowers of oil-seed rape (*Brassica napus*) when pollinated by bumblebees (*Bombus lapidarius*)", *Journal of Ecology*, Vol. 87, pp. 670-677.

Croissant, R.L., D.L. Johnson and J.F. Shanahan (1986), *Safflower Production in Colorado,* Report No. 111, Colorado State University Cooperative Extension.

Cummings, J.L. et al. (2008), "Dispersal of viable row-crop seeds of commercial agriculture by farmland birds: Implication for genetically modified crops", *Environmental biosafety research*, Vol. 7, pp. 241-252.

Deadman, M.L. et al. (2005), "First report of rust caused by *Puccinia carthami* on safflower in Oman", *Plant Disease*, Vol. 89, pp. 208.

Deshmukh, S.N., M.M. Wakode and R.D. Ratnaparakhi (2014), "Cytoplasmic male sterility development in safflower", *PKV Research Journal*, Vol. 38, pp. 1-3.

Deshpande, R.B. (1952), "Wild safflower (*Carthamus oxyacantha* Bieb.) - A possible oilseed crop for the desert and arid regions", *Indian Journal of Genetics and Plant Breeding*, Vol. 12, pp. 10-14.

Ellstrand, N.C., H.C. Prentice and J.F. Hancock (1999), "Gene flow and introgression from domesticated plants into their wild relatives", *Annual Review of Ecology and Systematics*, Vol. 30, pp. 539-563.

Emongor, V. (2010), "Safflower (*Carthamus tinctorius* L.) the underutilized and neglected crop: A review", *Asian Journal of Plant Sciences*, Vol. 9, pp. 299-306.

Erwin, D.C. (1950), "*Phytophthora* root rot of safflower in Nebraska caused by P*hytophthora drechsteri*", *Plant Disease Reporter*, Vol. 34, pp. 306.

Esfahani, M.N., J. Yazdi and T. Ostovar (2018), "The major diseases associated with safflower and some of the resistant sources", *Horticulture International Journal*, Vol. 2, pp. 185-192.

Esfahani, M.N. et al., (2018), "The major diseases associated with safflower and some of the resistant sources", *Horticulture International Journal*, Vol. 2, pp. 185-192.

Esfahani, M.N. et al. (2012), "The main insect pests of safflower on various plant parts in Iran", *Journal of Agricultural Science and Technology*, Vol. A2, pp. 1281-1288.

Estilai, A. and P.F. Knowles (1976), "Cytogenetic studies of *Carthamus divaricatus* with eleven pairs of chromosomes and its relationship to other *Carthamus* species (Compositae)", *American Journal of Botany*, Vol. 63, pp.771-782.

FAOSTAT (2022), *Crop Production Data*, Food and Agriculture Organization of the United Nations, Statistics Division online database, https://www.fao.org/faostat/ (accessed 3 February 2022).

FSANZ (n.d.), *Current GM Applications and Approvals*, Food Standards Australia New Zealand, https://www.foodstandards.gov.au/consumer/gmfood/applications/Pages/default.aspx.

Garnatje, T. et al. (2006), "Genome size variation in the genus *Carthamus* (Asteraceae, Cardueae): Systematic implications and additive changes during allopolyploidization", *Annals of Botany*, Vol. 97, pp. 461-467.

Gary, N. et al. (1977), "The interfield distribution of honey bees foraging on carrots, onions, and safflower", *Environmental Entomology*, Vol. 6, pp. 637-640.

GBIF (2020), *Global Biodiversity Information Facility*, Denmark, https://www.gbif.org/ (accessed 13 May 2020).

GBIF Backbone Taxonomy (2017), "*Carthamus* L.", in *GBIF Secretariat.*

Gilbert, J. (2008), "International safflower production - An overview", Paper presented at "Safflower: Unexploited Potential and World Adaptability, 7th International Safflower Conference", Wagga Wagga, NSW, Australia.

Govindappa, M., S. Lokesh and V. Ravishankar Rai (2005), "A new stem-splitting symptom in safflower caused by *Macrophomina phaseolina*", *Journal of Phytopathology*, Vol. 153, pp. 560-561.

Govindappa, M., V.R. Rai and S. Lokesh (2011), "*In vitro* and *in vivo* responses of different treating agents against wilt disease of safflower", *Journal of Cereals and Oilseeds*, Vol. 2, pp. 16-25.

GRDC (2017), *GrowNotes Safflower Northern*, Grains Research and Development Corporation, Australia.

GRDC (2010), *Raising the Bar with Better Safflower Agronomy*, ACT, Australia, Grains Research and Development Corporation.

Groves, R.H. et al. (2003), *Weed Categories for Natural and Agricultural Ecosystem Management*, Bureau of Rural Sciences, Canberra.

Hall, C. (2016), "Overview of the Oilseed Safflower (*Carthamus tinctorius* L.)", in *Reference Module in Food Science*, Elsevier.

Hamdan, Y. et al. (2009), "Inheritance of high oleic acid content in safflower", *Euphytica*, Vol. 168, pp. 61-69.

Hamdan, Y. et al. (2008), "Inheritance of very high linoleic acid content and its relationship with nuclear male sterility in safflower", *Plant Breeding*, Vol. 127, pp. 507-509.

Hanumantharaya, L. et al. (2008), "Pest status of safflower, *Carthamus tinctorius* L. in northern parts of Karnataka", Paper presented at: "Safflower: Unexploited Potential and World Adaptability, 7th International Safflower Conference", Wagga Wagga, NSW, Australia.

Harrigan, E.K.S. (1987), "Safflower registration of cv. Sironaria", *Sesame and Safflower Newsletter*, Vol. 3, pp. 47-49.

Haygood, R., A.R. Ives and D.A. Andow (2003), "Consequences of recurrent gene flow from crops to wild relatives", *Proceedings of the Royal Society of London Series B: Biological Sciences*, Vol. 270, pp. 1879-1886.

Heaton, T.C. and J.M. Klisiewicz (1981), "A disease-resistant safflower alloploid from *Carthamus tinctorius* L. x *C. lanatus* L.", *Canadian Journal of Plant Science*, Vol. 61, pp. 219-224.

HerbiGuide (2014a), *Safflower*, (accessed 13 May 2020).

HerbiGuide (2014b), *Weeds*, (accessed 13 May 2020).

Heritage, A.D. and E.K.S. Harrigan (1984), "Environmental factors influencing safflower screening for resistance to *Phytophthora cryptogea*", *Plant Disease*, pp. 767-769.

Heuzé, V. et al. (2015), *Safflower (*Carthamus tinctorius*) seeds and oil meal, Feedipedia: A programme by INRA, CIRAD, AFZ and FAO*, https://www.feedipedia.org/node/49 (accessed 30 July 2020).

Hoes, J.A. and H.C. Huang (1976), "Importance of disease to sunflower in Manitoba in 1975", *Canadian Plant Disease Survey*, Vol. 56, pp. 75-76.

Huang, H.C. and J.A. Hoes (1980), "Importance of plant spacing and sclerotial position to development of *Sclerotinia* wilt of sunflower", *Plant Disease*, Vol. 64, pp. 81-84.

Imrie, B.C. and P.F. Knowles (1970), "Inheritance studies in interspecific hybrids between *Carthamus flavescens* and *C. tinctorius*", *Crop Science*, Vol. 10, pp. 349-352.

Irwin, J.A.G. (1976), "*Alternaria carthami*, a seed-borne pathogen of safflower", *Australian Journal of Experimental Agriculture*, Vol. 16, pp. 921-925.

ISAAA , *GM Approval Database*, International Service for the Acquisition of Agri-biotech Applications, http://www.isaaa.org/gmapprovaldatabase/default.asp (accessed 13 May 2020).

Jackson, K.J., J.A.G. Irwin and J.E. Berthelsen (1982), "Effect of *Alternaria carthami* on the yield, yield components and seed quality of safflower", *Australian Journal of Experimental Agriculture and Animal Husbandry*, Vol. 22, pp. 221-225.

Jochinke, D. et al. (2008), "Growing safflower in Australia: Part 1- History, experiences and current constraints on production", Paper presented at: "Safflower: Unexploited Potential and World Adaptability, 7th International Safflower Conference", Wagga Wagga, NSW, Australia.

Joshi, A.B. (1979), "Breeding methodology for autogamous crops", *Indian Journal of Genetics and Plant Breeding*, Vol. 39, pp. 567-578.

Kadam, B.S. and V.K. Patankar (1942), "Natural cross-pollination in safflower", *Indian Journal of Genetics and Plant Breeding*, Vol. 2, pp. 69-70.

Kaffka, S.R. and T.E. Kearney (1998), "Safflower production in California", *University of California Agriculture and Natural Resources*, Vol. 21565.

Kammili, A. (2013), "Genetic linkage between male sterility and non-spiny trait in safflower (*Carthamus tinctorius* L.)", *Plant Breeding*, Vol. 132, pp. 180-184.

Kashtwari, M., A.A. Wani and R.N. Rather (2019), "TILLING: An alternative path for crop improvement", *Journal of Crop Improvement*, Vol. 33, pp. 83-109.

Kim, S.G. et al. (2016), "First report of Fusarium wilt caused by *Fusarium proliferatum* on safflower", *Research in Plant Disease*, Vol. 22, pp. 111-115.

Klisiewicz, J.M. (1968), "Relation of *Pythium spp.* to root rot and damping-off of safflower", *Phytopathology*, Vol. 58, pp. 1384-1386.

Knowles, P.F. (1989), “Safflower”, in G. Röbbelen, R.K. Downey and A. Ashri (eds.), *Oil Crops of the World: Their Breeding and Utilization*, McGraw Hill, New York, pp. 363-374.

Knowles, P.F. (1980), “Safflower”, in W.R. Fehr and H.H. Hadley (eds.), *Hybridization of Crop Plants*, American Society of Agronomy and Crop Science Society of America, Madison, pp. 535-548.

Knowles, P.F. (1969a), “Centers of plant diversity and conservation of crop germplasm: Safflower”, *Economic Botany*, Vol. 23, pp. 324-349.

Knowles, P.F. (1969b), “Modification of quantity and quality of safflower oil through plant breeding”, *Journal of the American Oil Chemists' Society*, Vol. 46, pp. 130-132.

Knowles, P.F. (1968), “Registration of UC-1 Safflower1 (Reg. No. 6)”, *Crop Science*, Vol. 8, pp. 641.

Knowles, P.F. and A. Ashri (1995), “Safflower: *Carthamus tinctorius* (Compositae)”, in: J. Smartt and N.W. Simmonds (eds.), *Evolution of Crop Plants*, Longman, Harlow, UK, pp. 47-50.

Knowles, P.F. and S.C. Schank (1964), “Artificial hybrids of *Carthamus nitidus* Boiss. and *C. tinctorius* L. (Compositae)”, *Crop Science*, Vol. 4, pp. 596-599.

Knowles, P.F. et al. (1965), *Safflower*, Report No. 532, Division of Agricultural Sciences University of California.

Kochman, J.K. and G. Evans (1969), “Fungi associated with root rot of irrigated safflower in the Namoi Valley, New South Wales”, *Australian Journal of Experimental Agriculture and Animal Husbandry*, Vol. 9, pp. 644-647.

Kotecha, A. and L.H. Zimmerman (1978), “Genetics of seed dormancy and its association with other traits in safflower”, *Crop Science*, Vol. 18, pp. 1003-1007.

Kumar, H. (1991), “Cytogenetics of Safflower”, in T. Tsuchiya and P.K. Gupta (eds.), *Chromosome Engineering in Plants: Genetics, Breeding and Evolution Part B*, *Development in Plant Genetics and Breeding: 2B*, Elsevier Science, pp. 251-277.

Kumar, S. et al. (2015), “Assessment of genetic diversity and population structure in a global reference collection of 531 accessions of *Carthamus tinctorius* L. (safflower) using AFLP markers”, *Plant Molecular Biology Reporter*, Vol. 33, pp. 1299-1313.

Kumar, S.P. and B.D.R. Kumari (2011), “Factors affecting on somatic embryogenesis of safflower (*Carthamus tinctorius* L) at morphological and biochemical levels”, *World Journal of Agricultural Sciences*, Vol. 7, pp. 197-205.

Kumari, A. and A.K. Pandey (2005), “Pollination mechanism and behaviour of pollinators in safflower (*Carthamus tinctorius* L.)”, *Journal of the Indian Botanical Society*, Vol. 84, pp. 57-61.

Kunin, W.E. (1997), “Population size and density effects in pollination: Pollinator foraging and plant reproductive success in experimental arrays of *Brassica kaber*”, *Journal of Ecology*, Vol. 85, pp. 225-234.

Langridge, D.F. and R.D. Goodman (1980), “A study of pollination of safflower (*Carthamus tinctorius*) cv. Gila.”, *Australian Journal of Experimental Agriculture*, Vol. 20, pp. 105-107.

Levin, M.D. and G.D. Butler (1966), “Bees associated with safflower in South Central Arizona”, *Journal of Economic Entomology*, Vol. 59, pp. 654-657.

Li, D. and H.H. Mündel (1996), *Safflower.* Carthamus tinctorius *L., Vol. 7*, Institute of Plant Genetics and Crop Plant Research, Gatersleben/International Plant Genetic Resources Institute, Rome.

López-González, G. (1990), “Acerca de la clasificación natural del género” Carthamus” L., s. I.”, *Anales del Jardín Botánico de Madrid*, Vol. 47, pp. 11-34.

Macas, J., A. Navrátilová and T. Mészáros (2003), “Sequence subfamilies of satellite repeats related to rDNA intergenic spacer are differentially amplified on *Vicia sativa* chromosomes”, *Chromosoma*, Vol. 112, pp. 152-158.

Mack, R.N. and W.M. Lonsdale (2001), “Humans as global plant dispersers: Getting more than we bargained for”, *BioScience*, Vol. 51, pp. 95-102.

MAGyP (n.d.), *Resolution RESOL-2017-103-APN-SECAV#MA Approving GM Safflower Varieties for Commercial Production*, Ministerio de Agricultura, Ganadería y Pesca (Ministry of Agriculture, Livestock and Fisheries), Argentina, https://www.magyp.gob.ar/sitio/areas/biotecnologia/ogm/_archivos/RS-2017-31775583.pdf.

Mailer, R.J. et al. (2008), “Quality evaluation of safflower (*Carthamus tinctorius* L.) cultivars”, Paper presented at: “Safflower: Unexploited Potential and World Adaptability, 7th International Safflower Conference”, Wagga Wagga, NSW, Australia.

Mattson, J.W., C. Sun and W.W. Koo (2004), *Analysis of the World Oil Crops Market*, Center for Agricultural Policy and Trade Studies, North Dakota University.

Mayerhofer, M. et al. (2011), “Introgression potential between safflower (*Carthamus tinctorius*) and wild relatives of the genus *Carthamus*", *BMC Plant Biology*, Vol. 11, pp. 47-57.

McPherson, M.A. et al. (2009a), "Pollen-mediated gene flow from transgenic safflower (*Carthamus tinctorius* L.) intended for plant molecular farming to conventional safflower", *Environmental Biosafety Research*, Vol. 8, pp. 19-32.

McPherson, M.A. et al. (2009b), "Potential for seed-mediated gene flow in agroecosystems from transgenic safflower (*Carthamus tinctorius* L.) intended for plant molecular farming", *Transgenic Research*, Vol. 18, pp. 281-299.

McPherson, M.A. et al. (2004), "Theoretical hybridization potential of transgenic safflower (*Carthamus tinctorius* L.) with weedy relatives in the New World", *Canadian Journal of Plant Science*, Vol. 84, pp. 923-934.

Meena, H.P. et al. (2012), "Heterosis breeding in safflower: Present status and future prospects under Indian scenario", *Journal of Oilseeds Research*, Vol. 29, pp. 164-167.

Mikkelsen, E. et al. (2008), "The effect of sowing depth on safflower germination and early growth in clay and sandy soils", Paper presented at: "Safflower: Unexploited Potential and World Adaptability, 7th International Safflower Conference", Wagga Wagga, NSW, Australia.

Mirshekari, M. et al. (2013), "Effect of sowing date and irrigation treatment on safflower seed quality", *Journal of Agricultural Science and Technology*, Vol. 15, pp. 505-515.

Morrall, R.A.A. and J. Dueck (1982), "Epidemiology of *Sclerotinia* stem rot of rapeseed in Saskatchewan", *Canadian Journal of Plant Pathology*, Vol. 4, pp. 161-168.

Mündel, H.H. et al. (2004), *Safflower Production on the Canadian Prairies: Revisited in 2004*, Agriculture and Agri-Food Canada.

Mündel, H.H. et al. (1985), "Sclerotinia head rot in safflower: Assessment of resistance and effects on yield and oil content", *Canadian Journal of Plant Science*, Vol. 65, pp. 259265.

Mündel, H.H., H.C. Huang and G.C. Kozub (1985), "Sclerotinia head rot in safflower: Assessment of resistance and effects on yield and oil content", *Canadian Journal of Plant Science*, Vol. 65, pp. 259-265.

Murumkar, D.R. et al. (2008), "Field evaluation of some newer fungicides against leaf spot of safflower caused by *Alternaria carthami*", Paper presented at: "Safflower: Unexploited Potential and World Adaptability, 7th International Safflower Conference", Wagga Wagga, NSW, Australia.

Nabloussi, A., L. Velasco and J.M. Fernandez-Martines (2013), "Cross pollination of safflower (*Carthamus tinctorius* L.) under Moroccan environmental conditions", *International Journal of Plant Breeding*, Vol. 7, pp. 145-147.

Nasehi, A. et al. (2013), "Screen of safflower (*Carthamus tinctorius* L.) genotypes against *Phytophthora drechsleri* and *Fusarium solani*, the causal agents of root rot disease", *Archives of Phytopathology and Plant Protection*, Vol. 46, pp. 2025-2034.

Nimbkar, N. (2008), "Issues in safflower production in India", Paper presented at: "Safflower: Unexploited Potential and World Adaptability, 7th International Safflower Conference", Wagga Wagga, NSW, Australia.

OECD, *BioTrack Product Database*, OECD, Paris, https://biotrackproductdatabase.oecd.org/ (accessed 13 May 2020).

Oelke, E.A. et al. (1992), *Safflower*, University of Wisconsin.

Oyen, L.P.A. and B.E. Umali (2007), *Carthamus tinctorius* L., Record from PROTA4U (Plant Resources of Tropical Africa/Ressources végétales de l'Afrique tropicale) (accessed 13 May 2020).

Ozkan, H., M. Tuna and K. Arumuganathan (2003), "Nonadditive changes in genome size during allopolyploidization in the wheat (*Aegilops*-Triticum) group", *Journal of Heredity*, Vol. 94, pp. 260-264.

Pahlavani, M.H. et al. (2009), "Influence of temperature and genotype on *Pythium* damping-off in safflower", *Journal of Plant Breeding and Crop Science*, Vol. 1, pp. 1-7.

Pandey, A.K. and A. Kumari (2008), "Pollination ecology of safflower (*Carthamus tinctorius* linn)", Paper presented at: "Safflower: Unexploited Potential and World Adaptability, 7th International Safflower Conference", Wagga Wagga, NSW, Australia.

Patel, M.Z. et al. (1989), "Genetic divergence in safflower (*Carthamus tinctorius* L.)", *Indian Journal of Genetics and Plant Breeding*, Vol. 49, pp. 113-118.

Pearl, S.A. et al. (2014), "Genetic analysis of safflower domestication", *BMC Plant Biology*, Vol. 14, pp. 43.

Pfister, S. et al. (2011), "Environmental impacts of water use in global crop production: Hotspots and trade-offs with land use", *Environmental Science and Technology*, Vol. 45, pp. 5761-5768.

Pillai, R.S.N., H. Kumar and R.B. Singh (1981), "Translocation homozygotes in safflower identification and frequency of chromosomes involved in the interchanges", *Crop Science*, Vol. 21, pp. 815-818.

Raina, S.N. et al. (2005), "Novel repeated DNA sequences in safflower (*Carthamus tinctorius* L.) (Asteraceae): Cloning, sequencing, and physical mapping by fluorescence in situ hybridization", *Journal of Heredity*, Vol. 96, pp. 424-429.

Randall, R.P. (2017), *A Global Compendium of Weeds*, Third edition, R.P. Randall, Perth, Western Australia.

Ranga Rao, V., M. Ramachandram and V. Arunachalam (1977), "An analysis of association of components of yield and oil in safflower (*Carthamus tinctorius* L.)", *Theoretical and Applied Genetics*, Vol. 50, pp. 185-191.

Rao, V.V. et al. (2015), "Traditional management methods used to minimize wild boar (*Sus scrofa*) damage in different agricultural crops at Telangana state, India", *International Journal of Multidisciplinary Research and Development*, Vol. 2, pp. 32-36.

Ricci, C. and E. Ciriciofolo (1983), "Osservazioni sull'*Acanthophilus helianthi* Rossi (Diptera Tephritidae) dannoso al cartamo in Italia centrale", *Redia*, Vol. 66, pp. 577-592.

Ridley, C.E. and L.C. Alexander (2016), "Applying gene flow science to environmental policy needs: A boundary work perspective", *Evolutionary Applications*, Vol. 9, pp. 924-936.

Rubis, D.D. (2001), "Developing new characteristics during 50 years of safflower breeding", Paper presented at the 5th International Safflower Conference, Williston, North Dakota and Sidney, Montana, US.

Rubis, D.D. (1981), "Development of root rot resistance in safflower by introgressive hybridization and thin-hull facilitated recurrent selection", Paper presented at the 1st International Safflower Conference, University of California, Davis, California, US.

Rudolphi, S., H.C. Becker and S. von Witzke-Ehbrecht (2008), "Outcrossing rate of safflower (*Carthamus tinctorius* L.) genotypes under the agro climatic conditions of northern Germany", Paper presented at: "Safflower: Unexploited Potential and World Adaptability, 7th International Safflower Conference", Wagga Wagga, NSW, Australia.

Sabetta, W. et al. (2011), "sunTILL: A TILLING resource for gene function analysis in sunflower", *Plant Methods*, Vol. 7, pp. 13.

Sabzalian, M.R. et al. (2010), "Wild safflower species (*Carthamus oxyacanthus*): A possible source of resistance to the safflower fly (*Acanthiophilus helianthi*)", *Crop Protection*, Vol. 29, pp. 550-555.

Saeidi, K., S. Mirfakhraei and F. Mehrkhou (2012), "Growth and development of *Acanthiophilus helianthi* Ross (Diptera: Tephritidae) feeding on safflower, *Carthamus tinctorius*", *Journal of Research in Agricultural Science*, Vol. 7, pp. 244-249.

Saeidi, K. et al. (2011a), "Efficacy of various insecticides on safflower fly, *Acanthiophilus helianthi* Rossi (Diptera: Tephritidae) in Kohgiloyeh and Boyerahmad province (Iran)", *Australian Journal of Basic and Applied Science*, Vol. 5, pp. 2660-2664.

Saeidi, K. et al. (2011b), "Pests of safflower (*Carthamus tinctorious* L.) and their natural enemies in Gachsara, Iran", *South Asian Journal of Experimental Biology*, Vol. 1, pp. 286-291.

Sastry, R.K. and C. Chattopadhyay (2003), "Development of Fusarium wilt-resistant genotypes in safflower (*Carthamus tinctorius*)", *European Journal of Plant Pathology*, Vol. 109, pp. 147-151.

Sehgal, D. and S.N. Raina (2011), "Carthamus", in C. Kole (ed.), *Wild Crop Relatives: Genomic and Breeding Resources*, Springer Berlin Heidelberg, pp. 63-95.

Sehgal, D. et al. (2009), "Nuclear DNA assay in solving issues related to ancestry of the domesticated diploid safflower (*Carthamus tinctorius* L.) and the polyploid (*Carthamus*) taxa, and phylogenetic and genomic relationships in the genus *Carthamus* L. (Asteraceae)", *Molecular Phylogenetics and Evolution*, Vol. 53, pp. 631-644.

Sheidai, M., M. Sotoode and Z. Nourmohammadi (2009), "Chromosome pairing and cytomixis in safflower (*Carthamus tinctorius* L., Asteraceae) cultivars", *Cytologia*, Vol. 74, pp. 43-53.

Siddiqui, M.H. and F.C. Oad (2006), "Nitrogen requirement of safflower (*Carthamus tinctorius* L.) for growth and yield traits", *Asian Journal of Plant Sciences*, Vol. 5, pp. 563-565.

Sikora, P. et al. (2011), "Mutagenesis as a tool in plant genetics, functional genomics, and breeding", *International Journal of Plant Genomics*, Vol. 2011.

Singh, N. and R. Kapoor (2018), "Quick and accurate detection of *Fusarium oxysporum* f. sp. *carthami* in host tissue and soil using conventional and real-time PCR assay", *World Journal of Microbiology and Biotechnology*, Vol. 34, pp. 175.

Singh, R.B., R.S.N. Pillai and H. Kumar (1981), "Induced translocations in safflower", *Crop Science*, Vol. 21, pp. 811-815.

Singh, V. (1997), "Identification of genetic linkage between male sterility and dwarfness in safflower", *The Indian Journal of Genetics and Plant Breeding*, Vol. 57, pp. 327-332.

Singh, V. (1996), "Inheritance of genetic male sterility in safflower", *The Indian Journal of Genetics and Plant*

Breeding, Vol. 56, pp. 490-494.

Singh, V. and N. Nimbkar (2006), "Safflower (*Carthamus tinctorius* L.)", in *Genetic Resources, Chromosome Engineering, and Crop Improvement: Oilseed Crops*, CRC Press, pp. 167-194.

Singh, V., M.B. Deshpande and N. Nimbkar (2003), "NARI-NH-1: The first non-spiny hybrid safflower released in India", *Sesame and Safflower Newsletter*, Vol. 18, pp. 77-79.

Singh, V., A.M. Ranaware and N. Nimbkar (2008), "Breeding for Fusarium wilt resistance in safflower", Paper presented at: *Safflower: Unexploited Potential and World Adaptability, 7th International Safflower Conference*, Wagga Wagga, NSW, Australia.

Smith, J.R. (1996), *Safflower*, Champaign, Illinois, AOCS Press.

Sujatha, M. (2008), "Biotechnological interventions for genetic improvement of safflower", Paper presented at: *Safflower: Unexploited Potential and World Adaptability, 7th International Safflower Conference*, Wagga Wagga, NSW, Australia.

Taware, M.R., V.M. Gholve and U. Dey (2014), "Bio-efficacy of fungicides, bioagents and plant extracts/botanicals against *Alternaria carthami*, the causal agent of *Alternaria* blight of safflower (*Carthamus tinctorius* L.)", *African Journal of Microbiology Research*, Vol. 8, pp. 1400-1412.

Teotia, D.S. et al. (2017), "Agro-ecological characteristics and ethanobotanical significance of safflower (*Carthamus tinctorius* L.): An overview", *Archives of Agriculture and Environmental Science*, Vol. 2, pp. 228-231.

Thalji, T. and B. Alqarallah (2015), "Study of safflower (*Carthamus Tinctorius* L.) cultivation under the Jordanian (Mediterranean) conditions", *International Journal of Agriculture Innovations and Research*, Vol. 3, pp. 2319-1473.

Thomas, C.A. (1970), "Effect of seedling age on *Pythium* root rot of safflower", *Plant Disease Reporter*, Vol. 54, pp. 1010-1011.

Thomas, C.A., D.D. Rubis and D.S. Black (1960), "Development of safflower varieties resistant to *Phytophthora* root rot", *Phytopathology*, Vol. 50, pp. 129-130.

Torchio, P.F. (1966), "A survey of alfalfa pollinators and pollination in the San Joaquin Valley of California with emphasis on establishment of the alkali bee", Master of Science Thesis, Oregon State.

Urie, A.L. and D.E. Zimmer (1970), "A reduced-hull seed character of safflower", *Crop Science*, Vol. 10, pp. 371-372.

USDA-APHIS (2008), *Finding of No Significant Impact and Decision Notice (Permit Application 06-363-103r)*, Animal and Plant Health Inspection Service, United States Department of Agriculture.

USDA-APHIS (2006), "Workshop on confinement of genetically engineered crops during field testing", Paper presented at USDA APHIS.

Vaani, M.N., S.S. Udikeri and S.S. Karabhantanal (2016a), "Baseline toxicology of insecticide for safflower aphid *Urolechon compositae* Theobald (Hemiptera: Aphididae)", *The Bioscan*, Vol. 11, pp. 841-845.

Vaani, M.N., S.S. Udikeri and S.S. Karabhantanal (2016b), "Bioefficacy, yield and economic impact of protecting aphid *Uroleucon compositae* (Theobald) pest in safflower through selected insecticides and biorationals", *Research in Environment and Life Sciences*, Vol. 9, pp. 826-829.

Van Deynze, A.E., F.J. Sundstrom and K.J. Bradford (2005), "Pollen-mediated gene flow in California cotton depends on pollinator activity", *Crop Science*, Vol. 45, pp. 1565-1570.

Vander Wall, S.B., K.M. Kuhn and M.J. Beck (2005), "Seed removal, seed predation, and secondary dispersal", *Ecology*, Vol. 86, pp. 801-806.

Vazačová, K. and Z. Münzbergová (2013), "Simulation of seed digestion by birds: How does it reflect the real passage through a pigeon's gut?", *Folia Geobotanica*, Vol. 48, pp. 257-269.

Velasco, L., M. Fischer and J.M. Fernandez-Martinez (2012), "Short communication. Estimation of cross-fertilization rate in safflower (*Carthamus tinctorius* L.)", *Spanish Journal of Agricultural Research*, Vol. 10, pp. 155-159.

Wachsmann, N. et al. (2008), "Growing safflower in Australia: Part 2-Agronomic research and suggestions to increase yields and production", Paper presented at: "Safflower: Unexploited Potential and World Adaptability, 7th International Safflower Conference", Wagga Wagga, NSW, Australia.

Wachsmann, N. et al. (2003), "The comparative growth, yield and water use of safflower, Linola™, mustard, canola and wheat in southern Australia", Paper presented at the 11th Australian Agronomy Conference, Australian Society of Agronomy.

Weiss, E.A. (2000), "Safflower", in *Oilseed Crops*, Blackwell Science Ltd, pp. 93-129.

Weiss, E.A. (1971), "Safflower", in *Castor, Sesame and Safflower*, Leonard Hill Books, London, pp. 529-746.

Wichelns, D., T.F. Weaver and P.M. Brooks (1992), "Estimating the impact of alkali bees on the yield and acreage of alfalfa seed", *Journal of Production Agriculture*, Vol. 5, pp. 512-518.

Wichmann, M.C. et al. (2008), "Human-mediated dispersal of seeds over long distances", *Proceedings of the Royal Society B: Biological Sciences*, Vol. 276, pp. 523-532.

Yan, H.H. et al. (2002), "A genome-specific repetitive DNA sequence from *Oryza eichingeri*: Characterization, localization, and introgression to *O. sativa*", *Theoretical and Applied Genetics*, Vol. 104, pp. 177-183.

Zayed, M.A. et al. (1980), "Studies on the host-parasite relationship of safflower root-rot disease caused by *Fusarium oxysporum* Schlecht", *Egyptian Journal of Phytopathology*, Vol. 12, pp. 63-70.

Zimmerman, L.H. (1972), "Variation and selection for preharvest seed dormancy in Safflower", *Crop Science*, Vol. 12, pp. 33-34.

Zohary, D., M. Hopf and E. Weiss (2012), "Dye crops", in Domestication of Plants in the Old World: The Origin and Spread of Domesticated Plants in Southwest Asia, Europe, and the Mediterranean Basin, Oxford University Press, pp. 166-168.

Note

[1] A protein complex that forms during meiosis between homologous chromosomes, which may modulate chromosome pairing, synapsis, and recombination.

4 Biology of Rice (*Oryza sativa*)

This chapter deals with the biology of rice (*Oryza sativa*), a revision of the original 1999 publication. It contains information for use during the risk/safety regulatory assessment of genetically engineered varieties of rice intended to be grown in the environment (biosafety). It includes elements of taxonomy, centres of origin, cultivation, reproductive biology, genetics, hybridisation and introgression, as well as ecology. Annexes present a glossary of rice ecological types, the common diseases, pests and weeds in rice fields, and current biotechnology developments.

Introduction

This chapter was prepared by the OECD Working Party on the Harmonisation of Regulatory Oversight in Biotechnology, with **Japan** as the lead country. It was initially issued in 2021 as the Revised Consensus Document on the Biology of Rice (*Oryza sativa* L.), replacing the original document issued in 1999. Production and trading data have been updated in this publication, based on FAOSTAT.

General description including taxonomy and morphology

Classification and nomenclature

Rice is the common name for all plant members belonging to the genus *Oryza* in the Poaceae (Gramineae) family. Cultivated rice includes two species: *Oryza sativa* L. and *Oryza glaberrima* Steud. Scientifically, wild rice refers to all other *Oryza* species, excluding the two cultivated species. However, when commonly used, the term wild rice additionally includes both cultivated and wild species from the genus *Zizania* and *Porteresia*, which are closely related but do not belong to the genus *Oryza*.

The cultivated rice species *O. sativa* is classified into two sub-species, *indica* and *japonica*, which are roughly characterised as long-grain rice and short-grain rice respectively (Figure 4.1). *Japonica* rice has been further classified into two ecotypes, temperate and tropical *japonica* according to the ecosystems where they have been evolved, whereas *indica* rice has been classified into ecotypes such as Aus, Amman, Rayada, and Boro according to their growing time and locations (Morinaga, 1968). Analysis by Wang et al. (2018) using genome sequencing of 3 010 accessions has revealed that *O. sativa* can be classified into nine sub-populations: four sub-populations for *indica*, three sub-populations for *japonica* and two single groups. These nine sub-populations could be related to geographic location and all these accessions are collectively called Asian cultivated rice. These Asian cultivated rice varieties have been widely grown in Asia, Oceania, Africa, North, Central, and South America, and Europe. More than 80% of these are represented by *indica* rice and approximately 15% by *japonica* rice. Another cultivated species, *O. glaberrima*, which is grown in limited areas in Africa, accounts for a small percentage (less than 5%) of global rice production and is known as African cultivated rice.

Figure 4.1. Panicle, seeds and brown rice of typical cultivated rice

Note: *Indica* rice (left), *japonica* rice (right).
Source: a) Photo zou (accessed 22 March 2022), http://photozou.jp/; b, c) courtesy of NARO; d) photo AC (accessed 22 March 2022), https://premium.photo-ac.com/; e, f) NARO (accessed 22 March 2022), *Genebank Project*, https://www.gene.affrc.go.jp/databases.php.

The genus *Oryza* comprises 23 species, including cultivated and wild species, and is divided into four major complexes (Table 4.1): the *sativa* complex with eight species, the *officinalis* complex, which is the largest with 11 species, the *ridleyanae* complex and the *granulata* complex, the latter two being remote relatives of *O. sativa* (Wing, Purugganan and Zhang, 2018; Zou et al., 2015; Joseph, Kuriachan and Thomas, 2008). Asian cultivated rice is thought to originate from an ancestor of perennial wild rice *O. rufipogon*, via multiple crossings between evolving plants that ultimately differentiated into the presently known species, sub-species and varieties (Chen et al., 2019; Choi et al., 2019). Another cultivated rice species, *O. glaberrima*, was found to have evolved from wild rice *O. barthii* (Wang et al., 2014). The habitats of eight species in the *sativa* complex, two cultivated species (*O. sativa* and *O. glaberrima*) and six close wild species relatives are shown in Figure 4.2.

Table 4.1. Classification and distribution of 23 species in the genus *Oryza*

Class	Species	Chromosome number	Genome	Genome size[1]	Genome size[2]	Distribution
Section *sativa*	*Oryza sativa* L.	24	AA		390	Asia
	O. rufipogon sensu lato	24	AA	439	381	Asia, Oceania
	O. nivara	24	AA	448		Asia, Oceania
	O. glaberrima Steud.	24	AA	357[3]		West Africa
	O. barthii A. Chev.	24	AA		403	Africa
	O. longistaminata Chev. & Roehr	24	AA		390	Africa
	O. meridionalis Ng	24	AA		381	Australia
	O. glumaepatula Steud.	24	AA		437	Central and South America
Section *officinalis*	*O. officinalis* Wall ex Watt	24	CC	651	549	Asia
	O. rhizomatis D.A. Vaughan	24	CC		823	Sri Lanka
	O. eichingeri Peter	24	CC		587	Africa, Sri Lanka
	O. minuta J.S. Presl ex C.B. Presl.	48	BBCC	1 124[3]		Philippines
	O. punctata Kotechy ex Steud.	24, 48	BB,BBCC	425	364	Africa
	O. latifolia Desv.	48	CCDD		806	Central and South America
	O. alta Swallen	48	CCDD	1 008	866	Central and South America
	O. grandiglumis (Döll.) Prod	48	CCDD		891	South America
	O. australiensis Domin	24	EE	965	827	Australia
Section *ridleyanae*	*O. brachyantha* Chev. & Roehr.	24	FF	362	265	Africa
	O. ridleyi Hook	48	HHJJ	1 283	1 080	Asia, New Guinea
	O. longiglumis Jansen	48	HHJJ		1 209	New Guinea
	O. schlechteri Pilger	48	unknown			Papua New Guinea
Section *granulata*	*O. granulata* Nees & Am ex Watt	24	GG	882	1 016	Asia
	O. meyeriana (Zoll. & Mor.ex Steud.) Baill	24	GG		1 003	Asia

1. Ammiraju, J.S.S. et al. (2006), "The *Oryza* bacterial artificial chromosome library resources: Construction and analysis of 12 deep-coverage large-insert BAC libraries that represent the 10 genome types of the genus *Oryza*", https://dx.doi.org/10.1101%2Fgr.3766306.
2. Calculated from Miyabayashi, T. et al. (2007), "Genome size of twenty wild species of *Oryza* Species determined by flow cytometric and chromosome analyses", https://doi.org/10.1270/jsbbs.57.73.
3. Martínez, C.P. et al. (1994), "Nuclear DNA content of ten rice species as determined by flow cytometry", https://doi.org/10.1266/jjg.69.513.
Other sources: Wing, R., M.D. Purugganan and Q. Zhang (2018), "The rice genome revolution: From an ancient grain to Green Super Rice", https://doi.org/10.1038/s41576-018-0024-z; Zou, X.H. et al. (2015), "Multiple origins of BBCC allopolyploid species in the rice genus (*Oryza*)", https://doi.org/10.1038/srep14876; Joseph, L., P. Kuriachan and G. Thomas, (2008), "Is *Oryza malampuzhaensis* Krish. et Chand. (Poaceae) a valid species? Evidence from morphological and molecular analyses", https://doi.org/10.1007/s00606-007-0606-2.

Figure 4.2. Habitats of eight species of the *sativa* complex in the genus *Oryza*

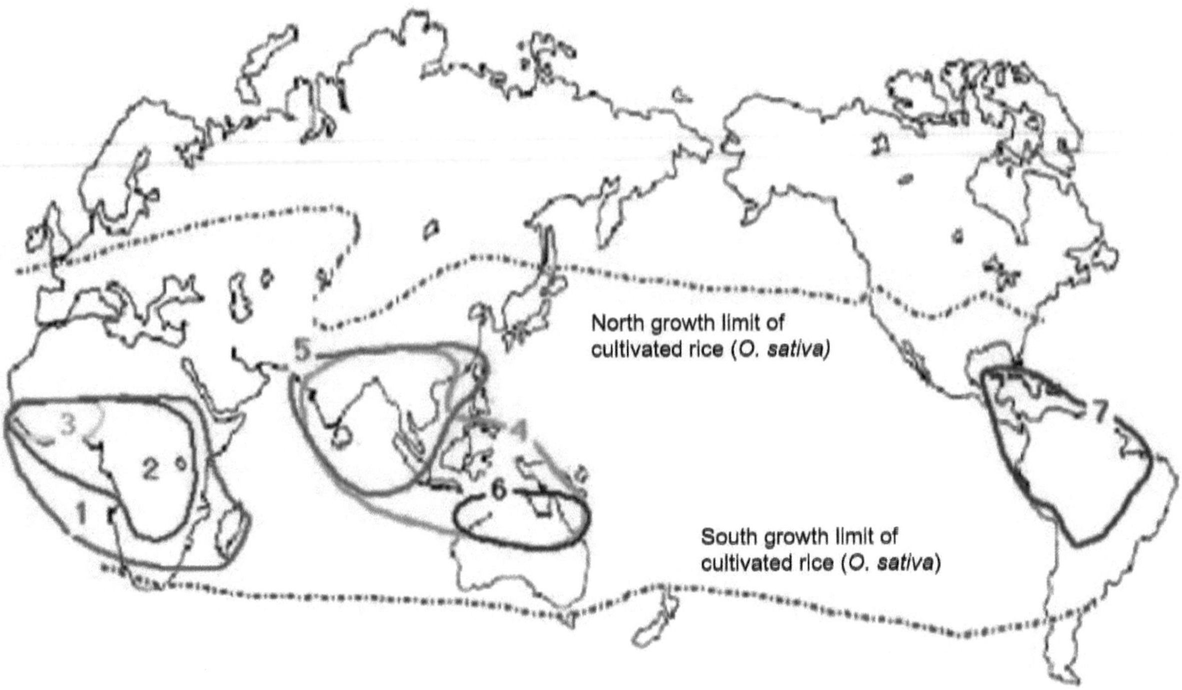

Note: 1. *O. longistaminata*; 2. *O. barthii*; 3. *O. glaberrima*; 4. *O. rufipogon* (perennial); 5. *O. nivara* (annual *O. rufipogon*); 6. *O. meridionalis*; 7. *O. glumaepatula*.
Source: Adapted from Stein, J.C. et al. (2018), "Genomes of 13 domesticated and wild rice relatives highlight genetic conservation, turnover and innovation across the genus Oryza", https://doi.org/10.1038/s41588-018-0040-0, and Oryzabase https://shigen.nig.ac.jp/rice/oryzabase/.

It has been suggested that Asian cultivated rice originated in the lower valley of the Yangtze River, People's Republic of China (hereafter 'China'), based on geographical, archaeological and folkloric traces (Fuller et al., 2009). However, more recent molecular biological analysis using a number of living rice accessions has indicated that the point of origin may be in the lower valley of Pearl River (Huang et al., 2012). Several hypotheses have been proposed regarding rice cultivation events, such as single cultivation events, independent multiple cultivation events and single cultivation followed by multiple crossing events. As of 2020, the results from the genome analyses of a large number of Asian cultivated and wild rice varieties/accessions support the hypothesis that multiple cultivated sub-species and varieties differentiated from a single cultivated variety, which was crossed with multiple wild/cultivated accessions. Details are also shown in the subsection on centres of origin and diversity, and geographical distribution.

Plants in the genus *Oryza* have a basis of 12 chromosomes, both in diploid species with two sets (2n = 24) and allotetraploid species with four sets (2n = 48). Each chromosome set is designated with 1 of the following 11 genome names: A, B, C, D, E, F, G, H, J, K or L, according to the chromosome pairing affinity of hybrid plants (Ge et al., 1999) or comparisons of the genome sequences (Wing, Purugganan and Zhang, 2018). The most popular species *O. sativa* was the first categorised as the "A" genome; subsequently, unknown species were given their alphabetical genome names in order of discovery (Kurata and Omura, 1984; Wing, Purugganan and Zhang, 2018). Genome size was found to vary between species ranging from 265 megabases (Mb) (*O. brachyantha*, an F genome species) to 827 Mb (*O. australiensis*, an E genome species), and the reference genome of *O. sativa, japonica* was 389 Mb (Miyabayashi et al., 2007). Table 4.1 summarises the chromosome number, ploidy level, genome name, genome size and habitats for all *Oryza* species.

The evolutionary relationships among all *Oryza* species have been clarified in previous studies (Figure 4.3) (Wing, Purugganan and Zhang, 2018). *O. granulata* emerged first approximately 14 million years ago (mya) and the AA genome species, including cultivated species, evolved most recently, approximately 3 mya (Stein et al., 2018). The *O. sativa* subsp. *japonica* rice genome was fully sequenced in 2004 by the International Rice Genome Sequencing Project (2005) and successive comparative genomic studies have been carried out for other species and genomes. These studies have found that genome construction appears to be similar among the different *Oryza* species, with genome-long homology and gene order conservation, while most of the variation in genome size was derived from amplification and defects of various types of transposable elements and from the copy numbers of specific gene families (Copetti and Wing, 2016; Wing, Purugganan and Zhang, 2018).

Figure 4.3. Evolutionary relationships of species in the genus *Oryza*

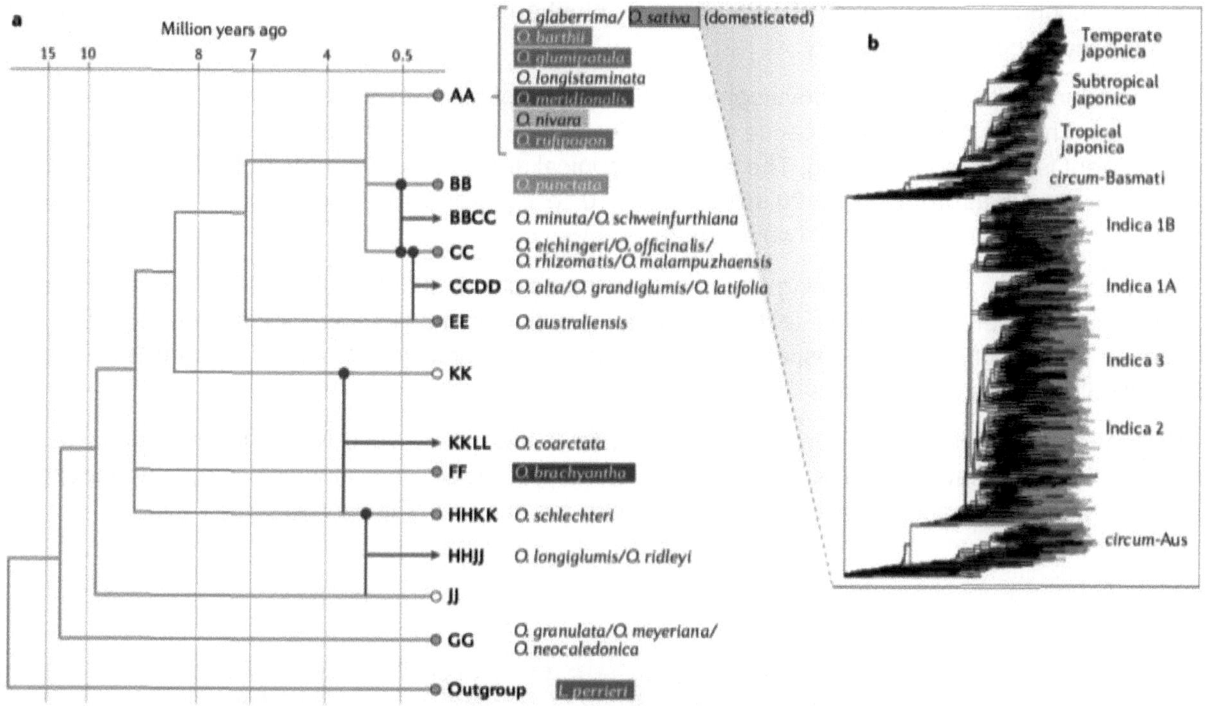

Source: Wing, R., M.D. Purugganan and Q. Zhang (2018), "The rice genome revolution: From an ancient grain to Green Super Rice", https://doi.org/10.1038/s41576-018-0024-z.

Asian cultivated rice *O. sativa* propagates by self-pollination, with up to 6.8% intraspecies outcrossing and cross-fertilisation with other species occurring at various rates. *O. rufipogon* and *O. nivara*, which are the closest relatives of *O. sativa*, have high cross-fertilisation abilities with *O. sativa* as they can easily cross with each other to yield offspring. Therefore, in habitats where the cultivated varieties and wild species overlap, weedy rice, which is derived from crosses between cultivated and wild rice, grows wildly and is problematic. Other AA genome species aside from these three closely-related species have relatively lower cross-fertilisation abilities and can yield hybrid embryos when crossed with the cultivated rice *O. sativa*. However, the embryos from such genetic combinations have various difficulties surviving because of the reproductive barriers that exist in their seed formation and/or hybrid plant growth. Meanwhile, the crossing of cultivated rice with wild *Oryza* species other than AA genome species is much more difficult and fertile seeds are rarely propagated.

In addition to the rice categories for the sub-species and ecotypes mentioned above, when considering the interactions between rice and other organisms (discussed in the section "Various interactions with other organisms (ecology)"), rice is also categorised into several ecological types: cultivated, volunteer, weedy, and wild rice types. The characteristics of each type and relationships among these types are described in Annex 4.A. These rice types can easily cross with each other, produce offspring and grow on and off farms as hybrid swarms. They consequently sometimes become problematic for rice farming.

Description

Cultivated rice is a herbaceous annual crop with an erect habit. Under standard cultivation conditions, the plant height ranges from 0.5 to 2 metres. The leaf blade ranges from 1 to 3 cm wide and from 20 to 50 cm long and is connected to the leaf sheath by a collar consisting of both the ligule and auricle. Tiller (culm) development is closely synchronised with leaf emergence in the upper three nodes on the corresponding stem; a total of 5-20 tillers per plant emerge, and the number depends on the total growth duration and planting density.

Under standard cultivation, floral development followed by panicle initiation starts 50 to 100 days after germination. The panicle or inflorescence emerges from the top of the culm after an additional 25-30 days and this event is defined as heading. The panicle is conical and its length ranges from 10 to 40 cm. Under normal growth, it sets from 50 to 400 spikelets on 10 to 20 branches. Each spikelet has six stamens (anthers) and one pair of pistils (i.e. two stigmas).

At the time of flowering, on the morning of a sunny summer's day, 6 000-12 000 pollen grains are dispersed from the split anthers and attach to the stigmas, resulting in fertilisation. During the 30 days after fertilisation, the embryo and endosperm develop into mature rice grains, which become seed for the propagation of the next generation.

Edible brown rice is yielded by removing the husk from the grain, while white rice is yielded by then removing the bran layers and embryo (germ) from the brown rice, leaving only the endosperm. The morphological characteristics of a typical rice plant are shown in Figure 4.4.

Figure 4.4. Phenotypic characteristics of cultivated rice *O. sativa*

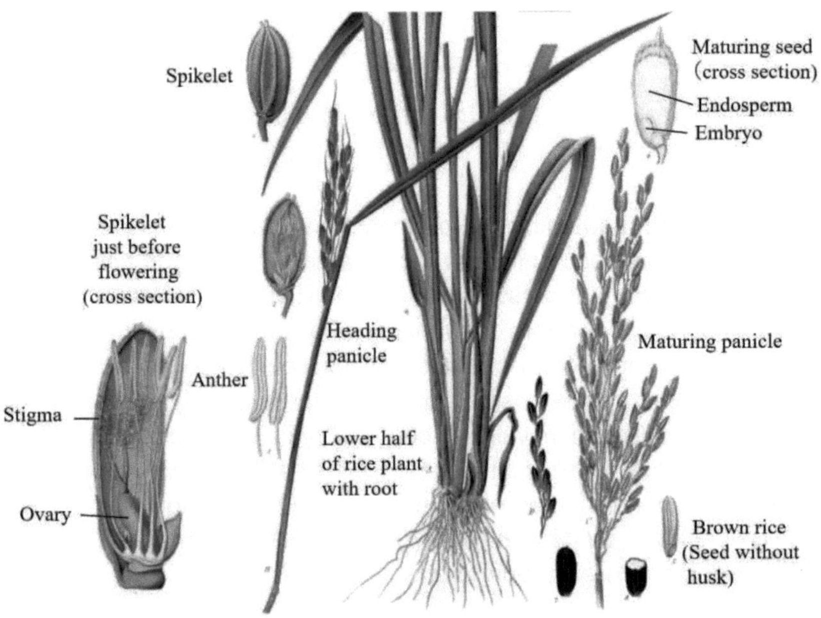

Source: Köhler, F.E. (1897), *Köhler's Medizinal-Pflanzen*; https://en.wikipedia.org/wiki/Rice.

The weight of fully matured seeds ranges from 10 to 46 mg (mode, 22-25 mg) among all varieties. The ratio of seed length to width varies widely from 1.6:1 for round grains to 4.0:1 for long grains. Generally, seeds retain dormancy traits that inhibit germination immediately after harvest. The degree of seed dormancy differs depending on the cultivar and environmental conditions, even though it is usually lost after a year in normal conditions (20-30°C). Dormancy can be coercively cancelled by heat treatment, hydrochloric acid treatment or the removal of the husk. If dormancy is broken, seeds start germination when their water content exceeds 30% after 24-48 hours of being soaked in water at 30°C. Seeds can maintain their germination ability for more than 10 years if they are kept at low temperatures and under dry conditions (less than 10% humidity).

The life cycle and morphological characteristics described above are typical of average rice plants grown around the world but they fluctuate greatly, even for the same cultivar, depending on the soil and weather conditions. Additionally, wild rice, mutant rice or cultivars grown in specific environments can exhibit extreme phenotypes deviating from the values described here.

Based on the starch content and utilisation of the edible grain, rice can be classified as glutinous or non-glutinous. Each of these types is further categorised by length as long grain or short grain, by fragrance (fragrant or not) and by colour (white, red, purple or black). According to these classifications, rice is processed in various styles such as boiled, stir-fried or steamed, for eating. Rice flour is kneaded and steamed or baked to produce various processed foods, such as noodles and cookies. Rice bran is an important material in cooking and industrial oils.

The inedible parts of the rice plant can also be used: for example, the husks can be used as fertiliser or animal feed, and the straw for packaging or rug-making. In some areas, farmers retain rice stubble on their fields after harvesting so that it can be grazed by cattle. The utilisation of the harvests and the residues of rice were well-documented in the OECD revised consensus document on compositional considerations for new varieties of rice (*Oryza sativa*) (OECD, 2016).

Rice adapts to a wide range of weather and soil environments. The Asian cultivated rice, *O. sativa*, is distributed from latitude 53°N – beside the Amur River on the border between the Russian Federation (hereafter 'Russia') and China – to latitude 40°S, in central Argentina (IRRI, 1985). The two sub-species of *O. sativa*, *indica* and *japonica*, are cultivated in the plains of a tropical zone and a mid-latitude high-rainfall temperate zone respectively. Typical characteristics of the two sub-species are compared in Table 4.2. (Watanabe, 1997). In the regions where seasonal flooding occurs, such as the deltas of Bangladesh, East India, Thailand and Viet Nam, a part of *indica* rice may be grown as floating or deepwater rice (Catling, 1992).

Table 4.2. Comparison of the main characteristics of japonica and indica rice

	Character	*japonica* rice	*indica* rice
1	Leaf shape and colour	Narrow and dark green	Wide and light green
2	Angle of flag leaf and rachis	Large	Small
3	Culm length	Short	Long
4	Culm strength	Lithe and hard to break	Hard and easy to break
5	Lodging property of culm	Hard to lodge	Easy to lodge
6	Grain shape	Wide and thick and round cross-section	Long, narrow and slightly flat
7	Shattering habit	Low shattering	High shattering
8	Awns	Mostly awnless, a few varieties with short awns	Awned with a variation of length
9	Length and number of glume trichomes	Relatively dense and short	Not dense and relatively long
10	Lengthwise ratio of grain	2.5 or less	2.5 or more
11	Germination	Slow	Quick
12	Phenol reactions	-	+
13	Potassium chlorate resistance	High	Susceptible
14	Low-temperature tolerance	High	Susceptible
15	Drought resistance	Low	High
16	Endosperm destruction by alkali	Easy	Hard

Source: Adapted from Matsuo, T. (1952), "Genecological studies on cultivated rice", *Bulletin of the National Institute of Agricultural Sciences Series D3*, pp. 1-111 (in Japanese).

The highest latitude at which rice is cultivated is in Heilongjiang Province, China and they grow early flowering cultivars with no photoperiod sensitivity. Sufficient growth volume is secured in the short summers as the long day length provides enough sunlight and the inland climate has high enough temperatures.

In contrast, in low-latitude areas, there are two types of cultivars. One type is strongly photosensitive and floral transition is initiated by sensing the short day length that coincides with the end of the rainy season. The other is the improved mid-flowering type, which has lost its photosensitivity and grows even in winter, with double or triple cropping thanks to an abundance of sunlight. On the other hand, the African species, *O. glaberrima*, is distributed in the basin of the Niger River in Sub-Saharan Africa, where it has adapted to high temperatures and a dry environment.

As paddy fields are excellent at maintaining high circulation levels for water and nutrients, the growth of lowland rice is not influenced as much by soil properties as the growth of dryland crops. Although rice can survive in saline, alkaline and acidic soils containing sulphur compounds, it prefers semi-acidic (pH 6.0-6.5) alluvial soils with a high degree of water retention.

In terms of water supplementation methods, there are four cropping systems: irrigated lowland (54% of the total world rice cultivation), rainfed lowland (25%), rainfed upland (13%) and deep water (8%). There are two systems of seedling establishment – direct seeding and transplanting – and system selection depends on the flatness of the field, the presence of irrigation systems, access to transplanting machines and the characteristics of the available cultivars. The use of direct seeding with small aircraft is widespread in the central plains of Australia and the United States.

Brown rice grains consist of bran layers (including the pericarp), an embryo and an endosperm. The endosperm consists of an aleurone layer and starch storage cells. Generally, starch in non-glutinous rice contains 10-30% amylose and 70-90% amylopectin. In glutinous rice, starch is composed of less than 5% amylose and mostly of amylopectin (Juliano and Villareal, 1993). The protein percentage ranges from

5% to 17% on a dry matter basis and the major protein in rice is glutelin (Juliano et al., 1968; Juliano, 1985). Fat, cellulose, minerals and vitamins are also present in brown rice (OECD, 2016).

As rice has a higher percentage of edible parts and a higher energy-conversion efficiency compared to other plants and because it is easily stored, it is a major source of calories in developing countries. Rice feeds more than half of the world's population and accounts for 20% of the total energy needs of humans, compared with 19% for wheat and 5% for maize in calorie consumption (FAO, 2005). Moreover, a diverse food culture has developed owing to the various methods of cooking with glutinous and non-glutinous rice.

Statistical data on the global cultivation areas and production are listed in Table 4.3. Total production in 2020 was 758.49 million tonnes and the largest producer was China, followed in decreasing order by India, Bangladesh, Indonesia and Viet Nam (FAOSTAT, 2020). The total global area under cultivation was 164.45 million hectares, with the greatest area in India, followed by China, Bangladesh, Indonesia and Thailand. The average yield was estimated 4.6 t/ha for that year, but this varied widely depending on the sunlight, soil conditions, rice cultivar and cultivation system. High-yielding areas commonly have a large supply of nutrients and water from upstream, as well as flat land with high levels of sunlight. The highest-yielding country is Australia (10 t/ha), followed in order by Tajikistan, Egypt, Uruguay and the United States. Rice is a subsistence crop in most countries, whereas other cereals, such as wheat, soybean and corn, are mainly supplied as commercial crops. According to the FAOSTAT (2020), typical exporting countries are India, Viet Nam and Thailand, and typical importing countries are China, Philippines and Saudi Arabia, although these roles change frequently with alterations in the balance between domestic production and consumption.

Table 4.3. Production and cultivation of rice in the world, 2020

	Country	Production (1 000 t)		Country	Area (1 000 ha)
1	China	213 611	1	India	45 000
2	India	178 305	2	China	30 342
3	Bangladesh	54 906	3	Bangladesh	11 418
4	Indonesia	54 649	4	Indonesia	10 657
5	Viet Nam	42 759	5	Thailand	10 402
6	Thailand	30 231	6	Viet Nam	7 223
7	Myanmar	25 100	7	Myanmar	6 656
8	Philippines	19 295	8	Nigeria	5 257
9	Brazil	11 091	9	Philippines	4 719
10	Cambodia	10 960	10	Pakistan	3 335

Source: FAOSTAT (2020). "Crops", https://www.fao.org/faostat/ (accessed 11 March 2022).

Centres of origin, geographical distribution and agronomic practices

Centres of origin and diversity, and geographical distribution

Asian cultivated rice landraces have a high level of genetic diversity, and areas from Assam, India, to Yunnan Province, China, are centres of rice biodiversity (Oka, 1988c). Some cultivars can be cultivated in the Equatorial region, while others can only be cultivated in subarctic zones such as Heilongjiang Province in China and Hokkaido in Japan, which indicates that each cultivar or strain has distinct locations for suitable cultivation. Based on the high-throughput sequencing data of more than 3 000 cultivars (3 000 genomes), Asian cultivated rice (*O. sativa*) can be divided into several sub-species and ecotypes containing *japonica*, *indica*, Aus and Basmati (Huang et al., 2012; Wang et al., 2018). Among them, the genetic distance timing between *japonica* and *indica* sub-species is estimated to be more than 350 000 years, suggesting complex domestication processes in rice (Figure 4.5).

The genetic diversity among rice cultivars that has formed after rice domestication is believed to have started 10 000-20 000 years ago and was extensively investigated using the 3 000 genome information (Wang et al., 2018). Bioinformatics analyses of genome sequences for more than 400 accessions of ancestral species of Asian cultivated rice (*O. rufipogon)* have revealed that the genomes of the *indica* accessions are very similar to some *O. rufipogon* accessions (these are same as *O. nivara* in Figure 4.5; *O. nivara* is also known as annual *O. rufipogon*), while the genomes of tropical and temperate *japonica* have clear evolutionary distances from all tested *O. rufipogon* lines (Huang et al., 2012). It is assumed that natural crossings between ancestral species of *indica* rice and *O. rufipogon* were caused presumptive gene flows.

Figure 4.5. Establishment of Asian cultivated rice and some key introgression events

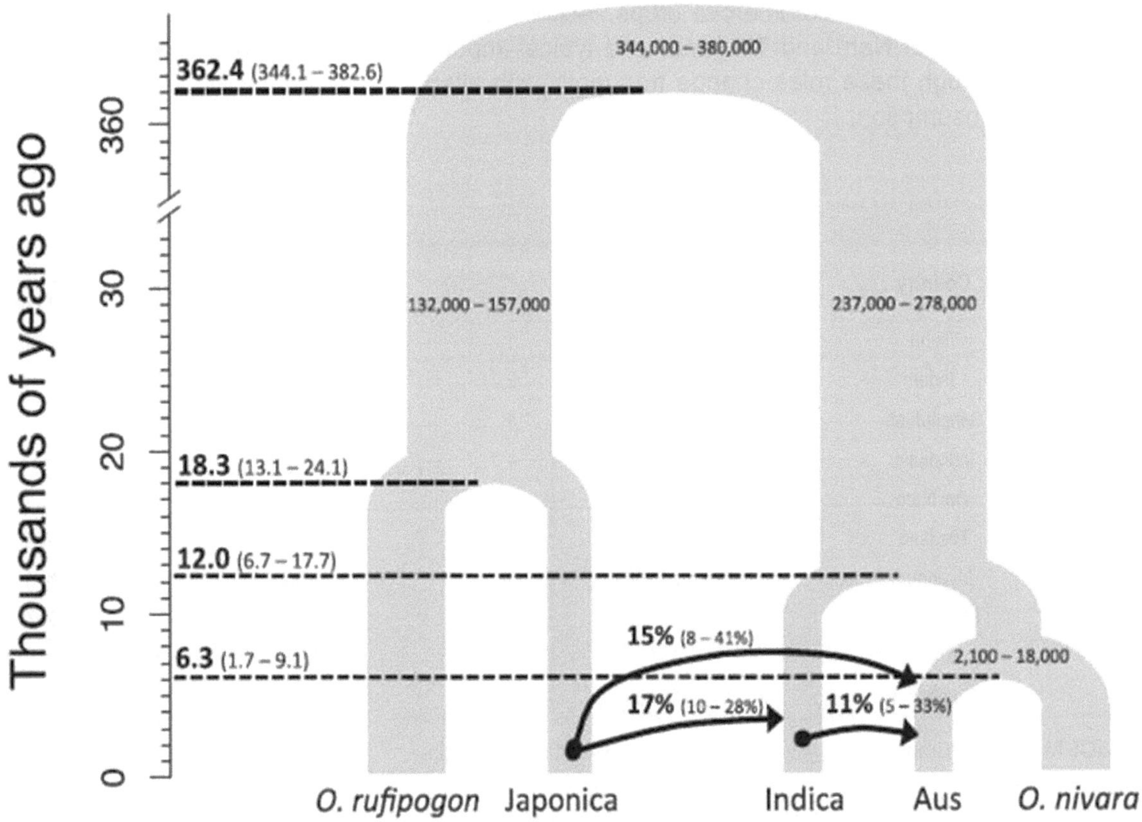

Note: Parameters were determined by a coalescent model. Left numbers are estimations of branching time. Arrows indicate the directions of introgressions. The numbers with the arrows are a median of estimation for introgressed genomic regions. The numbers in parenthesis indicate 95% confidence levels.
Source: Choi, J.Y. et al. (2017), "The rice paradox: Multiple origins but single domestication in Asian rice", https://doi.org/10.1093/molbev/msx049.

In addition, key natural variations in the genes selected for by humans during rice domestication have been identified, including *sh4* (seed shattering) (Li, Zhou and Sang, 2006), *PROG1* (erect leaf stature) (Jin et al., 2008; Tan et al., 2008), *rc* (rice pericarp colour) (Sweeney et al., 2007), *wx* (stickiness of cooked rice)

(Isshiki et al., 1998), *qSH1* (seed shattering) (Konishi et al., 2006), *Kala4* (black pericarp colour) (Oikawa et al., 2015) and *LABA1* (seed awn) (Hua et al., 2015), via quantitative trait locus (QTL) analyses and subsequent fine mapping. In some cases, there are clear remains of critical introgression events of genomic fragments having natural variations from an ancient sub-species. Although there are several controversial models proposed, it is strongly supported that *japonica* sub-species have been domesticated first and then key introgression events may have occurred through natural backcrossing to establish other sub-species/ecotypes, such as *indica* and Aus (Figure 4.5) (Choi et al., 2017; Chen et al., 2019)

The lower Yangtze River valley is a likely candidate area for the origin of rice domestication. This is supported by the discovery of a large-scale paddy field cultivation of rice around 8 000 years ago and this is mainly based on archaeological analysis of the remains of old paddy fields (Fuller et al., 2009). Furthermore, by analysing vascular bundles in rice antiquity grains found in historic remains, the natural variations in the *qSH1* seed shattering gene were found to have been selected in the lower valley area of the Yangtze River to reduce seed shattering (Zheng et al., 2016). On the other hand, as some tropical *japonica* cultivars have not been selected for key domestication-related genes, cultivation areas for the old tropical *japonica* cultivars may also be candidate areas for rice domestication (Konishi, Ebana and Izawa, 2008). The lower valley of Pearl River is also a candidate centre for rice domestication as some wild rice accessions of *O. rufipogon*, with genome sequences of 55 domestication sweep regions that are the most similar to those of some *japonica* cultivars, still grow wildly near the valley of Pearl River in the southern region of China (Huang et al., 2012). While all of this information is highly valuable, more research is required for a comprehensive understanding of the rice domestication processes.

African cultivated rice *O. glaberrima,* however, is thought to be derived from *O. barthii*, which is a wild rice species growing mainly in West African regions (Wang et al., 2014). It is believed that *O. glaberrima* has been domesticated in the delta region of the Niger River but rich genetic diversity has been observed in the upper swampy area of the Niger River. During the domestication of African cultivated rice, a few independent events that caused partial loss of seed shattering traits might have occurred, suggesting a complex domestication process (Choi et al., 2019). In East Africa, admix cultivars between *O. sativa* and *O. glaberrima*, termed New Rice for Africa (NERICA), have become promising owing to their higher productivity levels when compared with the local *O. glaberrima* landraces; however, critical improvements of the NERICA cultivars are still required (Yamamoto et al., 2018).

Weedy rice is geographically distributed in almost all rice-growing areas, such as in Brazil, Cambodia, China, Hungary, India, Italy, Japan, Korea, the Lao People's Democratic Republic, Malaysia, the Philippines, Sri Lanka, Thailand, the United States and Viet Nam, under different cultivation systems including upland/lowland, transplanted/wet sown/dry sown, and so forth (Kraehmer et al., 2016).

Ecosystems and habitats where the species occurs natively, and where it has naturalised

Asian cultivated rice, *O. sativa,* is derived from Asian wild rice *O. rufipogon* (Oka, 1988a). More than 100 000 entries for local varieties and breeding lines have been maintained in the worldwide gene banks (IRRI.org Archived, 2012). These cultivars share similar characteristics with wild rice, except for their domestication-related traits, such as seed shattering, seed dormancy and plant architecture. As wild rice has survived by adjusting to tropical environments, rice cultivars can also grow year-round under tropical conditions. If rice experiences low temperatures at the panicle initiation stage, seed fertility will decrease because of aberrant meiosis in the pollen mother cells (Nishiyama, 1995). Therefore, in low temperate and high-latitude temperate areas, some rice cultivars can be grown only in summer with high temperatures.

Rice is a short-day plant that produces flowers when the daylight period becomes short. In low-latitude tropical areas and high-latitude temperate areas, critical day-lengths of the photosensitive cultivars are around 13-13.5 and 14-14.5 hours respectively (Oka, 1954). This indicates that cultivars in low latitudes tend to have shorter critical day-lengths. Therefore, temperate cultivars planted in tropical areas often generate fewer tillers and panicles and most tropical cultivars cannot generate ear panicles under temperate conditions. After domestication, cultivated rice was distributed to various areas and varieties with local adaptations have been selected for. Such local varieties can be transferred to places with similar environmental conditions.

Modern breeding varieties with many useful traits have been produced through crossbreeding. They can be introduced to both tropical and temperate areas if they are grown under appropriate cultivation conditions for day length and temperature.

Asian cultivated rice, *O. sativa*, is mainly divided into *indica* and *japonica* sub-species. Varieties of *indica* are predominantly cultivated in the delta and plain regions in Southeast Asia and South Asia. While many *japonica* varieties are grown in East Asia. Upland varieties classified as tropical japonica are observed in the mountain areas in Indochina and tropical islands. In Africa, most of the paddy rice and rainfed rice is *indica* varieties, whereas tropical *japonica* is dominant among the upland varieties. African cultivated rice, *O. glaberrima*, is also planted but its cultivation area is more restricted to the west-coast area including Guinea, Senegal and Sierra Leone, than that of *O. sativa* (Linares, 2002).

Agronomic and other intensively managed ecosystems where the species is grown or occurs on its own, including management practices

Rice can grow in a wide range of hydrological and climate conditions, ranging from flooded to water deficit conditions. The growing environments of cultivated rice are categorised into irrigated lowland, rainfed lowland, rainfed upland and deep water. More than 75% of the global rice grain yield is produced in irrigated lowlands that make up 54% of its cultivation area (GRiSP, 2013; Saito et al., 2013). After irrigated lowlands, rainfed lowlands produce 20% of the global rice grain yield. About 90% of the production comes from Asia and 4-5% from Africa and Latin America. China is the largest producer, followed by India. Major growing environments differ between regions and countries worldwide. Irrigated lowland areas are dominant in Asia and America, whereas rainfed lowland and upland areas are major growing environments in Africa. Deepwater rice grows in the Deltas of the Brahmaputra, Ganga and Mekong where the water depth is greater than 50 cm. Floating rice grows in flooded areas in which the water depth exceeds 100 cm and remains at these depths for several months. Rice also grows in mangrove swamps in some parts of West Africa, particularly in tidal estuaries close to the sea.

Growing environments and management practices affect the growth and yield ability of rice plants. In general, irrigated lowland rice produces higher yields than other growing environments, because high-yielding semi-dwarf cultivars are adopted, there are high inputs of chemical fertilisers and irrigation contributes to the reduction of drought and flooding risks. Lower rice yields in growing environments other than irrigated lowlands are caused by the high risk of drought or flooding. Farmers tend to apply smaller amounts of fertiliser and other inputs in case of these conditions (Saito et al., 2018).

In most rainfed upland areas, the yield is less than 2 t/ha. In contrast, the highest rice yield is 9.8 t/ha in irrigated lowlands in high-latitude areas where rice is grown during long summer days, such as California (US) and Southwest Australia and, at low latitude, areas having high diurnal temperatures and strong sunlight, such as Yunnan Province in China, the Nile Delta in Egypt and Uruguay. In these areas, rice is cultivated once per year.

In the tropics, rice can be cultivated throughout the year, with two or three crops when irrigation water is available. In places where climate conditions clearly differ between the dry and wet seasons, the rice yield is higher in the dry season because of the increased sunlight.

In Asia, rice is cultivated in the vast delta regions in Bangladesh, Cambodia, East India, Myanmar, Thailand and Viet Nam. Although these regions have abundant water resources for rice production, they did not benefit from the Green Revolution because of flooding problems and water control difficulties. However, since low-cost pump technology and short-duration rice cultivars were introduced, rice production systems in the delta regions have shifted from low-production deepwater rice and floating rice to high-production irrigated lowland rice (GRiSP, 2013). However, the damage caused by flooding and salinity owing to rising sea levels remains a serious concern in these regions. In regions where water resources are limited, such as China and north-western parts of the Hindustan Plain, the sustainable use of water resources is required.

Rainfed lowland rice mainly grows in South and Southeast Asia and Africa. Its cultivation is strongly affected by rainfall in the wet season from May to November in the northern hemisphere. Rainfed lowland rice is cropped in coastal areas, inland valleys and delta regions in the above-mentioned areas.

Rainfed upland rice grows in Africa, Asia and Latin America. Among them, Asia and Africa occupy 65% and 25% of the total rainfed upland rice area respectively (Saito et al., 2018). Rainfed upland rice occupies 32% of the total rice area in Africa but only 6% in Asia. During the past 30 years, the upland rice area has increased in Africa, while it has reduced in Asia and Latin America.

Some resource-poor countries with higher annual rainfall and lower gross national incomes per capita tend to have a higher percentage of upland rice in their total area of rice cultivation. In Asia, upland rice cultivation areas are high in India, Indonesia, and China.

Upland rice was historically cultivated in shifting cultivation patterns on hilly slopes in the mountainous region of the Indochina Peninsula. In this region, high population pressure has caused the change from shifting cultivation to permanent farming systems in the limited fields.

In tropical Asia, cattle and water buffalo have been used for land preparation for many years. However, the use of agricultural machines such as hand tractors has become more popular with rice farmers. There are two crop establishment methods: direct seeding and transplanting.

Direct seeding dominates in South Asia, including Bangladesh, India and Sri Lanka. In Southeast Asia, transplanting is a major crop establishment method in inland areas, while direct seeding dominates in delta areas. In Africa, transplanting is widely used in irrigated lowlands, while direct seeding is common in rainfed conditions (Niang et al., 2017). Several different methods of direct seeding, such as broadcasting, dibbling and drilling, are used in the rainfed upland areas of Africa and Asia. Direct seeding areas have increased in both the irrigated and rainfed lowlands in Asia because of labour shortages. Direct seeding is a common crop establishment method in deepwater rice.

Transplanting is also used to avoid damage from flooding and weed infestation in some areas (Pandey and Velasco, 2005). For large-scale rice farming in the United States and Latin America, rice is directly sown in wet or dry fields using aircrafts or large seeding machines. Double rice cropping is practised by using ratooning in the southern states of the United States. In tropical Africa and Asia, transplanting and direct seeding are practised by hand, as the use of agricultural machines is still limited, while agricultural chemicals, such as fertiliser and herbicides, are commonly used (Rodenburg et al., 2019).

In the tropical areas of Asia and Africa, the use of agricultural machines for harvesting is still limited, except in Thailand, Viet Nam, and Senegal. Rice is thus usually harvested by hand. Harvested rice grains are usually threshed in the field using threshing equipment with or without a power source. In some areas, harvested panicle bundles are taken from the field for storage without threshing.

Large genetic variations among rice cultivars are observed in seed dormancy after ripening. Seed dormancy affects seed longevity and spontaneous growth as strong dormancy makes it possible to germinate and survive by avoiding unfavourable growth periods.

There is broad genetic variation at the level of seed shattering. In Japan, non-shattering cultivars have been selected to avoid grain loss in the field owing to the combine harvester. On the other hand, easy shattering cultivars are widely cultivated in tropical Asia, where some seeds drop on the ground during harvesting and threshing in the field. They germinate in the next cropping season and result in an increased risk of contamination of different rice cultivars and spontaneous growth.

Where cultivated rice is grown near populations of wild rice, hybrid populations derived from outcrossing between cultivated and wild rice are sometimes observed. Individual plants from hybrid populations have broad ranges of phenotypic variation in plant height, hull colour, awn length, seed colour and shattering habit. Some weedy rice lines have also originated from outcrossing between cultivated and wild rice (Akasaka et al., 2009; Brozynska et al., 2017).

Weedy rice includes wild rice, off-types of cultivated rice and hybrid swarm as volunteers from seeds that shattered in the previous cropping and germinated during the following rice-growing season. They frequently continue to grow repeatedly via fallen seeds. It is often observed in paddy fields. As the weedy rice has similar morphological and physiological characteristics to the rice cultivars, it is difficult to avoid contamination of crops during harvesting periods, causing yield loss, caused by competition during the growth stage and seed shattering, and the decline of grain quality. The management of weedy rice is more difficult with direct seeding methods than transplanting systems. It is an emerging problem in Asia as the direct seeding method has become more widespread than transplanting systems (Chauhan, 2013).

To control weedy rice, integrated weed management measures including the rotation of direct seeding and transplanting, rotation with other crops, the use of herbicides, puddling paddy fields before transplanting and manually pulling out weedy rice, are required. In addition, a wide range of herbicide susceptibility exists in cultivated rice, e.g. *indica* vs. *japonica* to acetolactate synthase (ALS) inhibitors (Kobayashi, Yogo and Sugiyama, 1995), and whether having functional *his1* gene which confers resistance to 4-HPPD inhibitors (Maeda et al., 2019). Moreover, herbicide-resistant rice cultivars are more frequently used as one of the management options in the United States and Latin America (Sudianto et al., 2013).

Reproductive biology

Generation time and duration under natural circumstances, and where grown or managed

Generation times for cultivated rice differ greatly among the varieties, ranging from approximately three to six months. During the vegetative growth period, which is followed by the reproductive growth period, the plant develops a dozen leaves and tillers. Environmental conditions, such as day length and temperature, affect plant growth and phase transitions to reproductive growth. Generally, long-day conditions lower plant height and deepen the green colour of the leaves. By contrast, short-day conditions are often required for phase transitions to reproductive growth.

Rice is commonly cultivated once per year and self-fertilised seeds are harvested. However, there are many *O. sativa* varieties that can be maintained as vegetative clones using axillary buds after bearing seeds, depending on the conditions. This characteristic enables newly elongated tillers from harvested stocks to grow again. Such tillers, called ratoons, can be harvested again. It is thought that this perennial property is derived from *O. rufipogon*, an ancestor species of Asian cultivated rice (*O. sativa*) (Morishima, Hinata and Oka, 1963). By contrast, another cultivated species (*O. glaberrima*) possesses more annual properties (Morishima, Hinata and Oka, 1962).

Reproduction (production of flowers, seeds and vegetative propagules)

Reproductive structure

O. sativa is a self-pollinating plant. A single rice flower, called a spikelet, contains 6 anthers, harbouring more than 1 000 pollen grains, and a pistil with furcate styles, each leading to stigmas. In concurrence with the opening of rice spikelets, pollen grains fall onto the stigmas, germinate and elongate their pollen tubes. One of the pollen tubes that reach the embryo sac takes part in double fertilisation.

The spikelet opening of rice starts on the day of or the day following panicle emergence. Spikelet opening proceeds from the panicle tip to the basal part (Moldenhauer and Gibbons, 2003). In detail, the top primary rachis-branch starts to open first and then the lower primary rachis-branches start to open in sequential order. In a primary rachis-branch, the top spikelet opens first and the lowest spikelet in the same primary rachis-branch opens next. Then, the lower spikelets start to open in sequence and the second-highest spikelet opens last. The spikelets in the secondary rachis-branches also start to open from the top and the sequence of spikelet opening in the secondary rachis-branch is the same as the one in the primary branch. The sequence of spikelet opening is identical to that of the differentiation of the flower in the young panicle (Hoshikawa, 1989).

Yoshida (1981) reported that it takes five days for most spikelets in a single panicle to open and seven to ten days for all spikelets. Sleper and Poehlman (2006) reported that the spikelet opening period of a single panicle lasts from three to seven days after the heading and most of them bloom two to four days after the spikelet opening begins.

The spikelet opening process of cultivated rice is as follows: immediately before spikelet opening, the filaments of the stamens become elongated and the anthers move to the upper part of the spikelet. Simultaneously, the stigmas standing straight begin to open and also their branches extend outward to increase the area available to receive pollen grains. The lodicule at the bottom of the palea takes in water and swells, and the swelling pressure pushes out the lemma. At the same time, the interlocking between the palea and the lemma is undone, and the top edges of the spikelet gradually start to open. Then spikelet opening starts. Anthers that reach the top of the spikelet start to dehisce and the pollen grains fall onto the pistil of the same spikelet. In most cases, the pollination process is complete at this stage. After that, the anthers are put out of the spikelet through the further opening of the lemma and the palea, and continuous elongation of the stamen filaments.

Extruded anthers release resting pollen grains to the outside. In 10-25 minutes after the spikelet opening starts, the opening between the lemma and the palea expands to an angle of 25-30 degrees. When the spikelet fully opens, both stigmas spread to an angle of 90 degrees compared to the apical-basal axis of the pistil and their apices become exposed through the opening between the lemma and the palea (Hoshikawa, 1989).

After spikelet opening, loss of moisture and subsequent shrinking of the lodicule cause the lemma to return to its previous position, resulting in spikelet closure, which terminates the spikelet opening process. Anthers and filaments extruded out of the spikelet remain outside of the spikelet. The spikelet opening period of a single spikelet ranges between 1 and 2.5 hours (Hoshikawa, 1989).

Although there are individual differences, pollen grains that fall on the stigmas start to germinate after two to three minutes in the shortest case and pollen tubes become elongated to the ovule in the ovary through the style. Under suitable conditions, the tip of the pollen tube reaches inside of the embryo sac within 15 minutes and then the fertilisation processes are completed during the next five to six hours (Hoshikawa, 1989).

The time of spikelet opening for cultivated rice varies depending on the weather conditions and genetic characteristics. Rice spikelet opening normally occurs between 9 a.m. and 2 p.m. (Moldenhauer and Gibbons, 2003) or 10 a.m. and 2 p.m. (Sleper and Poehlman, 2006). The spikelet opening times in tropical areas tend to be longer than those observed in temperate areas (Nagai, 1959). In detail, Hoshikawa (1989) reported that in temperate areas rice spikelet opening starts around 9 a.m., the peak of spikelet opening is around 11 a.m. and most spikelets close around 1 p.m. when the weather is fine and the temperatures are high enough. However, when the temperatures are around 20°C, spikelet opening starts around noon, lasts sluggishly until around 5 p.m. and ends around 6 p.m.

Yoshida (1981) and Moldenhauer and Gibbons (2003) also reported that the beginning and the end of spikelet opening could be delayed by low temperatures and cloudy conditions. Additionally, in severe weather, rice spikelets do not open but the elongation of the filaments and dehiscence of the anthers take place inside the spikelet, resulting in pollination without spikelet opening, which is called cleistogamy (Hoshikawa, 1989).

Yoshida (1981) reported genetic differences for the start and end times of rice spikelet opening in tropical areas. While the spikelet opening of *O. sativa* starts around 8 a.m. and ends around 1 p.m., the spikelet of *O. glaberrima* starts to open earlier at around 7 a.m. and ends after a shorter duration, around 11 a.m. There are also wild rice varieties whose spikelets start to open in the early morning or at night (Watanabe, 1993).

Pollination, pollen dispersal, pollen viability

As described in the previous subsection on reproductive structure, rice is a self-pollinating plant. However, natural crossings of rice can occur by the wind. When pollen fertility of recipient plants is decreased by low-temperature conditions in the pollen formation period, the crossing rate rises (Sato and Yokoya, 2008; Tanno et al., 2011). The crossing rate of cultivated rice is affected by other conditions, including the duration of spikelet opening, wind direction and speed, and the scale of the pollen source.

It is thought that the differences in the morphological characteristics of the stamens and pistils are responsible for the differences in the natural crossing rates of the rice. In a study on the seed production of hybrid rice cultivars, Virmani (1994) reported that the crossing rate was increased when the anthers and stigmas were larger, and with a higher frequency of exposure of the stigma out of the spikelet, which increased the probability of catching pollen in the air. These characteristics are more common in wild rice than in cultivated rice (Oka and Morishima, 1967; Uga et al., 2003). The length of anthers is highly correlated with the number of enclosed pollen grains. A single anther of cultivated or wild rice can contain approximately 700-2 500 or 700-9 000 pollen grains respectively (Oka and Morishima, 1967). Bakti and Tanaka (2019) reported that *O. rufipogon*, a wild rice species, tends to expose its stigma outside of the spikelet in contrast to cultivated rice.

The morphology of the panicle and the positional relationship between the panicle and the flag leaf also affect the natural crossing rate (Virmani, 1994). Some wild rice varieties have a time lag between spikelet opening and the release of pollen grains. This also contributes to an increase in the natural crossing rate (Oka and Morishima, 1967).

Nagao and Takano (1938) and Oka and Morishima (1967) characterised the viability time for pollen grains. In cultivated rice, the rate of fertilisation drops over time after the release of pollen grains from the anther, as the released pollen grains become infertile after five minutes. An immediate decrease in the number of fertile pollen grains after their release from the anther was also observed on artificial growth medium during germination tests and vital staining. It is considered that the loss of pollen viability results from desiccation (Nakayama, 1934; Koga et al., 1971; Khatun and Flowers, 1995). By contrast, in wild rice, fertilisation can occur in less than nine minutes after pollen grain release (Oka and Morishima, 1967).

However, once the stigma becomes competent, it maintains competency for three to seven days (Yoshida, 1981). Therefore, the natural crossing rate increases if the stigma remains out of the spikelet after the end of the spikelet opening (Kato and Namai, 1987; Xu and Shen, 1987; Yan and Li, 1987; Yan et al., 2009). Nagao and Takano (1938) found that the fertilisation ability of stigmas is greatly decreased three days after spikelet opening in artificial crossing experiments.

Completion in 2004 of the genome sequencing project for the rice cultivar, Nipponbare, enabled extensive analyses of the quantitative trait loci (QTL) between cultivars and various mutants related to the morphology and development of inflorescence and seed formation in rice. This work allowed for the identification of many of the causal genes regulating the morphology of seeds and panicles in rice.

It is well known that the characteristics controlling the variations of both seed length and width are genetically regulated in an independent manner (Zuo and Li, 2014). The differences in seed shape observed in various rice cultivars are commonly regulated by such characteristic QTL. Among the genes regulating seed width, *qSW5/GW5* is known to contribute markedly to rice variation and has been revealed to function as a genetic element in brassinosteroid signalling (Shomura et al., 2008; Weng et al., 2008; Liu et al., 2017a). Since *qSW5/GW5* narrows seed width, it is believed that the loss of these functional alleles was selected for during the early stages of rice domestication. Another main regulator gene of seed length in rice is *GS3*, which encodes a G protein γ-subunit (Fan et al., 2009; Mao et al., 2010).

Several genes related to awn formation have been identified. In the early stages of rice domestication, the defective alleles of *An-1* were selected and, subsequently, the defective alleles of *RAE2* and *An-2* were selected (Luo et al., 2013; Bessho-Uehara et al., 2016; Gu et al., 2015). This has led to the loss of awns in the spikelets of most rice cultivars.

Furthermore, *Gn1a* (Ashikari et al., 2005), *WFP/IPA* (Jiao et al., 2010; Miura et al., 2010) and *APO1* (Ikeda et al., 2007) function to control the panicle size and seed number (or the number of spikelets in a panicle). *Gn1a* encodes an enzyme for a phytohormone, cytokinin, whereas *WFP/IPA* encodes an SPL (SQUAMOSA Promoter binding protein-like)-type transcriptional factor. The *APO1* gene encodes an F-box protein related to specific protein degradation and is assigned as an orthologue of the *UFO* gene in *Arabidopsis thaliana.* In addition, it is known that the *WFP/IPA* gene is regulated epigenetically and affected by specific miRNAs.

Since sexual reproduction in rice is mainly mediated by self-pollination, there is no significant agricultural problem unless the fertility of plants decreases due to specific environmental conditions and/or genetic effects. Rice plants with the *spw1-cls* allele have a mutation in the *SPW1* (*SUPERWOMAN1*) gene that results in an amino acid change and consequently, a cleistogamous trait is exhibited (Yoshida et al., 2007). The use of this *SPW1* allele has been considered for genetically engineered (GE) rice cultivation. However, there is low stability of the cleistogamy trait under relatively low-temperature conditions and, consequently, its economic uses have not been pursued.

In wild rice, the abscission layers are formed at the base of the spikelet. After pollination, the layers start to be degraded and maturing seeds shatter to propagate seeds in the natural environment. In cultivated rice, non-shattering traits have been selected by humans. There are several natural mutations in various distinct genes that are involved in the diversity of seed shattering traits in rice cultivars. There are broad variations of these traits among different species/sub-species/varieties. The easy shattering cultivars, including many of the *indica* cultivars, are grown in developing countries with less access to agricultural implements and machinery. Most *japonica* cultivars, however, exhibit non-shattering traits, making them suitable for use with agricultural machinery. During domestication, a defective allele in *sh4,* a standing variation in wild rice, has been strongly selected for. Consequently, all of the cultivars tested have the same *sh4* allele (Li, Zhou and Sang, 2006).

In addition to the defective *sh4* allele, the non-shattering trait in most of the currently used Japanese cultivars is due to the natural variations in the *qSH1* gene (Konishi et al., 2006) and this mutation has been observed only in temperate *japonica* cultivars. Compared with the selection for the *sh4* gene, this mutation in *qSH1* was selected for during the establishment of the cultivar, or temperate *japonica*. Based on the analysis of the antique carbonised rice grains found in the paddy field remains from the lower valley of the Yangtze River, it is speculated that this mutation was selected approximately 7 500 years ago (Zheng et al., 2016). Rice plants having both defective alleles possess no abscission layer, making the cultivars suitable only for mechanical harvesting. Since *qSH1* is normally expressed at the shoot apex region and functions in the development and maintenance of the shoot meristems in rice, the selected natural mutation resides in the cis-regulatory region of the *qSH1* promoter and represses *qSH1* transcription only at the provisional abscission layers (Konishi et al., 2006).

There have been two genes identified as causal genes involved in the loss of seed shattering during the domestication of African cultivated rice (*O. glaberrima*). One is an orthologue of the *sh4* gene in Asian cultivated rice (*O. sativa*), the other is *SH3*, which encodes a YABBY-type transcription factor. Since the standing variations still exist in African wild rice (*O. barthii*), it is speculated that those mutations were selected sequentially to lose seed shattering traits in African cultivated rice (*O. glaberrima*) (Wu et al., 2017; Lv et al., 2018).

Seed viability, longevity, dormancy, natural seed bank, germination and seedling viability and establishment

The seeds of the varieties with strong dormancy maintain their viability for several seasons. For example, Surjamkhi, a cultivar with a strong dormancy, maintained viability after six years, whereas Fujiminori, a cultivar with weak dormancy, lost viability after three years (Takahashi and Suzuki, 1975). Seeds with no or weak dormancy germinate in the ear of standing rice (vivipary). When vivipary occurs, the grains lose their value as food. In the past, farmers and breeders have continuously selected cultivars with appropriate dormancy for their cultivation styles (Bewley et al., 2013).

The seeds of the varieties with strong dormancy can become weedy because the volunteer seeds from previous seasons would germinate sporadically in the field where new cultivars are grown. The factors responsible for seed dormancy reside in the chaff. The dormancy of seeds increases the potential weediness of the cultivars when the seeds are released from the ear. *Indica* cultivars have a wider range of dormancy than *japonica* cultivars and often become indigenous weeds. Red-kernelled rice cultivars also shed easily and have strong dormancy in both *indica* and *japonica*. They consequently become weeds frequently in rice fields, creating problems for farmers. The intercrossing between cultivated rice and indigenous weeds, including red-kernelled rice, occurs in many rice farming countries and has also become a widespread problem (Ziska et al., 2015).

The optimal temperature for rice seed germination ranges from 13°C to 30°C, and the highest temperature is 44°C; there are varietal differences associated with these variations. Varieties with outstanding germination properties at low temperatures are selected from wild varieties found in high-latitude regions. At optimal temperatures, rice seeds absorb approximately 25% of their air-dried seed weight in water and germinate in the presence of oxygen. Unlike other Poaceae (Gramineae) crops, rice seeds can germinate under conditions with low oxygen concentrations, through anaerobic respiration. It was thought that the germination of rice seeds was not affected by light. However, it has been reported that light promotes seed germination for some varieties of weedy rice (light-induced germination) (Chung and Paek, 2003). Although light weakly affects the promotion of seed germination in cultivated rice, there are varietal differences in the extent of the light induction (Lee et al., 2010).

The biological aspects of rice seeds in natural conditions have mostly been studied in weedy rice and volunteer rice. A difference was found in the survival rate of the seeds between the surface of the field and the soil layer. The survival rate of the seeds on the field surface dropped below 50% after 1 winter and all seeds died after 2 winters (Hosoi et al, 2010). The seeds buried in the soil layer (10-15 cm below ground), however, maintained their germination rate after 2 winters but died after 3 winters. It is known that the moisture content of the soil affects the maintenance of viability in buried conditions, with a report showing that the viability of red-kernelled rice seeds buried in irrigated fields was longer than when they were buried in non-irrigated fields (Suzuki, 2003).

In wild rice, the germination rate of seeds buried at 25°C for 40 months was higher than 40%, with the water content of the seeds exceeding 30%. However, when seeds were maintained at a water content of 16%, all seeds died after 16 months (Oka, 1992). In cultivated rice, it is known that viability decreases quickly in high-temperature and high-humidity conditions (Roberts, 1961). There are varietal differences in the viability of seeds. There are many reports in which seeds of *indica* rice cultivated in tropical areas tend to have a longer life duration than *japonica* rice cultivated in temperate areas at relatively high altitudes (Juliano, Perez and Chang, 1990; Chang, 1991; Ellis, Hong and Roberts, 1992; Rao and Jackson, 1996a, 1996b, 1996c, 1997; Ebina, Nakamura and Yamamoto, 1998; Padma and Reddy, 2000).

The sowing depth, that is the soil depth at which the seed starts to germinate, affects the germination of rice seeds (Ohno et al., 2018). In some cultivars, sowing depths that exceed five centimetres significantly inhibit germination. On the other hand, some weedy rice varieties can germinate even at 13 cm below ground, indicating that the tolerance of greater sowing depths is an effective trait for survival under natural conditions (Vidotto and Ferrero, 2000). Rice seeds can also germinate when submerged. However, when deeply submerged (2-8 cm), germination can be suppressed (Chauhan, 2012). In cultivated rice, red-kernelled rice is superior in terms of its resistance to submerged conditions and is used as a genetic resource to improve the submergence tolerance at the germination stage of cultivated rice (Septiningsih et al., 2013).

Asexual propagation (apomixis, vegetative reproduction)

O. sativa is cultivated as an annual crop. However, the plants can continue their vegetative growth cycle after bearing if the water and temperature conditions are suitable. It is thought that the perennial property of *O. sativa* is derived from an ancestral species *O. rufipogon* (Morishima, Hinata and Oka, 1963). In natural conditions, the tiller buds at the basal nodes begin to elongate after the harvesting of the ears. The new tillering buds, called ratoons, can elongate in long-day conditions. In some countries such as Brazil, China, the Dominican Republic, India and the United StatesUS, farmers grow the ratoons and harvest a second crop of the grains.

The rhizome is another characteristic related to perennial rice. A wild rice species, *O. longistaminata*, is perennial and has a strong rhizomatous nature, and several loci were identified that controlled this trait (Hu et al., 2003; Zhang et al., 2015). Rice rhizomes have several characteristics, including that the buds bend to elongate horizontally and, as the rhizome expands, it maintains its juvenile phase (Yoshida et al., 2016).

The perennial properties of rice can be beneficial, including its rhizomatous nature which competes with weeds and is useful for improving the soil environment in non-ploughing cultures. Consequently, there is an ongoing effort to introduce these perennial properties into cultivated rice varieties (Sacks, 2013).

Although there are many Poaceae (Gramineae) species that reproduce by apomixis, no apomictic species have been identified in the genus *Oryza* (Khush et al., 1994). The productivity of rice can be improved by breeding and especially through first-generation hybrid breeding if the apomictic property was introduced into existing cultivars. Thus, the idea that the apomictic property could be introduced into rice from genetic resources was proposed. Recently, a technique has been developed that introduces apomictic reproduction into rice by genetically engineering the reproductive process through genome editing (Xie et al., 2019). The apomixis was introduced into rice by mutating four responsible genes for meiotic recombination and the quadruple mutant line was named Apomictic Offspring Producer (AOP).

It is possible to induce and propagate rice calluses using tissue and cell culture methods. In the appropriate conditions, calluses re-differentiate into tissues and plantlets, and propagate asexually. Haploid plants of rice can be easily obtained by pollen cultures. The haploid plants sometimes become diploid plants by natural duplication. Diploid plants can also be easily obtained by chemically treating haploid plants (Niizeki and Oono, 1968).

Genetics

Relevant detailed genetic information on the species

Gene pool

The Asian cultivated rice, *O. sativa*, is an AA genome diploid species (2n = 2x = 24). The primary and secondary gene pools of this species are defined based on their level of reproductive isolation (Khush, 1997; Jena, 2010). One cultivated species (*O. glaberrima*) and six wild species (*O. rufipogon*, *O. nivara*, *O. longistaminata*, *O. barthii*, *O. glumaepatula*, and *O. meridionalis*) constitute the primary gene pool. They share the AA genome and are crossable with *O. sativa*. These species with AA genomes correspond to those in the *sativa* complex defined by Morishima and Oka (1960), based on the morphological characteristics of the genus *Oryza*. Among them, *O. rufipogon* have high crossability with *O. sativa*, because they are wild progenitors of common cultivated rice. They grow mainly in swampy and wet areas in tropical Asia and gene flow is often observed between cultivated and wild rice around the paddy fields (Oka, 1988b). The African cultivated rice, *O. glaberrima*, can be crossed with *O. sativa*; however, their hybrids cannot produce fertile seeds due to severe pollen sterility (Sano, Chu and Oka, 1979; Garavito et al., 2010).

The secondary gene pool consists of wild species in the *officinalis* complex (Table 4.1). This complex includes 11 wild species having BB, CC, BBCC, CCDD and EE genomes, such as *O. officinalis* and *O. minuta* (Khush, 1997; Jena, 2010). Crosses between *O. sativa* and these species can be accomplished by embryo rescue using tissue culture techniques (Brar and Khush, 1997). Their hybrids are completely sterile because normal pairing between their chromosomes for the different genomes in meiosis cannot occur.

Genome information

The nuclear genomes of the *O. sativa japonica* cultivar Nipponbare and the *indica* cultivar 93-11 have been sequenced and assembled as reference genomes (IRGSP, 2005; Yu et al., 2002, 2005). The genome size of Nipponbare was estimated to be 389 Mb and that of 93-11 was 466 Mb. The reference genome of Nipponbare has been improved by adding sequence information derived from short-read high-throughput sequencing, resulting in the correction of sequence errors and increasing genome coverage (Kawahara et al., 2013). Genome databases of Nipponbare with detailed gene annotation information have been developed as RAP-DB (Sakai et al., 2013) and MSU (Ouyang et al., 2007). Subsequently, the genomes of the Japanese elite cultivar Koshihikari and the African cultivated species *O. glaberrima* were sequenced and assembled, using the Nipponbare and 93-11 as reference genomes (Yamamoto et al., 2010; Sakai et al., 2011). More than 3 000 diverse Asian accessions have been made to the gene bank of the International Rice Research Institute (IRRI), revealing a large amount of structural variation among them (Wang et al., 2018; Fuentes et al., 2019).

Based on *de novo* assembly from high-throughput sequencing data, relatively high-quality reference genomes have been assembled for Shuhui498 (Du et al., 2017), *O. laberrima* (Wang et al., 2014) and several wild relatives with AA genomes: *O. rufipogon* (Zhao et al., 2018), *O. nivara*, *O.* barthii, *O. glumaepatula*, and *O. meridionalis* (Zhang et al., 2014). In addition, The International *Oryza* Map Alignment Project (Jacquemin et al., 2013) has made available the sequences of wild species other than those with AA genomes, such as *O. longistaminata* (Reuscher et al., 2018), *O. brachyantha* (Chen et al., 2013) and *O. granulata* (Wu et al., 2018).

Expression profiling has also been conducted for rice and several databases are available. For the *japonica* cultivar Nipponbare, transcriptome data for different growth stages and tissues are available in RiceXPro (Sato et al., 2010, 2013) and its co-expression database RiceFREND (Sato et al., 2012). For *indica* cultivars, similar expression profiling databases are available on Zhenshan 97 and Minghui 63, the parental lines of the primary F_1 hybrid variety grown in China (Wang et al., 2010). Proteome and metabolome databases were also constructed (Hong et al., 2019). As for the genetic DNA markers, 2 240 simple sequence repeat (SSR) markers have been identified and summarised (McCouch et al., 2002) and are widely used in genetic and molecular analyses and marker-assisted selection (MAS) in rice breeding. The resequencing of many cultivars identified single nucleotide polymorphisms (SNPs). These SNPs are used in genetic analysis and selection in breeding programmes (Huang et al., 2009, 2010; Eishire et al., 2011).

Genetic factors affecting maturity (heading date)

Heading date, or timing of heading, is the event during which the panicle emerges from the sheath of the final mature leaf, termed the flag leaf. The heading date can be considered an indicator of flowering time in rice and an important agricultural trait related to yield and suitability to cultivate in diverse geographical locations. Genetically, it is well known as a quantitative trait that is regulated by multiple loci. Based on genetic linkage analyses with known genetic markers in rice and using the progenies from between the cultivars, several loci having clear effects on heading date have been mapped using classical genetics approaches, such as *Se1*, *E1*, *E2*, *E3* and *Ef1*, although this information has been considered fundamental knowledge and has not been used for breeding (Hori, Matsubara and Yano, 2016).

In the late 1990s, many DNA markers were developed and subsequently, many QTL analyses were performed. As a result, many of the QTL that control heading dates were identified. Particularly, Yano's group in Japan performed an extensive QTL analysis using F_2 progenies and backcrossed progenies between Nipponbare (a temperate *japonica* cultivar) and Kasalath (an Aus cultivar) and identified more than 15 QTL affecting heading date between them (Yano et al., 2001). Although a few of those QTL are speculated to be due to the natural variations in the genes previously identified, it is not easy to identify all the relationships between them. This is because the positions of the QTL are based on the positions of DNA markers, whereas the positions of the previously identified genetic loci related to heading date were defined with genetic distances based on other known genetic loci that are easily phenotyped, such as *wx* (*waxy: glutinous endosperm*), *C* (*chromogen for anthocyanin*), and *Pl* (*purple leaf*). At present, more than 14 heading time-related genes have been identified genetically using QTL cloning in rice (Hori, Matsubara and Yano, 2016) (Table 4.4). In recent years, using the precise positional information of identified QTL affecting heading date but not using any phenotypic data, DNA-marker-assisted breeding has been performed to develop new cultivars that have preferable heading dates for their given cultivation areas (Hori, Matsubara and Yano, 2016).

Among the many heading date QTL in rice that have already been identified, several that make large contributions to rice breeding due to their critical effects are discussed here. The *Hd1* (*Heading date 1*) gene functions as a floral promoter under short-day conditions but as a floral repressor under long-day conditions (Yano et al., 2000). Thus, *Hd1* is bifunctional and can contribute to local adaptions in temperate cultivation areas. For tropical *japonica* and the Aus ecotype that are cultivated in tropical and sub-tropical areas, a defective allele of *Hd1* (*hd1*) has become dominant (Fujino et al., 2010). The *hd1* allele causes prolonged vegetative growth and reduces the photoperiodic responses of the floral transitions in cultivation areas at low latitudes. This defect may help crops adjust to different seasons and avoid the flooding seasons for major cultivars in Aus ecotypes (Fujino et al., 2010).

Generally, rice breeding cultivation areas in Asia have historically progressed northward. In particular, a defective natural mutation occurred in the *Ghd7* (*Grain number and heading date 7*) gene that contributed critically to the extension of rice cultivation into subarctic areas, such as Hokkaido in Japan and Heilongjiang Province in China (Xue et al., 2008). *Ghd7* functions as a very strong floral repressor under long-day conditions. All tested cultivars adapted to the Hokkaido areas possessed the defective *Ghd7* allele (*ghd7*). It has led to the development (or selection) of cultivars that flower in early August under long-day natural conditions with no responses to day length changes and consequently they are able to provide enough yield for the human populations in the subarctic climate of the Hokkaido area. Similarly, the defective alleles of the *Dth8/Hd5* gene and *OsPRR37/Hd2* gene have both clearly contributed to the northward progression of rice cultivation (Li et al., 2015). Both the reduction of photoperiod sensitivity and the early flowering phenotype due to the above natural variations may play pivotal roles in the progression of rice to the northern areas.

Table 4.4. Classical Mendelian genes and isolated genes for natural variation in heading date in rice

Gene symbol	Synonym	Effect on flowering[1]	Chromosome	RAP ID[2]	MSU ID[3]	Description	References[4]
Se	*Se1*, *K*, *Lm*, *Hd1*	SD promotion/ LD repression	6	Os06g0275000	LOC_Os06g16370	Zinc-finger protein	Chandraratna (1953, 1955), Yokoo and Fujimaki (1971), Yano et al. (1997, 2000)
E1	*M*, *m-Ef1*, *Ghd7*	LD repression	7	Os07g0261200	LOC_Os07g15770	CCT (CONSTANS, CONSTANS-LIKE, and TIMING OF CHLOROPHYLL A/B BINDING1) domain protein	Syakudo and Kawase (1953), Syakudo et al. (1954), Tsai and Oka (1966), Tsai (1976), Okumoto et al. (1992), Okumoto and Tanisaka (1997), Xue et al. (2008)
E2	*Hd17*, *Ef7*, *OsELF3-1*, *OsELF3*, *Hd-q*	SD/LD promotion	6	Os06g0142600	LOC_Os06g05060	Homolog of Arabidopsis EARLY FLOWERING 3 protein	Syakudo and Kawase (1953), Syakudo et al. (1954), Matsubara et al. (2008a), Monden et al. (2009), Yuan et al. (2009), Matsubara et al. (2012), Saito et al. (2012)
E3	*Hd6*	LD repression	3	Os03g0762000	LOC_Os03g55389	Similar to protein kinase CK2, alpha subunit	Syakudo and Kawase (1953), Syakudo et al. (1954), Takahashi et al. (2001)
E	*Ef1*, *Ehd1*	SD/LD promotion	10	Os10g0463400	LOC_Os10g32600	B-type response regulator	Tsai and Oka (1966), Tsai (1976), Sato et al. (1988), Doi et al. (2004), Saito et al. (2009)

Gene symbol	Synonym	Effect on flowering[1]	Chromosome	RAP ID[2]	MSU ID[3]	Description	References[4]
Hd3a		SD promotion	6	Os06g0157700	LOC_Os06g06320	Florigen	Kojima et al. (2002)
RFT1		LD promotion	6	Os06g0157500	LOC_Os06g06300	Florigen	Kojima et al. (2002), Ogiso-Tanaka et al. (2013)
DTH8	*Ghd8, LHD1, Hd5, LH8*	SD promotion/ LD repression	8	Os08g0174500	LOC_Os08g07740	Putative HAP3 subunit of CCAAT box-binding transcription factor	Wei et al. (2010), Dai et al. (2012), Fujino et al. (2013), Chen et al. (2014)
DTH3	*OsMADS50*	SD/LD promotion	3	Os03g0122600	LOC_Os03g03070; LOC_Os03g03100	MIKC-type MADS-box protein	Lee et al. (2004), Bian et al. (2011)
DTH2		LD promotion	2	Os02g0724000	LOC_Os02g49230	CONSTANS-like protein	Wu et al. (2013)
Hd16	*EL1*	LD repression	3	Os03g0793500	LOC_Os03g57940	Casein kinase I	Dai and Xue (2010), Hori et al. (2013), Kwon et al. (2014)
OsPRR37	*Hd2*	LD repression	7	Os07g0695100	LOC_Os07g49460	Pseudo-response regulator	Koo et al. (2013)
Ehd4		SD/LD promotion	3	Os03g0112700	LOC_Os03g02160	Zinc finger CCCH domain-containing protein	Gao et al. (2013)
Hd18		SD/LD promotion	8	Os08g0143400	LOC_Os08g04780	Amine oxidase domain-containing protein	Shibaya et al. (2016)

1. SD: Short days; LD: Long days.
2. Locus ID of the Rice Annotation Project, National Agriculture and Food Research Organization.
3. Locus ID of the Rice Genome Annotation Project, Michigan State University.
4. Short references listed here are detailed with their full mention in Hori, Matsubara and Yano (2016).

Source: Adapted from Hori, K., K. Matsubara and M. Yano (2016), "Genetic control of flowering time in rice: Integration of Mendelian genetics and genomics", https://doi.org/10.1007/s00122-016-2773-5.

It has been found that the *Hd1* protein can bind to the *Ghd7* protein both in rice protoplasts and in cells from rice plants (Nemoto et al., 2016). This *Hd1-Ghd7* complex may play an important role in repressing the *Ehd1* (*Early heading date 1*) gene, a flowering promoter in rice, under long-day conditions. Conversely, the activation of *Ehd1* under short-day conditions may not require *Ghd7* function. Although most key functional natural variations identified in QTL genes have resulted in defective alleles, a specific mutation resulting in amino acid changes in the *Hd17* (*Heading date 17*) gene was found to be beneficial for rice breeding as it improved *Hd17* activity, reducing the amount of *Ghd7* repressor mRNA (Matsubara et al., 2012). This selection occurred as a rare case during modern crossbreeding in rice.

Throughout the history of rice breeding, there are a few cases of cultivars that have progressed southward. A rare example of this is the major Chinese Taipei cultivar, Taichung 65, which has defective alleles in two heading date genes. One is a defective allele of the *Hd1* gene, while the other is the *Ehd1* gene; both of these defective alleles were introgressed from local landraces in Chinese Taipei into Japanese cultivar backgrounds to develop Taichung 65 (Doi et al., 2004; Wei et al., 2016). Here, both defective alleles of *Hd1* and *Ehd1* caused a late-flowering phenotype under short-day conditions. Thus, Taichung 65 possesses a long vegetative growth phase in subtropical areas of Chinese Taipei.

Itoh et al. (2018) evaluated the genetic contributions to the heading date of genome fragments from 10 distinct cultivars grown in various cultivation areas using 10 sets of chromosomal segment substitution lines (in total 429 lines). This work suggests that natural variations affecting heading date in various rice cultivars may be positioned at around 10-20 loci, although the same loci may have distinct heading date effects due to several distinct functional polymorphisms in a gene. In addition, many natural variations lead to neutral amino acid changes in genes or behave as silent mutations. Thus, phylogenetic trees tell the history (genetic distances) of genes and genomes but do not represent breeding selection due to functional changes of the target agricultural traits. Furthermore, some genomic regions contain clear signs of their past introgression events including selection for these heading date genes. These indicate complex genetic events for the heading date genes have been involved to establish each sub-species in rice.

Genetic factor affecting male sterility

Cytoplasmic male sterility (CMS) is a maternally inherited trait in which plants fail to produce functional pollen or anthers and is caused by interactions between the nuclei and mitochondria. A product of a CMS-causing gene encoded from the mitochondrial genome regulates nuclear genes via retrograde signalling, resulting in male sterility (reviewed in Fujii and Toriyama, 2008). However, a fertility restorer gene (*Rf* gene) in the nucleus genome suppresses the expression of the CMS-causing gene and recovers male fertility. A CMS line, a maintainer line and a fertility restorer line are thus often used for hybrid rice breeding and are known as a three-line system.

CMS plants are often obtained by successive backcrossing between distantly related species or sub-species yielding cytoplasmic substitutions, although they are sometimes found in wild rice populations. Pollen abortion was observed in different developmental stages depending on the origins of the cytoplasm. For example, microspores abort just after meiosis in wild-abortive (WA)-type CMS, which is derived from wild rice in Hainan Island, whereas pollen aborts at a tricellular pollen stage in Boro (BT)-type CMS, which is derived from an *indica* rice variety Chinsurah Boro II (Table 4.5). In another case, exemplified by Chinese wild rice (CW)-type CMS, pollen looks morphologically normal but lacks the ability to germinate. WA-type CMS is most widely used for female parents in hybrid rice breeding (reviewed in Huang et al., 2014). Other CMS types used for hybrid rice breeding include BT-type and Honglian (HL)-type CMS (reviewed in Huang et al., 2014).

Known CMS-causing genes from the mitochondrial genome are *WA352* for WA-type CMS (Bentolila and Stefanov, 2012; Luo et al., 2013; Tang et al., 2017) and *orf79* for BT-type CMS (Iwabuchi, Kyozuka and Shimamoto, 1993; Akagi et al., 1994; Kazama et al., 2016) (Table 4.5; reviewed in Huang et al., 2014; Kim and Zhang, 2018). *WA352/orf352* and their sequence variants are reported in other CMS types such as D, DA, GA, ID, K (Luo et al., 2013), and RT102 (Okazaki et al., 2013). *Orf79* and its sequence variants are reported in HL-type (Yi et al., 2002) and Lead rice (LD)-type CMS (Itabashi, Kazama and Toriyama, 2009; Table 4.5). *WA352/orf352* is composed of parts from three genes of unknown function in the Nipponbare mitochondrial genome, namely *orf284, orf224, and orf288*, and a sequence of unknown origin (Luo et al., 2013; Okazaki et al., 2013). It is co-transcribed with *rpl5*, encoding ribosomal protein large subunit 5. The *WA352* protein is reported to interact with a subunit of a respiration complex IV, resulting in reactive oxygen species (ROS) production and programmed cell death (PCD). *Orf79* consists of a part of a *coxI* encoding cytochrome oxidase subunit I and has a sequence of unknown origin. It is co-transcribed with *atp6* encoding ATP synthase subunit 6 (Iwabuchi, Kyozuka and Shimamoto, 1993; Akagi et al., 1994; Kazama et al., 2016). *ORFH79* of HL-CMS, which is encoded by a sequence variant of *orf79*, was reported to interact with a subunit of respiration complex III, resulting in ROS production and PCD leading to male sterility (Wang et al., 2013a).

Table 4.5. Type and characters of cytoplasmic male sterility (CMS)

CMS type	Cytoplasm source	Morphology of pollen[1]	Abortive stage	CMS-associated gene	Fertility restorer genes[2]
WA	Wild rice with abortive pollen	Unstained; irregular withered	Early uninucleate microspore	*WA352*	*Rf3, Rf4 (=PPR782a)*
HL	Wild rice (Hong Lian)	Unstained; spherical	Bicellular pollen	*orfH79*	*Rf5(='Rf1a),' Rf6 (PPR 894)*
BT	Chinsurah Boro II (*indica*)	Lightly stained; spherical	Tricellular pollen	*orf79*	*Rf1a(='PPR791),' Rf1b (=PPR506)*
LD	Lead rice (*indica*)	Lightly stained; spherical	Tricellular pollen	*L-orf79*	*Rf2 (glycine-rich protein)*
CW	Wild rice (W1)	Stained; round but no germination	Germination	*orf307*	*Rf17(='retrograde-regulated' male sterility)*

1. pollen stainability with I2-KI.
2. the names of the PPR genes are based on the number of encoded amino acids.
Sources: Li, S., D. Yang and Y. Zhu (2007), "Characterization and use of male sterility in hybrid rice breeding", https://doi.org/10.1111/j.1744-7909.2007.00513.x; Huang, J.Z. et al. (2014), "Workable male sterility systems for hybrid rice: Genetics, biochemistry, molecular biology, and utilization", https://doi.org/10.1186/s12284-014-0013-6; Kim, Y.-J. and D. Zhang (2018), "Molecular control of male fertility for crop hybrid breeding", https://doi.org/10.1016/j.tplants.2017.10.001.

Fertility *Rf* genes are present in the nuclear genome. *Rf1* for BT-type CMS is present in chromosome 10 and acts gametophytically for fertility restoration. *Rf3* and *Rf4* are in chromosomes 1 and 10 respectively, and sporophytically restore fertility. *Rf2* for LD-CMS has a weak restoration ability for BT-type CMS. There are some other *Rf* genes known to be responsible for weak fertility restoration (reviewed in Huang et al., 2014).

Molecular cloning has been performed for the following *Rf* genes: *Rf1a* and *Rf1b* for BT-type CMS (Kazama and Toriyama 2003; Komori et al., 2004; Akagi et al., 2004; Wang et al., 2006); *Rf4* for WA-type CMS (Kazama and Toriyama 2014; Tang et al., 2014), and *Rf5* (=*Rf1*) and *Rf6* for HL-type CMS (Huang et al., 2015) (Table 4.5; reviewed in Huang et al., 2014; Kim and Zhang, 2018). These genes all encode pentatricopeptide repeat (PPR) proteins, which are known to be sequence-specific RNA-binding proteins (Table 4.5). These PPR proteins are targeted into the mitochondria and bind to *orf79* or *WA352*-containing RNA, and promote RNA processing, such as RNA cleavage and degradation, resulting in the suppressed accumulation of products from CMS-causing genes. *Rf2* encodes a glycine-rich protein, although its restoration mechanisms are unknown (Itabashi et al., 2011).

Thermo-sensitive genic male sterility (TGMS) and photoperiod-sensitive genic male sterility (PGMS) have also been used for hybrid rice breeding (reviewed in Huang et al., 2014). They are also referred to as environment-sensitive genic male sterility (EGMS). In these cases, a maintainer line is no longer necessary because male-sterile lines can be propagated through self-pollination under designated conditions. Hybrid seeds are produced by crossing between these male-sterile lines and any pollen parents. Thus, this method is called the two-line method. An example of this is the super hybrid rice "Liangyoupei9 (LYP9)" that was obtained using a P/TGMS line, Peiai64S (PA64S) and pollen parent 93-11. The TGMS and PGMS lines are sterile in high-temperature (typically >25°C) and long-day conditions (typically >14 h) but fertile in lower temperature and short-day conditions.

Although most genic male sterility is caused by loss-of-function alleles of genes that are essential for anther and pollen development (reviewed in Wang et al., 2013b), dominant genic male-sterile mutants have also been reported in rice and are expected to be useful for recurrent selection breeding to facilitate population improvements. The Pingxiang dominant male-sterile gene was designated Ms-p and mapped to chromosome 10 (Huang et al., 2007). The gene for the Sanming dominant male sterility was named *SMS* and mapped to chromosome 8 (Pang et al., 2017). The *SMS* dominant male-sterile line has been effectively used for recurrent selection breeding to obtain multiple abiotic stress-tolerant rice cultivars (Pang et al., 2017).

Genetic factors affecting sterility and weakness in hybridisation between cultivated species

Fitness reductions, such as lethality, weakness and sterility, are observed both in intraspecific and interspecific rice hybrids. This phenomenon is referred to as hybrid incompatibility. This subsection describes the hybrid incompatibility found in intraspecific hybrids of the Asian cultivated species *O. sativa* and in the interspecific hybrids between *O. sativa* and closely related species.

Hybrid compatibilities of the *Oryza* species with AA genomes (*sativa* complex) are governed by nuclear gene interactions and cytoplasm-nucleus gene interactions have also been detected. Details of the cytoplasmic male sterility genes have been described in the preceding section ("Genetic factor affecting male sterility"). Regarding nuclear genes involved in hybrid sterility, no locus common to natural mutations and induced mutations have been detected so far.

Hybrid sterility refers to the sterility of male gametes, female gametes or both gametes of F_1 hybrids or hybrid progeny. Sterility can be sporophytic or gametophytic. Genetic studies of hybrid sterility have revealed two genetic models: i) allelic interactions at a single genetic locus (including tightly linked multiple genes) on heterozygotes; and ii) interactions at two independent genetic loci. In the allelic interaction model, selective abortion occurs depending on the genotype of the gametophyte but no sterility or other abnormal phenotype can be seen in either homozygote. In the intraspecific crosses of *O. sativa*, many genes corresponding to the allelic interaction types are reported, such as *Sa* (Zhuang et al., 1999), *Sc* (Zhuang et al., 2002), *S24* (Kubo et al., 2008), *S25* (Win et al., 2009), *S35* (Kubo et al., 2008) as male sterility genes and *S5* (Ikehashi and Araki, 1986) and *S7* (Yanagihara, Kato and Ikehashi, 1992) as female sterility genes. The cross combination of *O. rufipogon* and *O. sativa*, *S36* (Win et al., 2009) and *ESA1* (Hou et al., 2019) was found to cause hybrid sterility.

Some cases of hybrid sterility are governed by intergenic interactions at two or more loci. In intraspecific hybrids of the cultivated species, *DPL1*/*DPL2* genes for gametophytic pollen sterility (Mizuta, Harushima and Kurata, 2010) and *HSA1*, *HSA2*, and *HSA3* (Kubo and Yoshimura, 2005) for sporophytic embryo sac sterility have been reported. *DGS1*/*DGS2* is known for interspecific hybridisation between *O. sativa* and *O. nivara* (Nguyen et al., 2017).

More than 40 causal loci/QTL for hybrid sterility have been reported. These reported genes mainly consist of allelic interaction type genes. Incompatible genotypes of the sporophyte or gametophyte determine sterility. Out of these reported gene loci, 11 genes have been isolated and characterised (Table 4.6). Cloning studies have revealed that the allelic interaction type loci are composed of two or more genes encoding different protein families or a tandem duplication of gene copies. The causal genes of hybrid sterility do not likely function in a single or specific physiological pathway essential for gamete development. However, genes encoding proteinases or peptidases have often been found to be the causal molecules.

Table 4.6. Cloned genes affecting hybrid sterility in intraspecific crosses of *O. sativa* L.

Mendelian locus	Chr.	Affected gametophyte	Gene	Gene function	Reference
S5	6	Female	*ORF3*	Heat shock protein Hsp70	Yang et al. (2010)
			ORF4	Unknown protein with transmembrane region	Yang et al. (2010)
			ORF5	Eukaryotic aspartic proteases	Chen et al. (2008)
S7	7	Female	*ORF3*	Tetratricopeptide repeat domain-containing protein	Yu et al. (2016)
S-a	1	Male	*SaF*	F-Box Protein	Long et al. (2008)
			SaM	SUMO E3 Ligase-like Protein	Long et al. (2008)
S-c	3	Male	*S-c*	DUF1618 domain-containing protein	Shen et al. (2017)
DPL1	1	Male	*DPL1*	Unknown protein	Mizuta, Harushima and Kurata (2010)
DPL2	6	Male	*DPL2*	Unknown protein	Mizuta, Harushima and Kurata (2010)
hsa1	12	Female	*HSA1a*	DUF1618 domain-containing protein	Kubo et al. (2016)
			HSA1b	Uncharacterised protein	Kubo et al. (2016)

Sources: Chen, X.-P, et al. (2008), "Ammonia-oxidizing archaea: Important players in paddy rhizosphere soil?", https://doi.org/10.1111/j.1462-2920.2008.01613.x; Kubo, T. et al. (2016), "Two tightly linked genes at the *hsa1* locus cause both F_1 and F_2 hybrid sterility in rice", https://doi.org/10.1016/j.molp.2015.09.014; Long, Y. et al. (2008), "Hybrid male sterility in rice controlled by interaction between divergent alleles of two adjacent genes", https://doi.org/10.1073/pnas.0810108105; Mizuta, Y., Y. Harushima and N. Kurata (2010), "Rice pollen hybrid incompatibility caused by reciprocal gene loss of duplicated genes", https://doi.org/10.1073/pnas.1003124107; Shen, R. et al. (2017), "Genomic structural variation-mediated allelic suppression causes hybrid male sterility in rice", https://doi.org/10.1038/s41467-017-01400-y; Yang, J. et al. (2010), "A killer-protector system regulates both hybrid sterility and segregation distortion in rice", *Science*, Vol. 337, pp. 1336-1340; Yu, Y. et al. (2016), "Hybrid sterility in rice (*Oryza sativa* L.) involves the tetratricopeptide repeat domain containing protein", https://doi.org/10.1534/genetics.115.183848.

The gametophytic sterility genes cause skewed segregation in the progeny of the heterozygous hybrid due to their allelic interactions. This phenomenon is also called transmission ratio distortion (TRD). Both homozygotes in the progeny of the heterozygous plant do not cause remarkable phenotypes, including sterility. The positively selected alleles are expected to penetrate the population at a faster rate than normal Mendelian factors in the heterozygous population.

Some local varieties or wild species harbouring neutral alleles have been found to be compatible with any allelic type (Chen et al., 2008). Neutral alleles are in widespread use in crossbreeding and breeding programmes for the F_1 hybrids in some Asian countries (Chen et al., 2008). New Rice for Africa (NERICA), which is a hybrid cultivar derived from an interspecific hybrid between *O. sativa* and African cultivated species *O. glaberrima*, has been widely grown in Africa. The potential opportunities of hybridisation with *O. sativa* cultivars are increasing. Generally, the hybrid between *O. sativa* and *O. glaberrima* does not produce self-pollinated seeds due to complete pollen sterility. Many genes for hybrid sterility are reported in the *O. sativa/O. glaberrima* cross: *S1* (Sano, 1990), *S18* (Doi, Taguchi and Yoshimura, 1998), *S19* (Taguchi, Doi and Yoshimura, 1999; Zhang et al., 2011), *S20*, *S21* (Doi, Taguchi and Yoshimura, 1999), *S29* (Hu et al., 2006), *S33* (Ren et al., 2005), *S34 (t)* (Zhang et al., 2002), *S36* (Li et al., 2011) and *S37*, *S38*, *S39* (Xu et al., 2014). *S1* causes both pollen and seed sterility but the other genes cause only pollen sterility.

The hybrid weakness among the *O. sativa/O. rufipogon* gene pool is genetically divided into two classes, hybrid weakness or lethality found in the F_1 generation (F_1 hybrid weakness/lethality) and those found in the F_2 and subsequent generations (F_2 hybrid weakness/lethality or hybrid breakdown). *Hwa*, *Hwc* and

Hwi1 are reported as F_1 hybrid weakness genes (Kuboyama et al., 2009; Ichitani et al., 2011; Chen et al., 2014). Duplicate recessive genes such as *hwb1/hwb2* (Oka, 1957), *hwd1/hwd2* (Fukuoka, Namai and Okuno, 1998) and *hwe1/hwe2* (Kubo and Yoshimura, 2002) are known as causal genes for F_2 hybrid weakness. Further analyses of *Hbd2/Hbd3* (Yamamoto et al., 2007; Yamamoto, 2010), *Hwi1/Hwi2* (Chen et al., 2014) and *Hwc3* (Nadir et al., 2019) revealed that deleterious interactions between these genes cause an autoimmune response.

Breeding approaches

Rice breeding has been supported by a variety of breeding techniques based on accumulated research and traditional experience over many years. Traditional breeding methods include the collection and evaluation of genetic resources, induction of artificial mutations and the selection of individuals and lines. It is described in detail in the Kaneda publication (1993).

To achieve stable rice production, high yields, lodging resistance, resistance to pests and disease, tolerance to abiotic stress such as high and low temperature, drought, salinity as well as good eating quality and health functionality are the main targets for rice breeding programmes. With temperature increases due to global warming, responses to high-temperature damage such as reductions in yield, grain quality and sterility need to be improved. In Japan and Korea, rice has been used as a feed crop, as whole crop silage or grain. High biomass and digestibility by animals are target traits in breeding programmes.

The lodging resistant variety IR8 was the first variety developed with a semi-dwarfing gene, *sd1*, and contributed greatly to the Green Revolution in the 1960s (Khush, Coffman and Beachell, 2001). Since then, the development of semi-dwarfing varieties has been the main goal in most rice-producing countries. It was revealed that the *Sd1* gene encodes GA20-oxidase (Os20ox2) and that the short stature phenotype was caused by a loss-of-function *sd1* (Sasaki et al., 2002). Interestingly, different types of the *Sd1* alleles, which showed weak function, have independently been artificially induced in Japan and the United States. These several types of *sd1* alleles have been used to develop new varieties (Sasaki et al., 2002). Major targets of disease resistance in rice breeding are rice blast, bacterial leaf blight, brown spot, sheath blight, rice stripe, rice dwarf and yellow dwarf, and, for pest resistance, they are brown planthopper, green leafhopper, rice stem borer and pecky rice bug (Annex 4.A and Annex 4.B).

Crossbreeding and selection are standard methods in rice breeding programmes. In the 1960s, since the cytoplasmic male sterility and its restorer genes became available, the development of F_1 hybrid varieties began and their commercial production increased (Cheng et al., 2007; FAORAP and APSA, 2014; Xie and Zhang, 2018).

Initially, a three-line system (cytoplasmic male-sterile [CMS], maintainer and restorer lines) was employed to develop F_1 hybrid cultivars. However, later strategies involved male parents for two-line hybrids based on thermo- or photo-sensitive male sterile lines to enhance the effective F_1 seed production (FAORAP and APSA, 2014; Cheng et al., 2007). In Asia, following the success of producing F_1 rice hybrids China, several other countries such as Bangladesh, India, Indonesia, Myanmar, the Philippines and Viet Nam introduced the development and production of F_1 hybrids. The level of heterosis has been clear in *indica* and *japonica* crosses but a relatively small level of heterosis was observed between *japonica* crosses. This poor heterosis resulted in limitations for the F_1 hybrid cultivars in Japan and Korea.

To improve a particular trait of interest, induced mutations and marker-assisted selection (MAS) have been utilised. So far, lodging resistance, disease resistance and changes to chemical components in the endosperm have been achieved through the selection of mutants induced by gamma-ray and chemical mutagens (Rutger, 1992; Nakagawa and Kato, 2017).

Due to the progress in genome sequencing and methods for genetic analysis, QTL identification and cloning have been routinely performed (Yano, 2001; Yamamoto, Yonemaru and Yano, 2009). In association with the dramatic progress in the detection of sequence variations, MAS has already been an effective method for rice breeding programmes (Jena and Mackill, 2008; Cobb, Biswas and Platten, 2019).

The utilisation of biotechnology in rice breeding started with transformation technologies in the late 1980s. The use of developed genome editing technologies has been promoted since 2010 (Christian et al., 2010). Since the CRISPR/Cas9 system was published in 2012 (Gasiunas et al., 2012; Jinek et al., 2012), however, genome editing technologies have rapidly spread, and genome editing for rice was developed in 2013 utilising the CRISPR/Cas9 system (Annex 4.D).

Hybridisation and introgression

Outcrossing and gene flow in rice

Cultivated rice is a strictly self-pollinated species. However, cross-pollination and gene flow can occur if rice is growing in the vicinity of weedy rice or other AA genome wild species, which show some degree of sterility and whose flowers remain open at the time of pollination. Oka (1988a) reported that the natural crossing frequency of *japonica* ranges from 0.6% to 3.9% and that of *indica* ranges from 0.0% to 6.8% (Table 4.7). The natural crossing rate of wild rice is greater than that of cultivated rice. There are some wild rice varieties with crossing rates greater than 50% (Table 4.7). This variation could be due to different growing conditions, for example the distance between rice and weedy rice/wild species, wind speed, opening of flower, stigma protrusion or the degree of sterility of the weedy rice/wild species, thus allowing for open pollination.

Table 4.7. Outcrossing rates estimated in wild and cultivated rice species by different methods

Taxa/type	Origin	Method	No. of populations	Outcrossing (%)	Reference[1]
Asian *O. perennis* Perennial	Chinese Taipei	Marker gene	1	30.7	Oka (1956c)
	Thailand	Marker gene	1	44	Oka and Chang (1961)
	Thailand	Isozyme markers	1 (NE88)	50.6	Barbier (1987)
Intermediate	Thailand	Isozyme markers	1 (CP20)	55.9	Barbier (1987)
Perennial	India	Variance ratio	1	37.4	Oka and Chang (1959)
	Sri Lanka	Variance ratio	2	22.4-26.5	Sakai and Narise (1959)
Annual	India	Variance ratio	1	21.7	Oka and Chang (1959)
	India	Variance ratio	3	16.6-33.9	Sakai and Narise (1960)
	India	Marker gene	1	7.9	Roy (1921)
	Thailand	Isozyme markers	1 (NE4)	7.2	Barbier (1987)
Weedy	India	Variance ratio	2	17.3-20.6	Oka and Chang (1959)
breviligulata	Africa	Variance ratio	2	3.2-19.7	Morishima et al. (1963)
sativa	India	Marker gene	34	0-6.8	Butany (1957)
indica	Africa	Marker gene	2	0-1.1	Roberts et al. (1961)
indica	Chinese Taipei	Marker gene	4	0.1-0.3	Oka (unpublished)
japonica	Chinese Taipei	Marker gene	5	0.6-3.9	Oka (unpublished)
indica	Sri Lanka	Variance ratio	1	3.6	Sakai and Narise (1960)

1. Short references listed here are detailed with their full mention in Oka (1988a).
Source: Oka, H.-I. (1988a), "Ancestors of cultivated rice", in *Origin of Cultivated Rice*, Japan SSP, Tokyo/Elsevier, Amsterdam, pp. 18-22.

Wild relatives show outcrossing to a varying degree. In several wild species or weedy rice species, the anthers are long with extruded stigma, favouring outcrossing. The Asian forms of *O. perennis* complex showed outcrossing ranging from 7.0% to 55.9%, which was higher in perennial than annual types.

Outcrossing is dependent on flower morphology, stigma exertion, male sterility, the duration of flower opening and other environmental factors (Endo et al., 2009).

Outcrossing is also affected by the capacity of the stigma to receive alien pollen before self-pollination and the capacity of anthers to emit pollen to pollinate other plants in their proximity. Intervals from flowering to pollen emission, stigma size and extrusion of the stigmas from the flower are the other factors affecting outcrossing.

Lu, Yang and Ellstrand (2016) summarised the results of different studies conducted in China, Costa Rica, Korea, Spain and the US on pollen-mediated gene flow from transgenic to non-transgenic rice. Outcrossing was determined using molecular marker analysis. The gene flow frequency ranged from 0.0% to 0.47% except in one study where it ranged from 1.0% to 2.3% (Table 4.8).

Several studies have shown that the strictly self-fertilising nature and short life of the pollen grains of cultivated rice plants account for the extremely low gene flow from transgenic rice to other non-rice cultivars. However, through pollen-mediated gene flow, transgenes can move from cultivated rice to nearby weedy rice (*O. sativa f. spontanea*) or any of the six wild species (*O. rufipogon*, *O. nivara*, *O. breviligulata* (*O. barthii*), *O. longistaminata*, *O. meridionalis*, *O. glumaepatula*) belonging to *sativa* complex growing sympatrically or as intermixed populations.

Several studies have shown that the outcrossing of rice with weedy rice and AA genome wild species of rice, occurs in field conditions in natural habitats. However, it is not known precisely how fitness-enhancing transgenes will accumulate in these populations and how far these will have unwanted environmental consequences. The risks could be assessed by: i) estimating transgene frequencies; ii) assessing the expression levels of transgenes in wild populations; and iii) measuring the fitness change.

Rong et al. (2012) grew 3 genetically engineered (GE) insect-resistant lines with non-transgenic lines at four scales ranging from 9 m^2 to 576 m^2 (8 GE: 1 non-GE). Out of 1.3 million seeds examined from non-GE rice plots, very low frequencies of the transgene were detected (<0.1%). Chen et al. (2004) estimated outcrossing rate from cultivated to weedy rice (0.011-0.046%) and from cultivated to wild rice (1.21-2.19%). Thus, transgenes can be expressed in weedy rice and wild species and potentially alter the fitness of the wild/weedy plants and the dynamics of the wild population.

Table 4.8. Field experiments to detect the frequency of pollen-mediated (trans)gene flow from cultivated rice to weedy rice

Crop	(Trans)gene	Location	Marker used to detect gene flow	Observed gene flow frequency (%)	References[1]
Glufosinate-resistant rice	[2]	United States	Glufosinate-resistant marker	0	Sanders et al. (1998)
Imidazolinone-resistant rice	[2]	United States	Imidazolinone-resistant marker	0.00	Sanders et al. (2000)
Imidazolinone-resistant rice line 'CL 2551'	[2]	United States	Imidazolinone-resistant marker and SSR molecular fingerprinting	0.0-0.05	Estorninos et al. (2002)
GE rice	*gusA* and *bar* gene	Spain	Glucuronidase marker	0.036±0.006	Messeguer et al. (2004)
GE rice (Nam29/TR18)	*bar* gene	South Korea	Basta-resistance marker	0.011-0.046	Chen et al. (2004)
Imidazolinone-resistant Clearfield® rice	[2]	United States	Imidazolinone-resistant marker and SSR molecular fingerprinting	0.003-0.008	Shivrain et al. (2007)
GE rice	PPT-R	Costa Rica	Glufosinate-resistant marker	1.0-2.3	Olguin et al. (2009)
GE rice	*Protox* (protoporphyrino-gen oxidase) gene	South Korea	PPO-resistance marker	0.04	Chun et al. (2011)
GE rice	*bar* gene	China	Basta-resistance marker	0.002-0.342 and 0.090	Jia et al. (2014)
indica and tropical *japonica* rice cultivars	[2]	United States	SSR molecular fingerprinting	0	Gealy et al. (2015)
GE rice (Xiang 125S/Bar68-1)	*bar* gene	China	Glufosinate-resistant marker	0.395-0.470 and 0-0.187	Sun et al. (2015)

1. Short references listed here are detailed with full mention in Lu, Yang and Ellstrand (2016).
2. Non-transgenic variety
Source: Lu, B.R., X. Yang and N.C. Ellstrand (2016), "Fitness correlates of crop transgene flow into weedy populations: a case study of weedy rice in China and other examples", https://doi.org/10.1111/eva.12377.

Experimental production of interspecific hybrids

A number of studies have been conducted over the years on interspecific crosses for cytogenetic research involving genome analysis, chromosome pairing analysis in F_1 hybrids and more recently on the introgression of useful genes from wild species into cultivated rice for tolerance to biotic and abiotic stresses, diversification of cytoplasmic male sterility sources and to introgress QTLs or yield-enhancing loci "wild species alleles" (Brar and Singh, 2011; Brar and Khush, 2018). Hybrids have been successfully produced through crosses made between rice and all of the 22 wild species of *Oryza* except *O. schlechteri*. Several crossability barriers limit the transfer of genes from wild species into rice (Sitch, 1990; Khush and Brar, 1992). Nezu, Katayama and Kihara (1960) studied crossability and chromosome affinity among 17 species of *Oryza* and found that crossability differs in different cross-combinations.

Crossability amongst AA genome species is relatively high and crosses of rice with the six diploid wild species of the *sativa* complex (2n = 24, AA) can be made easily. These hybrids have been produced through direct crosses (without embryo rescue) of rice with all of the species of the *sativa* complex. Plant breeders make these crosses routinely by crossing elite breeding lines of rice (*O. sativa*) with the wild species accessions possessing the genes for the target agronomic traits. F_1 offspring are partially fertile and these are either selfed or backcrossed with the recurrent rice parent to develop elite breeding lines for the introgression of useful genes from wild species. Several institutes have produced a series of interspecific hybrids (rice × wild species) and introgression lines for cytogenetic and breeding research.

In natural conditions, where rice and diploid wild species of the *sativa* complex grow sympatrically, cross-hybridisation occurs frequently, resulting in the production of interspecific hybrids, intermediate progenies or hybrid swarms. Such types of cross-hybridisation in natural habitats are common among rice, weedy rice and AA genome wild species.

Unlike the AA genome wild species, hybrids cannot be produced through direct crosses between rice and wild species belonging to the *officinalis* complex (BB, CC, BBCC, CCDD, EE genomes) without embryo rescue in the F_1. No report is available on the natural crossing and production of hybrids between rice and species of this complex. Hybrids have been produced between rice and wild species of the *officinalis* complex through embryo rescue of developing F_1 seeds (Jena and Khush, 1990; Brar, Elloran and Khush, 1991). In one experiment, a total of 26 034 spikelets of three lines of *O. sativa* were pollinated with the CC genome wild species (*O. officinalis*) and the seed set ranged from 8.82% to 17.30% (Jena and Khush, 1990). From these F_1 seeds, embryos were rescued after 14 days of pollination and cultured on MS medium. While the germination ratios for the embryos were high (from 56.8% to 70.0%), the rate of plant survival after culture was lower. As a result, crossability (number of hybrid plants obtained/total number of spikelets pollinated) ranged from 1.0% to 2.3%.

Crosses of *O. sativa* with the CCDD genome species (*O. latifolia*) were made by Multani et al. (2003). The seed set was 19.8%, germination of the hybrid embryos was 85.5%, with crossability being 7.6%. In the BC_1, 10 144 spikelets of F_1, were pollinated with rice pollen and crossability was 0.11%, similarly in the BC_2 and BC_3 crossability was 0.21% and 0.62% respectively.

Multani et al. (1994) made crosses among rice and the EE genome wild species (*O. australiensis*). Seed set ranged from 2.3% to 2.9%. Although embryos germinated well in the culture medium (50.4-62.9%), however, crossability was extremely low (0.25-0.90%). Data on such a low crossability in controlled crosses of rice and distantly related wild species support the lack of any report of hybrids under natural field conditions. Low crossability and other barriers may be the reason why no natural hybrids exist between rice and wild species, except for the AA genome species.

A number of genes for several agronomic traits, brown planthopper (BPH) resistance, bacterial blight (BB) resistance and blast resistance, have been introgressed from wild species of the *sativa* complex into cultivated rice and improved varieties have been released for commercial cultivation (Brar and Khush, 1997, 2018; Table 4.9). Among the classical examples are the introgression of a gene for grassy stunt virus resistance from *O. nivara* to cultivated rice varieties (Khush, 1977) and the transfer of a cytoplasmic male-sterile (CMS) source from wild rice, *O. sativa f spontanea* (Lin and Yuan, 1980).

Other useful genes from wild species such as *Xa21*, *Xa23 and Xa38* for BB resistance have been introgressed into rice. *Xa21* has a broad spectrum of resistance and has been pyramided along with other genes for BB resistance (Singh et al., 2001). Many varieties have been released through marker-assisted selection (MAS) using *Xa21* and other stacked genes. Genes for tolerance to tungro and tolerance to acid sulphate soil conditions have been transferred from *O. rufipogon* into the *indica* rice cultivar (Table 4.9). Recently, at Punjab Agricultural University, India, *Xa38* and *xa45(t)* have been identified from *O. nivara* and *O. glaberrima* respectively for resistance to BB.

Advanced breeding lines carrying these genes have been developed and one of the lines (PR127) carrying *xa45(t)* has been released for commercial cultivation. Furthermore, many introgression lines harbouring variations for yield component traits from the five different wild species with AA genomes have been developed (Bhatia et al., 2017). The African rice (*O. glaberrima*) has been used extensively by the Africa Rice Center and a number of *indica* rice varieties NERICA have been released with introgressed genes for early heading, weed competitive ability and tolerance to biotic and abiotic stress.

Despite limited recombination between chromosomes of rice and wild species such as *O. officinalis, O. minuta, O. latifolia, O. australiensis,* and *O. grandiglumis* of the *officinalis* complex, some genes for resistance to BPH, BB, blast, and whitebacked planthopper (WBPH) have been successfully introgressed into rice (Table 4.9). Some varieties have also been released commercially.

Table 4.9. Introgression of genes from wild *Oryza* species into cultivated rice

Trait(s) transferred into *O. sativa* (AA)	Wild Species (donor)	Gene/QTLs	Genome
Grassy stunt resistance	*O. nivara*	*Gs*	AA
Bacterial blight resistance	*O. longistaminata*	*Xa21*	AA
	O. rufipogon	*Xa23*	AA
	O. nivara	*Xa38*	AA
	O. officinalis	*Xa 29(t)*	CC
	O. minuta	*Xa27*	BBCC
	O. latifolia	Unknown	CCDD
	O. australiensis	Unknown	EE
	O. brachyantha	Unknown	FF
	O. glaberrima	*xa45(t)*	AA
Blast resistance	*O. glaberrima*	Unknown	AA
	O. rufipogon	Unknown	AA
	O. nivara	Unknown	AA
	O. glumaepatula	Unknown	AA
	O. barthii	Unknown	AA
	O. minuta	*Pi9*	BBCC
	O. australiensis	*Pi40*	EE
Brown planthopper (BPH) resistance	*O. rufipogon*	*Bph35*	AA
	O. nivara	*Bph34*	AA
	O. officinalis	*Bph11, Bph12, Bph14, Bph15*	CC
	O. eichingeri	*Bph13*	CC
	O. minuta	*Bph20, Bph21*	BBCC
	O. latifolia	Unknown	CCDD
	O. australiensis	*Bph10, Bph18*	EE
Whitebacked planthopper (WBPH) resistance	*O. officinalis*	*Wbph7(t), Wbph8(t)*	CC
	O. latifolia	Unknown	CCDD
Cytoplasmic male sterility (CMS)	*O. sativa f spontanea*	Wild abortive (WA)	AA
	O. perennis	Unknown	AA
	O. glumaepatula	Unknown	AA
	O. rufipogon	Unknown	AA
Tungro tolerance	*O. rufipogon*	Unknown	AA
Tolerance to iron toxicity	*O. rufipogon*	Unknown	AA
	O. glaberrima	Unknown	AA
Drought-related traits	*O. glaberrima*	QTL	AA
Tolerance to aluminium toxicity	*O. rufipogon*	QTL	AA
Tolerance to acidic conditions	*O. glaberrima*	Unknown	AA
	O. rufipogon	Unknown	AA
Tolerance to phosphorus deficiency	*O. glaberrima*	Unknown	AA
	O. rufipogon	Unknown	AA
Yield-enhancing loci (wild species alleles)	*O. rufipogon*	QTL	AA
	O. nivara	QTL	AA
	O. grandiglumis	QTL	CCDD
Earliness, stress tolerance, weed competitive ability	*O. glaberrima*	Unknown	AA
Increased elongation ability	*O. rufipogon*	Unknown	AA

Note: QTL – Quantitative trait locus.
Source: Khush, G.S. and D.S. Brar (2017), "Alien introgression in rice", https://doi.org/10.1007/s13237-017-0222-7.

Introgression from the CC genome species: Several introgression lines have been produced from the crosses of *O. sativa* and *O. officinalis* (Jena and Khush, 1990). Genes for resistance to BPH, e.g. *Bph10, bph11, bph12* and *Bph18*, and two QTL, *qBph1, qBph2 and Xa29(t)* for BB resistance have been introgressed into the progenies. Four breeding lines have been released as varieties (MTL95, MTL98, MTL103, and MTL110) for commercial cultivation in the Mekong Delta of Viet Nam.

Introgression from the BBCC genome species: Interspecific hybrids have been produced between *O. sativa* and the tetraploid wild species *O. minuta* (BBCC). Advanced introgression lines were produced using the embryo rescue of F_1 hybrids followed by backcrossing with the *O. sativa* parent (Brar et al., 1996). Genes for resistance to BB and blast have been introgressed into rice. Blast resistance gene (*Pi9*) has a wide spectrum resistance and has been used in breeding programmes in India. Two genes (*Bph20* and *Bph21*) for BPH resistance have been introgressed from *O. minuta* into rice.

Introgression from the CCDD genome species: Previous investigations have developed hybrids between rice and *O. latifolia* (CCDD) (Sitch, 1990; Brar, Elloran and Khush, 1991). Several introgression lines derived from this cross have been evaluated for the introgression of useful traits (Multani et al., 2003). Ten allozymes of *O. latifolia*, such as Est5, Amp1, Pgi1, Mdh3, Pgi2. Amp3, Pgd2, Est9, Amp2 and Sdh1, located on 8 of the 12 chromosomes were observed in the introgression lines. Alien introgression was also detected for morphological traits such as long awns, earliness, black hull, purple stigma and apiculus. Genes for resistance to BB, BPH and WBPH have been introgressed into elite breeding lines from *O. latifolia*. Yield-enhancing loci in the population derived from crosses of the *japonica* cultivar Hwaseongbyeo × *O. grandiglumis* (CCDD) have been identified. Of the 39 QTL, *O. grandiglumis* contributed desirable alleles in 18 QTL.

Introgression from EE genome species: Hybrids between cultivated rice and the EE genome species *O. australiensis* were produced (Multani et al., 1994). Of the 600 BC_2F_4 progenies, four were resistant to BPH. Introgression was observed for morphological traits such as long awns and earliness and Amp3 and Est2 allozymes. Resistance to BPH was found to be under monogenic recessive control in two progenies and a dominant gene conveyed resistance in the other two. The dominant gene in one of the progenies designated as *Bph10* conferred resistance to three biotypes of BPH in the Philippines. Marker RG457 detected introgression from *O. australiensis*. Co-segregation for the BPH reaction and molecular markers showed a gene for BPH resistance linked to RG457, with a distance of 3.68 centimorgan (cM) (Ishii et al., 1994). Introgression was detected for two other genes from *O. australiensis*: Bph18 for BPH resistance and a major gene *Pi40 (t)* for blast resistance.

Introgression from FF genome species: A hybrid between cultivated rice and the FF genome species *O. brachyantha* was produced and 149 backcross progenies were obtained. Introgression was obtained for resistance to Philippines bacterial blight races 1, 4, and 6 (Brar et al., 1996). Gene transfer in the introgression lines was not associated with any undesirable traits of *O. brachyantha*.

Introgression from KKLL genome species: To introduce salt tolerance into cultivated rice, a hybrid of cultivated rice and *O. coarctata* Roxb (KKLL genome) was produced by embryo rescue method (Jena, 1994). Although salt tolerance level has not been evaluated, viable hybrid plants showed triploid nature and possessed several phenotypic characteristics resembling *O. coarctata*.

Information and data on natural introgression

Gene flow from cultivated rice to wild rice under experimental field conditions

Under experimental field conditions, gene flow from cultivated rice (*O. sativa*) to wild rice (*O. rufipogon*) was confirmed using simple sequence repeat (SSR) markers specific to cultivated rice (Song et al., 2003). Of the 23 776 seedlings from *O. rufipogon*, 294 were identified to be interspecific hybrids between *O. sativa* and *O. rufipogon*. The frequency of the gene flow significantly decreased with distance from the pollen sources of the cultivated rice. The maximum observed distance of the gene flow was 43.2 m.

Introgression from cultivated rice to wild rice under natural field conditions

Under natural field conditions, gene flow also occurs from cultivated rice to wild rice populations. In Thailand, 7 out of 13 wild rice populations were found to have glutinous genes specific to cultivated rice (Oka and Chang, 1961). Most of them seemed to be caused by occasional gene flow from cultivated rice but one maintained high frequency (28.3%) of the glutinous gene in these populations. This population may have survived beyond the initial hybrid generation with a large amount of genetic variability through introgression. In southern China, genetic variation among six wild populations in Guangdong Province was surveyed using SSR markers (Zhu et al., 2017; Jin et al., 2017). Of these, one population spatially close to rice fields showed less genetic differentiation from the local cultivated rice groups, indicating that introgression from cultivated rice considerably altered the genetic structure of the wild population.

Introgression from cultivated rice to weedy rice

Weedy rice is a conspecific form of cultivated rice. Some weedy groups seem to have evolved from cultivated ancestors according to whole-genome sequence analyses (Li et al., 2017) and others have been generated by gene flow between cultivated and wild rice in tropical Asia (Pusadee et al., 2013, Song et al., 2014). Under experimental field conditions, gene flow from cultivated rice to weedy rice was estimated to be about 0.036% when there was a 25 cm distance between the plants (Messeguer et al., 2004).

In the United States, herbicide-resistant rice varieties that were a result of mutation breeding were first marketed in 2001 (Tan et al., 2005). Low levels of natural hybrids were initially reported between resistant varieties and weedy rice (Shivrain et al., 2007, 2008). However, weed control using the herbicide has forced strong selection on weedy rice populations. In 2010, resistant weedy rice plants were detected in all 26 fields with a history of herbicide-resistant varieties in Arkansas (Burgos et al., 2014). Although most weedy rice offspring (63%) were still sensitive to the herbicide, introgression of resistant alleles to the weedy rice population, by outcrossing between weedy rice and the herbicide-resistant varieties, is highly likely to be ongoing.

Various interactions with other organisms (ecology)

Interactions in natural ecosystems and agroecosystems

Interaction with pests

Interaction with vertebrate pests

Various birds, such as sparrows, crows, pigeons, parrots, weaverbirds and ducks feed on rice around the world. Damage by birds occurs during the sowing and harvest periods. In Japan, rice crops were damaged mainly by tree sparrows, jungle crows, carrion crows, Oriental turtle doves and spot-billed ducks (Lane, Azuma and Higuchi, 1998; Fujioka and Yoshida, 2001). However, the ears of the harvested rice and gleanings were fed on mostly by ducks, geese and cranes in the winter (Shimada 2002; Fujioka et al., 2010). The Japanese Red List 2020 made the following designations: greater white-fronted geese (near threatened, NT), bean geese (vulnerable species, VU), hooded cranes (VU) and white-naped cranes (VU). Cackling geese (critically endangered, CR), snow geese (CR) and lesser white-fronted geese (endangered species, EN) were included, although there have been few arrivals (Fujioka et al., 2010).

Interaction with invertebrate pests

Many insect pests have been reported in rice cultivation areas around the world. Grist and Lever (1969) lists more than 800 insect pests but only approximately 20 species are usually important in tropical Asia (Dale, 1994). In China, it has been reported that 347 species of insects infest rice plants, of which 74 species cause economic damage, 5 species cause serious damage and 31 species cause problems depending on the region and year (Zhang, 1992).

In Japan, 232 species of insects have been reported to infest rice plants (Japanese Society of Applied Entomology and Zoology, 2006) and 8 species and 1 group (rice bugs) have been designated as Specified Pests by the Ministry of Agriculture, Forestry and Fisheries, Japan. In West Africa, 330 species of insects have been collected from paddy fields but only about 10 species are of major importance (Heinrichs and Barrion, 2004). In India, 71 species of insects have been observed in paddy fields, including root feeders, stem borers, defoliators, grain suckers, leafhoppers and plant hoppers (Ane and Hussain, 2015).

The major pest species that damage rice not only vary from region to region but also vary from year to year in the same region and by rice growth stage. The characteristics of pests are described below in terms of their feeding habits, host ranges and migration. The detailed classification and ecology of insect pests of rice plants have been previously described (Grist and Lever, 1969, Ressing et al., 1986, Khan et al., 1990; Pathak and Khan, 1994; Heinrichs, 1994; Heinrichs and Barrion, 2004).

Feeding habit

Stem borers: Fifty species have been reported worldwide, most of them in the order Lepidoptera (family: Crambidae, Noctuidae and Pyralidae) (Khan et al., 1990). The larvae infest widely from seedling to maturing stage of rice plant. Larvae penetrate the leaf sheath and stem of the rice, causing leaf death (dead heart), and no filling of the spikelets (white head). The host range varies greatly from monophagy and oligophagy to polyphagy, depending on the species (Khan et al., 1990). Major species reported are *Chilo suppressalis* and *Scirpophaga incertulas*, *Scirpophaga innotata, Sesamia inferens* in Asia and Oceania, *C. partellus*, *C. diffusilineus*, *Maliarpha separatella* in Africa (Pathak and Khan, 1994). *C. suppressalis* was one of the most important paddy rice pests in Japan but it decreased its number and infestation area rapidly from the 1960s, and damage from this pest is now hardly reported. The decrease in *C. suppressalis* is largely attributable to changes in rice varieties, earlier transplanting and the introduction of harvesting machines (Kiritani, 2007).

Stalk-eyed flies (Diptera: Diopsidae) are reported as stem borers only in Africa. The larvae penetrate the stem and produce a dead heart. Khan et al. (1990) reported five species but *Diopsis macrophthalma* (= *D. longicornis*) and *D. indica* (= *D. apicalis)* are considered the main species.

Foliage feeders: Lepidopteran insect larvae, such as armyworm, cutworm, rice green semilooper, rice caseworm, eat the leaf blade of rice plants and decrease the leaf area. The larvae of leaffolders and rice skippers fold rice leaf blade and remove leaf tissue and make white/transparent streams on the leaf blade, reducing the photosynthetic ability (Pathak and Khan, 1994; Dale, 1994). The adults and nymphs of grasshoppers (Orthoptera), locusts and field crickets can damage leaf blades and, in some circumstances, can cause outbreaks. Other known vegetative pests are rice leaf beetle, whorl maggot, leafminer, thrips and gall midge.

Plant sucking insects: Planthoppers and leafhoppers (Homoptera: Delphacidae and Cicadellidae) are the largest pest group that affect rice cultivation. *Nilaparvata lugens*, *Sogatella furcifera*, *Laodelphax striatellus* and some of the green leafhoppers (*Nephotettix* species) are distributed across large areas of Asia. *Tagosodes orizicolus* has been found in the Caribbean islands, South America and the southern United States. They suck the phloem and xylem sap and reduce photosynthesis assimilates in the rice plants. It is well known that infestations of *N. lugens* cause plant death (hopperburn) when their density on rice plants is extremely high.

The planthoppers and leafhoppers also act as vectors for many viral diseases. For example, *N. lugens* transmits the grass stunt and ragged stunt viruses in South and Southeast Asia; *L. striatellus* is a vector for the rice stripe virus and the black-streaked dwarf virus in East Asia; and the green rice leafhoppers are known for being vectors for the tungro viruses in South and Southeast Asia, and rice dwarf virus and yellow dwarf (Phytoplasma) disease in East Asia. *S. furcifera* is not known as a vector of viruses but, recently, it has been reported that it can transmit Southern rice black-streaked dwarf virus (Zhou et al., 2008; Zhang et al., 2008). Rice black bugs (*Scotinophara coarctata, Scotinophara lurida,* Hemiptera: Pentatomidae) also feed on plant sap from the rice sheath and reduce plant growth and yield (Joshi, Barrion and Sebastian, 2007).

Grain-sucking insects: After the heading stage of rice plants, many heteropteran insects move to rice paddies from surrounding grassy areas. They usually suck the endosperm of ears of mainly gramineous plants (weeds) around the rice fields. The most important species are rice bugs (Alydidae) and stink bugs (Pentatomidae), as they suck the growing spikelets and cause discolouration of the brown rice which degrades its quality and, in severe cases, sterility of the spikelets. In Japan, the quality degradation of rice grain by the sucking of leaf bugs (Miridae) is also a problem.

Insect pests of upland rice

Soil-inhabiting insects have been recorded in African and Asian countries, such as ants, termites, mole crickets, white grubs (larva of scarab beetle), rice root aphids and rice root weevils. They cause damage when the rice plants are cultivated in upland areas and well-drained conditions (Dale, 1994; Pathak and Khan, 1994).

Host range

The extent of the host range varies greatly among insect species. The planthoppers and the rice stem borers, which are important pests in a wide range of areas, are mostly monophagous or oligophagous. On the other hand, many rice bugs and stink bugs inhabit various gramineous plants and fly to paddy fields during rice heading. The southern green stink bug, *Nezara viridula*, utilises plants from 32 families and 145 species. In addition, the small brown planthopper, *Laodelphax striatellus,* lives in gramineous weeds, wheat and rice plants, and it changes hosts depending on the season. Although it is difficult to investigate the actual situation of host plant utilisation in the field, it is important to consider the developmental dynamics of insect species due to the spatiotemporal changes of rice cultivation.

Geographic/genetic variation

The introduction of pest-resistant varieties and the continuous use of pesticides leads to the development of pests that can infest these resistant varieties and are resistant to agricultural chemicals. Regional differences in chemical utilisation also lead to increased genetic variation in pests.

Long-distance migratory species

Some of the rice insect species are known to migrate exceptionally long distances. The brown planthopper *N. lugens*, whitebacked planthopper *S. furcifera*, leaffolder *Cnaphalocrocis medinalis* and armyworm *Mythimna separata* are representative of long-range migratory pests. *N. lugens* and *S. furcifera* pass the winter in the northern part of Viet Nam. After the beginning of the rice cultivation period, they increase their numbers and then start to migrate north to the Korean Peninsula and Japan via the continent. It is reported that rice planthoppers flying to Japan have changed their resistance to pesticides and biotype properties against resistant varieties (Tanaka and Matsumura, 2000; Matsumura et al., 2008; Matsumura and Sanada-Morimura, 2010), which may reflect the history of pesticide usage and resistant varieties in their original source areas. Two bugs, *Cyrtorhinus lividipennis* Reuter and *Tytthus chinensis* (Stål), are known to be the major predators of the rice planthoppers in Japan (Nakamura, 2003).

Invasive species

Some pest species are intentionally or unintentionally introduced into new environments from their origins, and cause outbreaks. The rice water weevil *Lissorhoptrus oryzophilus*, which is native to southern and eastern parts of the United States, was first detected in Aichi Prefecture, Japan, in 1976 and spread rapidly throughout Japan by 1986. It is estimated that they intruded in dry grass and were imported from the United States. It also invaded China and South Korea in 1988. It is now widely distributed in many countries including Chinese Taipei, Greece, India and Italy (Aghaee and Godfrey, 2014; CABI, 2020).

The golden apple snail *Pomacea canaliculata* (Gastropoda: Ampullariidae) is a large freshwater snail native to South America. After it was introduced to Asian countries for food purposes, individuals escaped and their populations have increased and spread through irrigation systems. It eats young rice plants and destroys the whole plant in the paddy field (Joshi and Sebastian, 2006). Damage to the rice plant is a serious problem in many countries (CABI, 2020) and *P. canaliculata* has been designated one of the top 100 of the World's Worst Invasive Alien Species (Invasive Species Specialists Group, 2020).

Predator insects including pollinator and pollen eater

Rice does not have an entomophilous flower but the pollen it produces is used by many organisms. Ladybird beetles and lacewings are natural predators that usually prey on aphids but they also feed on rice pollen when their food supply is low (Pathak and Khan, 1994). A survey in China showed that many insects use rice pollen and that leafcutter bees, sweet bees and honeybees, in particular, carry rice pollen, and *Apis mellifera* carries pollen for over 500 m (Pu et al., 2014).

Interaction with plants

Weeds

Wild, weedy and volunteer rice plants are described in the first five sections to some extent, from the viewpoints of classification, biology, genetics, introgression and so forth. Therefore, the description related to these plants here focuses on the ecology of wild rice, weedy rice (*Oryza sativa* L. [*f. spontanea*] in this document) and volunteer rice (*Oryza sativa* L. in this document). Weedy and volunteer rice behave as ecological competitors against wild rice in natural ecosystems and weedy rice results in more adverse effects than volunteer rice, from the viewpoint of weediness, such as seed shattering and dormancy. Furthermore, wild, weedy and volunteer rice are the competitors to cultivated rice in the farmland. They voluntarily grow in direct-seeded and transplanted rice areas, although they compete against cultivated rice and are more difficult to manage in direct-seeded rice than transplanted rice, due to the simultaneous growth of the cultivated rice.

Asian *O. rufipogon* is an ancestor of *O. sativa* and several factors have contributed to the so-called domestication of rice over a long historic period (Kovach, Sweeney and McCouch, 2007), as explained in the first section.

Throwback (off-type, transmogrify, de-domestication, voluntary) is the opposite of gene flow. It means that the unintentional outcrossing of the cultivated rice with wild relatives resulted in the degradation (off-type) of domestication syndrome towards weedy rice. Several examples have been reported on genetic erosion from cultivated (*indica* and *japonica*) cultivars to wild and weedy rice (Suh, Sato and Morishima, 1997; Tang and Morishima, 1998; Ishikawa et al., 2006). Many cross-hybridisations happened to generate weedy type rice or introduce various genetic components (Li et al., 2012; Huang et al., 2012). Some of them have been found as nuclear and cytoplasm substituted lines (Ishikawa et al., 2002a, 2002b; Kim et al., 2015), which may be partly due to the past cross-hybridisation presumed by Li et al. (2017). The introduction of modern varieties into different geographical areas have also resulted in weedy rice (Kawasaki et al., 2009), due to the *indica-japonica* hybridisation. The hybridisation broke seed shattering because of the inconsistency of gene components.

In addition, weedy rice is geographically distributed in almost all rice-growing areas such as in Brazil, Cambodia, China, Hungary, India, Italy, Japan, Korea, the Lao People's Democratic Republic, Malaysia, the Philippines, Sri Lanka, Thailand, the United States and Viet Nam, under different cultivation systems including upland/lowland, transplanted/wet sown/dry sown and so forth (Kraehmer et al., 2016). Herbicide-resistant red rice (*O. sativa var. sylvatica*) against acetolactate synthase (ALS) inhibitors distribute in several countries where Clearfield® rice had been cultivated several years continuously in combination with imazapic and/or imazethapyr (Burgos et al., 2014).

Since rice is grown in a wide range of farmland conditions, such as paddy (shallow/deep water) to upland fields, with different cultivation methods, and wet-/dry-sown to transplanted rice. The favourable conditions are different among the cultivars for the climates in the cultivation areas. Therefore, many kinds of weeds are grown with their own favourite habitats and/or cultivation conditions. Major weeds in the rice fields of the world are listed in Annex 4.C, except for weedy rice (Akanksha, 2009; Caton et al., 2010; IRRI, n.d.-a; n.d.-b; Kraehmer et al., 2016; Moody, 1989; Rao, Chandrasena and Matsumoto, 2017; IRRI, 1983).

The majority of weeds are grasses of Poaceae (Gramineae) species, such as *Echinochloa colona*, *E. crus-galli*, *E. glabrescens*, *Eleusine indica*, *Ischaemum rugosum*, *Leptochloa chinensis*, *Paspalum distichum*, followed by sedges (Cyperaceae), such as *Cyperus difformis*, *C. iria*, *C. rotundus*, *Fimbristylis miliacea*, the other monocotyledons (monocots) and dicotyledons (dicots). In the other monocots, *Monochoria vaginalis* is the major weed in paddy fields.

Parasitic plants (i.e. *Striga* spp.) are noxious weeds only under upland conditions, and a diversity of rice genotypes exists in *Striga* resistance (Gurney et al., 2006; Rodenburg et al., 2017). Aquatic plants, such as algae and floating plants, are also troublesome under shallow water conditions, such as transplanted rice in irrigated paddy conditions.

As these weedy plants are divergent from the *Oryza* genus, there is no possibility to cross-hybridise. Therefore, the decisive factors of their population dynamics in certain areas are as follows:

- **Competition between cultivated rice and weeds:** Weeds compete with cultivated rice for light, nutrition and water (upland soil condition only). In addition, allelopathy is also one of the important factors (see following sub-section on allelopathic interaction). On the other hand, water depth affects the population dynamics and deep water gives an advantage to cultivated rice growth in general.
- **Dormancy and longevity of seed and vegetative organs:** The dormancy changes under different seasonal, field, buried seed conditions and the longest period was ten years or more depending on the species and the above conditions. The crop rotations between paddy and upland field conditions are also effective tools for changing weed populations, which reduce their longevity and/or the amount of buried seed and vegetative organs.
- **Mitigation/invasion, acclimation, adaptation ability of weeds:** After/at seed shattering, weed seeds are carried by the wind, animals, cultivated soil, rivers and so forth. Cultivated soil can be contaminated with weed seeds attached to the tires of tractors or combine harvesters that move from field to field. Floating seeds in the paddy field flow the outlet to the river via the canal and go downstream. Riverside weeds directly go to the river and take root in the other riverbed in the downstream area. Floating seeds move to the other river basin via the irrigation canal. Import/export is also a crucial route for invasive alien species.

Competitiveness for rice and dormancy are distinctive factors in weeds in comparison to insects and diseases. The adverse effects of weeds on cultivated crops are not dramatic in the short term within the cultivation period but are long term once a weed has established its population in the area.

Allelopathic interaction

There are many reports on the allelopathy of rice. The allelopathic potential of rice might play an important role in improving weed control. There are two ways to research rice allelopathy. One is the screening of allelopathic rice cultivars or accessions. The other is the isolation and identification of allelochemicals from rice plants.

Historically, screening of rice cultivars for their allelopathic potential started in Japan and the United States around 1990. The USDA scientists, Dilday, Nastasi and Smith (1989), Dilday, Mattice and Moldenhauer (2000), Dilday, Lin and Yan (1994) and Dilday et al. (1992, 2001) evaluated allelopathic potential among thousands of rice cultivars collected worldwide. Of these, 412 among 12 000 rice cultivars exhibited allelopathic activity against ducksalad in a field assessment. The strongest cultivars were PI321777 and PI338046. In Japan, Fujii et al. screened allelopathic activity of 500 cultivars of rice in the Gene Bank of Japan by using a bioassay entitled the plant box method and found that traditional red rice such as Awa-akamai, Kouketsumochi and tropical *japonica* and African rice (*O. glaberrima*) possessed greater allelopathic potential to certain weeds than other types, especially the improved types (Fujii, 1992, 2001; Fujii and Shibuya, 1991; Fujii et al., 2001). At IRRI, Olofsdotter et al. tested actual allelopathic activity on the field and found Kouketsumochi showed the strongest suppression activity to certain weeds (Olofsdotter, Navarez and Moody, 1995; Olofsdotter, Navarez and Rebulanan, 1997; Olofsdotter et al., 1999).

Allelopathic potential may be a polygenic characteristic and its correlation with other rice characteristics has been controversial (Dilday et al., 1991). Ebana and Okuno reported QTL analysis with allelopathic rice (Ebana et al., 2001, Okuno and Ebana, 2003). Gu and Guo also did a screening of allelopathic rice varieties (Gu, Wang and Kong, 2008, 2009; Guo et al., 2009). Improved rice cultivars often exert weak allelopathic potential, which may be because of a lack of selection pressure for allelopathic characteristics during breeding (Olofsdotter, Navarez and Moody, 1995).

As for allelochemicals in rice, momilactones were identified from rice straws and leaves (Kato et al., 1973), rice hulls (Cartwright et al., 1981; Chung, Hahn and Ahmad, 2005) and root exudates (Kato-Noguchi and Ino, 2003, 2005; Kato-Noguchi and Peters, 2013). There are many phenolic acids reported. For example, benzoic acid, caffeic acid, salicylic acid and other phenolic acids were found in rice straws (Kuwatsuka and Shindo, 1973). Ferulic acid, coumaric acid, *p*-hydroxybenzoic acid and salicylic acid were identified in leaves and stems (Chou, Chang and Oka, 1991). Olofsdotter et al. (2002) doubted phenolic compounds as primary allelochemicals in rice because of their low concentration. Bioactive steroids were also reported (Macías et al., 2006). Other many compounds were reported (reviewed in Khanh, Xuan and Chung, 2007; Jabran, 2017; Fujii and Hiradate, 2007). There are many reports on the allelochemical candidates but the contribution of these chemicals was not well examined. There are several papers on how to evaluate the contribution by their total activity defined by the activity of each candidate and concentration *in situ* (Hiradate, 2006; Fujii and Hiradate, 2005; Hiradate et al., 2010).

Interaction with micro-organisms

Rhizosphere: The rhizosphere soil of rice enables the coexistence of aerobic and anaerobic microbes because the development of root aerenchyma allows microenvironments of aerobic areas in the anaerobic conditions of the paddy field (Shabuer et al., 2015). This also allows for radial O_2 loss which makes the difference in the redox potential and has an effect on the biogeochemistry of mineral elements in the rhizosphere, especially for C, N, P, and Fe (Kögel-Knabner et al., 2010).

Methanogens and methanotrophs are important microbes regulating methane dynamics in the rhizosphere. Methanogens that consist of domain archaea, *Methanosaeta*, *Methanocella* and *Methanobacterium*, are the main components (Imchen et al., 2019). It is known that large parts of produced methane are oxidised in the rhizosphere by methanotrophs (Kögel-Knabner et al., 2010). *Methylocystis* belonging to Type II methanotrophs are reported most abundantly in India (Pandit et al., 2016) and China (Liu et al., 2017b). Many types of nitrogen-fixing microbes have been discovered (59 genera) (Wang et al. 2019) and some of them are considered to play a beneficial role in the growth of rice (Banik, Mukhopadhaya and Dangar, 2016).

Continuous environmental changes from the root-rhizosphere-bulk soil make a large variety of biogeochemical pathways in this region. Nitrification occurred in aerobic conditions by ammonia oxidising archaea (AOA) and/or ammonia oxidising bacteria (AOB). Among AOA, *Nitrosocaldus* (Imchen et al., 2019) and/or *Nitrososphaera* (Chen et al., 2008) were reported to be abundant. In the case of AOB, *Nitrospira* was the most abundant in Japan (Bowatte et al., 2006) and China (Chen et al., 2008). The produced NO_3^- diffused into adjacent anaerobic conditions, and then denitrifiers led to gaseous nitrogen loss (N_2, NO, and N_2O) which is strongly dependent on carbon availability (Chen et al., 2018).

Anaerobic ammonia oxidation coupled with Fe^{3+} reduction, called Feammox, is driven by the Fe^{3+} reduction (Zhou et al., 2016) and then generates NO_2^-, NO_3^- and N_2 as the terminal product of the NH_3 oxidation pathway using different microbes (Yang, Weber and Silver, 2012).

The existence of fungi is limited under anaerobic conditions, while contributions of arbuscular mycorrhizal fungi (AMF) on the rice growth have been reported (Watanarojanaporn et al., 2013) but it has also been reported that only a few mycorrhizal species were functional under flooded conditions (Gutjahr, Casieri and Paszkowski, 2009). The AMF colonisation rate in the flooded conditions was about one-third to half that in the non-flooded conditions (Hajiboland, Aliasgharzad and Barzeghar, 2009). The role of the AMF for the rice was not only to increase nutrient uptake but some abiotic and biotic stress was alleviated by the infection (Mbodj et al., 2018). From the metagenomic analysis of the 16s rRNA gene, there was a substantial difference in the composition of rhizosphere micro-organisms within wild rice species and cultivated varieties (Shenton et al. 2016) and, furthermore, when comparing *indica* (68) and *japonica* (27) varieties, it was found that nitrogen utilising efficiency was more active under *indica* varieties (Zhang et al. 2019).

Phyllosphere (Surface area of plant shoot): As the phyllosphere is directly affected by environmental conditions, those microbes in the phyllosphere may act to alleviate the impacts from outside (Vacher et al., 2016). From the phyllosphere, researchers are investigating the beneficial microbes against pathogens (Harsonowati, Astuti and Wahyudi, 2017).

Endophytes: It is important to evaluate the role of endophytes regardless of their cultivability and to address this a metagenomic approach has been carried out to identify the endophytic bacteria of the rice roots (Sessitsch et al., 2015). Based on the metagenomic approach, Gammaproteobacteria, mostly Enterobacter-related endophytes and Alphaproteobacteria, which includes a large number of rhizobia, were identified as the most abundant group. This allowed for the prediction of traits and metabolic processes such as the nitrogen cycle involving nitrogen fixation, denitrification and nitrification.

The carbon cycle was also highlighted: though the relative abundance of methanogens (*Methanocella*, *Methanosarcina* and *Methanosaeta*) was higher in the rhizosphere than inside the rice roots, *Methanobacterium* was equal or higher inside the root (Edwards et al., 2015).

Influences of rice on organisms in usual close contact

Influences on pathogens

Fungi and oomycetes

Fungal and oomycete diseases (see Annex 4.B)

Rice blast is the most important air-borne paddy rice disease in the world, including in Southeast Asia and the United States. The pathogen is *Pyricularia oryzae (*syn.: *Magnaporthe oryzae)*, an ascomycete fungus, and infected seeds are the primary infection source; it occurs during the seedling stage. In the rice field, it forms spindle-shaped leaf blast lesions, spores and infects the upper leaves. Infection at the panicle emergence stage causes wilting and death of grain and neck, resulting in a large decrease in yield.

Rice sheath blight is the second most important soil-borne disease in the world, following rice blast. The pathogen is *Rhizoctonia solani*, a basidiomycete fungus and the sclerotium, which is the primary infection source, floats during pudding and attaches to the rice stem, forming a lesion. The lesions develop on the upper leaves and spread to neighbouring plants. If the disease is severe, even the flag leaves and panicles are affected. This disease can also cause lodging in strong winds such as typhoons.

Rice false smut is a disease that occurs in China and Southeast Asia and forms black spore balls on rice grains during the ripening stage. The pathogen is *Ustilaginoidea virens*, which belongs to Ascomycota. Chlamydospores contained in diseased grains fall into the soil and become the primary infection source. When rice plants are transplanted the following year, the fungus invades through the roots and reaches the spikelets during the panicle formation stage, leading to the disease.

Rice brown spot is an air-borne disease that occurs mainly in South and Southeast Asia. The pathogen is *Cochliobolus miyabeanus*, which belongs to Ascomycota. The primary infection source is infected seed and diseased straw. The fungus causes brown spots on leaves and when panicles are infected, panicles may die. The disease occurs often in soils that are deficient in microelements and fertilisers (Ou, 1985; Cartwright et al., 2018).

Mechanisms of symptom development and rice resistance for blast disease

The causal agent of blast disease, *Pyricularia oryzae* (syn.: *Magnaporthe oryzae*), is an ascomycete whose genome has been sequenced and made available to the public. The host-pathogen interactions in this disease are controlled under "Gene-for-Gene" interactions. Rice is resistant (incompatible interaction) or susceptible (compatible interaction) to *P. oryzae* if rice has a true resistance gene (*R*-gene, Kalia and Rathour, 2019) that recognises the fungal race-specific "effector" gene, or not respectively. Among these effectors, AvrPii and AvrPiz-t have been characterised for their biochemical roles in the host cell (Park et al., 2012, Singh et al., 2016). Thus, resistance regulated by the *R*-gene, called effector-triggered immunity (ETI), is highly race-specific. By 2019, 25 *R*-genes were cloned and characterised (Kalia and Rathour, 2019). The fungal invasion starts with the formation of dome-shaped specific structures, the appressorium, from which infectious hyphae penetrate the host epidermal cell (Howard and Valent, 1996).

In the incompatible interaction, hyphal extension is strongly restricted at the early stage of infection by programmed death of invaded rice cells, while in the compatible interaction, the fungal hyphae penetrate into the rice cell, keeping the plasma membrane and organelle, including the vacuole, intact. This observation strongly indicates that the virulent race of this fungus is able to suppress the host defence (Yan and Talbot, 2016).

Another class of immunity is called PAMP-triggered immunity (PTI), where cell components of pathogens, PAMPs (Pathogen-Associated Molecular Patterns), induce defence responses in rice (Liu et al., 2013). PTI is not race-specific and a main part of basal resistance. The most studied PAMP from *P. oryzae* is the chitin oligomer, hydrolysate of chitin which is a backbone structure of fungal cell walls. Rice recognises this elicitor using two sensors, OsCEBiP and OsCERK1 (Desaki et al., 2018). Recognition of chitin oligomers by rice have been demonstrated to contribute to basal resistance against *P. oryzae* (Kishimoto et al., 2010).

On the other hand, *P. oryzae* has developed novel strategies to avoid the host resistance induced by chitin oligomers. One is the masking of cell wall chitin with α-1,3-glucans after starting hyphal penetration into the host cell. As higher plants do not have α-1,3-glucanase activities, *P. oryzae* can protect the chitin backbone in the cell wall from attack by chitinase of the rice origin leading to the production of chitin oligomers (Fujikawa et al., 2012). Another strategy of the fungus is Slp1 secreted from infectious hyphae.

This protein has a high binding affinity to chitin oligomers and is considered to contribute to successful infections by preventing chitin oligomers from being recognised by CEBiP (Mentlak et al., 2012).

Both ETI and PTI of higher plants induce largely common defence responses such as the expressions of pathogenesis-related (PR) protein genes and the accumulation of anti-microbial metabolites, phytoalexins (Peng, van Wersch and Zhang, 2018). Therefore, the signalling pathway likely merges into a common pathway after perception of the effectors or PAMPs by *R*-gene or receptors respectively. Several key factors in the common signal pathway have been identified. A small GTP-binding protein, OsRac1, has been demonstrated to be deeply involved in both ETI and PTI through its activation/inactivation cycle (Liu et al., 2013). Salicylic acid (SA) was also observed to play essential roles in the defence responses in rice. Transgenic rice harbouring the SA-inactivating gene exhibits compromised resistance in ETI and PTI against *P. oryzae*. In the downstream of SA signalling, two signalling factors, OsNPR1 and OsWRKY45, have been identified as key factors. Constitutive expression of *OsWRKY45* confers strong resistance to the infection of *Xanthomonas oryzae*, a bacterial pathogen of rice leaf blight disease, in addition to *P. oryzae* (Takatsuji, H., 2014).

Bacterial pathogen (see Annex 4.B)

Eleven species of bacteria have been identified as a pathogen of rice and the site of infection for all bacteria is the above-ground parts of the plant. The main bacterial diseases of rice are bacterial grain rot, bacterial brown stripe, bacterial seedling blight, bacterial blight (BB) and bacterial leaf streak.

The bacterial grain rot is caused by *Burkholderia glumae* and occurs at the seedling stage. The leaf sheaths or leaf blades turn light or dark brown and decompose. Alternatively, the leaves become yellowing and curling, eventually leading to death. Symptoms initially appear in patches but then spread to the surrounding area. After the ear emergence stage (after the milk-ripening stage), the disease symptoms also appear on the panicle. The panicle wilts to a white, greyish-white or light yellowish-brown colour, resulting in poor fertility. *Burkholderia glumae* is a gram-negative, rod-shaped aerobic bacterium with an optimal growth temperature of around 30°C and an optimal pH of 6.0-7.5. Under natural conditions, rice is the only host of this bacterium, which is transmitted from infested seeds or soil and infects the panicle through the leaf sheath and leaf blade (Tsushima, 1996; Ura et al., 2006).

The bacterial brown stripe, caused by *Acidovorax avenae*, forms brown, elongated, streaky lesions on leaf sheaths and leaf blades of seedlings, resulting in stunting of growth and death. Subsequently, the whole plant turns brown mainly from curled leaf sheaths and brown streaky lesions, leading to death, but the disease is only dispersed throughout nursery boxes. *Acidovorax avenae* prefers high temperatures (optimal growth temperature: 35-40°C) and is transmitted by seeds (Kadota and Ohuchi, 1990).

The bacterial seedling blight caused by *Burkholderia plantarii* occurs only during seedling growth in nursery boxes and does not occur in adult rice. The early symptoms are browning of the basal part, chlorosis and wilting at the base of new leaves but no rotting at the base. Subsequently, leaves roll, wilt and turn brown, leading to death. In addition, this disease produces a toxin (tropolone) that inhibits root elongation and above-ground greening and often occurs in spots. This disease is transmitted from infected seeds of the previous year and secondary infection is promoted by high temperatures during germination and emergence. Although the disease develops remarkably at high temperatures (30-34°C) during germination and seedling growth, it develops less severely at temperatures below 30°C and does not develop at temperatures above 37°C. In addition, the optimum pH for this disease is lower than 5.0-5.5 (Azegami et al., 1987).

The BB is caused by *Xanthomonas oryzae* pv. *oryzae* which is a gram-negative, rod-shaped bacterium. The bacteria enter the leaf through the hydathodes or wounds, multiply in the intercellular spaces of the underlying epitheme, and propagate to reach the xylem vessels. They further move through the veins of leaves and spread into the plant. The water-soaked spots at the leaf tips and margins are first observed and then, the leaves become chlorotic and necrotic along the leaf veins. The bacteria can pass the winter in the seed, straw, stubble or the soil, but in case the disease is induced next year, the major origin is the Poaceae (Gramineae) family weeds that are growing in the ridge of the field or the irrigation canal. The bacteria enter the field on the water flow and thereafter are spread by the wind. If the rice nursery can be flooded easily, an excess of nitrogen during the fertilisation process stimulates a rapid vegetative overgrowth of the rice plants that favours the disease development (Niño-Liu Zohary, Ronald and Bogdanove, 2006).

The bacterial leaf streak is caused by *Xanthomonas oryzae* pv. *oryzicola*, a gram-negative rod-shaped bacterium with an optimal growth temperature of 25-28°C. The bacteria penetrate the leaf mainly through stomata or wounds, multiply in the substomatal cavity and then colonise the intercellular spaces of the parenchyma. Different from the BB, small, water-soaked lesions along the leaf between the veins were observed during the early stage of bacterial leaf streak infection, resulting in translucent and yellow streaks. The infected leaves turn greyish-white and die later on. This disease frequently occurs in the condition of high temperature and humidity, and, in severe cases, the field turns brown entirely (Niño-Liu, Ronald and Bogdanove, 2006).

Phytoplasmas (see Annex 4.B)

Two species of phytoplasmas have been identified as pathogens of rice, one for *Candidatus* Phytoplasma oryzae causing yellow dwarf and the other for *Candidatus* Phytoplasma asteris causing orange leaf.

The rice yellow dwarf phytoplasma is mediated by green rice leafhopper, for which the transovarial transmission does not occur. The symptoms of the disease are characterised by prominent stunting of plants and excessive tillering. Leaf colour changes from yellowish green to whitish green, and the leaf becomes soft and droops. The disease is transmitted by leafhopper vectors *Nephotettix* sp. with a latent period of 25-30 days in the vector. The pathogen also survives on several grass weeds (Muniyappa and Raychaudhuri, 1988; Nakashima and Hayashi, 1995).

Rice orange leaf disease phytoplasma causes moderate stunting and the appearance of a golden or orange leaf colouration that initiates at the tip and then progresses downward, followed by an inward rolling of leaves and eventually leading to leaf senescence in mature rice plants. Then the grain yield is seriously damaged. This disease also occurs at the seedling stage and often causes a lethal effect. Insects such as zigzag-striped leafhopper (*Recilia dorsalis* Motschulsky) and green leafhopper (*Nephotettix cincticeps* Uhler) are responsible for the spread of this phytoplasma (Valarmathi et al., 2013; Jonson et al., 2020).

Viruses (see Annex 4.B)

There are approximately 14 species of viruses that infect rice. The major vectors are pests, while in some cases, can be transmitted transovarially to their offspring. The characteristics of the major viruses are described below:

- The Rice dwarf virus (RDV) is transmitted among rice plants by green rice leafhopper (*Nephotettix cincticeps*). The virus multiplies in the pests and can be transmitted transovarially to their offspring (Honda et al., 2007). The virus infection occurs mainly just after the transplanting, through the feedings damage caused by infected leafhoppers. The infected rice plants transmit the virus to other rice plants via the pests, and the pests passing the winter transmit the virus to rice plants the following year. The symptom is the dwarfing of the stubble at the tillering stage, change in leaf colour to dark green and display of a series of vivid white spots along the leaf veins. In addition, if the infection occurs at the early stage of rice growth, the rice does not head, or even if the heading occurs, the panicle is small and becomes sterile (Morales, 2008).
- Rice ragged stunt virus (RRSV) is a double-stranded RNA virus that is classified in the *Oryzavirus* genus. It is transmitted by *Nilaparvata lugens* and transovarial transmission does not occur. The disease occurs in China, Chinese Taipei, India, Indonesia, Japan, Malaysia, Thailand and

the Philippines. The infection causes dwarfing of the whole stubble, change in leaf colour to dark green, and serration and twisting of the leaves (Hibino et al., 1986a).

- The Rice black-streaked dwarf virus (RBSDV) is a double-stranded RNA virus that is classified in the *Fijivirus* genus. It is transmitted by *Laodelphax striatellus* and causes damage in China, Japan and Korea. This virus also causes damage to the corn. The infection induces extreme stunting, darkening of the leaves and twisting of the distal portions of young rice leaves (Wu et al., 2020). During the last few years, Southern rice black-streaked dwarf virus (SRBSDV), a species that is closely related to the RBSDV and mediated by *Sogatella furcifera*, has rapidly spread throughout China, Japan and Viet Nam (Zhou et al., 2013).
- The Rice stripe virus (RSV) is an RNA virus that is classified in the Tenuivirus genus. This virus is spreading throughout East Asia, especially in China, Japan and Korea. The virus is mediated mainly by small brown planthopper *Laodelphax striatellus* or other planthoppers such as *Unkanodes sapporona* or *Terthron albovittatum*. The transmission occurs transovarially but neither seed transmission nor contagious transmission occurs. The major hosts of this virus are crops and weeds of the Poaceae (Gramineae) family. The disease frequently occurs at the tillering stage and the RSV-infected plants display chlorosis, weakness and necrosis in leaves, abnormal growth and result in death (Cho et al., 2013).
- Rice grassy stunt virus (RGSV) is an RNA virus that is classified in the *Tenuivirus* genus. The disease is occurring widely in East and Southeast Asia, including China, India, Japan and Sri Lanka. The virus is transmitted by *Nilaparvata lugens* and the transovarial transmission does not occur. The infection causes yellowing of the leaf, dwarfing of the plant, browning/dark-browning and poor fertility of the panicle (Hibino, 1986b).
- Rice tungro disease is causing damage in South and Southeast Asia, including Bangladesh and India. This disease is mediated by *Nephotettix impicticeps* and results in the yellowing of the leaf and leaf sheaths and dwarfing of the whole stubble. The disease is caused by the combination of two viruses, one for Rice tungro bacilliform virus (RTBV), classified in the *Tungro* genus and involved in pathogenesis, and the other for Rice tungro spherical virus (RTSV), classified in the *Waikavirus* genus and involved in the virus transmission (Hibino, 1983).

Influences on invertebrate pests

Plants have evolved a range of defence mechanisms to protect themselves from damage by herbivores (Mithöfer, Boland and Maffei, 2009; Erb and Reymond, 2019). Two such mechanisms of defence are mechanical protection and chemical protection. Plant defences can be further categorised into constitutive and induced defences following herbivore feeding (Mithöfer, Boland and Maffei, 2009). Insect-resistant varieties of rice have been screened to determine which varieties have resistance to which insect pests. It has been clarified that there are many varieties resistant to specific insect pests and that this is variety dependent (Heinrichs, Medrano and Rapusas, 1985).

Many species of sap-sucking pest insects ingest nutrients from the phloem of rice. Some rice varieties are resistant to these insect pests, for example delphacid planthoppers (the brown planthopper [BPH] *N. lugens*, the whitebacked planthopper [WBPH] *S. furcifera* and the small brown planthopper [SBPH] *L. striatellus*) and cicadellid leafhoppers (the green rice leafhopper [GRH] *Nephotettix cincticeps* and the green leafhopper [GLH] *Nephotettix apicalis*(. Some of the genes involved in rice resistance to insect pests have been mapped and used for breeding (Fujita, Kohli and Horgan, 2013). Secondary metabolites thought to be related to plant constitutive defence mechanisms have been analysed to reveal causative factors of varietal resistance. However, different sources reported that it is induced resistance that contributes to varietal resistance (Kaloshian and Walling, 2016; Ling, Ang and Weilin, 2019; Du et al., 2020). In this subsection, we focus mainly on BPH and GRH, and introduce studies on the resistance response of rice to these insect pest species.

Since the 1960s, many BPH resistant rice varieties have been discovered (Pathak and Khush, 1979). Based on the hypothesis that resistant rice varieties must contain feeding deterrents to pest species, it was first attempted to isolate feeding deterrents from resistant varieties using natural product chemistry techniques. Following these lines of enquiry, Yoshihara et al. (1980) reported oxalic acid as a feeding deterrent in rice leaf sheaths that carried the BPH resistance gene, *Bph1*. In addition, Shigematsu et al. (1982) reported β-sitosterol as a further feeding deterrent. Later, Stevenson et al. (1996) identified schaftoside as a feeding deterrent from the *indica* rice variety Rathu Heenati that carries the resistance gene *Bph3*. These feeding deterrent compounds are important substances in constitutive defences of rice against herbivorous insects. If these feeding deterrents were responsible for varietal resistance, then we would expect that the virulent biotype of BPH, which is known to feed on resistant varieties, would be adapted to these feeding deterrents. However, it has not yet been confirmed that these deterrents are not effective against the virulent biotype.

The feeding behaviour of BPH and GRH on resistant varieties has been analysed in detail using electric penetration graphs (Kawabe, 1985; Hattori, 2001). BPH is a monophagous insect that only feeds on rice. When BPH attempts to attack a non-host plant, such as the barnyard grass (*Echinochloa crus-galli* var. *oryzicola*), BPH probing is interrupted before the arrival of the stylets at the sieve elements of the rice (Hattori, 2001). It is thought that probing is interrupted by a feeding deterrent such as (E)-aconitic acid in the parenchyma of rice (Hattori, 2001). On the other hand, although the stylet mouth part of BPH reaches the sieve elements of the resistant rice variety, BPH can hardly suck the phloem sap of the resistant rice. Therefore, this sucking inhibition by resistant rice likely does not occur in the parenchyma but in the phloem sieve elements. Hattori (1997) reported that GRH could suck all of the phloem sap that was collected from three different GRH-resistant rice varieties by a stylectomy method using BPH that can feed on the GRH-resistant variety. Thus, it seems that non-constituents that are particularly unsuitable as gustatory stimuli are involved in the phloem sap of the tested GRH-resistant varieties.

Owing to genomic information, some BPH resistance genes have been isolated and characterised from BPH resistant rice varieties and wild rice spices (Ling et al., 2019; Du et al., 2020). *Bph14* derived from wild rice, which was first isolated as a resistance gene for BPH, and *BPH26*, which was subsequently isolated from an *indica* rice variety, encode nucleotide-binding site leucine-rich repeat (NBS-LRR) proteins (Du et al., 2009; Tamura et al., 2014).

Most of the disease resistance genes in plants encode NBS-LRR proteins and they are considered to induce a host plant defence response through directly or indirectly recognising a pathogen-derived effector (Elmore, Lin and Coaker, 2011). Since BPH resistance proteins are also NBS-LRRs, it is expected that they recognise injury signals, such as effectors, from BPH and induce the defence response, the same as for the disease resistance proteins. It is suggested that ETI may be present in the defence of rice against sucking insects as NBS-LRRs have been isolated as resistance proteins from rice.

When fed on rice, BPH secretes two kinds of saliva: gelling and watery saliva (Huang et al., 2016). The BPH resistance protein of the NBS-LRR family is predicted to recognise a saliva protein as an effector and become active. As a result, it induces sucking inhibition in the sieve elements of rice plants.

The BPH14 protein is thought to form homocomplexes that interact with the transcription factors WRKY46 and WRKY72 (Hu et al., 2017). WRKY46 and WRKY72 then bind to the promoters of the receptor-like cytoplasmic kinase gene *RLCK281* and the callose synthase gene *LOC_Os01g67364.1*, whose transactivation activity is dependent on WRKY46 or WRKY72. Sieve element occlusion through callose deposition is thought to be an important defence mechanism, induced by *Bph14*, which prevents planthoppers from ingesting phloem sap (Du et al., 2009; Hu et al., 2017).

The defence response mediated by the NBS-LRR resistance protein is characterised by a rapid, high specificity response and strong resistance. In resistant varieties carrying the NBS-LRR resistance protein, BPH does not settle and, when BPH is forcibly attached, the mortality rate of BPH increases, egg production decreases and the rice plant survives. These phenomena observed in resistant varieties are caused by an inhibition of sucking in the phloem (Sōgawa, 1982). It is expected that BPH survival and the development of the ovaries is affected by nutritional deficiency.

Other non-NBS-LRR BPH resistance genes have been cloned, suggesting that there may be various forms of plant defence responses other than ETI. *Bph3* (originally reported as *Bph17*), which was cloned from the *indica* rice variety Rathu Heenati, is a plasma membrane-localised lectin receptor kinase (OsLecRK1-OsLecRK3; Liu et al., 2015). *BPH15* is also thought to be a lectin receptor kinase (Du et al., 2020). *Bph3* is characterised by broad-spectrum and durable insect resistance. Although it is unknown what the ligands of lectin receptor kinases are, they may play a critical role in priming plant pattern-triggered immunity (PTI) responses to BPH infestation (Liu et al., 2015).

BPH6 encodes a previously uncharacterised protein that localises to exocysts and interacts with the exocyst subunit OsEXO70E1 (Guo et al., 2018). *BPH6* expression facilitates exocytosis and cell wall reinforcement and induces co-ordinated salicylic acid, cytokinin and jasmonic acid signalling. This gene is effective not only for BPH but also for WBPH. *BPH29* and *Bph32* also encode proteins different from NBS-LRR (Wang et al., 2015; Ren et al., 2016). Lu et al. (2018) have also reported that the resistance of rice to insect pests may be mediated by the suppression of serotonin biosynthesis.

Rice likely has various defence pathways against sucking insects and these have coevolved between rice and sucking insects over many years. Although there are still many unclear points concerning rice defence mechanisms to insect pests, the culmination of these research studies will likely lead to the production of rice varieties that are insect pest resistant.

Annex 4.A. Glossary of rice ecological types and their relationships

Annex Table 4.A.1. Characteristics of rice ecological types

Ecological type of rice	Description	Habitat	
		Natural ecosystem	Farmland
Wild rice	Ancestor and close relatives of cultivated rice which hold seed shattering and dormancy.	+++	+
Weedy rice	Mixture of wild rice and hybrid offspring derived from wild x wild, wild x cultivar and cultivar x cultivar. They are difficult to distinguish by species classification. Some weedy rices are cultivated rice but lost domestication characteristics due to outcrossing with wild relatives and others are adapted wild rice to the farmland.	+	+++
Volunteer rice	Voluntarily emerged cultivated rice. They are derived from dropped and buried seeds in the previous years, because of their seed shattering and dormant activities.	+	+++
Cultivated rice	Cultivars domesticated from wild rice. Their traits are almost fixed in each cultivar under cultivation condition.	-	+++

Annex Figure 4.A.1. Relationships among wild, weedy, volunteer and cultivated rice

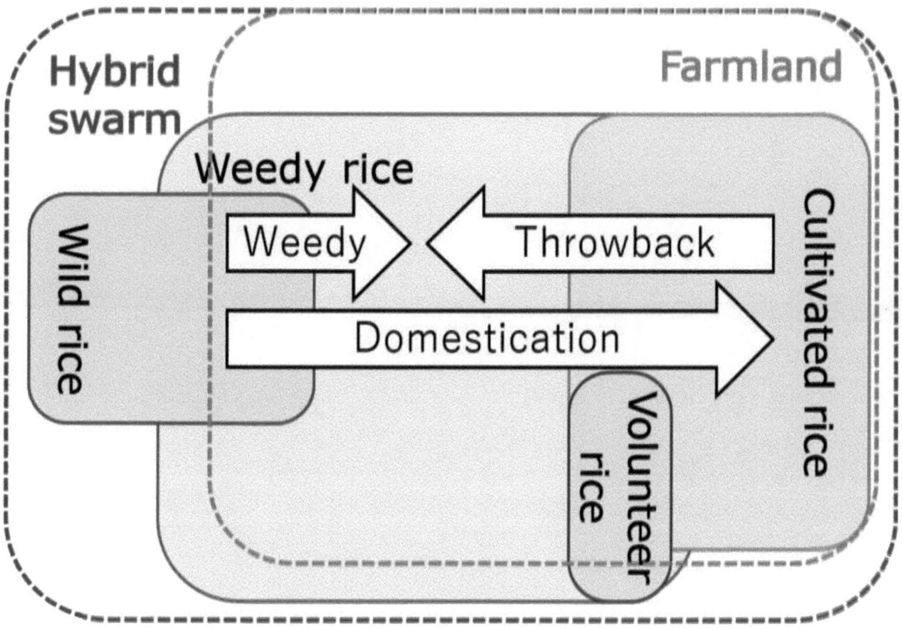

Annex 4.B. Rice diseases

Annex Table 4.B.1. Fungal and oomycete diseases

Common name of disease	Scientific name of pathogen	Affected parts
Aggregate sheath spot (Brown sclerotial disease)	*Ceratobasidium setariae* (Sawada) Oniki et al. (syn. *Ceratobasidium oryzae-sativae* P. S. Gunnell & R. K. Webster)	Sheath, Culm
Bakanae	*Fusarium fujikuroi* Nirenberg (syn. *Gibberella fujikuroi* (Sawada) S. Ito)	Seedling, Crown, Lower culm
Black kernel (Brown blotch of grains)	*Curvularia clavata* B.L. Jain *Curvularia inaequalis* (Shear) Boedijn *Curvularia intermedia* Boedijn *Curvularia lunata* (Wakker) Boedijn *Curvularia ovoidea* (Hiroë) Munt.-Cvetk. *Alternaria alternata* (Fr.) Keissl.	Grain
Blast	*Pyricularia oryzae* Cavara (syn. *Magnaporthe oryzae* B. C. Couch)	Seedling, Leaf, Culm, Panicle
Brown spot	*Bipolaris oryzae* (Breda de Haan) Shoemaker (syn. *Cochliobolus miyabeanus* (Ito & Kurib.) Drechsler ex Dastur) (syn. *Drechslera oryzae* (Breda de Haan) Subram. & P. C. Jain) (syn. *Helminthosporium oryzae* Breda de Haan)	Seedling, Leaf, Panicle
Crown sheath rot (Black sheath rot)	*Gaeumannomyces graminis* (Sacc.) Arx & D. L. Olivier	Lower leaf sheath
Downy mildew	*Sclerophthora macrospora* (Sacc.) Thirum. et al. (syn. *Sclerospora macrospora* Sacc.)	Leaf
Eyespot	*Drechslera gigantea* S. Ito	Leaf
False smut	*Ustilaginoidea virens* (Cooke) Takah. (syn. *Villosiclava virens* (Nakata) E. Tanaka & C. Tanaka)	Grain
Glume blight	*Microsphaeropsis glumarum* (Ellis & Tracy) Boerema *Epicoccum sorghinum* (Sacc.) Aveskamp et al.	Grain
Kernel smut	*Tilletia barclayana* (Bref.) Sacc. & P. Syd. (syn. *Neovossia barclayana* Bref.) (syn. *Tilletia horrida* Takah.)	Grain
Kernel discolouration (Grain discolouration, black kernel)	*Alternaria padwickii* (Ganguly) M.B. Ellis	Grain
Leaf scald	*Microdochium albescens* (Thüm.) Hern.-Restr. & Crous (syn. *Gerlachia oryzae* (Hashioka & Yokogi) W. Gams)	Leaf, Sheath
Leaf smut	*Eballistra oryzae* (Syd. & P. Syd.) R. Bauer et al. (syn. *Entyloma oryzae* Syd. & P. Syd.)	Leaf
Red blotch of grains	*Epicoccum nigrum* Link (syn. *Epicoccum purpurascens* Ehrenb.) *Epicoccum neglectum* Desm. *Epicoccum oryzae* S. Ito & Iwadare	Grain
Red stripe	*Gonatophragmium* sp. Some papers attributed the disease to bacteria.	Leaf
Scab	*Fusarium graminearum* Schwabe (syn. *Gibberella zeae* (Schwein.) Petch)	Grain, Culm

Common name of disease	Scientific name of pathogen	Affected parts
Seedling blight (Seedling damping-off)	*Fusarium* spp. *Pythium* spp. *Globisporangium spinosum* Uzuhashi et al. (syn. *Pythium spinosum* Sawada) *Rhizopus* spp. *Mucor fragilis* Bainier *Trichoderma viride* Pers. *Rhizoctonia solani* J.G. Kühn *Athelia rolfsii* (Curzi) C. C. Tu & Kimbr. (syn. *Sclerotium rolfsii* Sacc.)	Seedling
Sheath blight	*Rhizoctonia solani* J.G. Kühn (syn. *Thanatephorus cucumeris* (A. B. Frank) Donk)	Sheath, Leaf
Sheath blotch	*Sydowia polyspora* (Bref. & Tavel) E. Müll.	Sheath
Sheath net blotch	*Calonectria morganii* Crous et al. (syn. *Cylindrocladium scoparium* Morg.)	Sheath
Sheath rot	*Sarocladium oryzae* (Sawada) W. Gams & D. Hawksw. (syn. *Acrocylindrium oryzae* Sawada) (syn. *Sarocladium attenuatum* W. Gams & D. Hawksw.)	Flag leaf sheath, Grain
Sheath spot	*Waitea circinata* Warcup & P.H.B. Talbot (syn. *Rhizoctonia oryzae* Ryker & Gooch)	Sheath
Stackburn (Alternaria leaf spot)	*Alternaria padwickii* (Ganguly) M.B. Ellis	Leaf
Stem rot	*Nakataea oryzae* (Catt.) J. Luo & N. Zhang (syn. *Magnaporthe salvinii* (Catt.) R. A. Krause & R. K. Webster)	Stem
Udbatta (Black choke, incense rod, false ergot)	*Balansia oryzae-sativae* Hashioka (syn. *Balansia oryzae* (Syd.) Naras. & Thirum.)	Panicle
Water moulds	*Achlya* spp. *Pythium* app. *Dictyuchus* spp. *Globisporangium spinosum* Uzuhashi et al. Others	Seed, Seedling
White leaf streak	*Mycovellosiella oryzae* (Deighton & D.E. Shaw) Deighton (syn. *Ramularia oryzae* Deighton & D. E. Shaw)	Leaf

Annex Table 4.B.2. Bacterial diseases

Common name of disease	Scientific name of pathogen	Affected parts
Bacterial brown stripe	*Acidovorax avenae* subsp. *avenae* (Manns) Willems et al. (syn. *Pseudomonas avenae* Manns)	Seedling
Bacterial foot rot	*Dickeya zeae* Samson et al. (syn. *Erwinia chrysanthemi* pv. *zeae* (Sabet) Victoria et al.	Node, Culm, Crown
Bacterial grain rot(Bacterial seedling rot)	*Burkholderia glumae* (Kurita & Tabei) Urakami et al. (syn. *Pseudomonas glumae* Kurita & Tabei) *Burkholderia gladioli* (Severini) Yabuuchi et al. (syn. *Pseudomonas gladioli* Severini)	Spikelet, Seed, Seedling
Bacterial leaf blight	*Xanthomonas oryzae* pv. *oryzae* (Ishiyama) Swings et al.	Leaf
Bacterial leaf streak	*Xanthomonas oryzae* pv. *oryzicola* (Fang et al.) Swings et al.	Leaf
Bacterial palea browning	*Pantoea ananatis* (Serrano) Mergaert et al. (syn. *Erwinia herbicola* (Löhnis) Dye)	Panicle
Bacterial seedling blight	*Burkholderia plantarii* (Azegami et al.) Urakami et al.	Seedling
Halo blight	*Pseudomonas syringae* pv. *oryzae* (Kuwata) Young et al.	Leaf

Red stripe	*Microbacterium* sp. Some papers attributed the disease to fungi.	Leaf
Sheath brown rot	*Pseudomonas fuscovaginae* Miyajima et al.	Sheath (mainly flag leaf)
Stem necrosis	*Pantoea ananatis* Serrano	Node

Annex Table 4.B.3. Phytoplasmal diseases

Common name of disease	Scientific name of pathogen	Vector
Orange leaf	*Candidatus* Phytoplasma asteris	Zig-zag leafhopper
Yellow dwarf	*Candidatus* Phytoplasma oryzae	Green rice leafhopper (temperate) Green leafhopper (tropics)

Annex Table 4.B.4. Viral diseases

Common name of disease	Scientific name of pathogen	Vector
Black-streaked dwarf	*Rice black-streaked dwarf virus* genus *Fijivirus*; family *Reoviridae*	Small brown planthopper
Dwarf	*Rice dwarf virus* genus *Phytoreovirus*; family *Reoviridae*	Green rice leafhopper Green leafhopper Zig-zag leafhopper
Gall dwarf	*Rice gall dwarf virus* genus *Phytoreovirus*; family *Reoviridae*	Green leafhopper Zig-zag leafhopper
Giallume	*Barley yellow dwarf virus* genus *Luteovirus*; family *Luteoviridae*	Bird cherry-oat aphid
Grassy stunt	*Rice grassy stunt virus* genus *Tenuivirus*; family *Phenuiviridae*	Brown planthopper
Hoja blanca	*Rice hoja blanca virus* genus *Tenuivirus*; family *Phenuiviridae*	Rice delphacid
Necrosis mosaic	*Rice necrosis mosaic virus* genus *Bymovirus*; family *Potyviridae*	*Polymyxa graminis*
Ragged stunt	*Rice ragged stunt virus* genus *Oryzavirus*; family *Reoviridae*	Brown planthopper
Southern black-streaked dwarf	*Southern rice black-streaked dwarf virus* genus *Fijivirus*; family *Reoviridae*	Small brown planthopper Whitebacked planthopper
Stripe	*Rice stripe virus* genus *Tenuivirus*; family *Phenuiviridae*	Small brown planthopper
Stripe necrosis	*Rice stripe necrosis virus* genus *Benyvirus*; family *Benyviridae*	*Polymyxa graminis*
Tungro (dual infection) and Waika	*Rice tungro bacilliform virus* genus *Tungrovirus*; family *Caulimoviridae* *Rice tungro spherical virus* genus *Waikavirus*; family *Secoviridae*	Green leafhopper Green rice leafhopper Zig-zag leafhopper
Yellow mottle	*Rice yellow mottle virus* genus *Sobemovirus*; family *Solemoviridae*	Adult chrysomelid beetles
Yellow stunt (formerly Transitory yellowing)	*Rice yellow stunt nucleorhabdovirus* genus *Nucleorhabdovirus*; family *Rhabdoviridae*	Green rice leafhopper Green leafhopper

Sources (annex): American Phytopathological Society (2017), *Diseases of Rice (Oryza and Zizania spp.), Common Names of Plant Diseases*, https://www.apsnet.org/edcenter/resources/commonnames/Pages/Rice.aspx (accessed 11 June 2019); Cartwright, R.D. et al. (2018), *Compendium of Rice Diseases and Pests*, Second edition, APS Press, p. 145; Hiraguri, A. et al. (2010), "Complete sequence analysis of rice transitory yellowing virus and its comparison to rice yellow stunt virus", https://doi.org/10.1007/s00705-009-0557-8; Index Fungorum (2019), *The*

Global Database of Fungal Names, http://www.indexfungorum.org/ (accessed 11 June 2019); ICTV (2019), *International Committee on Taxonomy of Viruses*, https://talk.ictvonline.org (accessed 11 June 2019); IRRI (2016), *Rice Diseases: Biology and Selected Management Practices*, http://rice-diseases.irri.org/home/contents; Xie, L. and J. Lin (1980), "Studies on rice bunchy stunt disease of rice, a new virus disease of rice plant", https://doi.org/10.1360/sb1980-25-9-785; Zhu, Y. et al. (2017), "Draft genome sequence of rice orange leaf phytoplasma from Guangdong, China", https://doi.org/10.1128/genomeA.00430-17.

Annex 4.C. Rice pests

Annex Table 4.C.1. Arthropoda

Scientific name		Common name (English)
Hemiptera (planthoppers, leafhoppers and others)		
Alydidae	*Leptocorisa acuta* Thunberg	Rice bug
	Leptocorisa chinensis Dallas	
	Leptocorisa oratorius Fabricius	
	Stenocoris claviformis Ahmad	
	Stenocoris southwoodi Ahmad	
Aphididae	Hysteroneura (=Carolinaia) setariae Thomas	Rusty plum aphid
	Tetraneura nigriabdominalis Sasaki	Rice root aphid
Cicadellidae	*Cicadella viridis* Linnaeus	Green leafhopper
	Cofana (=Tettigella=Cicadella) spectra Distant	White leafhopper
	Nephotettix cincticeps Uhler	Green rice leafhopper
	Nephotettix malayanus Ishihara & Kawase	Green leafhopper
	Nephotettix nigropictus (=apicalis) Stål	Green leafhopper
	Nephotettix virescens (=impicticeps) Distant	Green leafhopper
	Recilia dorsalis Motschulsky	Zigzag leafhopper
Delphacidae	*Laodelphax striatellus* Fallén	
	Nilaparvata lugens Stål	
	Sogatella furcifera Horváth	
	Tagosodes (=Sogatodes) orizicolus Muir	
Miridae	*Stenotus rubrovittatus* Matsumura	Sorghum plant bug
	Trigonotylus caelestialium (Kirkaldy)	Rice leaf bug
Pentatomidae	*Eysarcoris (=Stollia) ventralis* Westwood	White-spotted stink bug
	Nezara viridula Linnaeus	Southern green stink bug
	Oebalus pugnax Fabricius	Rice stink bug
	Pygomenida varipennis Westwood	Stink bug
	Scotinophara coarctata Fabricius	Malayan rice black bug
	Scotinophara lurida Burmeister	Japanese rice black bug
Pseudococcidae	*Brevennia (=Heterococcus=Ripersia) rehi (=oryzae)* Lindinger	Rice mealybug
	Pseudococcus saccharicola Takahashi	Rice mealybug
Thysanoptera (thrips)		
Phlaeothripidae	*Haplothrips aculeatus* Fabricius	Rice aculeated thrips
Thripidae	*Stenchaetothrips (=Baliothrips=Thrips) biformis* Bagnall	Rice thrips
Lepidoptera (moths)		
Crambidae	*Chilo auricilius* Dudgeon	Gold-fringed stem borer
	Chilo polychrysus Meyrick	Dark-headed striped stem borer
	Chilo partellus Swinhoe	Sorghum stem borer
	Chilo suppressalis Walker	Striped stem borer
	Chilo zacconius Bleszynski	Striped stem borer
	Cnaphalocrocis medinalis Guenée	Rice leaffolder
	Diatraea saccharalis Fabricius	Sugarcane borer
	Nymphula depunctalis Guenée	Rice caseworm

Scientific name		Common name (English)
	Marasmia (=Susumia) exigua Butler	Rice leaffolder
	Marasmia patnalis Bradley	Rice leaffolder
	Marasmia trapezalis Guenée	Rice leaffolder
	Parapoynx diminutalis Snellen	Rice caseworm
	Parapoynx (=Nymphula) fluctuosalis Zeller	Rice caseworm
	Rupela albinella Cramer	White stem borer
	Scirpophaga (=Tryporyza=Schoenobius) incertulas Walker	Yellow stem borer
	Scirpophaga innotata Walker	White stem borer
Erebidae	*Rivula atimeta* Swinhoe	Green hairy caterpillar
Noctuidae	*Naranga aenescens* Moore	Green semilooper
	Mythimna (=Pseudaletia=Leucania=Cirphis) separata Walker	Rice ear-cutting caterpillar
	Mythimna unipuncta Haworth	True armyworm
	Sesamia calamistis Hampson	African pink borer
	Sesamia inferens Walker	Pink stem borer
	Spodoptera frugiperda J.E. Smith	Fall armyworm
	Spodoptera litura Fabricius	Common cutworm
	Spodoptera mauritia acronyctoides Guenée	Rice swarming caterpillar
Nymphalidae	*Melanitis leda ismene* Cramer	Greenhorned caterpillar
Pyralidae	*Elasmopalpus lignosellus* Zeller	Lesser cornstalk borer
	Maliarpha separatella Ragonot	African white rice borer
Coleoptera (beetles)		
Brachyceridae	*Lissorhoptrus oryzophilus Kuschel*	Rice water weevil
Chrysomelidae	*Dicladispa (=Hispa) armigera* Oliver	Rice hispa
	Dicladispa viridicyanea Kraatz	Rice hispa
	Oulema (=Lema) oryzae Kuwayama	Rice leaf beetle
	Trichispa sericea Guérin-Méneville	Rice hispa
Dryophthoridae	Echinocnemus squamous Billberg	Rice root weevil
Scarabaeidae	Lachnosterna serrata (Fabricius)	White grub
Diptera (flies)		
Cecidomyiidae	Orseolia (=Pachydiplosis) oryzae Wood-Mason	Rice gall midge
	Orseolia oryzivora Harris & Gagné	Rice gall midge
Chloropidae	Chlorops oryzae Matsumura	Rice stem maggot
Diopsidae	*Diopsis longicornis* Macquart	Stalk-eyed fly
	Diopsis indica Westwood	Stalk-eyed fly
Ephydridae	*Hydrellia griseola* Fallén	Rice leaf miner
	Hydrellia philippina Ferino	Rice whorl maggot
	Hydrellia sasakii Yuasa & Isitani	Paddy stem maggot
Muscidae	*Atherigona exigua* Stein	Rice seedling maggot
	Atherigona oryzae Malloch	Rice seedling maggot
Orthoptera (grasshoppers, locusts and crickets)		
Acrididae	Locusta migratoria manilensis Meyen	Oriental migratory locust
	Oxya hyla intricata Stål	Short-horned grasshopper
	Oxya japonica japonica Thunberg	Rice grasshopper
Gryllidae	*Euscyrtus concinnus* de Haan	Field cricket
Gryllotalpidae	*Scapteriscus borellii* Giglio-Tos	Mole cricket

Annex Table 4.C.2. Nematoda

Scientific name	Common name (English)
Aphelenchoides besseyi Christie	Rice white tip nematode
Ditylenchus angustus (Butler) Filipjev	Rice stem nematode
Heterodera oryzae Luc & Berdon	Rice cyst nematode
Hirschmanniella oryzae Luc & Goodey	Rice root nematode
Meloidogyne graminicola Golden & Birchfield	Rice root knot nematode

Annex Table 4.C.3. Mollusca

Scientific name	Common name (English)
Pomacea canaliculata (Lamarck)	Golden apple snail
Pomacea maculata	Golden apple snail

Sources (annex): Ane, N.U. and M. Hussain (2015), "Diversity of insect pests in major rice growing areas of the world", https://www.semanticscholar.org/paper/Diversity-of-insect-pests-in-major-rice-growing-of-Ane-Hussain/04615420a3c817a37ea6f494574772f84a2a3f09; EPPO (2019), *EPPO Global Database*, https://gd.eppo.int/ (accessed 11 June 2019); Heinrichs, E.A. and A.T. Barrion (2004), "Rice-feeding insects and selected natural enemies in West Africa: Biology, ecology, identification", International Rice Research Institute, Los Baños, Philippines, and WARDA–The Africa Rice Center, Abidjan, Côte d'Ivoire; IRRI (n.d.-c), *Learn About Best Practices in Rice Farming*, http://www.knowledgebank.irri.org/ (accessed 30 October 2020); Joshi and Sebastian (2006), Kyndt, T., D. Fernandez and G. Gheysen (2014), "Plant-parasitic nematode infections in rice: Molecular and cellular insights", https://www.annualreviews.org/doi/10.1146/annurev-phyto-102313-050111; Nicol, J.M. et al. (2011), "Current nematode threats to world agriculture", https://doi.org/10.1007/978-94-007-0434-3_2; Pathak, M.D. and Z.R. Khan (1994), *Insect Pests of Rice*, https://www.cabi.org/isc/abstract/19951100418; Shepard, B.M., A.T. Barrion and J.A. Litsinger (1995), *Rice-Feeding Insects of Tropical Asia*, International Rice Research Institute, Manila, Philippines, p. 228.

Annex 4.D. Weeds in rice fields

Annex Table 4.D.1. Weeds in rice fields (except for weedy rice (*Oryza sativa* L. [f. *spontanea*])

Class	Group	Species
Monocots	Grasses	*Brachiaria (B. plantaginea, B. platyphylla), Cynodon dactylon, Dactyloctenium aegyptium, Digitaria (D. ciliaris (adscendens), D. sanguinalis, D. setigera), Diplachne fusca, Echinochloa (E. colona, E. crus-galli, E. crus-pavonis, E. glabrescens, E. oryzicola (oryzoides, macrocarpa, phyllopogon)), Eleusine indica, Eragrostis parviflora, Imperata cylindrica, Ischaemum rugosum, Leersia (L. hexandra, L. japonica, L. oryzoides, L. sayanuka), Leptochloa (L. chinensis, L. panicea), Panicum repens, Paspalum (P. distichum, P. paspaloides, P. scrobiculatum), Rottboellia cochinchinensis, Setaria glauca*
	Sedges	*Bolboschoenus maritimus, Cyperus (C. aromaticus, C. compressus, C. difformis, C. esculentus, C. haspan, C. iria, C. polystachyos, C. rotundus, C. serotinus, C. sphacelatus, C. tenuispica), Eleocharis (E. acicularis, E. acuta, E. congesta, E. dulcis, E. geniculata, E. kuroguwai, E. tetraquetra, E. yokoscensis), Fimbristylis (F. dichotoma, F. diphylla, F. ferruginea, F. littoralis (miliacea)), Schoenoplectiella/Schoenoplectus (S. juncoides, S. mucronatus, S. pungens, S. scirpoides), Scirpus (S. erectus, S. grossus, S. maritimus, S. miliaceus, S. nipponicus, S. planiculmis, S. supinus, S. zeylanica)*
	Floating plants	*Eichhornia crassipes, Lemna (L. minor, L. paucicostata), Pistia stratiotes, Spirodela polyrhiza*
	Others	*Alisma (A. canaliculatum, A. lanceolatum, A. plantago-aquatica), Butomus umbellatus, Commelina (C. benghalensis, C. diffusa), Damasonium minus, Heteranthera (H. limosa, H. reniformis), Limnocharis flava, Monochoria vaginalis, Sagittaria (S. graminea, S. longiloba, S. montevidensis, S. platyphylla, S. pygmaea, S. trifolia), Typha orientalis*
Dicots		*Aeschynomene (A. aspera, A. indica), Ageratum conyzoides, Alternanthera (A. philoxeroides, A. sessilis), Amaranthus (A. spinosus, A. viridis), Ammannia (A. baccifera, A. multiflora), Bacopa rotundifolia, Celosia argentea, Chromolaena odorata, Eclipta prostrata, Elatine (E. gratioloides, E. triandra), Ipomoea aquatica, Lindernia procumbens, Ludwigia (L. adscendens (stipulacea), L. hyssopifolia, L. octovalvis, L. prostrata (epilobioides)), Lythrum hyssopifolia, Mimosa diplotricha, Oldenlandia corymbosa, Persicaria (Polygonum) hydropiper, Portulaca oleracea, Rotala Indica, Rumex crispus, Sesbania exaltata, Sphenoclea zeylanica, Trianthema portulacastrum*
	Parasites	*Striga (S. asiatica, S. hermonthica)*
Ferns		*Azolla filiculoides, Marsilea (M. drummondii, M. minuta)*
Algae	Blue-green algae	*Anabaena* spp., *Lyngbya* spp., *Nostoc* spp., *Phormidium* spp.
	Green algae	*Chara* spp., *Hydrodictyon* spp., *Pithophora* spp., *Spirogyra* spp.

Source: IRRI (n.d.-a), *How to Control Weeds*, http://www.knowledgebank.irri.org/step-by-step-production/growth/weed-management (accessed 2 September 2020); IRRI (n.d.-b), *Main Weeds of Rice in Asia*, http://www.knowledgebank.irri.org/training/fact-sheets/pest-management/weeds/main-weeds-of-rice-in-asia (accessed 2 September 2020); Kraehmer, H. et al. (2016), "Global distribution of rice weeds - A review", https://doi.org/10.1016/j.cropro.2015.10.027; Moody, K. (1989), *Weeds, Reported in Rice in South and Southeast Asia*, International Rice Research Institute, Philippines; Rao, A.N., N. Chandrasena and H. Matsumoto (2017), "Rice weed management in the Asian-Pacific region: An overview", http://oar.icrisat.org/10210/.

Annex 4.E. Transgenic and genome-edited rice (*Oryza sativa*)

Transgenic rice

At the dawn of transformation technology research, the production of transgenic rice was more difficult than for other plants. The reason for this was that Agrobacterium does not infect monocotyledons and is not a rice pathogen. Therefore, the transformation of rice required physical methods such as electroporation (Zhang et al., 1988; Shimamoto et al., 1989) and polyethylene glycol method (PEG) (Toriyama et al., 1988; Zhang and Wu, 1988), which are applied to protoplasts. Although transformations in protoplasts have been used, it is quite difficult to regenerate rice plants from them and the occurrence of many somaclonal variations is another serious problem.

The novel transformation method, particle bombardment, was then applied (Christou, Ford and Kofron, 1991). In this method, foreign genes are directly introduced into a callus derived from a cell with high re-differentiation ability, such as the scutellum. Using this method, the regeneration efficiency was higher than with the protoplasts and the somaclonal variations in the regenerated plants tended to be suppressed when compared to those from the protoplasts.

The next important step was the application of the Agrobacterium method with the Super Binary Vector for the transformation of rice (Hiei et al., 1994). After this research was published, Agrobacterium strains, culture conditions and selection markers were investigated and the transformation efficiency was improved (Toki et al., 2006). Currently, rice is widely used in experiments for monocotyledonous plants as the most easily transformed monocotyledonous crop. The advantages of the Agrobacterium method are its high transformation efficiency and accurate insertion of gene constructs on plasmids when compared to the physical methods, and the number of introduced copies tends to be lower compared to the other methods.

After inserting foreign genes into rice cells/tissues, a selection system for transformed cells was required. An antibiotic resistance gene is generally used as a selection marker. Initially, selection with kanamycin was used with the *neomycin phosphotransferase II* (*NPT-II*) gene but the selection efficiency was insufficient and, subsequently, geneticin (G418), to which resistance can be given by the *NPT-II* gene, was used. As it is a more reliable system, selection based on hygromycin resistance using the *hygromycin phosphotransferase* (*HPT*) gene has become more common. Subsequently, selection using glyphosate resistance with the *modified 3-phosphoshikimate-1-carboxyvinyltransferase* (*mEPSPS*) gene, using glufosinate resistance with the phosphinothricin acetyltransferase (Christou, Ford and Kofron, 1991), or using bispyribac salt with the *modified acetolactate synthase* (*mALS*) gene have also been developed (Li, Hayashimoto and Murai, 1992). Selection by herbicide tolerance was efficient and produced novel rice not affected by herbicides.

The target of transformation technologies was the insertion of marker genes in order to develop efficient transformation systems in the early research periods but gradually shifted to research for the introduction of practical traits that were being introduced in other crops, such as insect resistance and herbicide resistance. Subsequent research in rice has expanded into other useful agricultural traits such as disease resistance, environmental stress tolerance, high yield and quality improvement. Additionally, functional foods with high contents of useful components or genetically engineered plants for medical use have also been reported. Examples of research reported in the scientific literature are presented in the following paragraphs. No commercial cultivation of these transgenic examples has been conducted at the time of writing (2018).

Disease and pest resistance: In agricultural production, pest resistance traits are of crucial importance. Consequently, significant research effort has been made towards the development of transgenic rice lines exhibiting resistance to agronomically important viruses, rice blast, leaf blight, amongst others (Kathuria et al., 2007). Research on disease resistance mechanisms in rice has led to the identification of multiple pathways involving salicylic acid (SA) (Takatsuji, 2014). Rice transgenic plants overexpressing *WRKY45*, which is activated by SA signalling, were extremely resistant to rice blast disease, indicating that *WRKY45* plays a central role in inducing resistance to filamentous fungi and bacteria (Shimono et al., 2007). In addition, *Cry* genes (coding for Cry1A, Cry1B, Cry1C, Cry1Ab, and Cry9B) have been introduced to provide resistance to Lepidopteran pests and Galanthus nivalis agglutinin (GNA), which provide resistance to Hemipteran pests including planthoppers (Shabir et al., 2015).

Nutritional change: Rice is one of the most consumed food crops, so supplementing high-nutrient rice could contribute to the improved nutritional status of people in low-nutrition areas. Provitamin A enriched rice, i.e. 'Golden Rice', is a notable transgenic example (Ye et al., 2000; Paine et al., 2005). In transgenic research, a soybean ferritin synthesis gene (Vasconcelos et al., 2003) and a human lactoferrin synthesis gene (Nandi et al., 2002) were introduced into rice and shown to enrich its iron and zinc contents respectively. Transgenic rice with enhanced specific amino acid contents such as glycine (Lapitan et al., 2009), lysine (Wu, Chen and Folk, 2003), tryptophan (Tozawa et al., 2001) and cysteine (Lee et al., 2003), have also been reported.

Health functional food or medical use: The development of functional rice to promote human health or transformed rice for medical uses via the induction of intestinal tolerance has been investigated (Wakasa and Takaiwa, 2013; Takaiwa et al., 2015; Shabir et al., 2015). Cedar pollen rice (Takagi et al., 2005), anti-tick rice (Suzuki et al., 2011) and anti-rheumatic rice (Iizuka et al., 2014) may induce oral immune tolerance and Japanese cedar pollen rice is undergoing clinical research in several hospitals. Examples of the rice lines that may impart health functionalities with functional peptides include blood pressure-regulating rice (Yang et al., 2006; Wakasa et al., 2011) and blood sugar-regulating rice (Sugita et al., 2005). Furthermore, the safety and stability of a rice-based oral vaccine called MucoRice-CTB have also been demonstrated (Azegami et al., 2015).

Efficient transformation capability, in combination with its small diploid genome and the availability of genetic and genomic resources, has led to the use of rice as a model monocotyledonous crop species. Comparative genomics, particularly within the Poaceae family, has contributed to the understanding of cereal crop biology and genome evolution, and advanced crop improvement research and strategies.

Genome-edited rice

Genome editing technologies represent a new era of crop improvement beyond the limits of traditional breeding methods. Among its uses, genome editing can modify specific deoxyribonucleic acid (DNA) sequences at desired positions in the genome, including three categories (Site-Directed Nuclease (SDN)-1, SDN-2 and SDN-3) (Podevin et al., 2013), as well as be applied to induce chromosomal rearrangement (Beying et al., 2020; Schwartz et al., 2020), epigenetic changes and other outcomes that similarly occur in nature. Rice provides an excellent model system for investigating a broad range of agronomically important traits. At the same time, due to the importance of rice as a crop, genome editing technology is expected to be used for modifications that produce commercial traits. A non-exhaustive overview of the results of rice genome editing was compiled mainly with information from scientific papers until 2019 (Mishra, Joshi and Zhao, 2018; Fiaz et al. 2019) (Annex Table 4.E.1).

Yield: Rice yields are increased by improving yield components. Zhang et al. (2017) have previously produced high-yielding rice using knockouts of negative regulators of yield components such as *GS3, GS5, DEP1, GW2, Gn1,* and *TGW6*. A co-mutant of *GW2, GW5,* and *TGW6* reported an increase in its 1 000 grain weight of 29.3% (Xu et al., 2016). Heading date is also an important characteristic for yield and heading date has changed significantly in the target mutants of the three major genes (*Hd2, Hd4,* and *Hd5*) (Li et al., 2017). Lacchini et al. (2020) attempted to produce dwarf type by modifying *HTD1* and increasing the yield by introducing three genes (*GN1A, GS3* and *GW2*).

Disease resistance: The bacterial binding protein in the promoter region of *OsSWEET14* was destroyed to confer resistance to leaf blight (Li et al., 2012). Similarly, *OsSWEET13* was modified by CRISPR/Cas9 to prevent Transcription Activator-Like (TAL) effects (Zhou et al., 2015). Mutagenesis targeting the *ERF* transcription factor *OsERF922* introduced blast resistance (Wang et al., 2016). Attempts have been made to reduce the infectivity of rice tungro spherical virus (RTSV) and rice tungro bacilliform virus (RTBV) by disrupting the sequences essential for their infection (Macovei et al., 2018). This has implied that plant pest-resistant varieties could be bred by altering essential sequences for plant pest infection or the negative regulators for disease resistance.

Quality and functionality: *SBEI* and *SBEIIb* have been removed to produce high-amylose rice (Sun et al., 2017) and high oleic acid rice (Abe et al., 2018) has been produced by disrupting the *FAD2* gene.

Herbicide tolerance: Mutations were introduced into the *ALS* gene to cultivate herbicide-tolerant rice (Li, 2016d; Sun, Y., 2016b). Li et al. (2016d) achieved high tolerance by introducing double point mutations in *OsALS*. In addition, Sun et al. (2016b) introduced multiple point mutations in the *ALS* gene by homologous recombination.

Male sterility and fertility restoration: Male-sterile and restorer lines are key materials for hybrid breeding. CRISPR/Cas9 system was applied to develop a rice male-sterile line. A thermo-sensitive genic male sterility was induced by knockout of the *TMS5* gene (Zhou et al., 2016; Barman et al., 2019; Li et al., 2019). A photosensitive genic male sterility was also developed by mutagenesis of the *CSA* gene (Li et al., 2016c). Fertility was restored by a mutation that occurred in the promoter region of *RMS* gene in the cytoplasmic male-sterile line (Sukemoto, Kazama and Toriyama, 2020). Kazama et al. (2019) demonstrated that TALEN-mediated mutagenesis of the mitochondrial gene, *orf79*, restored the fertility of cytoplasmic male sterility.

Targeting: Through targeting, via positive-negative selection in addition to gene knockouts, the visualisation of endogenous gene expression will be possible via the knock-in of visible marker genes (Yamauchi et al., 2009). In addition, the precise modification of target genes could be applied to detailed functional analysis and molecular breeding in rice.

Expanding the genome editing toolbox: SpCas9 is widely used but the target site is restricted by the protospacer-adjacent motif (PAM) sequence called -NGG. Therefore, the utilisation of CRISPR/Cpf1 and CaCas9 which have different PAM sequences have been explored. Additionally, SpCas9 was engineered to recognise a single character (-NG) and developed to remove the restriction of PAM sequences consisting of multiple bases (Nishimasu et al., 2018). Furthermore, base editors have been developed as advanced approaches that allow for the direct and irreversible conversion of one target base to another without the need for a double-strand break or donor template (Komor et al., 2016; Nishida et al., 2016). The base editors have already been used in many crops, including rice (Gao, 2021). Genome editing has been successful in rice using a combination of single character PAM recognitions and a base editor (Endo et al., 2019).

Annex Table 4.E.1. List of gene modifications by genome editing in rice (till 2020)

	Targeted gene	Strategy	Molecular functions	References[1]
Yield and quality improvement	*LOX3*	TALENs	Enhanced storage tolerance	Ma et al. (2015)
	GW2, GW5, and *TGW6*	CRISPR/Cas9	Improvement of grain weight	Xu et al. (2016)
	Hd2, Hd4, and *Hd5*	CRISPR/Cas9	Early maturity of rice varieties	Li et al. (2017)
	Gn1a, DEP1, GS3 and *IPA1*	CRISPR/Cas9	Improvement of grain number, panicle architecture, grain size, and plant architecture	Li et al. (2016b)
	CCD7	CRISPR/Cas9	Increased tiller number	Butt et al. (2018)
	PYLs	CRISPR/Cas9	Improved growth and productivity	Miao et al. (2018)
	OsBADH2	TALENs	Enhanced fragrance	Shan et al. (2015)
	BADH2	CRISPR/Cas9	Enhanced fragrance	Shao et al. (2017)
Quality Improvement	*SBE1* and *SBEIIb*	CRISPR/Cas9	high-amylose rice	Sun et al. (2017)
	OsCYP97A4, OsDSM2, OsCCD4a, OsCCD4b, and *OsCCD7*	CRISPR/Cas9	increases -carotene accumulation in rice endosperm	Yang et al. (2017)
	OsNramp5	CRISPR/Cas9	Low Cd-accumulating	Tang et al. (2017)
Biotic stress tolerance	*OsSWEET13*	TALENs	Enhanced resistance to bacterial blight	Li et al. (2012)
	OsSWEET13	TALENs	Enhanced resistance to bacterial blight	Zhou et al. (2015)
	OsSWEET13	TALENs	Enhanced resistance to bacterial blight	Blanvillain-Bauf. et al. (2017)
	Os09g29100	TALENs	Enhanced resistance to bacterial leaf streak	Cai et al. (2017)
	OsERF922	CRISPR/Cas9	Enhanced resistance to blast disease	Wang et al. (2016)
Abiotic stress tolerance	*BEL*	CRISPR/Cas9	Herbicide-resistant	Xu et al. (2014)
	OsEPSPS	CRISPR/Cas9	Glyphosate resistant	Li et al. (2016a)
	OsALS	TALENs	Herbicide-resistant	Li et al. (2016d)
	ALS	CRISPR/Cas9	Herbicide-resistant	Sun et al. (2016)
	C287	Base editing	Herbicide-resistant	Shimatani et al. (2017)
	OsSAPK2	CRISPR/Cas9	Drought tolerance	Lou et al. (2017)
Nutritional improvement	*OsNRAMP5*	CRISPR/Cas9	Low cadmium content	Tang et al. (2017)
	SBEIIb and *SBEI*	CRISPR/Cas9	Generation of high-amylose rice	Sun et al. (2017)
	OsPDS and *OsSBEIIb*	CRISPR/Cpf1	carotenoid/starch biosynthesis	Li et al. (2018)
	OsFAD2	CRISPR/Cas9	High oleic/low linoleic	Abe et al. (2018)
	GR1, GR2	CRISPR/Cas9	Carotenoid-enriched	Dong et al. (2020)
Stomatal density	*OsEPFL9*	CRISPR/Cas9 CRISPR/Cpf1	Regulates leaf stomatal density	Yin et al. (2017)
Nitrogen use efficiency	*NRT1.1Bgene*	Base editing	Enhance nitrogen use efficiency	Lu and Zhu (2017)
Senescence and death	*OsCDC48*	Base editing	Regulate senescence and death	Zong et al. (2017)
Hybrid production	*TMS5*	CRISPR/Cas9	Thermo-sensitive male sterility	Zhou et al. (2016) ; Barman et al. (2019) ; Li et al. (2019)
	CSA	CRISPR/Cas9	Photoperiod controlled male-sterile lines	Li et al. (2016c)
	RMS	CRISPR/Cas9	Restoration of cytoplasmic male sterility	Sukemoto, Kazama and Toriyama (2020)
	Orf79 (mitochondria)	TALENs	Restoration of cytoplasmic male sterility	Kazama et al. (2019)

Note: This table provides examples of genes that have been modified by genome editing in rice and does not constitute an exhaustive list.
1. Short references are listed in full in the reference section below.

References

Abe, K. et al. (2018), "Production of high oleic/low linoleic rice by genome editing", *Plant Physiology and Biochemistry*, Vol. 131, pp. 58-62, https://doi.org/10.1016/j.plaphy.2018.04.033.

Aghaee, M.-A. and L.D. Godfrey (2014), "A century of rice water weevil (Coleoptera: Curculionidae): A history of research and management with an emphasis on the United States", *Journal of Integrated Pest Management*, Vol. 5, pp. 1-14, https://doi.org/10.1603/IPM14011.

Akagi, H. et al. (2004), "Positional cloning of the rice *Rf-1* gene, a restorer of BT-type cytoplasmic male sterility that encodes a mitochondria-targeting PPR protein", *Theoretical and Applied Genetics*, Vol. 108, p. 1449-1457, https://doi.org/10.1007/s00122-004-1591-2.

Akagi, H. et al. (1994), "A unique sequence located downstream from the rice mitochondrial *atp6* may cause male sterility", *Current Genetics*, Vol. 25, p. 52-58, https://doi.org/10.1007/BF00712968.

Akanksha (2009), "Important weeds of rice", *agropedia*, http://agropedia.iitk.ac.in/content/important-weeds-rice (accessed 2 September 2020).

Akasaka, M. et al. (2009), "Genetic relationships and diversity of weedy rice (*Oryza sativa* L.) and cultivated rice varieties in Okayama Prefecture, Japan", *Breeding Science*, Vol. 59, p. 401-409, https://doi.org/10.1270/jsbbs.59.401.

American Phytopathological Society (2017), *Diseases of Rice (Oryza and Zizania spp.), Common Names of Plant Diseases*, https://www.apsnet.org/edcenter/resources/commonnames/Pages/Rice.aspx (accessed 11 June 2019).

Ammiraju, J.S.S. et al. (2006), "The *Oryza* bacterial artificial chromosome library resources: Construction and analysis of 12 deep-coverage large-insert BAC libraries that represent the 10 genome types of the genus *Oryza*", *Genome Research*, Vol.16, pp.140-147, https://dx.doi.org/10.1101%2Fgr.3766306.

Ane, N.U. and M. Hussain (2015), "Diversity of insect pests in major rice growing areas of the world", *Journal of Entomology and Zoology Studies*, Vol. 4, pp. 36-41, https://www.semanticscholar.org/paper/Diversity-of-insect-pests-in-major-rice-growing-of-Ane-Hussain/04615420a3c817a37ea6f494574772f84a2a3f09.

Ashikari, M. et al. (2005), "Cytokinin oxidase regulates rice grain production", *Science*, Vol. 309, p. 741-745, https://doi.org/10.1126/science.1113373.

Azegami, K. et al. (1987), "*Pseudomonas plantarii* sp. nov., the causal agent of rice seedling blight", *International Journal of Systematic Bacteriology*, Vol. 37, p. 144-152, https://doi.org/10.1099/00207713-37-2-144.

Azegami, T. et al. (2015), "Novel transgenic rice-based vaccines", *Archivum Immunologiae et Therapiae Experimentalis*, Vol. 63, pp. 87-99, https://doi.org/10.1007/s00005-014-0303-0.

Bakti, C. and J. Tanaka (2019), "Detection of dominant QTLs for stigma exsertion ratio in rice derived from *Oryza rufipogon* accession 'W0120'", *Breeding Science*, Vol. 69, p. 143-150, https://dx.doi.org/10.1270%2Fjsbbs.18139.

Banik, A., S.K. Mukhopadhaya and T.K. Dangar (2016), "Characterization of N_2-fixing plant growth promoting endophytic and epiphytic bacterial community of Indian cultivated and wild rice (*Oryza* spp.) genotypes", *Planta*, Vol. 243, pp. 799-812, https://doi.org/10.1007/s00425-015-2444-8.

Barman, H.N. et al. (2019), "Generation of a new thermo-sensitive genic male sterile rice line by targeted mutagenesis of *TMS5* gene through CRISPR/Cas9 system", *BMC Plant Biology*, Vol. 19, Article 109, https://doi.org/10.1186/s12870-019-1715-0.

Bentolila, S. and S. Stefanov (2012), "A reevaluation of rice mitochondrial evolution based on the complete sequence of male-fertile and male-sterile mitochondrial genomes", *Plant Physiology*, Vol. 158, p. 996-1017, https://doi.org/10.1104/pp.111.190231.

Bessho-Uehara, K. et al. (2016), "Loss of function at *RAE2*, a previously unidentified EPFL, is required for awnlessness in cultivated Asian rice", *Proceedings of the National Academy of Sciences of the United States of America*, Vol. 113, pp. 8969-8974, https://doi.org/10.1073/pnas.1604849113.

Bewley, J.D. et al. (2013), "Germinability during development", in *Seeds: Physiology of Development, Germination and Dormancy*, 3rd edition, Springer, pp. 52-59.

Beying, N. et al. (2020), "CRISPR–Cas9-mediated induction of heritable chromosomal translocations in *Arabidopsis*", *Nature Plants*, Vol. 6, pp. 638-645, https://doi.org/10.1038/s41477-020-0663-x.

Bhatia, D. et al. (2017), "Introgression of yield component traits in rice (*Oryza sativa* ssp. *indica*) through interspecific hybridization", *Crop Science*, Vol. 57, pp. 1557-1573, https://doi.org/10.2135/cropsci2015.11.0693.

Blanvillain-Baufumé, S. et al. (2017), "Targeted promoter editing for rice resistance to *Xanthomonas oryzae* pv. *oryzae* reveals differential activities for *SWEET14*-inducing TAL effectors", *Plant Biotechnology Journal*, Vol. 15, pp. 306-317, https://doi.org/10.1111/pbi.12613.

Bowatte, S. et al. (2006), "Molecular analysis of the ammonia oxidizing bacteria community in the surface soil layer of Japanese paddy field", *Soil Science and Plant Nutrition*, Vol. 52, pp. 427-431, https://doi.org/10.1111/j.1747-0765.2006.00058.x.

Brar, D.S. and G.S. Khush (2018), "Wild relatives of rice: A valuable genetic resource for genomics and breeding research", in T.K. Mondal and R.J. Henry (eds.), *The Wild Oryza Genomes*, pp.1-25, https://doi.org/10.1007/978-3-319-71997-9_1.

Brar, D.S. and G.S. Khush (1997), "Alien introgression in rice", *Plant Molecular Biology*, Vol. 35, pp. 35-47, https://doi.org/10.1023/A:1005825519998.

Brar, D.S. and K. Singh (2011), "*Oryza*", in C. Kole (ed.), *Wild Crop Relatives: Genomic and Breeding Resources, Cereals*, Spring-Verlag, pp. 321-365.

Brar, D.S., R. Elloran and G.S. Khush (1991), "Interspecific hybrids produced through embryo rescue between cultivated and eight wild species of rice", *Rice Genetics Newsletter*, Vol. 8, pp. 91-93.

Brar, D.S. et al. (1996), "Gene transfer and molecular characterization of introgression from wild rice *Oryza* species into rice", in G.S. Khush (ed.), *Rice Genetics III*, Internat. Rice Research Instit., Manila, Philippines, pp. 477-486.

Brozynska, M. et al. (2017), "Sequencing of Australian wild rice genomes reveals ancestral relationships with domesticated rice", *Plant Biotechnology Journal*, Vol. 15, p. 765-774, https://doi.org/10.1111/pbi.12674.

Burgos, N.R. et al. (2014), "The impact of herbicide-resistant rice technology on phenotypic diversity and population structure of United States weedy rice", *Plant Physiology*, Vol. 166, p. 1208-1220, https://doi.org/10.1104/pp.114.242719.

Butt, H. et al. (2018), "Engineering plant architecture via CRISPR/Cas9-mediated alteration of strigolactone biosynthesis", *BMC Plant Biology*, Vol. 18, Article 174, https://doi.org/10.1186/s12870-018-1387-1.

CABI (2020), *Invasive Species Compendium*, https://www.cabi.org/isc/ (accessed 31 August 2020).

Cai, L. et al. (2017), "A transcription activator-like effector Tal7 of *Xanthomonas oryzae* pv. *oryzicola* activates rice gene *Os09g29100* to suppress rice immunity", *Scientific Reports*, Vol. 7, Article 5089, https://doi.org/10.1038/s41598-017-04800-8.

Cartwright, D.W. et al. (1981), "Isolation and characterization of two phytoalexins from rice as momilactones A and B", *Phytochemistry*, Vol. 20, pp. 535-537, https://doi.org/10.1016/S0031-9422(00)84189-8.

Cartwright, R.D. et al. (2018), *Compendium of Rice Diseases and Pests*, 2nd edition, APS Press.

Catling, D. (1992), *Rice in Deep Water*, International Rice Research Institute, MacMillan Press, London, https://doi.org/10.1007/978-1-349-12309-4.

Caton, B.P. et al. (2010), *A Practical Field Guide to Weeds of Rice in Asia*, 2nd edition, Internat. Rice Research Instit.

Chang, T.T. (1991), "Findings from a 28-year seed viability experiment", *International Rice Research Newsletter*, Vol.16, pp. 5-6.

Chauhan, B.S. (2013), "Strategies to manage weedy rice in Asia", *Crop Protection*, Vol. 48, pp. 51-56, https://doi.org/10.1016/j.cropro.2013.02.015.

Chauhan, B.S. (2012), "Weedy rice (*Oryza sativa*) II. Response of weedy rice to seed burial and flooding depth", *Weed Science*, Vol. 60, pp. 385-388, https://doi.org/10.1614/WS-D-11-00213.1.

Chen, C. et al. (2014), "A two-locus interaction causes interspecific hybrid weakness in rice", *Nature Communications*, Vol. 5, pp. 33-57, https://doi.org/10.1038/ncomms4357.

Chen, E. et al. (2019), "The genomics of *Oryza* species provides insights into rice domestication and heterosis", *Annual Review of Plant Biology,* Vol. 70, pp. 639-665, https://doi.org/10.1146/annurev-arplant-050718-100320.

Chen, J. et al. (2013), "Whole-genome sequencing of *Oryza brachyantha* reveals mechanisms underlying *Oryza* genome evolution", *Nature Communications*, Vol. 4, 1595, https://doi.org/10.1038/ncomms2596.

Chen, J. et al. (2008), "A triallelic system of *S5* is a major regulator of the reproductive barrier and compatibility of indica-japonica hybrids in rice", *Proceedings of the National Academy of Sciences of the United States of America,* Vol. 105, pp. 11436-11441, https://doi.org/10.1073/pnas.0804761105.

Chen, L.J. et al. (2004), "Gene flow from cultivated rice (*Oryza sativa*) to its weedy and wild relatives", *Annals of Botany*, Vol. 93, pp. 67-73, https://doi.org/10.1093/aob/mch006.

Chen, S. et al. (2018), "Organic carbon availability limiting microbial denitrification in the deep vadose zone", *Environmental Microbiology*, Vol. 20, pp. 980-992, https://doi.org/10.1111/1462-2920.14027.

Chen, X.-P, et al. (2008), "Ammonia-oxidizing archaea: Important players in paddy rhizosphere soil?", *Environmental Microbiology*, Vol. 10, pp. 1978-1987, https://doi.org/10.1111/j.1462-2920.2008.01613.x.

Cheng, S.-H. et al. (2007), "Progress in research and development on hybrid rice: A super-domesticate in China",

Annals of Botany, Vol. 100, pp. 959-966, https://doi.org/10.1093/aob/mcm121.

Cho, W.K. et al. (2013), "Current insights into research on *Rice stripe virus*", *The Plant Pathology Journal*, Vol. 29, pp. 223-233, https://doi.org/10.5423/PPJ.RW.10.2012.0158.

Choi, J.Y. et al. (2019), "The complex geography of domestication of the African rice *Oryza glaberrima*", *PLoS Genetics*, Vol. 15, e1007414, https://doi.org/10.1371/journal.pgen.1007414.

Choi, J.Y. et al. (2017), "The rice paradox: Multiple origins but single domestication in Asian rice", *Molecular Biology and Evolution*, Vol. 34, pp. 969-979, https://doi.org/10.1093/molbev/msx049.

Chou, C.-H., F.J. Chang and H.I. Oka (1991), "Allelopathic potentials of a wild rice, *Oryza perennis"*, *Taiwania*, Vol. 36, pp. 201-210, (in Chinese with English Abstract), https://doi.org/10.6165/tai.1991.36.201.

Christian, M. et al. (2010), "Targeting DNA double-strand breaks with TAL effector nucleases", *Genetics*, Vol. 186, pp. 757-761, https://doi.org/10.1534/genetics.110.120717.

Christou, P., T.L. Ford and M. Kofron (1991), "Production of transgenic rice (*Oryza sativa* L) plants from agronomically important Indica and Japonica varieties via electric discharge particle acceleration of exogenous DNA into immature zygotic embryos", *Nature Biotechnology*, Vol. 9, pp. 957-962, https://doi.org/10.1038/nbt1091-957.

Chung, I.-M., S.-J. Hahn and A. Ahmad (2005), "Confirmation of potential herbicidal agents in hulls of rice, Oryza sativa", *Journal of Chemical Ecology*, Vol. 31, pp. 1339-1352, https://doi.org/10.1007/s10886-005-5290-5.

Chung, N.-J. and N.-C. Paek (2003), "Photoblastism and ecophysiology of seed germination in weedy rice", *Agronomy Journal*, Vol. 95, pp. 184-190, https://doi.org/10.2134/agronj2003.1840.

Cobb, J.N., P.S. Biswas and J.D. Platten (2019), "Back to the future: Revisiting MAS as a tool for modern plant breeding", *Theoretical and Applied Genetics*, Vol. 132, pp. 647-667, https://doi.org/10.1007/s00122-018-3266-4.

Copetti, D. and R.A. Wing (2016), "The dark side of the genome: Revealing the native transposable element/repeat content of eukaryotic genomes", *Molecular Plant*, Vol. 9, pp. 1664-1666, https://doi.org/10.1016/j.molp.2016.09.006.

Dale, D. (1994), "Insect pests of the rice plant – Their biology and ecology", in E.A. Heinrichs (ed.), *Biology and Management of Rice Insects*, Wiley Eastern Ltd, pp. 363-485.

Desaki, Y. et al. (2018), "Plant immunity and symbiosis signaling mediated by LysM receptors", *Innate Immunity*, Vol. 24, pp. 92-100, https://doi.org/10.1177%2F1753425917738885.

Dilday, R.H., J. Lin and W. Yan (1994), "Identification of allelopathy in the USDA-ARS germplasm collection", *Australian Journal of Experimental Agriculture*, Vol. 34, pp. 907-910, https://doi.org/10.1071/EA9940907.

Dilday, R.H., J.D. Mattice and K.A. Moldenhauer (2000), "An overview of rice allelopathy in the USA", in *Proceedings of International Workshop in Rice Allelopathy*, 17-19 August 2000, Kyungpook National University, Taegu, Institute of Agricultural Science and Technology, Kyungpook National University, Korea, pp. 15-26.

Dilday, R.H., P. Nastasi and R.J. Smith Jr. (1989), "Allelopathic observations in rice (*Oryza sativa* L.) to ducksalad (Heteranthera limosa)", *Proceedings of the Arkansas Academy of Sciences*, Vol. 43, pp. 21-22.

Dilday, R.H. et al. (2001), "Allelopathic potential of rice germplasm against ducksalad, redstem and barnyard grass", *Journal of Crop Production*, Vol. 4, pp. 287-301, https://doi.org/10.1300/J144v04n02_11.

Dilday, R.H. et al. (1992), "Weed control with crop allelopathy", *Arkansas Farm Research*, Vol. 41, pp. 14-15.

Dilday, R.H. et al. (1991), "Allelopathic activity in rice (*Oryza sativa* L.) against ducksalad (*Heteranthera limosa* (Sw))", in J.D. Hanson et al. (eds.), *Sustainable Agriculture for the Great Plains, Symposium Proceedings*, 19-20 January 1989, USDA, Fort Collins, Colorado, ARS, Springfield, Maryland, pp. 193-201.

Doi, K. et al. (2004), "*Ehd1*, a B-type response regulator in rice, confers short-day promotion of flowering and controls *FT-like* gene expression independently of *Hd1*", *Genes and Development,* Vol. 18, pp. 926-936, https://doi.org/10.1101%2Fgad.1189604.

Doi, K., K. Taguchi and A. Yoshimura (1999), "RFLP mapping of *S20* and *S21* for F_1 pollen semi-sterility found in backcross progeny of *Oryza sativa* and *O. glaberrima*", *Rice Genetics Newsletter*, Vol. 16, pp. 65-68.

Doi, K., K. Taguchi and A. Yoshimura (1998), "A new locus affecting high F1 pollen sterility found in backcross progenies of Japonica rice and African rice", *Rice Genetics Newsletter*, Vol. 15, pp. 146-148.

Dong, O.X. et al. (2020), "Marker-free carotenoid-enriched rice generated through targeted gene insertion using CRISPR-Cas9", *Nature Communications*, Vol. 11, Article 1178, https://doi.org/10.1038/s41467-020-14981-y.

Du, B. et al. (2020), "Current understanding of the genomic, genetic, and molecular control of insect resistance in rice", *Molecular Breeding*, Vol. 40, Article 24, https://doi.org/10.1007/s11032-020-1103-3.

Du, B. et al. (2009), "Identification and characterization of *Bph14*, a gene conferring resistance to brown planthopper in rice", *Proceedings of the National Academy of Sciences of the United States of America*, Vol. 106, pp. 22163-

22168, https://doi.org/10.1073/pnas.0912139106.

Du, H. et al. (2017), "Sequencing and *de novo* assembly of a near complete *indica* rice genome", *Nature Communications*, Vol. 8, 15324, https://doi.org/10.1038/ncomms15324.

Ebana, K. et al. (2001), "Analysis of QTL associated with the allelopathic effect of rice using water-soluble extracts", *Breeding Science*, Vol. 51, p. 47-51, https://doi.org/10.1270/jsbbs.51.47.

Ebina, D., M. Nakamura and K. Yamamoto (1998), "Effect of storage period on the germination ability of rice seed", *Bulletin of the Yamaguchi Agricultural Experiment Station*, Vol. 49, pp.70-74, (in Japanese with English abstract).

Edwards, J. et al. (2015), "Structure, variation, and assembly of the root-associated microbiomes of rice", *Proceedings of National Academy of Science of the United States of America*, Vol. 112, pp. E911-E920, https://doi.org/10.1073/pnas.1414592112.

Elshire, R.J. et al. (2011), "A robust, simple genotyping-by-sequencing (GBS) approach for high diversity species", *PLoS ONE*, Vol. 6, e19379, https://doi.org/10.1371/journal.pone.0019379.

Ellis, R.H., T.D. Hong and E.H. Roberts (1992), "The low-moisture-content limit to the negative logarithmic relation between seed longevity and moisture content in three subspecies of rice", *Annals of Botany*, Vol. 69, pp. 53-58, https://doi.org/10.1093/oxfordjournals.aob.a088306.

Elmore, J.M., Z.-J.D. Lin and G. Coaker (2011), "Plant NB-LRR signaling: Upstreams and downstreams", *Current Opinion in Plant Biology*, Vol. 14, pp. 365-371, https://doi.org/10.1016/j.pbi.2011.03.011.

Endo, M. et al. (2019), "Genome editing in plants by engineered CRISPR–Cas9 recognizing NG PAM", *Nature Plants*, Vol. 5, pp. 14-17, https://doi.org/10.1038/s41477-018-0321-8.

Endo, T. et al. (2009), "Estimate of outcrossing rates in a rice plant (*Oryza sativa* L.) under field conditions using a purple grain rice cultivar, Okunomurasaki", *Breeding Science*, Vol. 59, pp. 195-202, https://doi.org/10.1270/jsbbs.59.195.

EPPO (2019), *EPPO Global Database,* European and Mediterranean Plant Protection Organization, https://gd.eppo.int/ (accessed 11 June 2019).

Erb, M. and P. Reymond (2019), "Molecular interactions between plants and insect herbivores", *Annual Review of Plant Biology*, Vol. 70, pp. 527-557, https://doi.org/10.1146/annurev-arplant-050718-095910.

Fan, C. et al. (2009), "A causal C-A mutation in the second exon of *GS3* highly associated with rice grain length and validated as a functional marker", *Theoretical and Applied Genetics*, Vol. 118, pp. 465-472, https://doi.org/10.1007/s00122-008-0913-1.

FAO (2005), *Rice is Life. International Year of Rice 2004 and its Implementation*, Food and Agricultural Organisation of the United Nations, Rome.

FAORAP/APSA (2014), *Hybrid Rice Development in Asia: Assessment of Limitation and Potential*, Proceedings of Expert Consultation, 2-3 July 2014 Bangkok Thailand, FAO Regional Office for Asia and the Pacific on the Food and Agriculture Organization of the United Nations and Asia and Pacific Seed Association.

FAOSTAT (2020), *Crop Production Data*, Food and Agriculture Organization of the United Nations, Statistics Division online database, https://www.fao.org/faostat/ (accessed 11 March 2022).

Fiaz, S. et al. (2019), "Applications of the CRISPR/Cas9 system for rice grain quality improvement: Perspectives and opportunities", *International Journal of Molecular Sciences*, Vol. 20, 888, https://doi.org/10.3390/ijms20040888.

Fuentes, R.R. et al. (2019), "Structural variants in 3000 rice genomes", *Genome Research*, Vol. 29, pp. 870-880, http://doi.org/10.1101/gr.241240.118.

Fujii, S. and K. Toriyama (2008), "Genome barriers between nuclei and mitochondria exemplified by cytoplasmic male sterility", *Plant and Cell Physiology*, Vol. 49, pp. 1484-1494, https://doi.org/10.1093/pcp/pcn102.

Fujii, Y. (2001), "Screening and future exploitation of allelopathic plants as alternative herbicides with special reference to hairy vetch", *Journal of Crop Production*, Vol. 4, pp. 257-275, https://doi.org/10.1300/J144v04n02_09.

Fujii, Y. (1992), "The allelopathic effect of some rice varieties", in *Proceedings of the International Symposium on Biological Control Integrated Management of Paddy and Aquatic Weeds in Asia*, 23 October 1992, Tsukuba, Japan, National Agricultural Research Center, pp. 1-6.

Fujii, Y. and S. Hiradate (eds.) (2007), *Allelopathy: New Concepts and Methodology,* Science Publishers, Inc., Enfield, NH, US.

Fujii, Y. and S. Hiradate (2005), "A critical survey of allelochemicals in action - The importance of total activity and the weed suppression equation", in *Proceedings of the 4th World Congress on Allelopathy*, pp. 73-76.

Fujii, Y. and T. Shibuya (1991), "Establishment of a new bioassay specific to allelopathy. Survey of allelopathic plant by the Plant Box Method" (in Japanese), *Weed Research* (Japan), Vol. 36 (Suppl.), pp. 152-153.

Fujii, Y. et al. (2001), "Screening of allelopathic activity and identification of "Awa-Akamai" (traditional red rice) as the most promising cultivar" (in Japanese), *Weed Research* (Japan), Vol. 46 (Suppl.), pp. 120-121, https://doi.org/10.3719/weed.46.Supplement_120.

Fujikawa, T. et al. (2012), "Surface α-1,3-glucan facilitates fungal stealth infection by interfering with innate immunity in plants", *PLoS Pathogens*, 8, e1002882, https://doi.org/10.1371/journal.ppat.1002882.

Fujino, K. et al. (2010), "Multiple introgression events surrounding the *Hd1* flowering-time gene in cultivated rice, *Oryza sativa*", *Molecular Genetics and Genomics,* Vol. 284, pp. 137-146, https://doi.org/10.1007/s00438-010-0555-2.

Fujioka, M. and H. Yoshida (2001), "The potential and problems of agricultural ecosystems for birds in Japan", *Global Environmental Research,* Vol. 5, pp. 151-161.

Fujioka, M. et al. (2010), "Bird use of rice fields in Korea and Japan", *Waterbirds*, Vol. 33 (Suppl.), pp. 8-29, https://doi.org/10.1675/063.033.s102.

Fujita, D., A. Kohli and F.G. Horgan (2013), "Rice resistance to planthoppers and leafhoppers", *Critical Reviews in Plant Sciences*, Vol. 32, pp. 162-191, https://doi.org/10.1080/07352689.2012.735986.

Fukuoka, S., H. Namai and K. Okuno (1998), "Geographical variation of the genes controlling hybrid breakdown and genetic differentiation of the chromosomal regions harboring these genes in Asian cultivated rice, *Oryza sativa* L.", *Genes and Genetic Systems*, Vol. 73, pp. 211-217, https://doi.org/10.1266/ggs.73.211.

Fuller, D.Q. et al. (2009), "The domestication process and domestication rate in rice: Spikelet bases from the Lower Yangtze", *Science*, Vol. 323, pp. 1607-1610, http://doi.org/10.1126/science.1166605.

Gao, C. (2021), "Genome engineering for crop improvement and future agriculture", *Cell*, Vol. 184, pp. 1621-1635, https://doi.org/10.1016/j.cell.2021.01.005.

Garavito, A. et al. (2010), "A genetic model for the female sterility barrier between Asian and African cultivated rice species", *Genetics*, Vol. 185, pp. 1425-1440, https://doi.org/10.1534/genetics.110.116772.

Gasiunas, G. et al. (2012), "Cas9-crRNA ribonucleoprotein complex mediates specific DNA cleavage for adaptive immunity in bacteria", *Proceedings of the National Academy of Sciences of the United States of America*, Vol. 109, E2579-E2586, https://doi.org/10.1073/pnas.1208507109.

Ge, S. et al. (1999), "Phylogeny of rice genomes with emphasis on origins of allotetraploid species", *Proceeding of the National Academy of Science of the United States of America*, Vol. 96, pp. 14400-14405, https://doi.org/10.1073/pnas.96.25.14400.

GRiSP (2013), *Rice Almanac*, 4th edition, Global Rice Science Partnership, International Rice Research Institute, Los Baos, Philippines.

Grist, D.H. and R.J.A.W. Lever (1969), *Pests of Rice*, Longmans, London, and Green and Co., Ltd. Harlow.

Gu, B. et al. (2015), "*An-2* encodes a cytokinin synthesis enzyme that regulates awn length and grain production in rice", *Molecular Plant*, Vol. 8, pp. 1635-1650, https://doi.org/10.1016/j.molp.2015.08.001.

Gu, Y., P. Wang and C.H. Kong (2009), "Urease, invertase, dehydrogenase and polyphenoloxidase activities in paddy soil influenced by allelopathic rice variety", *European Journal of Soil Biology*, Vol. 45, pp. 436-441, https://doi.org/10.1016/j.ejsobi.2009.06.003.

Gu, Y., P. Wang and C.H. Kong (2008), "Effects of rice allelochemicals on the microbial community of flooded paddy soil", *Allelopathy Journal*, Vol. 22, pp. 299-309.

Guo, J. et al. (2018), "*Bph6* encodes an exocyst-localized protein and confers broad resistance to planthoppers in rice", *Nature Genetics*, Vol. 50, pp. 297-306, https://doi.org/10.1038/s41588-018-0039-6.

Guo, Y. et al. (2009), "Allelopathic effects of rice cultivars on barnyardgrass growth to reduce the herbicide dose", *Allelopathy Journal*, Vol. 24, pp. 321-329.

Gurney, A.L. et al. (2006), "A novel form of resistance in rice to the angiosperm parasite *Striga hermonthica*", *New Phytologist*, Vol. 169, pp. 199-208, https://doi.org/10.1111/j.1469-8137.2005.01560.x.

Gutjahr, C., L. Casieri and U. Paszkowski (2009), "*Glomus intraradices* induces changes in root system architecture of rice independently of common symbiosis signaling", *New Phytologist*, Vol. 182, pp. 829-837, https://doi.org/10.1111/j.1469-8137.2009.02839.x.

Hajiboland, R., N. Aliasgharzad and R. Barzeghar (2009), "Phosphorus mobilization and uptake in mycorrhizal rice (*Oryza sativa* L.) plants under flooded and non-flooded conditions", *Acta agriculturae Slovenica*, Vol. 93, pp. 153-161, https://doi.org/10.2478/V10014-009-0010-4.

Harsonowati, W., R.I. Astuti and A.T. Wahyudi (2017), "Leaf blast disease reduction by rice-phyllosphere actinomyecetes producing bioactive compounds", *Journal of General Plant Pathology*, Vol. 83, pp. 98-108, https://doi.org/10.1007/s10327-017-0700-4.

Hattori, M. (2001), "Probing behavior of the brown planthopper, *Nilaparvata lugens* Stål (Homoptera: Delphacidae) on a non-host barnyard grass, and resistant and susceptible varieties of rice", *Applied Entomology and Zoology*, Vol. 36, pp. 83-89, https://doi.org/10.1303/aez.2001.83.

Hattori, M. (1997), "Feeding behavior of the green rice leafhopper, *Nephotettix cincticeps* (Homoptera: Cicadellidae) towards pure phloem sap collected from resistant and susceptible rice varieties", *Applied Entomology and Zoology*, Vol. 32, pp. 409-412, https://doi.org/10.1303/aez.32.409.

Heinrichs, E.A. (ed.) (1994) *Biology and Management of Rice Insects*, Wiley Eastern Ltd.

Heinrichs, E.A. and A.T. Barrion (2004), *Rice-feeding Insects and Selected Natural Enemies in West Africa: Biology, Ecology, Identification*, International Rice Research Institute, Los Baños, Philippines, and WARDA–The Africa Rice Center, Abidjan, Côte d'Ivoire.

Heinrichs, E.A., F.G. Medano and H.R. Rapusas (1985), *Genetics Evaluation for Insect Resistance in Rice*, International Rice Research Institute, Manila, Philippines.

Hibino, H. et al. (1986a), "Rice ragged stunt virus", *Technical Bulletin of the Tropical Agriculture Research Center*, Vol. 21, pp. 14-33.

Hibino, H. et al. (1986b), "Rice grassy stunt virus – Purification and serology –", *Technical Bulletin of the Tropical Agriculture Research Center*, Vol. 21, p. 34-40.

Hibino, H. (1983), "Relations of rice tungro bacilliform and rice tungro spherical viruses with their vector *Nephotettix virescens*", *Annals of Phytopathological Society of Japan*, Vol. 49, pp. 545-553, https://doi.org/10.3186/jjphytopath.49.545.

Hiei, Y. et al. (1994), "Efficient transformation of rice (*Oryza sativa* L.) mediated by *Agrobacterium* and sequence analysis of' the boundaries of the T-DNA", *The Plant Journal*, Vol. 6, pp. 271-282, https://doi.org/10.1046/j.1365-313X.1994.6020271.x.

Hiradate, S. (2006), "Isolation strategies for finding bioactive compounds: Specific activity vs. total activity", *Natural Products for Pest Management*, ACS Symposium Series, Vol. 927, pp. 113-126, https://doi.org/10.1021/bk-2006-0927.ch009.

Hiradate, S. et al. (2010), "Quantitative evaluation of allelopathic potentials in soils: Total activity approach", *Weed Science*, Vol. 58, pp. 258-264, https://doi.org/10.1614/WS-D-09-00085.1.

Hiraguri, A. et al. (2010), "Complete sequence analysis of rice transitory yellowing virus and its comparison to rice yellow stunt virus", *Archives of Virology*, Vol. 155, pp. 243-245, https://doi.org/10.1007/s00705-009-0557-8.

Honda, K. et al. (2007), "Retention of *Rice dwarf virus* by descendants of pairs of viruliferous vector insects after rearing for 6 years", *Phytopathology*, Vol. 97, pp. 712-716, https://doi.org/10.1094/PHYTO-97-6-0712.

Hong, W.-J. et al. (2019), "Infrastructures of systems biology that facilitate functional genomic study in rice", *Rice*, Vol. 12, Article 15, https://doi.org/10.1186/s12284-019-0276-z.

Hori, K., K. Matsubara and M. Yano (2016), "Genetic control of flowering time in rice: Integration of Mendelian genetics and genomics", *Theoretical and Applied Genetics*, Vol. 129, pp. 2241-2252, https://doi.org/10.1007/s00122-016-2773-4.

Hoshikawa, K. (1989), "Chapter X: Heading, anthesis and fertilization", in *The Growing Rice Plant*, Nobunkyo, Tokyo, pp. 237-253.

Hosoi, J. et al. (2010), "Viability dynamics of overwintering seeds of weedy rice in Nagano Prefecture placed on soil surface and buried in soil", *Japanese Journal of Crop Science*, Vol. 79, pp. 322-326, https://doi.org/10.1626/jcs.79.322.

Hou, J. et al. (2019), "*ESA1* is involved in embryo sac abortion in interspecific hybrid progeny of rice", *Plant Physiology*, Vol. 180, pp. 356-366, https://doi.org/10.1104/pp.18.01374.

Howard, R.J. and B. Valent (1996), "Breaking and entering: host penetration by the fungal rice blast pathogen *Magnaporthe grisea*", *Annual Review of Microbiology*, Vol. 50, pp. 491-512, https://doi.org/10.1146/annurev.micro.50.1.491.

Hu, F. et al. (2006), "Molecular mapping of a pollen killer gene *S29(t)* in *Oryza glaberrima* and co-linear analysis with *S22* in *O. glumaepatula*", *Euphytica*, Vol. 151, pp. 273-278, https://doi.org/10.1007/s10681-006-9146-z.

Hu, F.Y. et al. (2003), "Convergent evolution of perenniality in rice and sorghum", *Proceeding of the National Academy of Sciences of the United States of America,* Vol. 100, pp. 4050-4054, https://doi.org/10.1073/pnas.0630531100.

Hu, L. et al. (2017), "The coiled-coil and nucleotide binding domains of BROWN PLANTHOPPER RESISTANCE14 function in signaling and resistance against planthopper in rice", *The Plant Cell*, Vol. 29, pp. 3157-3185, https://doi.org/10.1105/tpc.17.00263.

Hua, L. et al. (2015), "*LABA1*, a domestication gene associated with long, barbed awns in wild rice", *The Plant Cell*,

Vol. 27, pp. 1875-1888, https://doi.org/10.1105/tpc.15.00260.

Huang, H.J. et al. (2016), "Screening and functional analyses of *Nilaparvata lugens* salivary proteome", *Journal of Proteome Research*, Vol. 15, pp. 1883-1896, https://doi.org/10.1021/acs.jproteome.6b00086.

Huang, J.Z. et al. (2014), "Workable male sterility systems for hybrid rice: Genetics, biochemistry, molecular biology, and utilization", *Rice,* Vol. 7, Article 13, https://doi.org/10.1186/s12284-014-0013-6.

Huang, T. et al. (2007), "Genetic analysis and mapping of genes involved in fertility of Pingxiang dominant genic male sterile rice", *Journal of Genetics and Genomics*, Vol. 34, pp. 616-622, https://doi.org/10.1016/S1673-8527(07)60070-8.

Huang, W. et al. (2015), "Pentatricopeptide-repeat family protein RF6 functions with hexokinase 6 to rescue rice cytoplasmic male sterility", *Proceedings of the National Academy of Sciences*, Vol. 112, pp. 14984-14989, https://doi.org/10.1073/pnas.1511748112.

Huang, X. et al. (2012), "A map of rice genome variation reveals the origin of cultivated rice", *Nature*, Vol. 490, pp. 497-501. https://doi.org/10.1038/nature11532.

Huang, X. et al. (2010), "Genome-wide association studies of 14 agronomic traits in rice landraces", *Nature Genetics*, Vol. 42, pp. 961-967, https://doi.org/10.1038/ng.695.

Huang, X. et al. (2009), "High-throughput genotyping by whole-genome resequencing", *Genome Research*, Vol. 19, pp. 1068-1076, http://www.genome.org/cgi/doi/10.1101/gr.089516.108.

Ichitani, K. et al. (2011), "Chromosomal location of *HWA1* and *HWA2*, complementary hybrid weakness genes in rice", *Rice*, Vol. 4, pp. 29-38, https://doi.org/10.1007/s12284-011-9062-2.

ICTV (2019), *International Committee on Taxonomy of Viruses*, https://talk.ictvonline.org (accessed 11 June 2019).

Iizuka, M. et al. (2014), "Suppression of collagen-induced arthritis by oral administration of transgenic rice seeds expressing altered peptide ligands of type II collagen", *Plant Biotechnology Journal*, Vol. 12, pp. 1143-1152, https://doi.org/10.1111/pbi.12223.

Ikeda, K. et al. (2007), "Rice *ABERRANT PANICLE ORGANIZATION 1*, encoding an F-box protein, regulates meristem fate", *The Plant Journal*, Vol. 51, pp. 1030-1040, https://doi.org/10.1111/j.1365-313X.2007.03200.x.

Ikehashi, H. and H. Araki (1986), "Genetics of F_1 sterility in remote crosses of rice", *Rice Genetics*, Vol. 1, pp. 119-130, https://doi.org/10.1142/9789812814265_0011.

Imchen, M. et al. (2019), "16S rRNA gene amplicon based metagenomic signatures of rhizobiome community in rice field during various growth stages", *Frontiers in Microbiology*, Vol. 10, 2103, https://doi.org/10.3389/fmicb.2019.02103.

Index Fungorum (2019), *The Global Database of Fungal Names*, http://www.indexfungorum.org/ (accessed 11 June 2019).

International Rice Genome Sequencing Project (2005), "The map-based sequence of the rice genome", *Nature*, Vol. 436, pp. 793-800, https://doi.org/10.1038/nature03895.

IRRI (2016), *Rice Diseases: Biology and Selected Management Practices*, International Rice Research Institute, http://rice-diseases.irri.org/home/contents.

IRRI (2012), *The International Rice Genebank – Conserving Rice*, International Rice Research Institute, https://web.archive.org/web/20121023054703/http:/irri.org/index.php?option=com_k2&view=item&id=9960&lang=en.

IRRI (1985), *International Rice Research: 25 Years of Partnership*, IRRI press, Manila, pp. 1-188.

IRRI (1983), *Field Problems of Tropical Rice*, Revised edition, International Rice Research Institute.

IRRI (n.d.-a), *How to Control Weeds*, Rice Knowledge Bank, International Rice Research Institute, http://www.knowledgebank.irri.org/step-by-step-production/growth/weed-management (accessed 2 September 2020).

IRRI (n.d.-b), *Main Weeds of Rice in Asia*, Rice Knowledge Bank, International Rice Research Institute, http://www.knowledgebank.irri.org/training/fact-sheets/pest-management/weeds/main-weeds-of-rice-in-asia (accessed 2 September 2020).

IRRI (n.d.-c), *Learn About Best Practices in Rice Farming*, Rice Knowledge Bank, International Rice Research Institute, http://www.knowledgebank.irri.org/ (accessed 30 October 2020).

Ishii, T., et al. (1994), "Molecular tagging of genes for brown planthopper resistance and earliness introgressed from *Oryza australiensis* into cultivated rice, *O. sativa*", *Genome*, Vol. 37, pp. 217-221, https://doi.org/10.1139/g94-030.

Ishikawa, R. et al. (2006), "Genetic erosion from modern varieties into traditional upland rice cultivars (*Oryza sativa* L.) in northern Thailand", *Genetic Resources and Crop Evolution*, Vol. 53, pp. 245-252, https://doi.org/10.1007/s10722-004-6132-y.

Ishikawa, R. et al. (2002a), "Origin of cytoplasm substituted rice cultivars found in Japan", *Theoretical and Applied*

Genetics, Vol. 105, pp. 608-613, https://doi.org/10.1007/s00122-002-0898-0.

Ishikawa, R. et al. (2002b), "Different maternal origins of Japanese lowland and upland rice populations", *Theoretical and Applied Genetics*, Vol. 104, pp. 976-980, https://doi.org/10.1007/s00122-001-0807-y.

ISSG (n.d.), *View 100 of the World's Worst Invasive Alien Species*, Invasive Species Specialist Group, http://www.issg.org/worst100_species.html (accessed 31 August 2020).

Isshiki, M. et al. (1998), "A naturally occurring functional allele of the rice *waxy* locus has a GT to TT mutation at the 5' splice site of the first intron", *The Plant Journal*, Vol. 15, pp.133-138, https://doi.org/10.1046/j.1365-313X.1998.00189.x.

Itabashi, E., T. Kazama and K. Toriyama (2009), "Characterization of cytoplasmic male sterility of rice with lead rice cytoplasm in comparison with that with Chinsurah Boro II cytoplasm", *Plant Cell Reports*, Vol. 28, pp. 233-239, https://doi.org/10.1007/s00299-008-0625-7.

Itabashi, E. et al. (2011), "The fertility restorer gene, *Rf2*, for lead rice-type cytoplasmic male sterility of rice encodes a mitochondrial glycine-rich protein", *The Plant Journal*, Vol. 65, pp. 359-367, https://doi.org/10.1111/j.1365-313X.2010.04427.x.

Itoh, H. et al. (2018), "Genomic adaptation of flowering-time genes during the expansion of rice cultivation area", *The Plant Journal,* Vol. 94, pp. 895-909, https://doi.org/10.1111/tpj.13906.

Iwabuchi, M., J. Kyozuka and K. Shimamoto (1993), "Processing followed by complete editing of an altered mitochondrial *atp6* RNA restores fertility of cytoplasmic male sterile rice", *The EMBO Journal*, Vol. 12, pp. 1437-1446, https://doi.org/10.1002/j.1460-2075.1993.tb05787.x.

Jabran, K. (2017), "Rice allelopathy for weed control", in K. Jabran. (ed.), *Manipulation of Allelopathic Crops for Weed Control*, Springer International Publishing AG, Switzerland, pp. 35-47, https://doi.org/10.1007/978-3-319-53186-1_5.

Jacquemin, J. et al. (2013), "The International Oryza Map Alignment Project: Development of a genus-wide comparative genomics platform to help solve the 9 billion-people question", *Current Opinion in Plant Biology*, Vol. 16, pp. 147-156, https://doi.org/10.1016/j.pbi.2013.02.014.

Japanese Society of Applied Entomology and Zoology (2006), *Major Insect and Other Pests of Economic Plants in Japan*, Revised edition, Tokyo.

Jena, K.K. (2010), "The species of the genus *Oryza* and transfer of useful genes from wild species into cultivated rice, *O. sativa*", *Breeding Science*, Vol. 60, pp. 518-523, https://doi.org/10.1270/jsbbs.60.518.

Jena, K.K. (1994) "Production of intergeneric hybrid between *Oryza sativa* L. and *Porteresia coarctata* T", *Current Science*, Vol. 67, pp. 744-746, http://www.jstor.org/stable/24095851.

Jena, K.K. and G.S. Khush (1990), "Introgression of genes from *Oryza offficinalis* Well ex Watt into cultivated rice, *O. sativa* L.", *Theoretical and Applied Genetics*, Vol. 80, pp. 737-745, https://doi.org/10.1007/BF00224186.

Jena, K.K. and D.J. Mackill (2008), "Molecular markers and their use in marker-assisted selection in rice", *Crop Science*, Vol. 48, pp. 1266-1276, https://doi.org/10.2135/cropsci2008.02.0082.

Jiao, Y. et al. (2010), "Regulation of *OsSPL14* by OsmiR156 defines ideal plant architecture in rice", *Nature Genetics*, Vol. 42, pp. 541-544, https://doi.org/10.1038/ng.591.

Jin, J. et al. (2008), "Genetic control of rice plant architecture under domestication", *Nature Genetics*, Vol. 40, pp.1365-1369, https://doi.org/10.1038/ng.247.

Jin, X. et al. (2017), "Introgression from cultivated rice alters genetic structures of wild relative populations: Implications for *in situ* conservation", *AOB Plants*, Vol. 10, plx055, https://doi.org/10.1093/aobpla/plx055.

Jinek, M. et al. (2012), "A programmable dual-RNA-guided DNA endonuclease in adaptive bacterial immunity", *Science*, Vol. 337, pp. 816-821, http://science.sciencemag.org/content/337/6096/816.

Jonson, G.B. et al. (2020), "Reemerging rice orange leaf phytoplasma with varying symptoms expressions and its transmission by a new leafhopper vector—*Nephotettix virescens* Distant", *Pathogens*, Vol. 9, p. 990, https://doi.org/10.3390/pathogens9120990.

Joseph, L., P. Kuriachan and G. Thomas, (2008), "Is *Oryza malampuzhaensis* Krish. et Chand. (Poaceae) a valid species? Evidence from morphological and molecular analyses", *Plant Systematics and Evolution*, Vol. 270, pp. 75-94, https://doi.org/10.1007/s00606-007-0606-2.

Joshi, R.C. and L.S. Sebastian (2006), *Global Advances in Ecology and Management of Golden Apple Snails*, Philippine Rice Research Institute, Nueva Ecija, Philippines.

Joshi, R.C., A.T. Barrion and L.S. Sebastian (eds.) (2007), "Rice black bugs: Taxonomy, ecology, biology, and management of invasive species", Philippines Rice Research Institute, p. 793.

Juliano, B.O. (1985), "Polysaccharides, proteins, and lipid of rice", in B.O. Juliano (ed.), *Rice: Chemistry and*

Technology, 2nd edition, American Association Cereal Chemists, St. Paul, Minnesota, pp 59-174.

Juliano, B.O. and C.P. Villareal (1993), *Grain Quality Evaluation of World Rices*, International Rice Research Institute (IRRI), p. 214.

Juliano B.O., C.M. Perez and T.T. Chang (1990), "Varietal differences in longevity of tropical rough rice stored under ambient conditions", *Seed Science and Technology*, Vol. 18, pp. 361-369.

Juliano, B.O. et al. (1968), "Screening for high protein rice varieties", *Cereal Science Today*, Vol. 13, pp. 299-301.

Kadota, I. and A. Ohuchi (1990), "Symptoms and ecology of bacterial brown stripe of rice", *Japan Agricultural Research Quarterly*, Vol. 24, pp. 15-21.

Kalia, S. and R. Rathour (2019), "Current status on mapping of genes for resistance to leaf- and neck-blast disease in rice", *3 Biotech.*, Vol. 9, p. 209, https://doi.org/10.1007/s13205-019-1738-0.

Kaloshian, I. and L.L. Walling (2016), "Hemipteran and dipteran pests: Effectors and plant host immune regulators", *Journal of Integrative Plant Biology*, Vol. 58, pp. 350-361, https://doi.org/10.1111/jipb.12438.

Kaneda, C. (1993), "Rice", in *Traditional Crop Breeding Practices: An Historical Review to Serve as a Baseline for Assessing the Role of Modem Biotechnology*, OECD, Paris, pp. 37-46.

Kathuria, H. et al. (2007), "Advances in transgenic rice biotechnology", *Critical Reviews in Plant Sciences*, Vol. 26, pp. 65-103, https://doi.org/10.1080/07352680701252809.

Kato, H. and H. Namai (1987), "Floral characteristics and environmental factors for increasing natural out crossing rate for F_1 hybrid seed production of rice *Oryza sativa* L.", *Japanese Journal of Breeding*, Vol. 37, pp. 318–330, https://doi.org/10.1270/jsbbs1951.37.318 (in Japanese with English abstract).

Kato, T. et al. (1973), "Momilactones are growth inhibitors from rice, Oryza sativa L.", *Tetrahedron Letters*, Vol. 39, pp. 3861-3864, https://doi.org/10.1016/S0040-4039(01)87058-1.

Kato-Noguchi, H. and R.J. Peters (2013), "The role of momilactones in rice allelopathy", *Journal of chemical Ecology*, Vol. 39, pp. 175-185, https://doi.org/10.1007/s10886-013-0236-9.

Kato-Noguchi, H. and T. Ino (2005), "Possible involvement of momilactone B in rice allelopathy", *Journal of Plant Physiology*, Vol. 162, pp. 718-21, https://doi.org/10.1016/j.jplph.2004.11.009.

Kato-Noguchi, H. and T. Ino (2003), "Rice seedlings release momilactone B into the environment", *Phytochemistry*, Vol. 63, pp. 551-554, https://doi.org/10.1016/S0031-9422(03)00194-8.

Kawabe, S. (1985), "Mechanism of varietal resistance to the rice green leafhopper (*Nephotettix cincticeps* Uhler)", *Japan Agricultural Research Quarterly*, Vol. 19, pp. 115-124.

Kawahara, Y. et al. (2013), "Improvement of the *Oryza sativa* Nipponbare reference genome using next generation sequence and optical map data", *Rice*, Vol. 6/4, https://doi.org/10.1186/1939-8433-6-4.

Kawasaki, A. et al. (2009), "Molecular constitution of weedy rice (*Oryza sativa* L.) found in Okayama prefecture, Japan", *Breeding Science*, Vol. 59, pp. 229-236, https://doi.org/10.1270/jsbbs.59.229.

Kazama, T. and K. Toriyama (2014), "A fertility restorer gene, *Rf4*, widely used for hybrid rice breeding encodes a pentatricopeptide repeat protein", *Rice*, Vol. 7, Article 28, https://doi.org/10.1186/s12284-014-0028-z.

Kazama, T. and K. Toriyama (2003), "A pentatricopeptide repeat-containing gene that promotes the processing of aberrant *atp6* RNA of cytoplasmic male-sterile rice", *FEBS Letters*, Vol. 544, pp. 99-102, https://doi.org/10.1016/S0014-5793(03)00480-0.

Kazama, T. et al. (2019), "Curing cytoplasmic male sterility via TALEN-mediated mitochondrial genome editing", *Nature Plants*, Vol. 5, pp. 722-730, https://doi.org/10.1038/s41477-019-0459-z.

Kazama, T. et al. (2016), "Mitochondrial ORF79 levels determine pollen abortion in cytoplasmic male sterile rice", *The Plant Journal*, Vol. 85, pp. 707-716, https://doi.org/10.1111/tpj.13135.

Khan, Z.R. et al. (1990), "World Bibliography of Rice Stem Borers 1794-1990", International Rice Research Institute.

Khanh T.D., T.D. Xuan and I.M. Chung (2007), "Rice allelopathy and the possibility for weed management", *Annals of Applied Biology*, Vol. 151, pp. 325-339, https://doi.org/10.1111/j.1744-7348.2007.00183.x.

Khatun, S. and T.J. Flowers (1995), "The estimation of pollen viability in rice", *Journal of Experimental Botany*, Vol. 46, pp. 151-154, www.jstor.org/stable/23694857.

Khush, G.S (1997), "Origin, dispersal, cultivation and variation of rice", *Plant Molecular Biology*, Vol. 35, pp. 25–34.

Khush, G.S. (1977), "Disease and insect resistance in rice", *Advances in Agronomy*, Vol. 29, pp. 265-341, https://doi.org/10.1016/S0065-2113(08)60221-7.

Khush, G.S. and D.S. Brar (2017), "Alien introgression in rice", *Nucleus*, Vol. 60, pp. 251-261, https://doi.org/10.1007/s13237-017-0222-7.

Khush, G.S. and D.S. Brar (1992), "Overcoming barriers in hybridization", in G. Kalloo and J.B. Chowdhury (eds.), *Distant Hybridization of Crop Plants*, Monographs on Theoretical and Applied Genetics, Vol. 16, pp. 47-61, https://doi.org/10.1007/978-3-642-84306-8_4.

Khush, G.S., W.R. Coffman and H.M. Beachell (2001), "The history of rice breeding: IRRI's contribution", in W.G. Rockwood (ed.), *Rice Research and Production in the 21st Century: Symposium Honoring Robert F. Chandler, Jr.*, International Rice Research Institute, Los Baños, Philippines, pp. 117-135, http://books.irri.org/9712201635_content.pdf.

Khush, G.S. et al. (1994), "*Apomixis for rice improvement*", in G.S. Khush (ed.), *Apomixis: Exploiting Hybrid Vigor in Rice,* pp. 1-21.

Kim, K. et al. (2015), "Complete chloroplast and ribosomal sequences for 30 accessions elucidate evolution of Oryza AA genome species", *Scientific Reports*, Vol. 5, 15655, https://doi.org/10.1038/srep15655.

Kim, Y.-J. and D. Zhang (2018), "Molecular control of male fertility for crop hybrid breeding", *Trends in Plant Science*", Vol. 23, pp. 53-65, https://doi.org/10.1016/j.tplants.2017.10.001.

Kiritani, K. (2007), "Implications of an unintended area-wide IPM for *Chilo suppressalis* in Japan", *Extension Bulletin 588*, Food and Fertilizer Technology Center, pp. 1-9.

Kishimoto, K. et al. (2010), "Perception of the chitin oligosaccharides contributes to disease resistance to blast fungus *Magnaporthe oryzae* in rice", *The Plant Journal*, Vol. 64, pp. 343-354, https://doi.org/10.1111/j.1365-313X.2010.04328.x.

Kobayashi, K., Y. Yogo and H. Sugiyama (1995), "Differential growth response of rice cultivars to pyrazosulfuron-ethyl", *Journal of Weed Science and Technology*, Vol. 40, pp. 104-109, https://doi.org/10.3719/weed.40.104.

Koga, Y. et al. (1971), "Studies on the longevity of pollen grains of rice, *Oriza sativa* L., I. Morphological change of pollen grains after shedding", *Cytologia*, Vol. 36, pp. 104-110, https://doi.org/10.1508/cytologia.36.104.

Kögel-Knabner, I. et al. (2010), "Biogeochemistry of paddy soils", *Geoderma*, Vol. 157, pp. 1-14, https://doi.org/10.1016/j.geoderma.2010.03.009.

Köhler, F.E. (1897), *Köhler's Medizinal-Pflanzen.*

Komor, A.C. et al. (2016), "Programmable editing of a target base in genomic DNA without double-stranded DNA cleavage", *Nature*, Vol. 533, pp. 420-424, https://doi.org/10.1038/nature17946.

Komori, T. et al. (2004), "Map-based cloning of a fertility restorer gene, *Rf-1*, in rice (*Oryza sativa* L.)", *The Plant Journal*, Vol. 37, pp. 315-325, https://doi.org/10.1046/j.1365-313X.2003.01961.x.

Konishi, S., K. Ebana and T. Izawa (2008), "Inference of the *japonica* rice domestication process from the distribution of six functional nucleotide polymorphisms of domestication-related genes in various landraces and modern cultivars", *Plant and Cell Physiology*, Vol. 49, pp. 1283-1293, https://doi.org/10.1093/pcp/pcn118.

Konishi, S. et al. (2006), "An SNP caused loss of seed shattering during rice domestication", *Science*, Vol. 312, pp. 1392-1396, https://doi.org/10.1126/science.1126410.

Kovach, M.J., M.T. Sweeney and S.R. McCouch (2007), "New insights into the history of rice domestication", *Trends in Genetics*, Vol. 23, pp. 578-587, https://doi.org/10.1016/j.tig.2007.08.012.

Kraehmer, H. et al. (2016), "Global distribution of rice weeds - A review", *Crop Protection*, Vol. 80, pp. 73-86, https://doi.org/10.1016/j.cropro.2015.10.027.

Kubo, T. and A. Yoshimura (2005), "Epistasis underlying female sterility detected in hybrid breakdown in a Japonica-Indica cross of rice (*Oryza sativa* L.)", *Theoretical and Applied Genetics*, Vol. 110, pp. 346-355, https://doi.org/10.1007/s00122-004-1846-y.

Kubo, T. and A. Yoshimura (2002), "Genetic basis of hybrid breakdown in a Japonica/Indica cross of rice, *Oryza sativa* L.", *Theoretical and Applied Genetics*, Vol. 105, pp. 906-911, https://doi.org/10.1007/s00122-002-1059-1.

Kubo, T. et al. (2016), "Two tightly linked genes at the *hsa1* locus cause both F_1 and F_2 hybrid sterility in rice", *Molecular Plant*, Vol. 9, pp. 221-232, https://doi.org/10.1016/j.molp.2015.09.014.

Kubo, T. et al. (2008), "A novel epistatic interaction at two loci causing hybrid male sterility in an inter-subspecific cross of rice (*Oryza sativa* L.)", *Genes and Genetic Systems*, Vol. 83, pp. 443-453, https://doi.org/10.1266/ggs.83.443.

Kuboyama, T. et al. (2009), "Fine mapping of *HWC2*, a complementary hybrid weakness gene, and haplotype analysis around the locus in rice", *Rice*, Vol. 2, pp. 93-103, https://doi.org/10.1007/s12284-009-9026-y.

Kurata, N. and T. Omura (1984), "Chromosome analysis", *Developments in Crop Science*, Vol. 7, pp. 305-320, https://doi.org/10.1016/B978-0-444-99615-2.50017-X.

Kuwatsuka, S. and H. Shindo (1973), "Behavior of phenolic substances in the decaying process of plants. I. Identification and quantitative determination of phenolic acids in rice straw and its decayed product by gas chromatography", *Soil Science and Plant Nutrition*, Vol. 19, pp. 219–227, https://doi.org/10.1080/00380768.1973.10432591.

Kyndt, T., D. Fernandez and G. Gheysen (2014), "Plant-parasitic nematode infections in rice: Molecular and cellular insights", *Annual Review of Phytopathology*, Vol. 52, pp. 135-153, https://www.annualreviews.org/doi/10.1146/annurev-phyto-102313-050111.

Lacchini, E. et al. (2020), "CRISPR-mediated accelerated domestication of African rice landraces", *PLoS One*, Vol. 15, e0229782, https://doi.org/10.1371/journal.pone.0229782.

Lane, S.J., A. Azuma and H. Higuchi (1998), "Wildfowl damage to agriculture in Japan", *Agriculture, Ecosystems and Environment*, Vol. 70, pp. 69-77, https://doi.org/10.1016/S0167-8809(98)00114-5.

Lapitan, V.C. et al. (2009), "Mapping of quantitative trait loci using a doubled-haploid population from the cross of *Indica* and *Japonica* cultivars of rice", *Crop Science*, Vol. 49, pp. 1620-1628, https://doi.org/10.2135/cropsci2008.11.0655.

Lee, H.S. et al. (2010), "Identification of molecular markers for photoblastism in weedy rice", *Korean Journal of Breeding Science*, Vol. 42, pp. 144-150.

Lee, T.T.T. et al. (2003), "Enhanced methionine and cysteine levels in transgenic rice seeds by the accumulation of sesame 2S albumin", *Bioscience, Biotechnology, and Biochemistry*, Vol. 67, p. 1699-1705, https://doi.org/10.1271/bbb.67.1699.

Li, C., A. Zhou and T. Sang (2006), "Rice domestication by reducing shattering", *Science*, Vol. 311, pp. 1936-1939, https://doi.org/10.1126/science.1123604.

Li, F. et al. (2011), "A new gene for hybrid sterility from a cross between *Oryza sativa* and *O. glaberrima*", *Plant Breeding*, Vol. 130, pp. 165-171, https://doi.org/10.1111/j.1439-0523.2010.01845.x.

Li, J. et al. (2016a), "Gene replacements and insertions in rice by intron targeting using CRISPR-Cas9", *Nature Plants*, Vol. 2, 16139, https://doi.org/10.1038/nplants.2016.139.

Li, L.-F. et al. (2017), "Signatures of adaptation in the weedy rice genome", *Nature Genetics*, Vol. 49, pp. 811-814, https://doi.org/10.1038/ng.3825.

Li, M. et al. (2016b), "Reassessment of the four yield-related genes *Gn1a*, *DEP1*, *GS3*, and *IPA1* in rice using a CRISPR/Cas9 system", *Frontiers in Plant Science*, Vol. 7, 377, https://doi.org/10.3389/fpls.2016.00377.

Li, Q. et al. (2016c), "Development of japonica photo-sensitive genic male sterile rice lines by editing carbon starved anther using CRISPR/Cas9", *Journal of Genetics and Genomics*, Vol. 43, pp. 415-419, https://doi.org/10.1016/j.jgg.2016.04.011.

Li, S., D. Yang and Y. Zhu (2007), "Characterization and use of male sterility in hybrid rice breeding", *Journal of Integrative Plant Biology*, Vol. 49, pp. 791-804, https://doi.org/10.1111/j.1744-7909.2007.00513.x.

Li, S. et al. (2019), "Developing disease-resistant thermosensitive male sterile rice by multiplex gene editing", *Journal of Integrative Plant Biology*, Vol. 61, pp. 1201-1205, https://doi.org/10.1111/jipb.12774.

Li, T. et al. (2016d), "TALEN-mediated homologous recombination produces site-directed DNA base change and herbicide-resistant rice", *Journal of Genetics and Genomics*, Vol. 43, pp. 297-305, https://doi.org/10.1016/j.jgg.2016.03.005.

Li, T. et al. (2012), "High-efficiency TALEN-based gene editing produces disease-resistant rice", *Nature Biotechnology*, Vol. 30, pp. 390-392, https://doi.org/10.1038/nbt.2199.

Li, X. et al. (2018), "Expanding the scope of CRISPR/Cpf1-mediated genome editing in rice", *Molecular Plant*, Vol. 11, pp. 995-998, https://doi.org/10.1016/j.molp.2018.03.009.

Li, X. et al. (2017), "High-efficiency breeding of early-maturing rice cultivars via CRISPR/Cas9-mediated genome editing", *Journal of Genetics and Genomics*, Vol. 44, pp. 175-178, https://doi.org/10.1016/j.jgg.2017.02.001.

Li, X. et al. (2015), "Combinations of *Hd2* and *Hd4* genes determine rice adaptability to Heilongjiang province, northern limit of China", *Journal of Integrative Plant Biology,* Vol. 57, pp. 698-707, https://doi.org/10.1111/jipb.12326.

Li, Z., A. Hayashimoto and N. Murai (1992), "A sulfonylurea herbicide resistance gene from Arabidopsis thaliana as a new selectable marker for production of fertile transgenic rice plants", *Plant Physiology*, Vol. 100, pp. 662-668, https://www.jstor.org/stable/4274685.

Lin, S.C. and L.P. Yuan (1980), "Hybrid rice breeding in China", in *Innovative Approaches in Rice Breeding*, International Rice Research Institute, pp. 35-51.

Linares, O.F. (2002), "African rice (*Oryza glaberrima*): History and future potential", *Proceedings of the National Academy of Sciences of the United States of America*, Vol. 99, pp. 16360–16365, https://doi.org/10.1073/pnas.252604599.

Ling, Y., L. Ang and Z. Weilin (2019), "Current understanding of the molecular players involved in resistance to rice planthoppers", *Pest Management Science*, Vol. 75, pp. 2566-2574, https://doi.org/10.1002/ps.5487.

Liu, J. et al. (2017a), "*GW5* acts in the brassinosteroid signalling pathway to regulate grain width and weight in rice", *Nature Plants*, Vol. 10, 17043, https://doi.org/10.1038/nplants.2017.43.

Liu, J. et al. (2017b), "Methane emissions and microbial communities as influenced by dual cropping of Azolla along with early rice", *Scientific Reports*, Vol. 7, 40635, https://doi.org/10.1038/srep40635.

Liu, W. et al. (2013), "Recent progress in understanding PAMP- and effector-triggered immunity against the rice blast fungus *Magnaporthe oryzae*", *Molecular Plant*, Vol. 6, pp. 605-620, https://doi.org/10.1093/mp/sst015.

Liu, Y. et al. (2015), "A gene cluster encoding lectin receptor kinases confers broad-spectrum and durable insect resistance in rice", *Nature Biotechnology*, Vol. 33, pp. 301-305, https://doi.org/10.1038/nbt.3069.

Long, Y. et al. (2008), "Hybrid male sterility in rice controlled by interaction between divergent alleles of two adjacent genes", *Proceedings of the National Academy of Sciences of the United States of America*, Vol. 105, pp. 18871-18876, https://doi.org/10.1073/pnas.0810108105.

Lou, D. et al. (2017), "OsSAPK2 confers abscisic acid sensitivity and tolerance to drought stress in rice", *Frontiers in Plant Science*, Vol. 8, pp. 993-1007, https://doi.org/10.3389/fpls.2017.00993.

Lu, B.R., X. Yang and N.C. Ellstrand (2016), "Fitness correlates of crop transgene flow into weedy populations: a case study of weedy rice in China and other examples", *Evolutionary Applications*, Vol. 9, p. 857-870, https://doi.org/10.1111/eva.12377.

Lu, H.P. et al. (2018), "Resistance of rice to insect pests mediated by suppression of serotonin biosynthesis", *Nature Plants*, Vol. 4, pp. 338-344, https://doi.org/10.1038/s41477-018-0152-7.

Lu, Y. and J.-K. Zhu (2017), "Precise editing of a target base in the rice genome using a modified CRISPR/Cas9 system", *Molecular Plant*, Vol. 10, p. 523-525, https://doi.org/10.1016/j.molp.2016.11.013.

Luo, D. et al. (2013), "A detrimental mitochondrial-nuclear interaction causes cytoplasmic male sterility in rice", *Nature Genetics*, Vol. 45, pp. 573-577, https://doi.org/10.1038/ng.2570.

Luo, J. et al. (2013), "*An-1* encodes a basic helix-loop-helix protein that regulates awn development, grain size, and grain number in rice", *The Plant Cell*, Vol. 25, pp. 3360-3376, https://www.jstor.org/stable/23598355.

Lv, S. et al. (2018), "Genetic control of seed shattering during African rice domestication", *Nature Plants*, Vol. 4, pp. 331-337, https://doi.org/10.1038/s41477-018-0164-3.

Ma, L. et al. (2015), "TALEN-based mutagenesis of lipoxygenase LOX3 enhances the storage tolerance of rice (*Oryza sativa*) seeds", *PLoS ONE.*, Vol. 10, e0143877, https://doi.org/10.1371/journal.pone.0143877.

Macías, F.A. et al. (2006), "Bioactive steroids from *Oryza sativa* L", *Steroids*, Vol. 71, pp. 603-608, https://doi.org/10.1016/j.steroids.2006.03.001.

Macovei, A. et al. (2018), "Novel alleles of rice *eIF4G* generated by CRISPR/Cas9-targeted mutagenesis confer resistance to *Rice tungro spherical virus*", *Plant Biotechnology Journal*, Vol. 16, pp. 1918-1927, https://doi.org/10.1111/pbi.12927.

Maeda, H. et al. (2019), "A rice gene that confers broad-spectrum resistance to β-triketone herbicides", *Science*, Vol. 365, pp. 393-396, https://doi.org/10.1126/science.aax0379.

Mao, H. et al. (2010), "Linking differential domain functions of the GS3 protein to natural variation of grain size in rice", *Proceedings of the National Academy of Sciences of the United States of America*, Vol. 107, pp. 19579-19584, https://doi.org/10.1073/pnas.1014419107.

Martínez, C.P. et al. (1994), "Nuclear DNA content of ten rice species as determined by flow cytometry", *The Japanese Journal of Genetics*, Vol. 69, pp. 513-523, https://doi.org/10.1266/jjg.69.513.

Matsubara, K. et al. (2012), "Natural variation in *Hd17*, a homolog of Arabidopsis *ELF3* that is involved in rice photoperiodic flowering", *Plant and Cell Physiology*, Vol. 53, pp. 709-716, https://doi.org/10.1093/pcp/pcs028.

Matsumura, M. and S. Sanada-Morimura (2010), "Recent status of insecticide resistance in asian rice planthoppers", *Japan Agricultural Research Quarterly*, Vol. 44, pp. 225-230, https://doi.org/10.6090/jarq.44.225.

Matsumura, M. et al. (2008), "Species-specific insecticide resistance to imidacloprid and fipronil in the rice planthoppers *Nilaparvata lugens* and *Sogatella furcifera* in East and South-east Asia", *Pest Management Science*, Vol. 64, pp. 1115–1121, https://doi.org/10.1002/ps.1641.

Matsuo, T. (1952), "Genecological studies on cultivated rice", *Bulletin of the National Institute of Agricultural Sciences Series D3*, pp. 1-111 (in Japanese).

Mbodj, D. et al. (2018), "Arbuscular mycorrhizal symbiosis in rice: Establishment, environmental control and impact on plant growth and resistance to abiotic stresses", *Rhizosphere*, Vol. 8, pp. 12-26, https://doi.org/10.1016/j.rhisph.2018.08.003.

McCouch, S.R. et al. (2002), "Development and mapping of 2 240 new SSR markers for rice (*Oryza sativa* L.)", *DNA Research*, Vol. 9, pp. 199-207, https://doi.org/10.1093/dnares/9.6.199.

Mentlak, T.A. et al. (2012), "Effector-mediated suppression of chitin-triggered immunity by *Magnaporthe oryzae* is necessary for rice blast disease", *The Plant Cell*, Vol. 24, pp. 322-335, https://doi.org/10.1105/tpc.111.092957.

Messeguer, J. et al. (2004), "A field study of pollen-mediated gene flow from Mediterranean GM rice to conventional rice and the red rice weed", *Molecular Breeding*, Vol. 13, pp. 103-112, https://doi.org/10.1023/B:MOLB.0000012285.39859.9d.

Miao, C. et al. (2018), "Mutations in a subfamily of abscisic acid receptor genes promote rice growth and productivity", *Proceeding of the National Academy of Sciences of the United States of America*, Vol. 115, pp. 6058-6063, https://doi.org/10.1073/pnas.1804774115.

Mishra, R., R.K. Joshi and K. Zhao (2018), "Genome editing in rice: Recent advances, challenges, and future implications", *Frontiers in Plant Science*, Vol. 9, 1361, https://doi.org/10.3389/fpls.2018.01361.

Mithöfer, A., W. Boland and M.E. Maffei (2009), "Chemical ecology of plant-insect interactions", *Annual Plant Reviews Book Series*, Vol. 34, pp. 261-291, https://doi.org/10.1002/9781119312994.apr0369.

Miura, K. et al. (2010), "*OsSPL14* promotes panicle branching and higher grain productivity in rice", *Nature Genetics*, Vol. 42, pp. 545-549, https://doi.org/10.1038/ng.592.

Miyabayashi, T. et al. (2007), "Genome size of twenty wild species of *Oryza* Species determined by flow cytometric and chromosome analyses", *Breeding Science*, Vol. 57, pp. 73-78, https://doi.org/10.1270/jsbbs.57.73.

Mizuta, Y., Y. Harushima and N. Kurata (2010), "Rice pollen hybrid incompatibility caused by reciprocal gene loss of duplicated genes", *Proceedings of the National Academy of Sciences of the United States of America*, Vol. 107, pp. 20417-20422, https://doi.org/10.1073/pnas.1003124107.

Moldenhauer, K.A.K and J.H. Gibbons (2003), "Rice morphology and development", in C.W. Smitha and R.H. Didlay (eds.), *Rice: Origin, History, Technology, and Production*, John Wiley and Sons, New York, pp. 103-127.

Moody, K. (1989), *Weeds, Reported in Rice in South and Southeast Asia*, International Rice Research Institute, Philippines.

Morales, F.J. (2008), "Cereal viruses: Rice", in B.W.J. Mahy and M.H.V. van Regenmortel (eds.), *Encyclopedia of Virology*, 3rd edition, pp. 482-489, https://doi.org/10.1016/B978-012374410-4.00699-3.

Morinaga, T. (1968), "Origin and geographic distribution of Japanese rice", *Tropical Agriculture Research Series*, Vol. 3, pp. 1-15.

Morishima, H. and H.-I. Oka (1960), "The pattern of interspecific variation in the genus *Oryza*: Its quantitative representation by statistical methods", *Evolution*, Vol. 14, pp. 153-165, https://doi.org/10.1111/j.1558-5646.1960.tb03074.x.

Morishima, H., K. Hinata and H.-I. Oka (1963), "Comparison of modes of evolution of cultivated forms from two wild rice species, *Oryza breviligulata* and *O. perennis*", *Evolution*, Vol. 17, pp. 70-181, https://doi.org/10.1270/jsbbs1951.12.153.

Morishima, H., K. Hinata and H.-I. Oka (1962), "Comparison between two cultivated rice species, *Oryza sativa* L. and *O. glaberrima* Steud.", *Japanese Journal of Breeding Science*, Vol. 12, pp. 153-165.

Multani, D.S. et al. (2003), "Alien genes introgression and development of monosomic alien additional lines from *Oryza latifolia* Desv. to rice, *Oryza sativa* L.", *Theoretical and Applied Genetics*, Vol. 107, p. 395-405, https://doi.org/10.1007/s00122-003-1214-3.

Multani, D.S. et al. (1994), "Development of monosomic alien addition lines and introgression of genes from *Oryza australiensis* Domin. to cultivated rice *O. sativa* L.", *Theoretical and Applied Genetics*, Vol. 88, pp. 102-109, https://doi.org/10.1007/BF00222401.

Muniyappa, V. and S.P. Raychaudhuri (1988), "Rice yellow dwarf disease", in K. Maramorosch and S.P. Raychaudhuri (eds.), *Mycoplasma Diseases of Crops*, Springer, pp. 233-284, https://doi.org/10.1007/978-1-4612-3808-9_14.

Nadir, S. et al. (2019), "A novel discovery of a long terminal repeat retrotransposon-induced hybrid weakness in rice", *Journal of Experimental Botany*, Vol. 70, pp. 1197-1207, https://doi.org/10.1093/jxb/ery442.

Nagai, I. (1959), "Procedure", in *Japonica Rice – Its Breeding and Culture*, Yokendo, Tokyo, pp. 408-435.

Nagao, S. and T. Takano (1938), "Duration of fertilizing capacity of pollen and stigma in rice", in S. Nagano (ed.), *Commemoration Papers in honour of Prof M. Akemine*, Yokendo, Tokyo, pp. 88-92 (in Japanese).

Nakagawa, H. and H. Kato (2017), "Induced mutations for food and energy security: Challenge of inducing unique mutants for new cultivars and molecular research", *NARO Bulletin, Crop Science Institute*, Vol. 1, pp. 33-124.

Nakamura, T. (2003), "A method for discriminating the nymphs of two species of predacious mirid bug, *Cyrtorhinus lividipennis* Reuter and *Tytthus chinensis* (Stål), and their occurrence in paddy fields", *Kyushu Plant Protection Research*, Vol. 49, pp. 77-82, https://jglobal.jst.go.jp/en/detail?JGLOBAL_ID=200902205564728147 (in Japanese with English abstract).

Nakashima, K. and T. Hayashi (1995), "Multiplication and distribution of rice yellow dwarf phytoplasma in infected tissues of rice and green rice leafhopper *nephotettix cincticeps*", *Japanese Journal of Phytopathology*, Vol. 61, pp. 451-455, https://doi.org/10.3186/jjphytopath.61.451.

Nakayama, R. (1934), "The artificial germination of rice pollen", *Agriculture and Horticulture*, Vol. 9, pp. 1917-1926 (in Japanese).

Nandi, S. et al. (2002), "Expression of human lactoferrin in transgenic rice grains for the application in infant formula", *Plant Science*, Vol. 163, pp. 713-722, https://doi.org/10.1016/S0168-9452(02)00165-6.

NARO (accessed 22 March 2022), *Genebank Project*, National Agriculture and Food Research Organization, Japan, https://www.gene.affrc.go.jp/databases.php.

Nemoto, Y. et al. (2016), "*Hd1*, a *CONSTANS* ortholog in rice, functions as an *Ehd1* repressor through interaction with monocot-specific CCT-domain protein Ghd7", *The Plant Journal,* Vol. 86, pp. 221-233, https://doi.org/10.1111/tpj.13168.

Nezu, M., T.C. Katayama and H. Kihara (1960), "Genetic study of the genus *Oryza*. Crossability and chromosome affinity among 17 species", *Seiken Zihô* (*Reports of Kihara Institute for Biological Researches*), Vol. 11, pp. 1-11.

Nguyen, G.N. et al. (2017), "Duplication and loss of function of genes encoding RNA polymerase III subunit C4 causes hybrid incompatibility in rice", *G3: Genes, Genomes Genetics,* Vol. 7, pp. 2565-2575, https://doi.org/10.1534/g3.117.043943.

Niang, A. et al. (2017), "Variability and determinants of yields in rice production systems of West Africa", *Field Crops Research*, Vol. 207, pp. 1-12, https://doi.org/10.1016/j.fcr.2017.02.014.

Nicol, J.M. et al. (2011), "Current nematode threats to world agriculture", in J. Jones, G. Gheysen and C. Fenoll (eds.), *Genomics and Molecular Genetics of Plant-Nematode Interactions*, Springer, Dordrecht, pp. 21-43, https://doi.org/10.1007/978-94-007-0434-3_2.

Niizeki, H. and K. Oono (1968), "Induction of haploid rice plant from anther culture", *Proceedings of the Japan Academy,* Vol. 44, pp. 554-557, https://doi.org/10.2183/pjab1945.44.554.

Niño-Liu, D.O., P.C. Ronald and A.J. Bogdanove (2006), "*Xanthomonas oryzae* pathovars: Model pathogens of a model crop", *Molecular plant pathology.* Vol. 7, pp. 303-324, https://doi.org/10.1111/j.1364-3703.2006.00344.x.

Nishida, K. et al. (2016), "Targeted nucleotide editing using hybrid prokaryotic and vertebrate adaptive immune systems", *Science*, Vol. 353/6305, https://doi.org/10.1126/science.aaf8729.

Nishimasu, H. et al. (2018), "Engineered CRISPR-Cas9 nuclease with expanded targeting space", *Science*, Vol. 361, pp. 1259-1262, https://doi.org/10.1126/science.aas9129.

Nishiyama, Y. (1995), "Factors and mechanisms causing cool weather damage", in T. Matsuo et al. (eds.), *Science of the Rice Plant: Physiology*, Food and Agriculture Policy Research Center, Tokyo, pp. 776-793.

OECD (2016), "Revised Consensus Document on Compositional Considerations for New Varieties of Rice (*Oryza sativa*): Key Food and Feed Nutrients, Anti-nutrients and Other Constituents", *Series on the Safety of Novel Foods and Feeds*, No. 28, OECD Publishing, Paris, http://www.oecd.org/officialdocuments/publicdisplaydocumentpdf/?cote=env/jm/mono(2016)38&doclanguage=en.

Ohno, H. et al. (2018), "Longer mesocotyl contributes to quick seedling establishment, improved root anchorage, and early vigor of deep-sown rice", *Field Crops Research*, Vol. 228, pp. 84–92, https://doi.org/10.1016/j.fcr.2018.08.015.

Oikawa, T. et al. (2015), "The birth of a black rice gene and its local spread by introgression", *The Plant Cell,* Vol. 27, pp. 2401-2414, https://doi.org/10.1105/tpc.15.00310.

Oka, H. (1954), "Varietal variation of the responses to day-length and temperature and the number of the days to growth period", *Japanese Journal of Breeding,* Vol. 4, pp. 92-100, https://doi.org/10.1270/jsbbs1951.4.92 (in Japanese with English abstract).

Oka, H.-I. (1992), "Ecology of wild rice planted in Taiwan III. Differences in regenerating strategies among genetic stocks", *Botanical Bulletin of Academia Sinica*, Vol. 33, pp. 133-140.

Oka, H.-I. (1988a), "Ancestors of cultivated rice", in *Origin of Cultivated Rice*, Japan Scientific Societies Press, Tokyo/Elsevier, Amsterdam, pp. 18-22.

Oka, H.-I. (1988b), "Variations in the breeding systems", in *Origin of Cultivated Rice*, Japan Scientific Societies Press, Tokyo/Elsevier, Amsterdam, pp. 32-36.

Oka, H.-I. (1988c), "The dynamics of domestication", in *Origin of Cultivated Rice*, Japan Scientific Societies Press Tokyo/Elsevier Amsterdam, pp. 114-123.

Oka, H.-I. (1957), "Genic analysis for the sterility of hybrids between distantly related varieties of cultivated rice", *Journal of Genetics*, Vol. 55, pp. 397-409, https://doi.org/10.1007/bf02984059.

Oka, H.-I. and H. Morishima (1967), "Variations in the breeding systems of a wild rice, *Oryza perennis*", *Evolution*, Vol. 21, pp. 249-258, https://doi.org/10.1111/j.1558-5646.1967.tb00153.x.

Oka, H.-I. and W.T. Chang (1961), "Hybrid swarms between wild and cultivated rice species, *Oryza perennis* and *O. sativa*", *Evolution*, Vol. 15, pp. 418-430, https://doi.org/10.2307/2406310.

Okazaki, M. et al. (2013), "Whole mitochondrial genome sequencing and transcriptional analysis to uncover an RT102-type cytoplasmic male sterility-associated candidate gene derived from *Oryza rufipogon*", *Plant and Cell Physiology*, Vol. 54, pp. 1560-1568, https://doi.org/10.1093/pcp/pct102.

Okuno, K and K. Ebana (2003), "Identification of QTL controlling allelopathic effects in rice: Genetic approaches to biological control of weeds", *Japan Agricultural Research Quarterly*, Vol. 37, p. 77-81, https://doi.org/10.6090/jarq.37.77.

Olofsdotter, M., D. Navarez and K. Moody (1995), "Allelopathic potential in rice (*Oryza sativa* L.) germplasm", *Annals of Applied Biology*, Vol. 127, pp. 543-560, https://doi.org/10.1111/j.1744-7348.1995.tb07611.x.

Olofsdotter, M., D. Navarez and M. Rebulanan (1997), "Rice allelopathy - Where are we and how far can we get?", *Brighton Crop Protection Conference: Weeds*, Vol. 1, pp. 99-104.

Olofsdotter, M.et al. (2002), "Why phenolic acids are unlikely primary allelochemicals in rice", *Journal of Chemical Ecology*, Vol. 28, pp. 229-242, https://doi.org/10.1023/A:1013531306670.

Olofsdotter, M.et al. (1999), "Weed suppressing rice cultivars - Does allelopathy play a role?", *Weed Research*, Vol. 39, pp. 441-454, https://doi.org/10.1046/j.1365-3180.1999.00159.x.

Oryzabase (n.d.), website, https://shigen.nig.ac.jp/rice/oryzabase/

Ou, S.H. (1985), *Rice Diseases*, 2nd edition, Commonwealth Mycological Institute, p. 380.

Ouyang, S. et al. (2007), "The TIGR Rice Genome Annotation Resource: Improvements and new features", *Nucleic Acids Research*, Vol. 35, pp. 883-887, https://doi.org/10.1093/nar/gkl976.

Padma, V. and B.M. Reddy (2000), "Evaluation of rice genotypes for dormancy duration and seed storability under natural and accelerated ageing", *Seed Research*, Vol. 28, pp. 158-165.

Paine, J. et al. (2005), "Improving the nutritional value of Golden Rice through increased pro-vitamin A content", *Nature Biotechnology*, Vol. 23, pp. 482-487, https://doi.org/10.1038/nbt1082.

Pandey, S. and L. Velasco (2005), "Trends in crop establishment methods in Asia and research issues", in K. Toriyama, K.L. Heong and B. Hardy (eds.), *Rice is Life: Scientific Perspectives for the 21st Century*, IRRI and JIRCAS, pp. 178-181.

Pandit, P.S. et al. (2016), "Deciphering community structure of methanotrophs dwelling in rice rhizospheres of an Indian rice field using cultivation and cultivation-independent approaches", *Microbial Ecology*, Vol. 71, pp. 634-644, https://doi.org/10.1007/s00248-015-0697-1.

Pang, Y. et al. (2017), "Recurrent selection breeding by dominant male sterility for multiple abiotic stresses tolerant rice cultivars", *Euphytica*, Vol. 213, Article 268, https://doi.org/10.1007/s10681-017-2055-5.

Park, C.H. et al. (2012), "The *Magnaporthe oryzae* effector AvrPiz-t targets the RING E3 ubiquitin ligase APIP6 to suppress pathogen-associated molecular pattern–triggered immunity in rice", *The Plant Cell*, Vol. 24, pp. 4748-4762, https://doi.org/10.1105/tpc.112.105429.

Pathak, M.D. and Z.R. Khan (1994), *Insect Pests of Rice*, International Rice Research Institute, Manila, Philippines, https://www.cabi.org/isc/abstract/19951100418.

Pathak, M.D. and G. Khush (1979), "Studies of varietal resistance in rice to the brown planthopper at the International Rice Research Institute", in International Rice Research Institute (ed.), *Brown Planthopper: Threat to Rice Production in Asia*, International Rice Research Institute, Manila, Philippines, pp. 285-301.

Peng, Y., R. van Wersch, Y. Zhang (2018), "Convergent and divergent signalling in PAMP-triggered immunity and effector-triggered immunity", *Molecular Plant-Microbe Interactions Journal*, Vol. 31, pp. 403-409, https://doi.org/10.1094/MPMI-06-17-0145-CR.

Podevin, N. et al. (2013), "Site-directed nucleases: A paradigm shift in predictable, knowledge-based plant breeding", *Trends in Biotechnology*, Vol. 31, pp. 375-383, https://doi.org/10.1016/j.tibtech.2013.03.004.

Pu, D.-q. et al. (2014), "Flower-visiting insects and their potential impact on transgene flow in rice", *Journal of Applied Ecology*, Vol. 51, pp. 1357-1365, www.jstor.org/stable/24032573.

Pusadee, T. et al. (2013), "Population structure of the primary gene pool of *Oryza sativa* in Thailand", *Genetic Resources and Crop Evolution*, Vol. 60, pp. 335-353, https://doi.org/10.1007/s10722-012-9839-1.

Rao, A.N., N. Chandrasena and H. Matsumoto (2017), "Rice weed management in the Asian-Pacific region: An overview", in A.N. Rao and H. Matsumoto (eds.), *Weed Management in Rice in the Asian-Pacific Region*, Asian-Pacific Weed Science Society, Hyderabad, pp.1-41, http://oar.icrisat.org/10210/.

Rao, N.K. and M.T. Jackson (1997), "Variation in seed longevity of rice cultivars belonging to different isozyme groups", *Genetic Resources and Crop Evolution*, Vol. 44, pp. 159-164, https://doi.org/10.1023/A:1008642318474.

Rao, N.K. and M.T. Jackson (1996a), "Seed longevity of rice cultivars and strategies for their conservation in genebanks", *Annals of Botan*, Vol. 77, pp. 251-260, https://doi.org/10.1006/anbo.1996.0029.

Rao, N.K and M.T. Jackson (1996b), "Effect of sowing date and harvest time on longevity of rice seeds", *Seed Science Research*, Vol. 7, pp. 13-20, https://doi.org/10.1017/S0960258500003317.

Rao N.K. and M.T. Jackson (1996c), "Seed production environment and storage longevity of *japonica* rices (*Oryza sativa* L)", *Seed Science Research*, Vol. 6, pp. 17-21, https://doi.org/10.1017/S0960258500002956.

Ren, G. et al. (2005), "A new gamete eliminator from *Oryza glaberrima*", *Rice Genetics Newsletter*, Vol.22, pp.45-47.

Ren, J. et al. (2016), "*Bph32*, a novel gene encoding an unknown SCR domain-containing protein, confers resistance against the brown planthopper in rice", *Scientific Reports*, Vol. 6, 37645, https://doi.org/10.1038/srep37645.

Ressing, W.H. et al. (1986), *Illustrated Guide to Integrated Pest Management in Rice in Tropical Asia*, International Rice Research Institute, p. 411.

Reuscher, S. et al. (2018), "Assembling the genome of the African wild rice *Oryza longistaminata* by exploiting synteny in closely related *Oryza* species", *Communications Biology*, Vol. 1, Article 162, https://doi.org/10.1038/s42003-018-0171-y.

Roberts, E.H. (1961), "The viability of rice seed in relation to temperature, moisture content, and gaseous environment", *Annals of Botany*, Vol. 25, pp. 381-390, https://www.jstor.org/stable/42907599.

Rodenburg, J. et al. (2019), "Status quo of chemical weed control in rice in sub-Saharan Africa", *Food Security*, Vol. 11, p. 69-92, https://doi.org/10.1007/s12571-018-0878-0.

Rodenburg, J. et al. (2017), "Genetic variation and host-parasite specificity of *Striga* resistance and tolerance in rice: The need for predictive breeding", *New Phytologist*, Vol. 214, pp. 1267-1280, https://doi.org/10.1111/nph.14451.

Rong, J. et al. (2012), "Scale effect on rice pollen-mediated gene flow: Implications in assessing transgene flow from genetically engineered plants", *Annals of Applied Biology*, Vol. 161, pp. 3-12, https://doi.org/10.1111/j.1744-7348.2012.00545.x.

Rutger, J.N. (1992), "Impact of mutation breeding in rice – A review", *Mutation Breeding Review*, Vol. 8, pp. 2-23.

Sacks, E.J. (2013), "Perennial rice: Challenges and opportunities", in *Perennial Crops for Food Security: Proceedings of the FAO Expert Workshop*, Food and Agriculture Organization of the United Nations, pp. 16-26.

Saito, K. et al. (2018), "Progress in varietal improvement for increasing upland rice productivity in the tropics", *Plant Production Science,* Vol. 21, pp. 145-158, https://doi.org/10.1080/1343943X.2018.1459751.

Saito, K. et al. (2013), "Towards a better understanding of biophysical determinants of yield gaps and the potential for expansion of the rice area in Africa", in M.C.S. Wopereis et al. (eds.), *Realizing Africa's Rice Promise*, CABI, pp. 188-203, https://doi.org/10.1079/9781845938123.0188.

Sakai, H. et al. (2013), "Rice Annotation Project Database (RAP-DB): An integrative and interactive database for rice genomics", *Plant and Cell Physiology*, Vol. 54, e6, https://doi.org/10.1093/pcp/pcs183.

Sakai, H. et al. (2011), "Distinct evolutionary patterns of *Oryza glaberrima* deciphered by genome sequencing and comparative analysis", *The Plant Journal*, Vol. 66, pp. 796–805, https://doi.org/10.1111/j.1365-313X.2011.04539.x.

Sano, Y. (1990), "The genic nature of gamete eliminator in rice", *Genetics*, Vol. 125, pp. 183-191.

Sano, Y., Y.-E. Chu and H. Oka (1979), "Genetic studies of speciation in cultivated rice. 1. Genetic analysis for the F_1 sterility between *O. sativa* L. and *O. glaberrima* Steud", *The Japanese Journal of Genetics*, Vol. 54, pp. 121-132, https://doi.org/10.1266/jjg.54.121.

Sasaki, A. et al. (2002), "A mutant gibberellin-synthesis gene in rice", *Nature*, Vol. 416, pp. 701-702, https://doi.org/10.1038/416701a.

Sato, Y. and S. Yokoya (2008), "Effects of male sterility caused by low temperature at the booting stage on out-crossing rates in rice (*Oryza sativa* L.)", *Breeding Research*, Vol. 10, pp. 127-134, https://doi.org/10.1270/jsbbr.10.127 (in Japanese with English abstract).

Sato, Y. et al. (2013), "RiceXPro version 3.0: Expanding the informatics resource for rice transcriptome", *Nucleic Acids Research*, Vol. 41, pp. D1206-D1213, https://doi.org/10.1093/nar/gks1125.

Sato, Y. et al. (2012), "RiceFREND: A platform for retrieving coexpressed gene networks in rice", *Nucleic Acids*

Research, Vol. 41, pp. D1214-D1221, https://doi.org/10.1093/nar/gks1122.

Sato, Y. et al. (2010), "RiceXPro: A platform for monitoring gene expression in *japonica* rice grown under natural field conditions", *Nucleic Acids Research*, Vol. 39 (Suppl. 1), pp. D1141-D1148, https://doi.org/10.1093/nar/gkq1085.

Schwartz, C. et al. (2020), "CRISPR–Cas9-mediated 75.5-Mb inversion in maize", *Nature Plants*, Vol. 6, pp. 1427-1431, https://doi.org/10.1038/s41477-020-00817-6.

Septiningsih, E.M. et al. (2013), "QTL mapping and confirmation for tolerance of anaerobic conditions during germination derived from the rice landrace Ma-Zhan Red", *Theoretical and Applied Genetics*, Vol. 126, pp. 1357-1366, https://doi.org/10.1007/s00122-013-2057-1.

Sessitsch, A. et al. (2015), "Functional characteristics of an endophyte community colonizing rice roots as revealed by metagenomic analysis", *Molecular Plant-Microbe Interactions*, Vol. 25, pp. 28-36, https://doi.org/10.1094/MPMI-08-11-0204.

Shabir, H.W. et al. (2015), "Transgenic rice: Advancements and achievements", *Advancements in Genetic Engineering*, Vol. 4, pp. 1-3, https://doi.org/10.4172/2169-0111.1000133.

Shabuer, G. et al. (2015), "Plant pathogenic anaerobic bacteria use aromatic polyketides to access aerobic territory", *Science*, Vol. 350, pp. 670-674, https://doi.org/10.1126/science.aac9990.

Shan, Q. et al. (2015), "Creation of fragrant rice by targeted knockout of the *OsBADH2* gene using TALEN technology", *Plant Biotechnology Journal*, Vol. 13, pp. 791-800, https://doi.org/10.1111/pbi.12312.

Shao, G. et al. (2017), "CRISPR/CAS9-mediated editing of the fragrant gene *Badh2* in rice", *Chinese Journal of Rice Science*, Vol. 31, pp. 216-222, https://doi.org/10.16819/j.1001-7216.2017.6098 (in Chinese).

Shen, R. et al. (2017), "Genomic structural variation-mediated allelic suppression causes hybrid male sterility in rice", *Nature Communications*, Vol. 8, p. 1310, https://doi.org/10.1038/s41467-017-01400-y.

Shenton, M. et al. (2016), "Effect of wild and cultivated rice genotypes on rhizosphere bacterial community composition", *Rice*, Vol. 9, Article 42, https://doi.org/10.1186/s12284-016-0111-8.

Shepard, B.M., A.T. Barrion and J.A. Litsinger (1995), *Rice-Feeding Insects of Tropical Asia*, International Rice Research Institute, Manila, Philippines, p. 228.

Shigematsu, Y. et al. (1982), "Sterols and asparagine in the rice plant, endogenous factors related to resistance against the brown planthopper (*Nilaparvata lugens*)", *Agricultural and Biological Chemistry*, Vol. 46, pp. 2877-2879, https://doi.org/10.1271/bbb1961.46.2877.

Shimada, T. (2002), "Daily activity pattern and habitat use of Greater White-fronted Geese wintering in Japan: Factors of the population increase", *Waterbirds*, Vol. 25, pp. 371-377, https://doi.org/10.1675/1524-4695(2002)025[0371:DAPAHU]2.0.CO;2.

Shimamoto, K. et al. (1989), "Fertile transgenic rice plants regenerated from transformed protoplasts", *Nature*, Vol. 338, pp. 274-276, https://doi.org/10.1038/338274a0.

Shimatani, Z. et al. (2017) "Targeted base editing in rice and tomato using a CRISPR-Cas9 cytidine deaminase fusion", *Nature Biotechnology*, Vol. 35, pp. 441-443, https://doi.org/10.1038/nbt.3833.

Shimono, M. et al. (2007), "Rice WRKY45 plays a crucial role in benzothiadiazole-inducible blast resistance", *The Plant Cell*, Vol. 19, pp. 2064-2076, https://doi.org/10.1105/tpc.106.046250.

Shivrain, V.K. et al. (2008), "Maximum outcrossing rate and genetic compatibility between red rice (*Oryza sativa*) biotypes and Clearfield™ rice", *Weed Science*, Vol. 56, pp. 807-813, https://doi.org/10.1614/WS-08-026.1.

Shivrain, V.K. et al. (2007), "Gene flow between Clearfield™ rice and red rice", *Crop Protection*, Vol. 26, pp. 349-356, https://doi.org/10.1016/j.cropro.2005.09.019.

Shomura, A. et al. (2008), "Deletion in a gene associated with grain size increased yields during rice domestication", *Nature Genetics*, Vol. 40, pp. 1023-1028, https://doi.org/10.1038/ng.169.

Singh, R. et al. (2016), "*Magnaporthe oryzae* effector AVR-Pii helps to establish compatibility by inhibition of the rice NADP-Malic enzyme resulting in disruption of oxidative burst and host innate immunity", *Molecules and Cells*, Vol. 39, pp. 426-438, https://doi.org/10.14348/molcells.2016.0094.

Singh, S. et al. (2001), "Pyramiding three bacterial blight resistance genes (*xa5, xa13* and *Xa21)* using marker-assisted selection into *indica* rice cultivar PR106", *Theoretical and Applied Genetics*, Vol. 102, pp. 1011-1015, https://doi.org/10.1007/s001220000495.

Sitch, L.A. (1990), "Incompatibility barriers operating in crosses of *Oryza sativa* with related species and genera", in J.P. Gustafson (ed.), *Gene Manipulation in Plant Improvement II*, Plenum Press, New York, pp. 77-93, https://doi.org/10.1007/978-1-4684-7047-5_5.

Sleper, D.A. and J.M. Poehlman (2006), "Breeding rice", in *Breeding Field Crops, 5th edition*, Blackwell Publishing, Ames, pp. 239-257.

Sōgawa, K. (1982), "The rice brown planthopper: Feeding physiology and host plant interactions", *Annual Review of Entomology*, Vol. 27, pp. 49-73, https://doi.org/10.1146/annurev.en.27.010182.000405.

Song, B.K. et al. (2014), "Malaysian weedy rice shows its true stripes: Wild *Oryza* and elite rice cultivars shape agricultural weed evolution in Southeast Asia", *Molecular Ecology*, Vol. 23, pp. 5003-5017, https://doi.org/10.1111/mec.12922.

Song, Z.P. et al. (2003), "Gene flow from cultivated rice to the wild species *Oryza rufipogon* under experimental field conditions", *New Phytologist*, Vol. 157, pp. 657-665, https://doi.org/10.1046/j.1469-8137.2003.00699.x.

Stein, J.C. et al. (2018), "Genomes of 13 domesticated and wild rice relatives highlight genetic conservation, turnover and innovation across the genus Oryza", *Nature Genetics,* Vol. 50, pp. 285-296, https://doi.org/10.1038/s41588-018-0040-0.

Stevenson, P.C. et al. (1996), "Schaftosides from rice phloem as feeding inhibitors and resistance factors to brown planthoppers, *Nilaparvata lugens*", *Proceedings of the 9th International Symposium on Insect-Plant Relationships*, Vol. 53, pp. 246-249, https://doi.org/10.1007/978-94-009-1720-0_56.

Sudianto, E. et al. (2013), "Clearfield® rice: Its development, success, and key challenges on a global perspective", *Crop Protection*, Vol. 49, pp. 40-51, https://doi.org/10.1016/j.cropro.2013.02.013.

Sugita, K. et al. (2005), "Genetically modified rice seeds accumulating GLP-1 analogue stimulate insulin secretion from a mouse pancreatic beta-cell line", *FEBS Letters*, Vol. 579, pp. 1085-1088, https://doi.org/10.1016/j.febslet.2004.12.082.

Suh, H.S., Y.I. Sato and H. Morishima (1997), "Genetic characterization of weedy rice (*Oryza sativa* L.) based on morpho-physiology, isozymes and RAPD markers", *Theoretical and Applied Genetics,* Vol. 94, pp. 316-321, https://doi.org/10.1007/s001220050417.

Suketomo, C., T. Kazama and K. Toriyama (2020), "Fertility restoration of Chinese wild rice-type cytoplasmic male sterility by CRISPR/Cas9-mediated genome editing of nuclear-encoded *RETROGRADE-REGULATED MALE STERILITY*", *Plant Biotechnology*, Vol. 37, pp. 285-292, https://doi.org/10.5511/plantbiotechnology.20.0326b.

Sun, Y. et al. (2017), "Generation of high-amylose rice through CRISPR/Cas9-mediated targeted mutagenesis of starch branching enzymes", *Frontiers in Plant Science*, Vol. 8, 298, https://doi.org/10.3389/fpls.2017.00298.

Sun, C. et al. (2016a), "RPAN: Rice pan-genome browser for ~3 000 rice genomes", *Nucleic Acids Research*, Vol. 45. pp. 597-605, https://doi.org/10.1093/nar/gkw958.

Sun, Y. et al. (2016b), "Engineering herbicide-resistant rice plants through CRISPR/Cas9-mediated homologous recombination of acetolactate synthase", *Molecular Plant*, Vol. 9, pp. 628-631, https://doi.org/10.1016/j.molp.2016.01.001.

Suzuki, K. et al. (2011), "Prevention of allergic asthma by vaccination with transgenic rice seed expressing mite allergen: Induction of allergen-specific oral tolerance without bystander suppression", *Plant Biotechnology Journal*, Vol. 9, pp. 982-990, https://doi.org/10.1111/j.1467-7652.2011.00613.x.

Suzuki, Y. (2003), *Seed Biology*, Tohoku-University Press, Sendai, p. 204 (in Japanese).

Sweeney, M.T. et al. (2007), "Global dissemination of a single mutation conferring white pericarp in rice", *PLoS Genetics*, Vol. 3, e133, https://doi.org/10.1371/journal.pgen.0030133.

Taguchi, K., K. Doi and A. Yoshimura (1999), "RFLP mapping of *S19*, a gene for F_1 pollen semi-sterility found in backcross progeny of *Oryza sativa* and *O. glaberrima*", *Rice Genetics Newsletter*, Vol. 16, p. 70-71, https://archive.gramene.org/newsletters/rice_genetics/rgn16/v16p70.html.

Takagi, H. et al. (2005), "Oral immunotherapy against a pollen allergy using a seed-based peptide vaccine", *Plant Biotechnology Journal*, Vol. 3, pp. 521-533, https://doi.org/10.1111/j.1467-7652.2005.00143.x.

Takahashi, N. and Y. Suzuki (1975), "Factor affecting the viability of seed with special references to maturity and longevity", *Japanese Committee for the International Biological Program synthesis*, Vol. 5, pp. 63-69.

Takaiwa, F. et al. (2015), "Rice seed for delivery of vaccines to gut mucosal immune tissues", *Plant Biotechnology Journal*, Vol. 13, pp. 1041-1055, https://doi.org/10.1111/pbi.12423.

Takatsuji, H. (2014), "Development of disease-resistant rice using regulatory components of induced disease resistance", *Frontiers in Plant Science*, Vol. 5, 630, https://doi.org/10.3389/fpls.2014.00630.

Tamura, Y et al. (2014), "Map-based cloning and characterization of a brown planthopper resistance gene *BPH26* from *Oryza sativa* L. ssp. *indica* cultivar ADR52", *Scientific Reports*, Vol. 4, Article 5872, https://doi.org/10.1038/srep05872.

Tan, L. et al. (2008), "Control of a key transition from prostrate to erect growth in rice domestication", *Nature Genetics*, Vol. 40, pp. 1360-1364, https://doi.org/10.1038/ng.197.

Tan, S. et al. (2005) "Imidazolinone-tolerant crops: History, current status and future", *Pest Management Science*,

Vol. 61, pp. 246-257, https://doi.org/10.1002/ps.993.

Tanaka, K. and M. Matsumura (2000), “Development of virulence to resistant rice varieties in the brown planthopper, *Nilaparvata lugens* (Homoptera: Delphacidae), immigrating into Japan”, *Applied Entomology and Zoology*, Vol. 35, pp. 529-533, https://doi.org/10.1303/aez.2000.529.

Tang, H. et al. (2017), “Multi-step formation, evolution, and functionalization of new cytoplasmic male sterility genes in the plant mitochondrial genomes”, *Cell Research*, Vol. 27, pp. 130-146, https://doi.org/10.1038/cr.2016.115.

Tang, H. et al. (2014), “The rice restorer *Rf4* for wild-abortive cytoplasmic male sterility encodes a mitochondrial-localized PPR protein that functions in reduction of *WA352* transcripts”, *Molecular Plant*, Vol. 7, pp. 1497-1500, https://doi.org/10.1093/mp/ssu047.

Tang, L. et al. (2017), “Knockout of *OsNramp5* using the CRISPR/Cas9 system produces low Cd-accumulating *indica* rice without compromising yield”, *Scientific Reports*, Vol. 7, Article 14438, https://doi.org/10.1038/s41598-017-14832-9.

Tang, L.H. and H. Morishima (1998), “Characteristics of weed rice strains”, *Rice Genetics Newsletter,* Vol. 5, pp. 70-72, https://archive.gramene.org/newsletters/rice_genetics/rgn5/v5II12.html.

Tanno, H. et al. (2011), “Relation between out-crossing rate and isolation distance under cool temperature conditions at the booting stage that causes the occurrence of male sterility in rice”, *Japanese Journal of Crop Science*, Vol. 80, pp. 49-58, https://doi.org/10.1626/jcs.80.49 (in Japanese).

Toki, S. et al. (2006), “Early infection of scutellum tissue with *Agrobacterium* allows high-speed transformation of rice”, *The Plant Journal*, Vol. 47, pp. 969-976, https://doi.org/10.1111/j.1365-313X.2006.02836.x.

Toriyama, K. et al. (1988), “Transgenic rice plants after direct gene transfer into protoplasts”, *Nature Biotechnology*, Vol. 6, pp. 1072-1074, https://doi.org/10.1038/nbt0988-1072.

Tozawa, Y. et al. (2001), “Characterization of rice anthranilate synthase α-subunit genes *OASA1* and *OASA2*. Tryptophan accumulation in transgenic rice expressing a feedback-insensitive mutant of OASA1”, *Plant Physiology*, Vol. 126, pp. 1493-1506, https://doi.org/10.1104/pp.126.4.1493.

Tsushima, S. (1996), “Epidemiology of bacterial grain rot of rice caused by *pseudomonas glumae*”, *Japan Agricultural Research Quarterly*, Vol. 30, pp. 85-89, https://www.semanticscholar.org/paper/Epidemiology-of-Bacterial-Grain-Rot-of-Rice-Caused-Tsushima/1e7032400ed6702ea1dafb5cd0e85244d7e18bc2.

Uga, Y. et al. (2003), “Variations of floral traits in Asian cultivated rice (*Oryza sativa* L.) and its wild relatives (*O. rufipogon* Griff.)”, *Breeding Science*, Vol. 53, pp. 345-352, https://doi.org/10.1270/jsbbs.53.345.

Ura, H. et al. (2006), “*Burkholderia gladioli* associated with symptoms of bacterial grain rot and leaf-sheath browning of rice plants”, *Journal of General Plant Pathology*, Vol. 72, pp. 98-103, https://doi.org/10.1007/s10327-005-0256-6.

Vacher, C. et al. (2016), “The phyllosphere: Microbial jungle at the plant-climate interface”, *Annual Review of Ecology, Evolution, and Systematics*, Vol. 47, pp. 1-24, https://doi.org/10.1146/annurev-ecolsys-121415-032238.

Valarmathi, P. et al. (2013), “First report of Rice orange leaf disease phytoplasma (16 SrI) in rice (*Oryza sativa*) in India”*, Australasian Plant Disease Notes*, Vol. 8, pp. 141-143, https://doi.org/10.1007/s13314-013-0117-7.

Vasconcelos, M. et al. (2003), “Enhanced iron and zinc accumulation in transgenic rice with the *ferritin* gene”, *Plant Science*, Vol. 164, pp. 371-378, https://doi.org/10.1016/S0168-9452(02)00421-1.

Vidotto, F. and A. Ferrero (2000), “Germination behaviour of red rice (*Oryza sativa* L.) seeds in field and laboratory conditions”, *Agronomie*, Vol. 20, pp. 375-382, https://doi.org/10.1051/agro:2000134.

Virmani, S.S. (1994), “Natural outcrossing mechanisms in rice”, in *Heterosis and Hybrid Breeding*, Monographs on Theoretical and Applied Genetics, Vol. *22*, pp. 82-96, https://doi.org/10.1007/978-3-642-85115-5_3.

Wakasa, Y. and F. Takaiwa (2013), “The use of rice seeds to produce human pharmaceuticals for oral therapy”, *Biotechnology Journal*, Vol. 8, pp. 1133-1143, https://doi.org/10.1002/biot.201300065.

Wakasa, Y. et al. (2011), “The hypocholesterolemic activity of transgenic rice seed accumulating lactostatin, a bioactive peptide derived from bovine milk β-lactoglobulin”, *Journal of Agricultural and Food Chemistry*, Vol. 59, pp. 3845-3850, https://doi.org/10.1021/jf200044j.

Wang, F. et al. (2016), “Enhanced rice blast resistance by CRISPR/Cas9-targeted mutagenesis of the ERF transcription factor gene *OsERF922*”, *PLoS ONE*, Vol. 11, e0154027, https://doi.org/10.1371/journal.pone.0154027.

Wang, K. et al. (2013a), “ORFH79 impairs mitochondrial function via interaction with a subunit of electron transport chain complex III in Honglian cytoplasmic male sterile rice”, *New Phytologist,* Vol. 198, pp. 408-418, https://doi.org/10.1111/nph.12180.

Wang, K. et al. (2013b), “Gene, protein, and network of male sterility in rice”, *Frontiers in Plant Science*, Vol. 4, 92, https://doi.org/10.3389/fpls.2013.00092.

Wang, L. et al. (2010), “A dynamic gene expression atlas covering the entire life cycle of rice”, *The Plant Journal*,

Vol. 61, pp. 752-766, https://doi.org/10.1111/j.1365-313X.2009.04100.x.

Wang, M. et al. (2014), "The genome sequence of African rice (*Oryza glaberrima*) and evidence for independent domestication", *Nature Genetics*, Vol. 46, pp. 982-988, https://doi.org/10.1038/ng.3044.

Wang, Q. et al. (2019), "Research progress on effects of straw returning on nitrogen cycling microbes and functional genes in paddy soil", *Acta Agriculturae Zhejiangensis*, Vol. 31, pp. 333-342, https://doi.org/10.3969/j.issn.1004-1524.2019.02.20 (in Chinese with English abstract).

Wang, W. et al. (2018), "Genomic variation in 3,010 diverse accessions of Asian cultivated rice", *Nature*, Vol. 557, pp. 43-49, https://doi.org/10.1038/s41586-018-0063-9.

Wang, Y. et al. (2015), "Map-based cloning and characterization of *BPH29*, a B3 domain-containing recessive gene conferring brown planthopper resistance in rice", *Journal of Experimental Botany*, Vol. 66, pp. 6035-6045, https://doi.org/10.1093/jxb/erv318.

Wang, Z. et al. (2006), "Cytoplasmic male sterility of rice with Boro II cytoplasm is caused by a cytotoxic peptide and is restored by two related PPR motif genes via distinct modes of mRNA silencing", *The Plant Cell*, Vol. 18, pp. 676-687, https://doi.org/10.1105/tpc.105.038240.

Watanabe, Y. (1997), "Phylogeny and geographical distribution of genus *Oryza*", in T. Matsuo et al. (eds.), *Science of the Rice Plant: Genetics*, Vol. 3, Genetics, Food and Agriculture Policy Research Center, Tokyo, pp. 29-39.

Watanabe, Y. (1993), "Classification and morphological characters of plants in genus Oryza", in T. Matsuo and K. Hoshikawa (eds.), *Science of the Rice Plant, Vol. 1. Morphology*, Food and Agricultural Policy Research Center, Tokyo, pp. 23-30.

Watanarojanaporn, N. et al. (2013), "Effect of rice cultivation systems on indigenous arbuscular mycorrhizal fungal community structure", *Microbes and Environments*, Vol. 28, pp. 316-324, https://doi.org/10.1264/jsme2.ME13011.

Wei, F.J. et al. (2016), "Both *Hd1* and *Ehd1* are important for artificial selection of flowering time in cultivated rice", *Plant Science,* Vol. 242, pp. 187-194, https://doi.org/10.1016/j.plantsci.2015.09.005.

Weng, J. et al. (2008), "Isolation and initial characterization of *GW5*, a major QTL associated with rice grain width and weight", *Cell Research*, Vol. 18, pp. 1199-1209, https://doi.org/10.1038/cr.2008.307.

Win, K.T. et al. (2009), "Identification of two loci causing F_1 pollen sterility in inter- and intraspecific crosses of rice", *Breeding Science*, Vol. 59, pp. 411-418, https://doi.org/10.1270/jsbbs.59.411.

Wing, R., M.D. Purugganan and Q. Zhang (2018), "The rice genome revolution: From an ancient grain to Green Super Rice", *Nature Reviews Genetics*, Vol. 19, pp. 505-517, https://doi.org/10.1038/s41576-018-0024-z.

Wu, N. et al. (2020), "*Rice black-streaked dwarf virus*: From multiparty interactions among plant–virus–vector to intermittent epidemics", *Molecular Plant Pathology*, Vol. 21, pp. 1007-1019, https://doi.org/10.1111/mpp.12946.

Wu, W. et al. (2017), "A single-nucleotide polymorphism causes smaller grain size and loss of seed shattering during African rice domestication", *Nature Plants*, Vol. 3, Article 17064, https://doi.org/10.1038/nplants.2017.64.

Wu, X.R., Z.H. Chen and W.R. Folk (2003), "Enrichment of cereal protein lysine content by altered $tRNA^{lys}$ coding during protein synthesis", *Plant Biotechnology Journal*, Vol. 1, pp. 187-194, https://doi.org/10.1046/j.1467-7652.2003.00017.x.

Wu, Z. et al. (2018), "De novo genome assembly of *Oryza granulata* reveals rapid genome expansion and adaptive evolution", *Communications Biology*, Vol.1, Article 84, https://doi.org/10.1038/s42003-018-0089-4.

Xie, E. et al. (2019), "A strategy for generating rice apomixis by gene editing", *Journal of Integrative Plant Biology*, Vol. 61, pp. 911-916, https://doi.org/10.1111/jipb.12785.

Xie, F. and J. Zhang (2018), "Shanyou 63: An elite mega rice hybrid in China", *Rice*, Vol. 11, Article 17, https://doi.org/10.1186/s12284-018-0210-9.

Xie, L. and J. Lin (1980), "Studies on rice bunchy stunt disease of rice, a new virus disease of rice plant", *Chinese Science Bulletin*, Vol. 25, pp. 785-789, https://doi.org/10.1360/sb1980-25-9-785.

Xu, P. et al. (2014), "Mapping three new interspecific hybrid sterile loci between *Oryza sativa* and *O. glaberrima*", *Breeding Science*, Vol. 63, pp. 476-482, https://doi.org/10.1270/jsbbs.63.476.

Xu, R. et al. (2016), "Rapid improvement of grain weight *via* highly efficient CRISPR/Cas9-mediated multiplex genome editing in rice", *Journal of Genetics and Genomics*, Vol. 43, pp. 529-532, https://doi.org/10.1016/j.jgg.2016.07.003.

Xu, R. et al. (2014), "Gene targeting using the *Agrobacterium tumefaciens*-mediated CRISPR-Cas system in rice", *Rice*, Vol. 7, Article 5, https://doi.org/10.1186/s12284-014-0005-6.

Xu, Y.-B. and Z.-T. Shen (1987), "Inheritance of stigma exsertion in rice", *Rice Genetics Newsletter*, Vol. 4, pp. 76-77, https://shigen.nig.ac.jp/rice/oryzabase/asset/rgn/vol4/v4p76.html.

Xue, W. et al. (2008), "Natural variation in *Ghd7* is an important regulator of heading date and yield potential in rice", *Nature Genetics,* Vol. 40, pp. 761-767, https://doi.org/10.1038/ng.143.

Yamamoto, E. (2010), "Gain of deleterious function causes an autoimmune response and Bateson-Dobzhansky-Muller incompatibility in rice", *Molecular Genetics and Genomics*, Vol. 283, pp. 305-315, https://doi.org/10.1007/s00438-010-0514-y.

Yamamoto, E. et al. (2007), "Interaction of two recessive genes, *hbd2* and *hbd3*, induces hybrid breakdown in rice", *Theoretical and Applied Genetics*, Vol. 115, pp. 187-194, https://doi.org/10.1007/s00122-007-0554-9.

Yamamoto, N. et al. (2018), "Comparative whole genome re-sequencing analysis in upland New Rice for Africa: Insights into the breeding history and respective genome compositions", *Rice*, Vol.11, Article 33, https://doi.org/10.1186/s12284-018-0224-3.

Yamamoto, T. et al. (2010), "Fine definition of the pedigree haplotypes of closely related rice cultivars by means of genome-wide discovery of single-nucleotide polymorphisms", *BMC Genomics*, Vol. 11, Article 267, https://doi.org/10.1186/1471-2164-11-267.

Yamamoto, T., J. Yonemaru and M. Yano (2009), "Towards the understanding of complex traits in rice: Substantially or superficially?", *DNA Research*, Vol. 16, pp. 141-154, https://doi.org/10.1093/dnares/dsp006.

Yamauchi, T. et al. (2009), "Homologous recombination-mediated knock-in targeting of the *MET1α* gene for a maintenance DNA methyltransferase reproducibly reveals dosage-dependent spatiotemporal gene expression in rice", *The Plant Journal*, Vol. 60, pp. 386-396, https://doi.org/10.1111/j.1365-313X.2009.03947.x.

Yan, W.G. and S.F. Li (1987), "Study on out-crossing characteristics among male sterile lines containing same nucleus in rice", *Hybrid Rice*, Vol. 4, pp. 8-11.

Yan, W.G. et al. (2009), "Association mapping of stigma and spikelet characteristics in rice (*Oryza sativa* L.)", *Molecular Breeding*, Vol 24, pp. 277-292, https://doi.org/10.1007/s11032-009-9290-y.

Yan, X. and N.J. Talbot (2016), "Investigating the cell biology of plant infection by the rice blast fungus Magnaporthe oryzae", *Current Opinion in Microbiology*, Vol. 34, pp. 147-153, https://doi.org/10.1016/j.mib.2016.10.001.

Yanagihara, S., H. Kato and H. Ikehashi (1992), "A new locus for multiple alleles causing hybrid sterility between an Aus variety and Javanica varieties in rice (*Oryza sativa* L.)", *Japanese Journal of Breeding*, Vol. 42, pp. 793-801, https://doi.org/10.1270/jsbbs1951.42.793.

Yang, J. et al. (2010), "A killer-protector system regulates both hybrid sterility and segregation distortion in rice", *Science*, Vol. 337, pp. 1336-1340.

Yang, L. et al. (2006), "A transgenic rice seed accumulating an anti-hypertensive peptide reduces the blood pressure of spontaneously hypertensive rats", *FEBS Letters*, Vol. 580, pp. 3315-3320, https://doi.org/10.1016/j.febslet.2006.04.092.

Yang, W., K.A. Weber and W.L. Silver (2012), "Nitrogen loss from soil through anaerobic ammonium oxidation coupled to iron reduction", *Nature Geoscience*, Vol. 5, pp. 538-541, https://doi.org/10.1038/ngeo1530.

Yang, X. et al. (2017), "Knocking out of carotenoid catabolic genes in rice fails to boost carotenoid accumulation, but reveals a mutation in strigolactone biosynthesis", *Plant Cell Reports*, Vol. 36, pp. 1533-1545, https://doi.org/10.1007/s00299-017-2172-6.

Yano, M. (2001), "Genetic and molecular dissection of naturally occurring variation", *Current Opinion in Plant Biology*, Vol. 4, pp. 130-135, https://doi.org/10.1016/S1369-5266(00)00148-5.

Yano, M. et al. (2000), "*Hd1*, a major photoperiod sensitivity quantitative trait locus in rice, is closely related to the Arabidopsis flowering time gene *CONSTANS*", *The Plant Cell*, Vol. 12, pp. 2473-2483, https://doi.org/10.1105/tpc.12.12.2473.

Yano, M. et al. (2001), "Genetic control of flowering time in rice, a short-day plant", *Plant Physiology,* Vol. 127, pp. 1425-1429, https://www.ncbi.nlm.nih.gov/pmc/articles/PMC1540174/.

Ye, X. et al. (2000), "Engineering the provitamin A (β-carotene) biosynthetic pathway into (carotenoid-free) rice endosperm", *Science*, Vol. 287, pp. 303-305, https://doi.org/10.1126/science.287.5451.303.

Yi, P. et al. (2002), "Discovery of mitochondrial chimeric-gene associated with cytoplasmic male sterility of HL-rice", *Chinese Science Bulletin*, Vol. 47, pp. 744-747, https://doi.org/10.1360/02tb9168.

Yin, X. et al. (2017), "CRISPR-Cas9 and CRISPR-Cpf1 mediated targeting of a stomatal developmental gene *EPFL9* in rice", *Plant Cell Reports*, Vol. 36, pp. 745-757, https://doi.org/10.1007/s00299-017-2118-z.

Yoshida, A. et al. (2016), "Analysis of rhizome development in *Oryza longistaminata*, a wild rice species", *Plant and Cell Physiology*, Vol. 57, pp. 2213-2220, https://doi.org/10.1093/pcp/pcw138.

Yoshida, H. et al. (2007), "*superwoman1-cleistogamy*, a hopeful allele for gene containment in GM rice", *Plant Biotechnology Journal*, Vol. 5, pp. 835-846, https://doi.org/10.1111/j.1467-7652.2007.00291.x.

Yoshida, S. (1981), “Heading and anthesis”, in *Fundamentals of Rice Crop Science*, International Rice Research Institute, Los Baños, Philippines, p. 55-58, http://books.irri.org/9711040522_content.pdf.

Yoshihara, T. et al. (1980), “Oxalic acid as a sucking inhibitor of the brown planthopper in rice (*Delphacidae, Homoptera*)”, *Entomologia Exp. et Applicata*, Vol. 27, pp. 149-155, https://doi.org/10.1111/j.1570-7458.1980.tb02959.x.

Yu, J. et al. (2005), “The genomes of *Oryza sativa*: A history of duplications”, *PLoS Biology*, Vol. 3, e38, https://doi.org/10.1371/journal.pbio.0030038.

Yu, J. et al. (2002), “A draft sequence of the rice genome (*Oryza sativa* L. ssp. *indica*)”, *Science*, Vol. 296, pp. 79-92, https://doi.org/10.1126/science.1068037.

Yu, Y. et al. (2016), “Hybrid sterility in rice (*Oryza sativa* L.) involves the tetratricopeptide repeat domain containing protein”, *Genetics*, Vol. 203, pp. 1439-1451, https://doi.org/10.1534/genetics.115.183848.

Zhang, H. et al. (2017), “Genome editing—principles and applications for functional genomics research and crop improvement”, *Critical Reviews in Plant Sciences*, Vol. 36, pp. 291-309, https://doi.org/10.1080/07352689.2017.1402989.

Zhang, H.-M. et al. (2008), “A black-streaked dwarf disease on rice in China is caused by a novel fijivirus”, *Archives of Virology*, Vol.153, pp.1893-1898, https://doi.org/10.1007/s00705-008-0209-4.

Zhang, H.M. et al. (1988), “Transgenic rice plants produced by electroporation-mediated plasmid uptake into protoplasts”, *Plant Cell Reports*, Vol. 7, pp. 379-384, https://doi.org/10.1007/BF00269517.

Zhang, J. et al. (2019), “*NRT1.1B* is associated with root microbiota composition and nitrogen use in field-grown rice”, *Nature Biotechnology*, Vol. 37, pp. 676-684, https://doi.org/10.1038/s41587-019-0104-4.

Zhang, Q.J. et al. (2014), “Rapid diversification of five *Oryza* AA genomes associated with rice adaptation”, *Proceedings of the National Academy of Sciences of the United States of America*, Vol. 111, pp. E4954-E4962, https://doi.org/10.1073/pnas.1418307111.

Zhang, W. and R. Wu (1988), “Efficient regeneration of transgenic plants from rice protoplasts and correctly regulated expression of the foreign gene in the plants”, *Theoretical and Applied Genetics*, Vol. 76, pp. 835-840, https://doi.org/10.1007/BF00273668.

Zhang, Y. et al. (2015), “Genome and comparative transcriptomics of African wild rice Oryza longistaminata provide insights into molecular mechanism of rhizomatousness and self-incompatibility”, *Molecular Plant*, Vol. 8, pp. 1683–1686, https://doi.org/10.1016/j.molp.2015.08.006.

Zhang, Y. et al. (2011), “Fine mapping of a gene responsible for pollen semi-sterility in hybrids between *Oryza sativa* L. and *O. glaberrima* Steud”, *Molecular Breeding*, Vol. 28, pp. 323-334, https://doi.org/10.1007/s11032-010-9485-2.

Zhang, Z. (1992), “Pest insects of rice in China”, in Z. Xiong et al. (eds.), *Rice in China,* China Agricultural Science and Technology Press, Beijing, pp. 130-149.

Zhang, Z. et al. (2002), “A new sterile gene from *Oryza glaberrima* on chromosome 3”, *Rice Genetics Newsletter*, Vol. 22, pp. 26-28, https://archive.gramene.org/newsletters/rice_genetics/rgn22/v05.html.

Zhao, Q. et al. (2018), “Pan-genome analysis highlights the extent of genomic variation in cultivated and wild rice”, *Nature Genetics*, Vol. 50, pp. 278-284, https://doi.org/10.1038/s41588-018-0041-z.

Zheng, Y. et al. (2016), “Rice domestication revealed by reduced shattering of archaeological rice from the lower Yangtze valley”, *Scientific Reports,* Vol. 6, Article 28136, https://doi.org/10.1038/srep28136.

Zhou, G. et al. (2013), “Southern rice black-streaked dwarf virus: A white-backed planthopper-transmitted fijivirus threatening rice production in Asia”, *Frontiers in Microbiology,* Vol. 4, 270, https://doi.org/10.3389/fmicb.2013.00270.

Zhou, G. et al. (2008), “Southern rice black-streaked dwarf virus: A new proposed *Fijivirus* species in the family *Reoviridae*”, *Chinese Science Bulletin*, Vol. 53, pp. 3677-3685, https://doi.org/10.1007/s11434-008-0467-2.

Zhou, G.W. et al. (2016), “Electron shuttles enhance anaerobic ammonium oxidation coupled to iron (III) reduction”, *Environmental Science and Technology*, Vol. 50, pp. 9298-9307, https://doi.org/10.1021/acs.est.6b02077.

Zhou, H. et al. (2016), “Development of commercial thermo-sensitive genic male sterile rice accelerates hybrid rice breeding using the CRISPR/Cas9-mediated *TMS5* editing system”, *Scientific Reports*, Vol. 6, Article 37395, https://doi.org/10.1038/srep37395.

Zhou, J. et al. (2015), “Gene targeting by the TAL effector PthXo2 reveals cryptic resistance gene for bacterial blight of rice”, *The Plant Journal*, Vol. 82, pp. 632-643, https://doi.org/10.1111/tpj.12838.

Zhu, Y. et al. (2017), “Draft genome sequence of rice orange leaf phytoplasma from Guangdong, China”, *Genome Announcements*, Vol. 5/22, https://doi.org/10.1128/genomeA.00430-17.

Zhuang, C. et al. (2002), “Molecular mapping of *S-c*, an F_1 pollen sterility gene in cultivated rice”, *Euphytica*, Vol. 127, pp. 133-138, https://doi.org/10.1023/A:1019973110467.

Zhuang, C. et al. (1999), "Molecular mapping of the *S-a* locus for F_1 pollen sterility in cultivated rice (*Oryza sativa* L.)", *Acta Genetica Sinica,* Vol. 26, pp. 213-218, https://europepmc.org/article/med/10589160.

Ziska, L.H. et al. (2015), "Weedy (red) rice: An emerging constraint to global rice production", *Advances in Agronomy*, Vol. 129, pp. 181-228, https://doi.org/10.1016/bs.agron.2014.09.003.

Zong, Y. et al. (2017), "Precise base editing in rice, wheat and maize with a Cas9-cytidine deaminase fusion", *Nature Biotechnology*, Vol. 35, pp. 438-440, https://doi.org/10.1038/nbt.3811.

Zou, X.H. et al. (2015), "Multiple origins of BBCC allopolyploid species in the rice genus (*Oryza*)", *Scientific Reports*, Vol. 5, Article 14876, https://doi.org/10.1038/srep14876.

Zuo, J. and J. Li (2014), "Molecular genetic dissection of quantitative trait loci regulating rice grain size", *Annual Review of Genetics*, Vol. 48, pp. 99-118, https://doi.org/10.1146/annurev-genet-120213-092138.

Annex A. List of OECD consensus documents on environmental safety assessment, 1996-2021

Consensus document	Lead country(ies)	Year of issue	Volume
Facilitating harmonisation			
Designation of a Unique Identifier for Transgenic Plants – 2006 revised version (guidance document)	Working Party	2006	Vol. 3
Introduction to the OECD Biosafety Consensus Documents – *updated for each volume*	Working Party	2005	Vol. 1, 3, 4, 5, 6, 7, 8, 9
Low-Level Presence of Transgenic Plants in Seed and Grain Commodities: Environmental Risk/Safety Assessment, and Availability and Use of Information	Working Party	2013	Vol. 6
Molecular Characterisation of Plants Derived from Modern Biotechnology	Canada	2010	Vol. 3
Revised Points to Consider for Consensus Documents on the Biology of Cultivated Plants – *replacing the 'Points to Consider' section of Vol.3*	Working Party	2020	Vol. 9
Traits			
Crop Plants Made Virus Resistant through Coat Protein Gene-Mediated Protection	Task Group	1996	Vol. 1
Genes and their Enzymes that Confer Tolerance to Glyphosate Herbicide	Germany, Netherlands, United States	1999	Vol. 1
Genes and their Enzymes that Confer Tolerance to Phosphinothricin Herbicide	Germany, Netherlands, United States	1999	Vol. 1
Herbicide Metabolism and the Residues in Glufosinate Ammonium (Phosphinothricin) – Tolerant Transgenic Plants	Germany	2002	Vol. 1
Transgenic Plants Expressing Bacillus thuringiensis Derived Insect Control Protein	United States	2007	Vol. 3
Micro-organisms			
Information used in the assessment of environmental applications of micro-organisms			
Acidithiobacillus	Canada	2006	Vol. 2
Acinetobacter	Canada	2008	Vol. 4
Baculovirus	Germany	2002	Vol. 2
Pseudomonas	United Kingdom	1997	Vol. 2
Guidance documents on biosafety aspects of bacteria			
Horizontal Gene Transfer Between Bacteria	Germany	2010	Vol. 4
Methods for Detection of Micro-organisms Introduced into the Environment: Bacteria	Netherlands	2004	Vol. 4
Use of Information on Pathogenicity Factors: Bacteria	Canada, Netherlands	2011	Vol. 5
Use of Taxonomy in Risk Assessment of Micro-organisms: Bacteria	Canada, United States	2003	Vol. 4
Biology of crops			
Apple (*Malus domestica*)	Belgium, Germany	2019	Vol. 9
Bananas and plantains (*Musa* spp.)	Spain	2009	Vol. 4
Brassica crops (*Brassica* spp.) *– replacing, and completing with other species, the Oilseed rape chapter of Vol.1*	Canada	2012	Vol. 5

Consensus document	Lead country(ies)	Year of issue	Volume
Cassava (*Manihot esculenta*)	Brazil, AUDA-NEPAD, ILSI-CERA	2014	Vol. 6
Chili, hot and sweet peppers (*Capsicum annuum*)	Korea, Mexico, United States	2006	Vol. 1
Common bean (*Phaseolus vulgaris*)	Brazil, ILSI-CERA	2015	Vol. 6
Cotton (*Gossypium* spp.)	Spain	2008	Vol. 4
Cowpea (*Vigna unguiculata*)	Australia	2015	Vol. 6
Maize (*Zea mays* subs. *mays*)	Mexico	2003	Vol. 1
Oyster mushroom (*Pleurotus* spp.)	Korea	2005	Vol. 1
Papaya (*Carica papaya*)	United States	2005	Vol. 1
Potato (*Solanum tuberosum* subsp. *tuberosum*)	Netherlands, United Kingdom	1997	Vol. 1
Revised Rice (*Oryza sativa*) – *replacing the Rice chapter of Vol.1*	Japan	2021	Vol. 9
Safflower (*Carthamus tinctorius*)	Australia	2020	Vol. 9
Sugar beet (*Beta vulgaris*)	Switzerland	2001	Vol. 1
Sugarcane (*Saccharum* spp.)	Australia	2013	Vol. 6
Sunflower (*Helianthus annus*)	France	2004	Vol. 1
Sorghum (*Sorghum bicolor*)	South Africa, United States	2016	Vol. 7
Soybean (*Glycine max*)	Canada	2000	Vol. 1
Squashes, pumpkins, zucchinis and gourds (*Cucurbita*)	Mexico, United States	2012	Vol. 5
Tomato (*Solanum lycopersicum*)	Mexico, Spain	2016	Vol. 7
Wheat (*Triticum aestivum*)	Germany	1999	Vol. 1
Biology of trees			
Timber trees			
Birch: European white birch (*Betula pendula*)	Finland	2003	Vol. 2
Douglas fir (*Pseudotsuga menziesii*)	Canada	2008	Vol. 3
Eucalyptus (*Eucalyptus* spp.)	Australia	2014	Vol. 6
Larches: North American larches (*Larix lyalli, Larix occidentalis, Larix laricina*)	Canada	2007	Vol. 3
Pines: Eastern white pine (Pinus strobus)	Canada	2002	Vol. 2
Pines: Jack pine (*Pinus banksiana*)	Canada	2006	Vol. 3
Pines: Lodgepole pine (*Pinus contorta*)	Canada	2008	Vol. 3
Pines: White pine (*Pinus monticola*)	Canada	2008	Vol. 3
Poplars (*Populus* spp.)	Canada	2000	Vol. 2
Spruces: Black spruce (*Picea mariana*)	Canada	2010	Vol. 3
Spruces: Norway spruce (*Picea abies*)	Norway	1999	Vol. 2
Spruces: Sitka spruce (*Picea sitchensis*)	Canada	2002	Vol. 2
Spruces: White spruce (*Picea glauca*)	Canada	1999	Vol. 2
Fruit trees			
Apple (*Malus domestica*) [also listed above in "Biology of crops"]	Belgium, Germany	2019	Vol. 9
Bananas and plantains (*Musa* spp.) [also listed above in "Biology of crops"]	Spain	2009	Vol. 4
Papaya (*Carica papaya*) [also listed above in "Biology of crops"]	United States	2005	Vol. 1
Stone fruits (*Prunus* spp.)	Austria	2002	Vol. 2
Biology of animals			
Atlantic salmon (*Salmo salar*)	Finland, Norway, United States	2017	Vol. 7
Mosquito *Aedes aegypti*	Brazil, Mexico, ILSI-RF	2018	Vol. 8

9 789264 375758

Printed by Libri Plureos GmbH in Hamburg,
Germany